SAUL BELLOW
AND
THE STRUGGLE AT THE CENTER

GEORGIA STATE LITERARY STUDIES SERIES: No 12

General Editor Victor A. Kramer

ISSN: 0884-8696

SAUL BELLOW

—AND—

THE STRUGGLE AT THE CENTER

Edited by

Eugene Hollahan

AMS PRESS
New York

Library of Congress Cataloging-in-Publication Data

Saul Bellow and the struggle at the center/edited by Eugene Hollahan
    (Georgia State literary studies, ISSN 0884-8696:12)
    Includes bibliographical references and index.
    ISBN 0-404-63212-2
        1. Bellow, Saul—Criticism and interpretation. I. Hollahan, Eugene. II. Series:
    Georgia State literary studies; v. 12. PS3503. E4488Z8472 1994
    813'.52—dc20   91-58150
                                                                       CIP

All AMS books are printed on acid-free paper that meets the guidelines for
performance and durability of the Committee on Production Guidelines for
Book Longevity of the Council on Library Resources.

COPYRIGHT ©1996 BY AMS PRESS, INC.

AMS PRESS
56 East 13th Street
New York, N.Y. 10003 U.S.A.

Manufactured in the United States of America

This book is for

Capt. Mark Ransom Hollahan, USMC

. . . but the son can shield the father . . .

and for

Saul Bellow

scribit ut scribam

A BODY OF WORK
(after reading *Humboldt's Gift*)

Today's lesson. Read it like a good book,
this naked chemical lump.
Anatomize this sack of blood and guts
by the number, provided you yield back
so many of nails, nerves, knuckles, joints,

grinders, tongues, toes, skulls, organs
(things of that kidney)
ears, bones, hairs, veins, arteries,
diaphragms, glands, tubes, and bladders.
Code them by form and function,

arrange them in systems
for feeling, bleeding, twitching, standing, moving,
breathing and breeding. Still you miss the main thing.
The scoop, the lunge, the seize, lift, and thrust,
the press and the pump, the blather and all the bother.

Recall how with one quick puff of breath
you impelled an object toward a goal,
skittering little dust men across a polished floor.
Work is the quintessence of dust.
As you scald your scalpel, recall:

given occasion, this earthwork,
our barrier against the null and void,
this little dustup
all compound of quirk and torque,
will rise up and fall to.

Eugene Hollahan   *Phase and Cycle* (Colorado)
Fall, 1992

CONTENTS

PREFATORY NOTE

Saul Bellow's work of more than five decades is a jewel of America's Urban-Jewish fiction. As with so much successful art that has ethnic and religious roots, such storytelling must grow out of the particulars of specific places imagined while suggesting much about the universal qualities of the human spirit. Surely a healthy provinciality, seriousness, and humor inform all of Bellow, while in so being these qualities help readers to appreciate the spiritual struggle to which the volume editor Eugene Hollahan alludes in his Introduction, a struggle in which all persons must engage – even though they may never be able to understand the complexity of what it is they sense about human love, a striving frequently referred to within this collection as being at the center of existence.

This gathering of essays, like others in the Georgia State Literary Studies Series, builds systematically insight-by-insight so that we can better perceive what Bellow is about. Ellen Pifer's bold *Saul Bellow Against the Grain* (University of Pennsylvania Press, 1990), one of the more interesting recent investigations about Bellow, reminds us of the implicit agenda within his fiction ultimately concerned with matters of spirituality and transcendence. This is increasingly obvious as Bellow has matured. In her analysis of *More Die of Heartbreak* Pifer stressed (using Bellow's words) that there is always something "behind the appearances" (253). Characters, such as the hero Benn in that novel, Pifer reminds us, are searching for what must remain below the surface, indeed beyond the physical. Thus, "[i]n Bellow's . . . fiction . . . it is the 'secret' of the human being, his 'hidden design' that the novelist's art is increasingly dedicated to unfolding" (163). So also therefore must this be the case with the essays of this book, including a new essay by Pifer about success.

With the continuing investigation of scholars, such as those included in this new collection, we see that even the first hero, Joseph, in *Dangling Man,* is suspended because of spiritual questions. The essays gathered here derive from a *Studies in the Literary Imagination* issue (Fall 1984), yet almost all of this material is completely new. (Some of the material of that original issue has already been reprinted elsewhere.) This reflects current high interest in the Nobel Prize winning author, Bellow. It also

ix

says a lot about the complexity of serious scholarship as a continuing exercise. It is perhaps ironic that as Bellow has developed skill and confidence as a writer, his characters must frequently come to admit their difficulties as they seek to articulate the mystery of being. In this way Bellow, like his fellow philosophical journeyer, Walker Percy, crafts moments of illumination which allow glimpses into the transcendent.

While the essays of this book are sophisticated in their analysis of Bellow's thought, they also constantly remind us that Saul Bellow usually insists that our world is first one of the ordinary, even mundane; and that it is through the ordinary that we are made aware of what may be beyond. We would do well also to remember that before we can expend energy at the rarefied levels of critical and philosophical thought basic to the many essays which together make this book, many quite practical matters of research, manuscript preparation, proofing, double-checking – even making an index – must precede. Many hands and minds are involved.

Once again, therefore, I take this opportunity to acknowledge the support provided for the Georgia State Literary Studies Series in the form of released time for faculty editors, graduate research support, and the staff services and sacrifices that have continued to make it possible for this Series (conceived in 1983; first book published in 1987; twelve books now in print) to develop. We think this book, like others in the Series which are completed, or now in process, and which range from Medieval to Contemporary, will stimulate thinking which goes beyond the immediate moment, and therefore beyond the limited world of academe about which Bellow often has expressed his displeasure.

Victor A. Kramer
General Editor

NOTES ON CONTRIBUTORS

GERHARD BACH is professor of American Studies at the Paedagogische Hochschule in Heidelberg, Germany. Since 1990, he has been Visiting Professor in the Department of English of Brigham Young University. His publications include books and articles on modern American fiction and drama, film and literature, educational psychology, and instructional methodology. Essays on Saul Bellow have appeared in *Saul Bellow Journal, Studies in American Jewish Literature,* and various anthologies. He edited *Saul Bellow at 75: A Collection of Critical Essays* (1991).

ALLAN CHAVKIN is Professor of English at Southwest Texas State University (San Marcos). He has published numerous essays on English romanticism and modern literature, including fifteen articles on Bellow's fiction. Most recently, he compiled and edited *Conversations with John Gardner* (1990), and *English Romanticism and Modern Fiction* (1993).

NANCY FEYL CHAVKIN is Associate Professor of Social Work at Southwest Texas State University. She has published on the underclass in Bellow's fiction, on problems of minorities, multicultural education, and other social issues. Her recent book *Families and Schools in a Pluralistic Society* was published by SUNY Press (1993).

GLORIA L. CRONIN is Professor of English at Brigham Young University. She is founding editor of the *Saul Bellow Journal,* which in 1992 began its second decade as a focal point of Bellovian studies. She is also a founding member of the Saul Bellow Society, serving as its official bibliographer. She has authored and edited numerous books and research guides on 20th Century American Literature, including *A Mosaic: Critical Essays on the Novels of Saul Bellow* (1992) and *Saul Bellow: Annotated Bibliography and Research Guide* (1987).

FREDERICK GLAYSHER studied writing with Robert Hayden and has edited Hayden's prose and poetry. He has published essays and reviews, including a review of Bellow's *Him with His Foot in His Mouth and Other Stories,* and has poems forthcoming in *Literature East & West.*

ANDREW GORDON is Associate Professor of English at the University of Florida. He authored *An American Dreamer: A Psychoanalytic Study of the Fiction of Norman Mailer* (Fairleigh Dickinson Univ. Press, 1980), as well as essays on Barth, Le Guin, and Kosinski. He has published numerous articles on Below, in the *Saul Bellow Journal, Modern Fiction Studies,* and other journals.

MICHAEL GREENSTEIN is Adjunct Professor of Literature at the University of Sherbrooke (Québec). He has authored *Third Solitudes: Tradition and Discontinuity in Jewish-Canadian Literature* (winner of the Toronto Jewish Congress book award, 1990), as well as more than forty articles on Victorian, Jewish, and Canadian literature. He is currently writing a study of Jewish Nobel laureates.

BLAINE H. HALL has been English Language and Literature Librarian at Brigham Young University since 1972. Among other work, he has authored or co-authored *Jewish American Fiction Writers: An Annotated Bibliography* (Garland, 1991) and *Saul Bellow: An Annotated Bibliography* (1987).

EUGENE HOLLAHAN edits *Studies in the Literary Imagination.* He teaches literary criticism and nineteenth-century English literature in the graduate program at Georgia State University (Atlanta). His critical history of the crisis-trope, *Crisis-Consciousness and the Novel* (1992), culminates with a chapter on Bellow as a crisis-watcher.

ROBERT F. KIERNAN is Professor of English and World Literature at Manhattan College in New York, as well as a former editor of *Literary Research Newsletter.* He has authored six books: *Katherine Anne Porter: A Reference Guide* (1976), *Gore Vidal* (1982), *American Writing Since 1945: A Critical Survey (1983), Noel Coward* (1986), *Saul Bellow* (1989), and *Frivolity Unbound: Six Masters of the Camp Novel* (1990).

S. LILLIAN KREMER is a member of the faculty of the Department of English at Kansas State University. She is the author of numerous articles of literary criticism and *Witness Through the Imagination: Jewish American Holocaust Literature.*

G. NEELAKANTAN is Lecturer in English in Cuddalore, India. He is preparing a book-length study of the waste-land problematic in Bellow and in Western culture generally.

ELLEN PIFER is Professor of English and Comparative Literature at the University of Delaware. Her most recent book, *Saul Bellow Against the Grain* (1990), won the 1990–91 Outstanding Academic Book Award from *Choice;* it is now available in paperback. Her previous books include *Nabokov and the Novel* (1980), and *Critical Essays on John Fowles* (1986). Her critical essays appear in *Modern Fiction Studies* and other standard journals. She recently served as visiting professor at Berkeley and at the University of Lyon (France).

DAVID RAMPTON is an assistant professor of American Literature at the University of Ottawa. His publications include a study of Nabokov's fictions (1984). He has edited several freshman anthologies.

EUSEBIO L. RODRIGUES is Professor of English at Georgetown University. His book *Quest for the Human: An Exploration of Saul Bellow's Fiction* (1984) is a landmark in the global enlargement of Bellow's reputation.

MARILYN SATLOF recently retired from the Department of Language and Literature of Columbus College, way down in Columbus, Georgia. Among her publications is the essay "Bellow's Modern Lamed Vovniks" in the *Saul Bellow Journal.*

WALTER SHEAR specializes in American prose of the Romantic period and of the mid-twentieth century. His publications include articles on Irving, Hawthorne, Poe, Twain, Peter Taylor, Flannery O'Connor, and Bernard Malamud.

BEN SIEGEL is Professor of English at California State Polytechnic University (Pomona). His books, solo or in collaboration, include *The Puritan Heritage: America's Roots in the Bible, Biography Past and Present, Isaac Bashevis Singer, The Controversial Sholem Asch,* and *The American Writer and the University.* His critical essays deal with Bellow, Malamud, Philip Roth, Singer, and Daniel Fuchs. He is a member of the advisory editorial boards of six journals, including the *Saul Bellow Journal.*

INTRODUCTION
Looking for the Center

Eugene Hollahan

The center, as aesthetic image and cultural problematic, has become, since Yeats, both crucial to human life and boldly foregrounded for critical consideration. The center cannot hold, complained Yeats. Agreed. But Saul Bellow insisted in his Nobel acceptance speech that individual human beings must not cease to struggle toward some imagined center and, arrived there, must not cease to struggle at the center.

> Out of the struggle at the center has come an immense, painful long-ing for a broader, more flexible, fuller, more coherent, more compre-hensive account of what we human beings are, who we are, and what this life is for. At the center, mankind struggles with collective powers for its freedom; the individual struggles with dehumanization for the possession of his soul. If writers do not come again into the center it will not be because the center is preempted. It is not. They are free to enter. If they so wish.[1]

Bellow obviously knew and embraced the other, the unspoken, part of Yeats's perception, that is, the principle that human life necessitates the beleaguered individual's trying to reach the center, and then to engage in a struggle for being at the center.

My own attempt to find a center in and for Bellow takes the form of *Crisis-Consciousness and the Novel* (Univ. of Delaware Press, 1992), where I examine the emergence of modern consciousness developing historically in prose fiction narrative. I represent a critical history of *crisis*, arguably the most characterizing single word in the modern world and a major figuration or trope, by studying the history of this important word within the development of the English-language novel, from Samuel Richardson to Saul Bellow. After establishing a heuristic model for such a critical history, I track the word (characterized by George Eliot in *Felix Holt, the Radical* as a "great noun") through two-and-a-half centuries of

narratives by major novelists, with contextualizing excursions into discourses in related fields such as autobiography, philosophy, theology, and
social science.

As a means of historically backgrounding and foregrounding exemplary novels from a major tradition of English-language narrative fiction, I
glance at writings by crisis-rhetoricians in the eighteenth century (Thomas
Paine), nineteenth century (Thomas Carlyle, J. S. Mill, J. H. Newman),
and twentieth century (Karl Barth, Edmund Husserl, T. S. Kuhn, Richard
M. Nixon). In my own understanding of the problem, such varied and
powerful crisis-rhetorics establish a matrix of language and ideas for a tradition of crisis-centered novels, for the most part masterpieces, including
major works by Richardson, Walter Scott, Jane Austen, George Eliot,
George Meredith, George Gissing, George Moore, D. H. Lawrence, E. M.
Forster, James Joyce, Lawrence Durrell, Robert Coover, and Bellow.

In *Louis Lambert,* Balzac urged: "What a wonderful book one would
write by narrating the life and adventures of a word." Forms of consciousness in fact attach themselves to and center upon specific words. The
story I narrate in *Crisis-Consciousness and the Novel* fulfills Balzac's
expectations as it depicts writer after writer working out influential rep-
resentations of human life in terms of crisis-consciousness centering
upon George Eliot's "great noun" *crisis.* Historically, it would appear,
such consciousness comes to define modern humanity.

My study teases out numerous implications of Eliot's ironical assertion
that one single word was taking on a special rhetorical role. I seek to discover why – by the fateful year 1832 – *crisis* had become peculiarly important
and would become steadily more so in the unfolding story of modern life.
What makes this noun so variable and yet so constant? Does it serve many
different purposes? What, if any, specifically rhetorical, figurative, or
critical function does the word serve in a novel? What I discover is that *crisis,* meaning judgment, is a writer's special invitation to the critic to criticize.

Following a hint from Paul de Man, I examine the processes by which
crisis-rhetoric historically converts a word of limited technical use into
one of the most flexible and conceptually loaded narrative tropes, how it
contributes to the novel's generic power to render the complex, fluid, at
times violent actualities of modern life. Richardson, for example, was
unable to compose his masterpiece *Clarissa* without distributing *crisis-*
signifiers that complicate vital stages in the conflict between Clarissa
Harlowe and Robert Lovelace. Likewise, Eliot could not construct her
masterpiece *Middlemarch* without insinuating a systematic *crisis*-trope
that establishes Dorothea Brooke and Will Ladislaw as the bearers of her
most compelling truth-effects.

To be aware of the potential power of Eliot's great noun means to witness to a central dynamic of modern life. Thus, within a framework of revolutionary passion given political expression by Thomas Paine, the first English novelist Richardson depicts a headlong collision between English aristocracy and an emergent middle class. Henry Mackenzie exhibits the tragic encounter between pre-Romantic humanitarianism and old-fashioned human greed. Scott marks the end of the eighteenth century's pure sentimentalism by positing a seriousness latent in Gothic emotionalism. Jane Austen smuggles into one of her novels the Romantic philosophy of esemplastic imagination only to judge it harshly. Eliot includes in three novels much carefully researched materials drawn from the reform period of 1832 and an incipient European Zionism. Meredith witnesses to the dead-end failure of an obtuse aristocracy; Gissing and Moore attest to inherent economic contradictions lurking within Victorian prosperity; Henry James builds class-consciousness into his novels in the form of a conflicted aestheticism. Lawrence provides a compelling portrayal of the mechanization that was ruining the English countryside. Forster sadly notes the failure of Anglo-Indian rapprochement. Lawrence Durrell invents a convoluted literary form in order to suggest the maddening intricacies of Middle-Eastern politics. Robert Coover makes literary substance and form out of a tormented reactionary ideology espoused by Richard Nixon. Finally, Bellow repeatedly attests to a culture-wide exploitation of crisis-mentality as a form of sociopolitical manipulation and escapism.

My representation of the crisis-trope attempts to demonstrate that the crisis-riddled modern world and the crisis-conscious novel are analogous and coeval. It confronts numerous vexing questions. Why has *crisis* become historically and culturally so important? What about the very word itself? What makes this single noun so variable and yet so constant? What constitutes the presumed rhetorical, figurative, or critical importance of *crisis* in a novel? How and why has it become a twisting trope that serves so many different rhetorical purposes?

Crisis begins as Aristotle's term for logical plot structuring, becomes Longinus's term for emotional exacerbation, and eventually enters into a variety of critical and narrative formulations: Matthew Arnold's cultural centrality, Henry James's existential aestheticism, Lawrence's self-defining sexuality, Marshall Brown's revolutionary turning point, Paul de Man's error-ridden criticism, Floyd Merrell's cut into the primordial flux, Durrell's reborn self, and Bellow's analysis of hysterical escapism. Broadly speaking, I urge that any *crisis*-trope will enable or even necessitate a unique confluence of writerly and readerly skills.

A *crisis*-trope may trigger other major figurations partly by coming nearest to the root meaning of *trope,* that is, a turning away from literal meaning. It thus enables and induces an extraordinary range of rhetorical effects, including major metaphors and ironies. It also enters into the radical problematics of authorship and authority. By inducing critical self-reflexivity, it activates salient critical and philosophical issues. It may prove to be the case that *crisis* achieves greatness simply by triggering a rhetorical tension adequate to the tensions of modern life.

Saul Bellow experiments throughout his career with crisis-tropes, arriving thereby in *Humboldt's Gift* at a succinct statement of his major theme: "Under pressure of public crisis, the private sphere is being surrendered." Thus Bellow joins his beleaguered fellow man in the struggle for the center and at the center. The essays in the present volume testify eloquently and strenuously to the ongoing struggle.

A 1991 biography, *Saul Bellow: A Biography of the Imagination,* contains an anecdote of a 1977 chat between Bellow, the recent Nobel laureate, and Edward Shils, Bellow's colleague at the University of Chicago. Shils, as Ruth Miller recalls, wryly declared that he must regretfully miss Bellow's prize-related speeches in Washington and Chicago because "he had no tuxedo."[2] This skew-whiffed anecdote, whether regarded as amusing or pathetic, should remind us of an off-the-wall fact bearing obliquely upon the concerns of *Saul Bellow and the Struggle at the Center.* In his situation as a member of Chicago's Committee on Social Thought, Bellow was ideally placed – should I say ideally centered? – to perceive and struggle with an extraordinarily influential sociological theory of social power informed by the metaphor of the *center* per se. I refer, of course, to Edward Shils's groundbreaking *Center and Periphery,* published the same year as Bellow's masterpiece *Humboldt's Gift* (1975).[3]

How broadly and deeply Shils's career-long meditation upon the center has influenced other thinkers can be seen in an intelligently edited book which grew out of the 1985 Chicago symposium on "The Authority of Intellectual Enterprises and the Center."[4] Happily, Shils himself provides a closural essay, "Center and Periphery: An Idea and Its Career, 1935–1987" (250–282) that describes how he came to regard the center as perhaps the most crucial single metaphor, at once concept and methodology, in sociological analysis. I will not at this time attempt a detailed summary of Shils's essay, with its compelling interpretations of charisma and secrecy, but will merely remind my reader of its existence and relevance. Here, I will briefly sketch the contents of Greenfeld's and Martin's collection of symposium proceedings gathered together under the title *Center.*

Shils's concept of the center finds its *raison* in the very constitution of society. Society is the outermost social structure for a given collection of individuals; by virtue of a sort of "genetic code" or central mechanism, they manage productively to relate to each other. Sometimes spatial and sometimes non-spatial, the center carries two meanings. First, it emerges as a dynamic process of values or central system of values by which peripheries or scattered materials are to be cohesively organized. Here, the mechanism is necessarily that of consensus; society is a consensual reality (p. ix). Second, center can also mean "central institutional system" when it refers to the mechanisms by which the genetic code or value system realizes itself. Human life is largely a function of the dialectics between centers and peripheries.

To turn from Greenfeld's and Martin's rendering of Shils's generalizations about the center to the fourteen essays they have collected under the title *Center*, in effect practical applications of Shils's theory, is to encounter a dizzying multiplicity of data and explanation. Certain themes provide some continuity, such as that symbolic systems function as centers, under certain conditions, in certain ways, with intellectuals having crucial roles to play in the dynamic interaction between center and periphery; in addition, there exists the very great likelihood that any given center tends to extend its power into any given periphery. Specific essays focus on historical or possible centers: religion, universities, specific places (e.g., St. Petersburg), intellectualism, humanistic scholarship, public service, and privacy. From various angles of vision, these Shilsian sociologists confront issues of German history, paradigm shifts from sacred life to secular life, Jewish history, monotheism and the modern state, Mandelstam versus Soviet power, brain versus technological brawn, social science per se, the *imperium* of the center, families and schools, and the general symbolism of any and all construals of any and all centers.

It seems abundantly clear that the next generation of Bellow critics must take up in multitudinous detail and strenuous depth the relations between Bellow's centering enterprise and the centering speculations worked out and encouraged by his colleague Edward Shils.

In one sense, the present collection of critical essays focusing upon Bellow's confrontation with a decentered or at least badly rattled universe has its genesis in an earlier collection of essays, *Philosophical Dimensions of Saul Bellow's Fiction*.[5] There, seven critics engaged their critical wits with Bellow's oeuvre in a collective effort to locate an intellectual center. As a happy result, we witnessed strenuous efforts to situate Bellow in Romanticism (Chavkin), Transcendentalism (Porter), Pessimism (Trachtenberg), anti-Freudianism (Fuchs), Judaism (Goldman), Nihilism (Newman), or in some dreamy/risky, empyrean/existential realm beyond all philosophies (Rodrigues). Reviewed as perhaps the most valuable collection of essays to date on Bellow's achievement,[6] that centralizing enterprise subsequently provided three essays (by Chavkin, Fuchs, and Goldman) for inclusion in a "best essays on" volume, *Saul Bellow in the 1980s.*[7] In the present collection, Allan Chavkin collaborates with N. F. Chavkin generously to provide a new essay that builds upon and extends the splendid insights of his original essay on Bellow and Romanticism. I have chosen to reprint here the essay by Eusebio Rodrigues which effectively extended our critical understanding of Bellow's fiction into the east.

In each novel, Bellow seeks for a center; his critics accordingly seek to identify the presumed center their novelist either stipulates for or conjectures. Among European readers, for example, Bellow's position as a novelist of ideas engaged with problems of displacement and marginalization places him at the shifting center of the stressful emergence of a new central Europe. Bellow's involvement with contemporary social concerns qualifies him to be included within this stressful context. He insists that the "inner voice" of the writer, seemingly distant from current political issues and developments, provides a social and cultural bond among writers and intellectuals across national boundaries, even boundaries of iron (Bach).

One of the preoccupations of Bellow's later fiction is the role of the modern writer in a society indifferent or hostile to art. The artist may degenerate into a "farcical martyr," as in *Humboldt's Gift*, but subsequently transform himself into a "moralist of seeing," as in *The Dean's December.* In Bellow's complicated vision of human life, then, one center of value locates itself in nineteenth-century English romanticism, which called for just such a liberation from the slavery of routine perceptions (Chavkin).

As a novelist, Bellow necessarily grounds his meditation on human life in the quagmire of relations between the sexes. In *More Die of Heartbreak,* two types of male consciousness alternately collide and fuse so as to depict for the reader a puzzling but convincing core experience of what it means to belong to one sex and thereby be fated to work out one's destiny in terms of the other sex (Cronin).

Like Tennyson in *In Memoriam,* Bellow posits one kind of center in something he calls the "soul." Bellow's sense of social decline in both the East and the West, and his conception of the bankruptcy of many Enlightenment ideas, should be given particular attention. Bellow's reassessment of modernism is made possible by the very decline of modernism itself, but he is in no way suggesting or urging a retrogression of man's soul (Glaysher).

One Bellovian center, in truth a constant center, is the suffering human person. Moses Herzog is not out of his mind but simply working through normal grief associated with divorce. *Herzog* is essentially Bellow's *Tender is the Night*, that is, a psychologically acute depiction of a major American social problem. Divorce is a kind of psychic death, and Herzog must mourn over his failed marriage and also the numerous other griefs and failures it calls to his mind. Herzog goes through the classic pattern: shock and denial; depression; homicidal anger and suicidal thoughts; finally, recuperation and acceptance (Gordon).

Bellow never loses sight of the human body as being, in at least one important sense, the true locus of at least one center of human reality. At the functional center of this physical center he discovers the human hand, with its forefinger and opposable thumb, together capably forming the circle (and center) that constitutes the O in OK! Bellow's highest flights of philosophical fancy are thus linked with the human hand, the agent, so to speak, of a necessarily tactile imagination. Palpability, or, more literally, tactility, thus constitues the dialectical center between *vita activa* and *vita contemplativa* (Greenstein).

A prevailing view that Bellow shifted decisively in the early 1950s from the pronunciative style of the French existentialists to a more ample and rhetorically indulgent nineteenth-century style fails to recognize that an ongoing counterpoint of the two styles is a technique of characterization in the oeuvre from *Dangling Man* to *More Die of Heartbreak*. The multiple awarenesses that threaten to unbalance Bellow's protagonists find in the counterpoint their symbol and cypher (Kiernan).

In some cases, the center is to be searched for in somewhat predictable places and ways. The Montreal chapter of *Herzog* must be read together with "The Old System." Each work is colored and informed by Bellow's knowledgeable incorporation of Jewish religious and cultural traditions, of the sociology of Russian-Jewish immigrant patterns of acculturation in Canada and the U.S.A. Even the comedic scenes derive from the conflicting historic attitudes of two major philosophic antagonists within the Eastern European Jewish community, the *Hasidim* and their opponents the *mitnagdim* (Kremer).

The center may reside in the east, as Rodrigues would have it, or perhaps be recognized by a critic residing in the east, for example, in India.

More Die of Heartbreak foregrounds and intensifies Bellow's brooding upon the modern world as a waste land. In its treatment of the evils of sexuality, death, money, and politics, Bellow surprisingly elucidates a belief that, via the sufferings undergone by a human person such as the character Benn Crader, we may be redeemed, revivified, or centered as if by a veritable holy knight of faith, one who redeems the waste land (Neelakantan).

In America, winning is everything; in America (as the song writer Randy Newman puts it), it's money that matters. However, to win may be to lose; to lose may be to win. So, where are we to find the stable center of some putative value structure in modern life? Bellow dwells upon the complex relations between the material demands of life and its no less insistent spiritual requirements. He plays with appearances in order to delve beneath appearances, and he unsettles his reader by radically questioning values we all enact in our lives. Bellow brings a bit of ancient wisdom to light: knowledge of the winner's hidden losses and the loser's hidden gains (Pifer).

Bellow is capable of understanding that the center to be located via literature may in fact be ontologically itself a literary phenomenon. Thus, in *More Die of Heartbreak*, the protagonist Kenneth Trachtenberg is an assistant professor of Russian literature at a midwest university. In the course of narrating his uncle's problems with women, he makes numerous erudite references to his academic specialty, including the Symbolists, Acmeists, and sexual mystics whose work dominated Russian literature at the beginning of the century. Bellow uses these ideas about life and death, history and culture, to develop his own multilayered and multicentered investigation of these crucial matters (Rampton).

Consciousness itself, together with the humanly understandable desire to escape from the more agonizing forms and contents of consciousness, represent another Bellovian center. In *The Bellarosa Connection*, Bellow utilizes the polarity of remembering and forgetting as the centralizing dynamic of American Jewry. The narrator, an assimilated Jew who has made a fortune by exploiting his "innate gift of memory," recounts the tale of a Holocaust survivor who is constrained by his rescuer, Billy Rose, from any further contact. Bellow thus takes us perilously close to a nearly unbearable center of twentieth-century experience (Satlof).

From Bellow's earliest fictions onward, the novelist examines characters who awaken to some surprising new dimension of existence. Wandering, then, in defamiliarized new worlds of sensation and thought, each character proceeds to discover some sign of personhood and integrity. Accordingly, another startling center of concern develops: the self's encounter with a mode of potential otherness (Shear).

Finally, the center of Bellow's oeuvre is said to reside in his ferreting out anew the "bitch-goddess Success" that had been first identified and labelled by the great pragmatic philosopher William James. We ought not to be too surprised to encounter, at the last, an explanation of Bellow's central concern in the very heart of American literary art and in the rigorous demands Bellow would place upon American writers (Siegel).

NOTES

1. Saul Bellow, "The Nobel Lecture," *The American Scholar* 46 (Summer 1977), 316–25.

2. Ruth Miller, *Saul Bellow: A Biography of the Imagination* (New York: St. Martin's Press, 1991), p. xxii. Further references are given in parentheses in the text.

3. Edward Shils, *Center and Periphery: Essays in Macrosociology* (Chicago: Univ. of Chicago Press, 1975).

4. *Center: Ideas and Institutions,* ed. Liah Greenfeld and Michael Martin (Chicago: Univ. of Chicago Press, 1988). Specific citations will be given parenthetically in the text.

5. Edited by Eugene Hollahan, in *Studies in the Literary Imagination,* 17:2 (Fall 1984).

6. Gloria L. Cronin, *Saul Bellow Journal* 5 (Winter 1986): 75–79.

7. *Saul Bellow in the 1980s: A Collection of Critical Essays,* ed. Gloria L. Cronin and L. H. Goldman (East Lansing: Michigan State Univ. Press, 1989).

Margin as Center:
Bellow and the New Central Europe

Gerhard Bach

B ELLOW'S PUBLIC appearances, at least in his native country,[1]
have become rare, so spaced in fact that one might suspect either
that the author wishes to underscore his rarity value or that he
has resigned himself to disinterestedness – both stances being sig-
natures of his ongoing revaluation of the writer's responsibility to
the public. The most recent occasion to hear Bellow address matters of public concern came on April 9, 1992, at Rutgers University's Newark campus, where the author participated in a conference on "Intellectuals and Social Change in Central and Eastern
Europe." It was an occasion characteristic of the kind of ambiguities that have come to be a Bellow trademark – ambiguities made
paramount by the localities, contexts, and themes repeatedly
chosen by the author for his fictional settings.

Such settings usually speak of displacement and of the individual character's specific response to such displacement from an
imagined center, which usually comes across as an inextricable
combination of physical, psychological, and spiritual states of
marginalization. As a novelist of ideas, whose major concern appears to be with such "displaced persons," Bellow has been popular with European readers since the 1950s. As a post-war generation German/European, I have found myself choosing Bellow as
an antidote to the noise generated by the cold-war years – the
physical noise of the presence of foreign armies exercising their
legal rights to refine their military skills on divided German
ground, the psychological noise of military (including nuclear)
threat, and the linguistic noise of star wars scenarios. Displaced

1

by the history-shaping noise of a cold war into which I find myself born, and from which, I am assured, my generation has recently been liberated, Bellow – and with him Günter Grass, Elias Canetti, Paul Celan, Alexandr Solzhenitsyn, and others – has served as a stabilizing center of consciousness, similar to the pattern laid out as "plain facts" in Bellow's recent story, "Something to Remember Me By": "Remember," the narrator cautions the reader,

> there were no redeemers in the streets, no guides, no confessors, comforters, enlighteners, communicants to turn to. You had to take teaching wherever you could find it. Under the library dome downtown, in mosaic letters, there was a message from Milton, so moving but perhaps of no utility, perhaps aggravating difficulties: A GOOD BOOK, it said, IS THE PRECIOUS LIFE'S BLOOD OF A MASTER SPIRIT.[2]

For me – as I have learned to turn the following banality into a cause – "good books" turned out to be a stabilizing counterforce to the centripetal forces of the cold-war vortices pulling post-war Europe apart into "democratic" and "communist" segments. The two Europes created after World War II quickly became margins of their respective superpowers, but "margins of centrality": where the margins met, the tensions created by the cold-war rhetoric, ironically so, gave my generation a sense of centrality. Emerging from that center of noisy margins and high tensions, we now find ourselves *not* settling comfortably on the periphery of events, but instead positioned in a new center whose geographical, political, and cultural boundaries are in the process of self-definition. Looking out from that center, the situation is much less emblazoned than the media desire us to believe. In fact, it is a center in which we currently confront a peculiar stillness: the recent absence of systemic definitions of who we are and where we belong makes this stillness audible much in the way the presence of silence is made audible and visible in *Waiting for Godot*.

Such stillness, sometimes numbing, marks a sharp contrast to the noise generated, for instance, in the United States over Germany's unification and the fall of the Iron Curtain and the emergence of Eastern Europe into "freedom." It took only a "zero wait-state" for business entrepreneurs to realize the advertising value of pictures of youngsters popping champagne bottles on the Berlin Wall. While this (Western) material force of entering and conquering new frontiers in the East is in the process of finally making the world safe for democracy, artists, writers, and intellectuals from Eastern and Central Europe[3] (including its previously "Western" segment) are, in my view, moving in the opposite direction. They appear to be more concerned with the cultural patterns emerging from their nations, states, or peoples, as counter-forces — the forces of stillness, self-silencing. In general, there is a sense of spiritual loss in the realization of a material gain. German novelist Christa Wolf expresses this most poignantly when she says that the disintegration of East Germany has been confronted by many intellectuals with a stubborn, often silent, resistance. Wolf calls this disposition towards self-silencing vis-à-vis the noise of exuberant change "the melancholy of the intellectuals," a state conditioned by the recognition of a double defeat, namely the loss of a nation *and* of a utopia. Neither loss, Wolf claims, is made any less painful by the knowledge and acceptance of its necessity.[4] Thomas Rosenlöcher, a young poet from eastern Germany, on the eve of the opening of the Berlin Wall, has this entry in his diary: "The borders are open/I have no words" (45).[5]

This ambiguity — of East and West meeting face to face and then finding themselves at a loss for words — invariably surfaces wherever writers and artists from both sides of the Iron Curtain (now allegedly extinct) meet. In many cases, the dialogue begins with a search for common words beyond the well-practiced cold-war language. As Richard Rorty states in a recent essay on America's political culture, the loss of an enemy has resulted in a loss, primarily for the American leftist intellectual, of a theoretical basis for thought and political action. Thus, and in view of the challenge to "make sense" of the historical events, American intellectuals find themselves at a loss for words much like Thomas Rosenlöcher. Terms like "capitalist economy" or "bourgeois culture" simply fail to impact any longer. And Rorty suggests that Americans should accept the fact "that from here on in we are going to have to be as crudely experimental as the new governments of Poland and Lithuania are being forced to be."[6]

While from Rorty's essay there speaks a prominent sense of loss and sadness, and a fear of banality, the author points to the possibility of turning this loss into gain, of giving up freely the idea that we will be able, in the foreseeable future, to come up with a "large theoretical framework that will enable us to put our society in an excitingly new context."[7] It is primarily from this sense of no longer viable systemic social theories, and from the sense of having been freed from prescribed order and a predefined utopia (both East and West), that writers and intellectuals gathered in the urban center of Newark in April of 1992 to speak to each other, and in doing so to develop a new post-cold-war language and poetics. In several ways, then, the context of the conference provides for an arena in which Saul Bellow's mind should feel very much at home. The four corners of this arena are: (1) the physical setting; (2) the current historical events; (3) the limits of communication; and (4) the question of historical identity. All of these need to be addressed briefly as an introduction to Bellow's actual presentation. At the same time, they provide more than a mere background to Bellow's presence at Rutgers. Reflecting on Bellow in this arena I again realize the intricate and delicate nature of his attempt to build bridges for Americans and Europeans to access the historical dimensions of their cultural selves.

The setting. A flyer "welcoming" the conference participants to Rutgers University in the heart of Newark, first of all *cautions* them about this urban metropolis with all its "hazards that befall such an environment," a phrase almost scriptural, as though the conditions it details are part of a providential apocalyptic design. Dean Corde comes to mind, as he flees such an environment only to witness the apocalypse unfolding more clearly from a distance: "Cities . . . were moods, emotional states, for the most part collective distortions, where human beings thrived and suffered, where they invested their souls in pains and pleasures, taking these pleasures and pains as proofs of reality."[8]

The current historical events. The political, geographical, and social changes resulting from the peaceful or violent restructuring of Europe are addressed and assessed by writers and intellectuals from western and eastern nations – to use the terms outdated now. Some of those nations, like Yugoslavia, no longer exist as a result of civil war and global indecisiveness or indifference, and "assessment" in this case finds its expression in the affliction of rage and/or speechlessness. The writers present are (or once were) dissidents to a greater or lesser degree, many of them exiled and involuntarily estranged from their national backgrounds and heritage. The common purpose, to investigate Central European intellectual life as destabilizing old regimes and restabilizing new conditions, with artists currently assuming the responsibilities formerly held by politicians and policy makers, touches a Bellow nerve: such cultural concerns have been on his mind and in his books for the past decade at least. Witnessing the actual changes in Eastern European countries as implemented by the actions of such individuals as Vaclav Havel in Czechoslovakia, Adam Michnik in Poland, or Blaga Dimitrova in Bulgaria, would have thawed the ice in Benn Crader's and Dean Corde's hearts to a dangerous degree: these two might have been forced to actually do something about their utopias beyond mere investigation.

The limits of communication. The first session of the conference brings together Saul Bellow, Ralph Ellison, Czeslaw Milosz, and Joseph Brodsky – all marginalized or exiled at some point by specific historical, racial, ethnic, or religious conditions. A singular tension is created when each briefly addresses the ongoing social and cultural changes in Europe in terms of loss and gain. For all, the loss of an enemy is a gain for humanity. But there are distinct Western and Eastern variants. While Bellow and Ellison address recent events retrospectively and in more general terms, with a view to the inadequacies of the *contrat social* in both the Eastern and the Western world, for Milosz and Brodsky the changes are more imminently related to the undercurrents of empowerment and disempowerment: these two writers express existential concerns to counterbalance the philosophical-historical analysis and reminiscences of their American colleagues.

The question of historical identity. Partisan Review, co-sponsor of the conference and at present the Western intellectual home-base for Eastern European voices, takes Bellow back to his own beginnings, and his association as a modest literary "radical" with the journal half a century ago, at a time of political and social restructuring equally powerful and yet incomparable to the present one. In the forties and fifties, Bellow's stories, book reviews, and essays characterize *Partisan Review*'s literary and intellectual divergence from what was then the mainstream.[9] Bellow's dissident voice of that time, as heralded by his literary and critical associates of the time – Delmore Schwartz, Robert Penn Warren, Alfred Kazin, and Philip Rahv – echoes faintly at Rutgers only. Here Bellow is the acute observer, the diagnostician, and the compassionate if distant companion of the new dissidents: Vassily Aksyonov, expelled from the former Soviet Union for his satirical novel *The Burn;* Joseph Brodsky, exiled from the same country for "poetic disobedience," and American Poet Laureate in 1991/92; Blaga Dimitrova, poet, novelist, and, as of January, 1992, elected Vice President of the new Republic of Bulgaria; Slavenka Drakulic and Dubrovka Ugresic, poets of the former Yugoslavia; Gyorgy Konrad, Hungarian novelist and essayist; Norman Manea, the Romanian writer forced to emigrate when he refused to affiliate himself with the Communist Party; Adam Michnik, a prominent driving force behind the Solidarity movement and now member of Poland's elected Parliament; Czeslaw Milosz, author of the famous *The Captive Mind,* published after the writer took political asylum in France in the early 1950s; Tatyana Tolstaya, Russian writer and outspoken anti-communist who decided to stay and lives in what is once again St. Petersburg; Adam Zagajewski, poet, member of the Polish opposition, who since the early 1980s has lived in Paris; and the list continues. On the Western side of the podium there are, among others, Bellow and Ellison, Doris Lessing, Hans Magnus Enzensberger, Susan Sontag, and William Phillips (the founding editor of *Partisan Review*). Thus it appears that, for its life-blood, *Partisan Review* has drawn on its long-time Western associates, while for its muscle it now resorts to Eastern and Central Europeans. This combination provides for a synthesis of analysis and experience which provides the audience with far more than a distant view of events allegedly taking place "elsewhere."

In this context, then, it is appropriate that Bellow should be speaking first, on "Transcending National Boundaries."[10] Bellow speaks from what can best be described as a "compassionate distance," a stance which the writer portrays with dramatic force in Artur Sammler and Moses Herzog. Bellow begins with the lament over the loss and/or depravity of values in Western and Eastern societies alike. While in totalitarian systems the individual has been *deprived* of such "higher values," the loss in the West has been *self-inflicted*. Bellow reiterates his basic tenet, projected repeatedly in his fictions, critical essays, and numerous interviews, that this self-inflicted loss in the West is rooted in the Enlightenment, that is, in the idea that a new egalitarian system would be able to overcome the pervasive "challenge of scarcity" (531). No longer would humanity need to strive for an Aristotelian *summum bonum;* the new *contrat social,* founded on reason, would allow the individual to be content with satisfying material needs and to avoid a "summum malum" – the internal chaos of civil war, tyranny, and poverty. "It was felt that it might be better to forget about high ceilings when what we wanted was a solid floor under our feet" (532). The spiritual deserts created by such mere-existential self-definition *ex negativo,* preclude any promise of a "higher life" that would reach beyond individualistic pleasure principles. As a consequence, a life of the spirit or the intellect has become a matter of private concerns; it no longer is a part of the social contract of the cultural community at large. The American variant of this experience has been a prolonged, purely pragmatic effort to achieve material abundance, physical completeness, and technological superiority.

So much for the standard Bellovian jeremiad, which takes up the greater part of Bellow's address. What keeps it from being repetitious or becoming formulaic are the few poignant observations Bellow adds on

the Eastern variant of this development, and the decidedly dialectic conclusion he then offers. The failure of the Russian Revolution of 1917 and
the ensuing reign of terror, Bellow argues, have deprived the East completely from participating even liminally in the pursuance of the dream
of self-realization, leaving the West to fill out the dream on its own and
according to its singular pragmatic dream formula. This American effort, however, has always been an effort to fulfill "certain perennial
dreams of a virtual utopia" (532), and prevented from achieving it,
Americans (and stand-in Western Europeans) have contented themselves with a virtual reality.

Bellow laments this deprivation of the full potential of life in the
East and the virtualization of reality in the West as equally efficient in
decomposing social contexts and cultural bonds, and he concludes: In the
(former) East "truth" has always been a scarcity, imprisoned, and
decreed by the isolated source of dictatorship, as a virtual truth to which
everyone succumbed but few would listen; conversely, in the West there
has been an overabundance of "truths," democratically equal, so much so
that nobody cares anymore which truth anyone else speaks. Both versions are dicated by their apparent value of marketability – the Bellow
reader here visualizes Doctor Tamkin (*Seize the Day*), Dewey Spangler
(*The Dean's December*), and Uncle Vilitzer (*More Die of Heartbreak*) – and
the difference between the economic systems which market them
becomes marginal. Virtual realities on both sides successfully conceal
the underlying *real* realities (Bellow's own category of "truth") and thus
are equally a threat to the "higher life" of mankind.

Truth, as becomes evident once more, for Bellow is a central and
normative issue, as it is for many European writers for that matter, including the expatriates, such as Milosz and Brodsky. Bellow's normative
truths, troubling many of his American readers and critics, are confirmed
and shared by his Eastern colleagues who simply point to the recent
developments in their countries as evidence. The point they make by way
of simple illustration and/or exemplification – in their (auto)biographical
fictions, essays, and poetry – is what for Bellow has always been the center of his fictional narratives and the predicament of his protagonists:
only the arts can protect (and successfully have protected in the past half
century) these truths for a new era. To support their argument, the
Eastern writers recall Vaclav Havel's observation on the dialectic of the
power of language – where systemic forces are at work, whether dic-
tated or freely accepted, writers find themselves to be the prisoners of
language *and* its protectors. This is the nature of their dissidence. It is a

condition of the self that exists and operates in ways most often not planned or even outside of any possibility of prognostication, as Havel says looking back on his nation's response to the 1968 invasion:

> Who would have believed . . . that a year later this recently apa-
> thetic, skeptical and demoralized society would stand up with such
> courage and intelligence to a foreign power! And who would have
> suspected that, after scarcely a year had gone by, this same society
> would, as swiftly as the wind blows, lapse back into a state of demor-
> alization far deeper than its original one! After all these experiences,
> one must be very careful about coming to any conclusions about the
> way we are, or what can be expected from us.[11]

Havel's major concern here is the unpredictable force of systemic influences on the individual. It is a concern shared widely by writers from
the East and the West alike. The question is, whether they respond similarly to the usurpation of truth and reality by systemic forces. According
to Bellow, the answer for the nineties is "Yes!" The triumph of the material over the spiritual that has recently been sweeping the Central European nations, whether in business, technology, or in the media, promises
to culminate in a mental misery and spiritual emptiness from which
there is no escape, and, what is worse, from which few will desire to
escape. Technological advances, Bellow suggests, all of them creations
of the human mind, will come to dominate human minds, East *and* West,
the more such minds lack even a rudimentary understanding of the basic
functioning of certain technologies. Vis-à-vis the technological revolution we have become savages, Bellow maintains, ignorant and bereft of
nobility the more we bow to the media's messages of "truth": "let's not
kid ourselves," Bellow cautions, "the prevailing culture is what we see on television"; what we observe there resembles "a kind of assembly of the country's mental life" (542). As a result, the public worship of such messages
and their proponents contributes to a shrinking of the writer's space.

Increasingly, then, functional illiteracy will lead to aesthetic illiteracy.
America's "mental misery," augured in *Humboldt's Gift* and *The Dean's
December,* seems to bring Bellow out in the open, eliciting from the artist
the message of concern commonly reserved for the elder statesman. In
the essay on Mozart, for example, Bellow comments on individual genius
in comparison to our contemporary desires for cultural collectivization.

> To congratulate ourselves . . . on our educated enlightenment is sim-
> ply an evasion of the real truth. We the "educated" cannot even begin

to explain the technologies of which we make daily use. . . . Face to face with the technological miracles without which we could not live our lives, we are as backward as any savage, though education helps us to conceal this from ourselves and others. Indeed it would utterly paralyze us to ponder intricate circuits or minicomputers, or attempt to gain a clear understanding of the translation of the discoveries of particle physics into modern arms.

These, however, are the miracles for which we have a very deep respect, and which, perhaps, dominate our understanding of what a miracle is. A miracle is what brings people to Australia in ten hours. And we owe this to the scientific revolution.[12]

Where miracles are the domain of technology, writers and poets – the "Mozarts of conversation"[13] – are an endangered species, since they are threatened with losing their audiences to the technological innovations of communication. It is a scenario already more real than imagined, Bellow says: "I think we're in danger of seeing a new dark age come over the mental life of the country" ("Intellectuals" 546). An illustration of this new age of darkened sensibilities is given by Bellow in his "state of the nation" analysis for *Forbes* (75th anniversary issue; 14 September 1992). Here Bellow deplores the tendency of contemporary Americans to surrender their mental freedom to the noise-makers of contemporary culture – from the Michael Jacksons to the Dan Rathers – to those who ostensibly wield a position of prominence in the cultural landscape of the American nation today. Lacking the sustaining traditions of the old world, "we cast about for prescriptions," and "given the oceanic proliferating complexity of things [most of us are] paralyzed by the very suggestion that we assume responsibility for so much."[14]

Even so, Bellow maintains, writers cannot simply relinquish their task, which is to reveal the powers of a deeper level of humanity's potential. The greater the pressure of the complex world, the greater the need "to think hard, to reject what is mentally dishonorable."[15] While Bellow acknowledges a certain lack of commitment to this goal among Western writers, he concedes a resistance and perseverance of dissident hope among his Eastern colleagues who, he senses, do not tire, more so now than ever before, to show by example that a country cannot live without art, as little as it can live without salt ("Intellectuals" 551). The salt of dissidence is the force sustaining writers and intellectuals in Eastern and Central Europe as their nations complete their cycles of change.

At the same time, Bellow is cautious to predict whether these changes towards democratic societies will eventually eliminate the need for dissidence. What he stresses instead is the constant necessity, under any system, for the writer to step aside and look into his or her own soul for answers to what is truly significant. In his essay on Mozart, Bellow explains this need: "[As human beings] we have transhistorical powers. The source of these powers is in our curious nature. We have concentrated with immense determination on what forms us externally, but that need not actually govern us internally. It can do that only if we grant it the right."[16] Here Bellow reiterates a hope he also projects as a "truth" in his presentation at the conference, namely that "our resistance cannot be eradicated" ("Intellectuals" 555). And he reminds the audience of Mandelstam as a case in point. Osip Mandelstam (1891–1938), poet, critic, and dissident of the early Stalin era, would not tire of projecting living truths against indoctrinated truths. In 1934, Mandelstam was arrested and sentenced to exile for publicly reading a trenchant poem condemning Stalin as "murderer and peasant slayer." His example shows that even the smallest group makes a "public," able to raise and maintain a voice against the common noise. According to Bellow, such side-stepping of the world of oppression and desire-manipulation, although it may not command the attention of millions, is worth every effort.

As the contemporary Central European dissidents, raised on cold-war rhetoric only to become its adversaries, have been showing by example, maintaining the inner voice is a sure sign of survival – of the individual writer, her or his intellectual history, and its surrounding culture; and if anything, it is the glue that will prove its strength in holding together the social fabric of the European nations emerging from the cold war into a new center.

NOTES

1. Foreign invitations to which Bellow has responded in recent years came from Oxford University (May 1990) and from Florence (December 1991), where he spoke at a celebration of Mozart's bicentenary on the nature of the artist as genius.

2. Saul Bellow, "Something to Remember Me By" [1990], *Something to Remember Me By: Three Tales* (New York: Signet, 1991), 220.

3. The search for a post-cold-war identity is adequately reflected in the search for a term acceptable to all of the nations and cultures which find themselves part of the new center. While the designation of Eastern and Western Europe is now either defunct (viz., united Germany) or misleading (how much more or less "Eastern" is Poland than the former East Germany?), the term "Central

Europe" takes hold, more so however, in the former "East" than the former "West" where the term still harbors negative historical implications of "centrality combined with power." My choice of "Central Europe" rests with the hope that Europeans will realize that they now have a chance to move beyond the established East-West bipolarity and establish a third and idiosyncratic way of cultural and political self-definition. I support this position specifically as a response to the current (late 1992) resurgence of right-wing nationalism in post-unification Germany.

4. See Christa Wolf, *What Remains, and Other Stories* (New York: Farrar Straus Giroux, 1992); see also Peter Schneider, *The German Comedy: Scenes of Life After the Wall* (New York: Farrar Straus Giroux, 1991).

5. Thomas Rosenlöcher, *Die verkauften Pflastersteine: Dresdner Tagebuch* (Frankfurt: Suhrkamp, 1990), 45. ["Die Grenzen sind offen/Mir fehlen die Worte." Translation mine].

6. Richard Rorty, "For a More Banal Politics," *Harper's* (May 1992): 17.

7. Ibid., 21.

8. Saul Bellow, *The Dean's December* [1982], (New York: Simon & Schuster Pocketbooks, 1983), 316.

9. Several of Bellow's early short stories first appeared in *Partisan Review*, as did the original version of *Seize the Day*. Bellow also contributed to the journal as a reviewer. On his association with *Partisan Review*, see Ruth Miller, *Saul Bellow: A Biography of the Imagination* (New York: St. Martin's, 1991), 49–53, and James Atlas, "Starting Out in Chicago," *Granta* 41 (1992): 39–68.

10. This is the title as given in the program notes. The proceedings of the conference have been published in *Partisan Review* 4 (1992). Bellow's impromptu remarks are grouped with those of other panelists under the session heading "Intellectuals and Writers Since the Thirties," pp. 531–58. Page references in the text are to this publication.

11. Vaclav Havel, *Disturbing the Peace*, qtd. in Rorty, 20.

12. Saul Bellow, "Mozart," *Bostonia* (Spring 1992): 32.

13. Saul Bellow, *Humboldt's Gift* (New York: Viking, 1975), 12.

14. Saul Bellow, "There Is Simply Too Much to Think About," *Forbes* (14 Sep. 1992): 104, 106.

15. Ibid., 100.

16. Bellow continues, with a view to current developments: "But we as individuals, in inner freedom, need not grant any such thing. This is a good moment to remind ourselves of this – now that the great ideological machines of the century have stopped forever and are already covered with rust." "Mozart," 35.

Saul Bellow's Martyrs & Moralists: The Role of the Writer in Modern Society

Allan Chavkin & Nancy Feyl Chavkin

O NE OF THE preoccupations of Bellow's later fiction is the role of the modern writer in a society indifferent or hostile to literary art. The dire situation of the modern writer is shown in all its complexities in *Humboldt's Gift,* but the solution to the writer's problem of what kind of writer he should aspire to be is best revealed in *The Dean's December.* This essay will explore the problematic situation of the modern writer who has degenerated into a "farcical martyr" in *Humboldt's Gift* and will then examine his transformation in *The Dean's December* to a "moralist of seeing."[1] The authentic role of the modern writer as a moralist of seeing owes a large debt to nineteenth-century English romanticism and should be contrasted to the inauthentic role of the powerful "big-name" journalist who is unable to convey what is occurring in modern society.

I

Bellow's focus in *Humboldt's Gift* is upon the absurd situation of the modern writer in a materialistic society marked by the cynical "realism" of "deeper thieves" (259). In such a society, the idealistic writer who hopes to play a great role in the fate of mankind feels as if power has been stolen from him, so that he becomes a "farcical martyr," performing the role of failed artist to the satisfaction of ubiquitous cynical "realists." When Von Humboldt Fleisher, who aspired to be "the great American poet of the century" (340), exults in being "the first poet in America with power brakes" and

13

speculates on what kind of drivers certain famous writers would have been (20, 21), his artistic collapse and farcical martyrdom are then adumbrated.[2]

Humboldt's Gift is actually a long desultory meditation prompted by the need of the narrator to understand the cause of the failure, madness, and premature demise of his friend and mentor Von Humboldt Fleisher. Though it often substitutes a comic tone for the solemnity of the romantics, the novel can be considered as an elaborate variation on the discursive meditative ode, the genre initiated by Wordsworth to present the gradual process of the mind's coming to terms with its own anxiety.[3] In an essay published in the same year as *Humboldt's Gift* and appropriately entitled "A World Too Much with Us," Bellow observes that the spiritual crisis which afflicted the English romantics, what "in our modern jargon" we call "alienation," is our problem today.[4] The form of *Humboldt's Gift* is a crisis meditation in which Charlie finds himself confronted with two radically different "teachers," Ronald Cantabile, a vibrant representative of modern materialistic society, and Humboldt, a spiritual mentor. To illuminate this crisis and its resolution, we will focus upon two failed writers, Humboldt and Charlie Citrine, and their automobiles, which function symbolically in the novel.

By conventional standards, Charlie is a successful writer who takes pride in the emblems of his success, especially a Mercedes 280-SL coupe that his voluptuous young girlfriend Renata coerced him into buying. Charlie has won prizes for his books on historical figures, has written a popular Broadway play based on his friend and mentor Humboldt, and has been commissioned by major magazines to write stories on the Kennedys and other national figures. For these accomplishments, he has earned a great deal of money, and the French government has made him a Chevalier of the French Legion of Honor. Yet Charlie suffers from writer's block and feels dissatisfied. In an early draft of the novel, it is especially clear that Charlie's belief in "realism" has resulted in his forsaking his potential as a serious artist: "Hamilcar [Humboldt] had always been good natured with him – almost always. Nevertheless, he had not liked being told that the real Orlansky [Citrine] was a strong realist. Not an artist" (MS 7.6, pp. 18–19).[5] This passage makes clear the basic opposition between "realism" and art that is at the core not only of this novel but also Bellow's other work. In its most extreme form, the "realism" that Humboldt refers to here, and which is the dominant modern sensibility, is a brutal cynicism and materialism; it is opposed to the values and outlook of the romantic writer, who believes that there is "the deeper life"[6] or added dimension to existence that cannot be scientifically verified or logically explained.

Although Charlie intended to resist materialism, the fact of the matter is that Charlie abandoned the search for "the deeper life" for easy money and social status. He realizes now that his success is superficial, and his fame temporary. His award given by the French government is a trivial one, the equivalent of one given to those who breed pigs or "improve the garbage cans" (187), and even the inept, comical hood Ronald Cantabile knows the insignificance of the award when he ridicules the writer by reading him part of Mike Schneiderman's column which refers to Charlie the Chevalier as "the Chevrolet of the French Legion" (258).

The distorted values of contemporary society in which worship of materialism results in excessive admiration for an expensive car is suggested when the amoral opportunist Ronald Cantabile insists that it was Charlie's fault that Cantabile deliberately battered the writer's silver Mercedes: "You made me. Yes, you. You sure did. You think I don't have feelings? You wouldn't believe how I feel about a car like that" (45). Charlie makes clear that an attack on the car is also an attack on himself (and a low blow at that) because he has allowed the car to become an extension of himself.

Stunned by the attack on his car, Charlie describes the damaged Mercedes in graphic detail. His excessive love for his car is revealed by the fact that he unconsciously anthropomorphizes it when he describes the damage to the vehicle.

> My loveliest of machines, my silver Mercedes 280, my gem, my love offering, stood mutilated in the street. Two thousand dollars' worth of bodywork would never restore the original smoothness of the metal skin. The headlights were crushed blind. . . . (47) The windshield was covered with white fracture-blooms. It had suffered a kind of crystalline internal hemorrhage. (35–36)

When Humboldt, a reckless, distracted driver, finally wrecks his car (53), the accident aptly symbolizes the "smash-up" of his life. Just before they are supposed to leave for Europe, Kathleen escapes from Humboldt, and he degenerates into madness. This downward turn into paranoia leaves no doubt that Humboldt's potential to be the great American poet of the century has been torpedoed. His life quickly deteriorates into ridiculous clowning as he plays with great energy the role of pathetic victim, the sensitive poet crucified by a harsh world full of enemies. Humboldt becomes the star performer in a circus of absurd drama, wild emotions, and scandal, as he involves himself with police, psychiatrists, lawyers, and private detectives. Charlie suggests that Humboldt has "a grand time being mad in New York" (53), and although there is much truth to that statement, Humboldt is not playacting. In his delusions, he believes that an innocent man named Magnasco is living with Kathleen, and the enraged poet repeatedly threatens him with a gun.[7] When the police come to arrest Humboldt, he fights like an ox. He ends up in Bellevue, soiled from diarrhea, locked away for the night in a filthy cell.

When Kathleen dumps Humboldt, the poet's paranoia knows no bounds, and even his "blood brother" Charlie becomes the focus of his rage. Humboldt cannot forgive Charlie for his success, especially since his Broadway play *Von Trenck* "exploited" Humboldt's character. "But who the hell is Citrine to become so rich?" (2); "And I don't say he actually pla-giarized, but he did steal something from me – my personality. He built my personality into his hero [Von Trenck]" (3–4). Humboldt satisfies some of his feelings for revenge by drawing his emergency "blood-brother" check on Charlie's account for $6,763.58. In his posthumously delivered letter to Charlie, Humboldt explains that he bought an Oldsmobile with part of the money, but states that he didn't really know what he was going to do with "this big powerful car on Greenwich street." In fact, the expense of keeping the car in a garage was more than the rent in his fifth-floor walk-up apartment. For a while he "drove a hell of a car" and would say to his buddies when he drove past the theater where *Von Trenck* was playing – "There's the hit that paid for this powerful machine" (340).

Ironically, after receiving shock treatment, he could not remember where he had left the car, the claim check, or the registration; thus, he lost the Oldsmobile. Humboldt confesses that he "had it in" for Charlie because Citrine expected Humboldt to be the great American poet of the century who would "purge consciousness of its stale dirt" and teach us about "the three-fourths of life that are obviously missing!" (340). Unfor-tunately, Humboldt explains, he has not been able to read or write poetry in "these last years": "Opening the *Phaedrus* a few months ago, I just couldn't do it. I broke down. My gears are stripped. My lining is shot. It is all shattered. I didn't have the strength to bear Plato's beautiful words, and started to cry. The original, fresh self isn't there any more" (340). It is revealing that Humboldt describes his mental collapse with automotive metaphors; the implication is that Humboldt inordinately identifies with his car and that he is excessively absorbed in materialism with the consequent loss of his poetic powers.

Humboldt's posthumous gift to Charlie, a film script, contains a description of the situation of the contemporary artist as farcical martyr which applies to both Charlie and Humboldt and clarifies Bellow's view of the fundamental situation of the modern artist in a materialistic society unsympathetic to his purpose.

> To the high types of Martyrdom the twentieth century has added the farcical martyr. This, you see, is the artist. By wishing to play a great role in the fate of mankind he becomes a bum and a joke. A double punishment is inflicted on him as the would-be representative of meaning and beauty. When the artist-agonist has learned to be sunk and shipwrecked, to embrace defeat, and assert nothing, to subdue his will and accept his assignment to the hell of modern truth perhaps his Orphic powers will be restored. . . . (345–46)

In contrast to the artist as tragic martyr (e.g., Gauguin, Melville), contemporary society has created the artist as self-indulgent buffoon. Having lost all discipline and thoroughly compromised himself, Humboldt stars in the farce of his own failed career, becoming an absurd caricature of the suffering artist-hero.

Humboldt is only partially responsible for his sad fate, as Charlie implies. Society must share a large part of the blame, for while it provides the poet with material comfort, it renders him socially insignificant and powerless, so that he becomes a tragic-comic figure. In the scene in which Cantabile kidnaps Charlie to take him to see Stronson, his Thunderbird is delayed in traffic by those who hold *real* power in the country – by "the deeper thieves":

> We turned into La Salle Street where we were held up by taxicabs and newspaper trucks and the Jaguars and Lincolns and Rolls-Royces of stockbrokers and corporation lawyers – of the deeper thieves and the loftier politicians and the spiritual elite of American business, the eagles in the heights far above the daily, hourly, and momentary destinies of men. (259)

The expression "deeper thieves" refers not only to the fact that the wealthy as a result of their power can steal more money than ordinary thieves, but also to their cynical "realism" which has resulted in their "stealing" the respect, stature, and power that artists once had. This cynical "realism" is largely accepted by society as a whole and is held by such disparate types as Renata, her mother the Sēnora, Charlie's brother

Ulick, Thaxter, and Cantabile, all of whom might be described with the language Charlie uses to describe the inept hoodlum – as parts of "the new mental rabble of the wised-up world" (107). This cynical "realism" disseminated by the powerful and widely adopted by much of society results in the artist's values being considered as insignificant or bogus, "children's play" or "fairy tale stuff." According to the literal-minded, the realist can make things happen, while the idealistic artist with his belief in such scientifically unverifiable ideas as the "soul" and "the imagination" cannot do useful work in the real world. Charlie reflects on this cynical point of view held by many in the country: a poem cannot pick you up in Chicago and land you in New York a few hours later; "it had no such powers. And interest was where power was" (155). Whereas in ancient times the poet possessed power in the material world, he no longer does. The "deeper thieves" respect those who can "make things happen" in the material world; "a poet can't perform a hysterectomy or send a vehicle out of the solar system" (118).

Charlie reflects that the poet's main occupation is to be a martyr – that is, to fail and to suffer. In fact, society is proud of its dead poets because their failures validate its cynical "realism." The poet's failure proves that in the U.S.A. only those who are "tough-minded" and devoted to the material world can be triumphant. Poets such as Humboldt are loved only because these martyrs "can't make it here." When a poet such as Humboldt goes mad, the "realist" exults. Citrine asserts: "If *I* were not such a corrupt, unfeeling bastard, creep, thief, and vulture, I couldn't get through this either. Look at these good and tender and soft men, the *best* of us. They succumbed, poor loonies" (118). It is Humboldt's feeling of social insignificance and powerlessness that results in his doing exactly what society expects and encourages him to do – to become "a hero of wretchedness" and to enact the "Agony of the American Artist" (155, 156). Charlie reflects that Humboldt "consented to the monopoly of power and interest held by money, politics, law, rationality, technology because he couldn't find the next thing, the new thing, the necessary thing for poets to do" (155).

In the film treatment in which Humboldt represents the role of the modern artist as farcical martyr, he implies that Charlie himself must transcend this role and find the "next thing" for the poet to do. Like Corcoran, the writer in the script, Charlie has lost both his wife and mistress and has compromised his integrity and prostituted the powers of his imagination for commercial gain. Humboldt's gift and an accompanying letter contain quotations from and allusions to the English romantic poets, especially Blake, which suggest the efficacy of the power of the imagination to help the individual achieve spiritual rebirth. At the end of his letter to Charlie, Humboldt reminds his friend that "we are not natural beings but supernatural beings" (347).

By the end of the novel, Charlie has struggled through his crisis and concluded that he must seek higher values than the materialism that is aptly symbolized by luxury cars. In an attempt to win Renata back when she left him for Flonzaley, Charlie had suggested that he would purchase a new Mercedes. Now that idea is forgotten, however, for Charlie intends to "take up a different kind of life" (483), one that will focus on spiritual matters and "The Messiah, that savior faculty the imagination" that can illuminate the commonplace world and help to redeem a society suffering from false values (396). The implication at the end of *Humboldt's Gift* is that a new role for the writer in marked contrast to that of the farcical martyr is needed, but exactly what this new role should be is not explained. In *The Dean's December,* however, Bellow does reveal what this new role will be.

II

The Dean's December is a tale of two cities in which the protagonist Albert Corde meditates upon life and death in Chicago and Bucharest, cities which represent the opposing civilizations of East and West. During his reflections on his experiences in the two cities, Bellow's protagonist and spokesman ponders the major problems that plague modern society, such as the threat of nuclear and ecological holocausts, crime, anarchy, authoritarianism, the plight of minorities, and the decline of the city. "Speaking up for the noble ideas of the West in their American form" (124), Corde is particularly concerned about the decline of the modern city and the worsening situation of the underclass. He sees a connection between our cultural impoverishment and the poverty of the ghetto. They have the same source, imaginative impoverishment. Modern man suffers from moral and emotional atrophy, and Corde predicts dire consequences unless the present course is altered and a new path is taken.

The communications industry, which should provide insight into this perplexing situation and help to show us the way out of our spiritual wilderness, only breeds misunderstanding, burying reality under a garbage heap. Corde emphasizes the need for "poetry" to uncover reality which has become buried under the debris of the contemporary dump heap. "The first act of morality was to disinter the reality, retrieve reality, dig

it out from the trash, represent it anew as art would represent it" (123).
In the tradition of Blake, Shelley, and other romantics, whom he quotes,
Corde stresses the power of the imagination to go beyond customary
perception, prejudice, and platitudes and to illuminate reality and to provide real understanding.

Although he has doubts that he can measure up to the kind of writer
he desires to be, Corde feels the need to write a higher kind of journalism
which incorporates "poetry" that is in many ways the antithesis of Dewey
Spangler's journalism. When the dean recalls the beginning line from
Shelley's "England in 1819" ("An old, mad, blind, despised, and dying
King"), he suggests that he would like to include that "wonderful hard
music" in his writing (59). To some extent, Corde was able to write this
kind of journalism in his *Harper's* articles, though he finds some faults
with them, such as a histrionic style at times. The powerful and influential Spangler, "ten times more important than any U. S. Senator you
could name" (121) and symbolic not only of modern journalism but also of
the mass media in all its forms, fails to explore and understand the moral,
emotional, and imaginative life, in short, "the true life" of people.
Moreover, the immense power of the mass media prevents human beings
from gaining access to "this true life." In fact, it deprives people of the
capacity to apprehend and to experience what is happening around them.

Spangler considers Corde's idea of incorporating poetry into journalism a regression to naive adolescence, and "pouring scorn" on this
"poetry," "the smart little monster" Spangler (300) ridicules the dean's
new role as poet-prophet, and criticizes him for viewing his work as "a
visionary project" (243). Corde reflects upon the hostility of the powerful
"back-stabbing" journalist:

> But perhaps Spangler's main charge against me was that I was
> guilty of poetry. And I don't know exactly what to make of that. He
> himself was keen on poetry in his youth. He's now a spokesman,
> though, and poets never really were liked in America. Benjamin
> Franklin said better one good schoolmaster than twenty poets.
> That's why when we have most need of the imagination we have only
> "special effects" and histrionics. But for a fellow like me, the real
> temptation of abyssifying is to hope that the approach of the "last
> days" might be liberating, might compel us to reconsider deeply,
> earnestly. In these last days we have a right and even a duty to purge
> our understanding. In the general weakening of authority, the
> authority of the ruling forms of thought also is reduced, those forms
> which have done much to bring us into despair and into the abyss. I

don't need to mind them anymore. For science there can be no good or evil. But I personally think about virtue, about vice. (278)

Embodying the ubiquitous communications industry which titillates and distorts as it attempts to satisfy the public's appetite for sensationalism, Spangler only "increases" the "debris of false description or non-experience" (243). Bellow himself in an interview that appeared shortly after the publication of the novel echoes Corde:

> although you are reading about it all the time, you can't find out what is happening in this world . . . and you can't find out what's happening humanly. . . . We live in this alleged age of communication, which comes in the form of distracting substitutes for reality. But the reality in our day comes from art. And we live in a country that has ruled this off limits.[8]

Only in poetry can one penetrate through the veil of facts and theories to reality, so Corde suggests that Spangler's kind of journalism only helps foster a "false consciousness" that pervades society. Spangler, the master of "crisis chatter," is part of America's "cultural intelligentsia," from whom "issues the real danger of self-perpetuating thought control in the form of ignorant, philistine culture discourse."[9] Moreover, Spangler's belief in "realism" is a cynical ideology that allows him selfishly to manipulate the honest and the vulnerable, as he does when he pretends to renew an old friendship with the dean while actually exploiting him. Bellow implies in his novel that there is a connection between seeing accurately and acting morally. His allusion to Shelley's poem "England in 1819" reinforces this idea, for in that poem, Shelley, like Bellow, attacks the ruling elite of his day when he refers to "Rulers who neither see nor feel nor know." Bellow twice alludes to the beginning line of Shelley's poem when he discusses Maxie Detillion, who is a good example of insensitive people who wield at least some power over the underclass. The line refers equally well to others, whose transgressions are more subtle than those of the outrageous Detillion. Dewey Spangler, Provost Witt, and Mason Zaehner, Sr., for example, are blind to the realities of the contemporary situation, and they are not only ignorant but also morally bankrupt. Unlike Shelley at the end of "England in 1819," Corde does not predict a violent revolution, but he does desire a revolutionary change of consciousness, as Blake and Wordsworth also did. Like the nineteenth-century romantics, the dean has an almost apoc-

alyptic faith in the powers of poetry to initiate this change of consciousness. In his *Harper's* articles, he had written about the profound effect a
line from *Macbeth* had on a class of African–American school children
and then had speculated that perhaps only poetry had the strength "to
rival the attractions of narcotics, the magnetism of TV, the excitements
of sex, or the ecstasies of destruction" (187).

Although Spangler mocks the dean's belief in Keatsian "realms of
gold" (249), Corde maintains that we can understand both external and
internal reality only by the power of the imagination. Modern man lacks
human knowledge, knowledge of his environment and his own self, and
chooses to live vicariously. The problem of modern man is that he is a
divided self who is detached from reality and from his fellow men and
thus can no longer experience reality or establish a common bond with
others. The romantics called this state "dejection"; in the modern jargon
it is called alienation, or as Corde suggests, it can be viewed as a kind of
schizophrenia in which the feelings atrophy and nihilism replaces humanism. In short, the modern problem is a problem that preoccupied the
romantics, but there is one important difference, as Bellow insists –
the problem has become much worse since Wordsworth's day, and the
eschatological tone that Corde assumes at times can be partially explained
because of this worsening of the problem. The romantics suggested that
recovery resided only in the imagination, and though he is more skeptical and self-mocking than the romantics, this solution is also Bellow's.
Like Blake, whom he quotes from and alludes to repeatedly, Corde
believes that man must free himself from spiritual incarceration, the
product of the atrophying of imagination and emotion.

In fact, *The Dean's December* is preoccupied with modern man's lack of
freedom. The novel bemoans the political bondage of both the underclass
of the non-Communist West and the populations in the penitentiary Communist East. Sympathetic to those who do not have equality – African–
Americans, women, and others – the novel reveals the violent as well as
subtle exploitations associated with authoritarianism, racism, and sex-
ism. Bellow is aware of the complexities of this theme of freedom. Inex-
tricably connected to political freedom is spiritual liberty. In the modern
city, which threatens to cripple people's creative capacities, they must
liberate themselves from their "mind-forged manacles" if they are to attain any degree of freedom.

Like the romantics, Bellow calls not only for political liberation but
also liberation of the mind from the mortmain of custom and the slavery
of routine perception so that the imagination can transform a "universe

of death" into one of life. This new kind of seeing, without the beclouding fog of prejudices, preconceptions, abstract theories, and a multitude of facts, is the first act of morality and a prerequisite for recovering the power to experience reality again and initiate social change. By the end of the novel, Bellow, a twentieth-century heir to the romantic tradition, reveals a qualified hope that the modern writer will assume his proper role and help man to recognize the powers of the imagination and use them to redeem himself and his world and reclaim the great positives of the Western past.

NOTES

We are grateful for a Southwest Texas State University Research Enhancement Award which enabled us to complete the research for this essay, and we also appreciate the editors of *The Kansas Quarterly* allowing us to use in the first section of this article parts of our article "'Farcical Martyrs' and 'Deeper Thieves' in Bellow's *Humboldt's Gift*," Kansas Quarterly, 21, no. 4 (1989): 77–88. We express thanks to Saul Bellow for allowing us to examine and quote from his unpublished manuscripts.

1. Saul Bellow, *Humboldt's Gift* (New York: Viking, 1975), p. 345 and *The Dean's December* (New York: Harper and Row, 1982), p. 123. Subsequent references will be given parenthetically in the text.

2. The extensive automotive references help clarify the main theme of *Humboldt's Gift*, but critics have neglected them. Barbara L. Estrin, "Recomposing Time: *Humboldt's Gift* and *Ragtime*," Denver Quarterly, 17 (1982): 16–31, mentions that the destruction of a car "sets into action the most dramatic sequence of both novels," but she does not discuss in any detail the importance of the automotive references in *Humboldt's Gift*.

3. For a discussion of Bellow's debt to English romanticism in *Humboldt's Gift*, see Michael G. Yetman, "Who Would Not Sing for Humboldt?" *ELH*, 48 (1981): 935–51, and Allan Chavkin, "*Humboldt's Gift* and the Romantic Imagination," *Philological Quarterly*, 62 (1983): 1–19, and Chavkin's "Bellow and English Romanticism," in *Saul Bellow in the 1980s: A Collection of Critical Essays*, ed. Gloria L. Cronin and L. H. Goldman (East Lansing, MI: Michigan State Univ. Press, 1989), pp. 67–79; originally published in *Studies in the Literary Imagination*, 17 (1984): 7–18.

4. Saul Bellow, "A World Too Much with Us," *Critical Inquiry*, 21, No. 1 (1975): 1.

5. This quotation is from unpublished drafts of the novel that are part of the Special Collections at the University of Chicago Library, where most of

Bellow's manuscript material is held. Occasionally, unpublished passages from the manuscripts confirm what is subtly suggested in the novel. As we do here, when we refer to these manuscripts we shall use the abbreviation MS and the identifying numbers used by the Special Collections staff. Thus: 7.9, pp. 18–19, refers to Box #7, Folder #9, pp. 18–19. In this article, the quotations from Bellow's early unpublished manuscripts of *Humboldt's Gift* are taken from "Deposit: 1978 group."

6. This expression refers to a spiritual state that modern society does not acknowledge. See *The Dean's December,* p. 105.

7. Humboldt is modelled on Delmore Schwartz, as James Atlas, *Delmore Schwartz: The Life of an American Poet* (New York: Farrar Straus Giroux, 1977) makes clear. Atlas reveals that Schwartz believed that his wife was unfaithful and had numerous lovers.

8. William Kennedy, "If Saul Bellow Doesn't Have a True Word to Say, He Keeps His Mouth Shut," *Esquire,* Feb. 1982: 50.

9. Gerhard Bach, "The Dean Who Came In from the Cold: Saul Bellow's America of the 1980s," in *Saul Bellow in the 1980s,* p. 308.

Two Not-So-Farcical Misogynists in *More Die of Heartbreak*

Gloria L. Cronin

Representation of the world, like the world itself, is the work of men; they describe it from their own point of view, which they confuse with absolute truth.

—Simone de Beauvoir

A radical critique of literature, feminist in its impulse, would take the work first of all as a clue to how we live, how we have been living, how we have been led to imagine ourselves, how our language has trapped as well as liberated us, how the very act of naming has been till now a male prerogative, and how we can begin to see and name—and therefore live—afresh.

—Adrienne Rich

B ELLOW'S LAST major novel, *More Die of Heartbreak*[1] (1987), functions as a Prufrockian lament about failed men and absent mermaids. Full of misogynous love-lore, comic characters, botched loves, fatal forays into the danger zones of sex and romance, farcical retreats, and serio-crackpot sexual philosophizings, this text provides an analogue of Bellow's end-of-the-century comic despair over the impasse of heterosexual relations. Misogynous in its narrative construction, the novel unfolds as the self-ironic report of two men exchanging battle wounds with each other and with a "mock reader" or "narratee" at the expense of women whom they perceive to have failed their romantic expectations.

Bellow's narrational structure provides the first clue that this novel's rhetorical strategies align it with a long Greco-Roman, medieval, and modern tradition of misogynous texts. Other clues include its male center of perception, its objectification of women,

25

its staging only the scoptophilic male gaze, its sympathetic exoneration of misogynist men, and its framing of stereotypical binary gender patterns. Such patterns typically dichotomize men as rational, good, intellectually competent, spiritually valuable, and sexually honorable, whereas women are merely "lack" or "other." Through these gender ideologies, the ontological status of woman disappears as she becomes aligned only with the senses. Intellectually passive, metaphysically liable, "Woman" in texts such as these is usually shrewish, depraved, androgynous, or, worse still, unintelligible. Such a female figure is integral to the misogynous plot which usually hinges on the dissuasion of men from marriage and the company of women.

The center of consciousness located in Kenneth Trachtenberg is what principally stages this text's enactment of misogyny. Not only is it an account told by one male character to another. It also creates a sympathetic listener or mock reader who is clearly a male intimate of the narrator. It further creates a sympathetic reader outside of the text who is scripted by the strategies of the text as a like-minded intimate, a reflective sharer of experience, or close companion of the writer. What the text forms, then, is a sympathetic male listening circle. If we are unresisting readers, we are compelled to play our role by conforming ourselves to the textual cues, learning the rules of the misogynous reading as we proceed. But what of the resisting reader, say perhaps a woman who finds herself being coerced into an intimate listening circle of male misogynists? Does she abandon her resisting female self and allow some kind of gender transformation to occur? Should she retreat in polite puzzlement? Should she allow herself to feel alienated or outraged, or should she perhaps read the text as it was not meant to be read – read it against itself in an act of resistance? Not to do so would be to render oneself morally inert or self-divided. A reading which focuses as much on the resisting female reader as on the text will hopefully yield useful insights into both meaning and the differing effects of the text on its male and female readers. As Judith Butler reminds the would-be gender critic:

> The critical task is . . . to locate strategies of subversive repetition enabled by those constructions, to affirm the local possibilities of intervention through participating in precisely those practices of repetition that constitute identity and, therefore, present the immanent possibility of contesting them.[2]

Bellow's menu of complaints against women in *MDH* is lengthy: the triple failure of science, religion, and belles lettres to illuminate love, modern distortions in human relations, the meaning of sado-masochism, the interconnection of love and death, the failure of modern marriage, the ironies of biological sexuality, the contemporary failure of "poetry" in human relations, and the comic incompatibility of heterosexual love with the male quest for higher consciousness.

The genre Bellow has chosen to explore these gender complaints is suggested by his adaptation of the Gogolian farce, "The Bridegroom," with its classic misogynist tale of the flight of the bridegroom from entrapment by marriage. Hence the aptness of a Charles Addams cartoon:

"Are you unhappy, darling?" [he asks Morticia.]
"Oh yes, *yes!* Completely." [she replies.] (10)

The gender anxieties in this late twentieth-century text parallel those of late nineteenth-century Anglo-American writers. As Gilbert and Gubar argue in *No Man's Land,* though the plot of sexual battle is timeless, during the late Victorian and early modern periods the simultaneous appearance of the woman writer and activist feminists provoked an anxious and sometimes violent male literary backlash.[3] "The Love Song of J. Alfred Prufrock," a key proof text, offers an interesting parallel with *MDH* in its depiction of an emasculated male convinced that mermaids of fabled romance are dangerous and will not sing to him. Prufrock's gender anxieties at the beginning of the century and Kenneth's at the end of it share remarkable similarities.

Between the dual consciousness of Kenneth and Benn, the "narratee," and the listening circle, Bellow constructs a drama about the male evasion of marriage and the banishment of women from the male republic of higher consciousness. In this economy, "Woman" is reduced to the signifier of masculine desire as fantasy object. Motivated by such an old misogynist agenda and fueled by anger at his father's libertinage and wasted intellectual gifts, his emasculating liaison with Treckie, and his childish fear of losing Benn to the ladies, Kenneth becomes violent in his attempt to dissuade Benn from marriage. He attempts a search-and-destroy mission targeting Benn's Poe-like quest for love with the classic beauty, Matilda Layamon. His explicit goal is to preserve both Benn and himself for the grail quest for higher consciousness. The upshot of this destructive endeavor is that both protagonists viciously condemn women for their collective failure to accept, arouse, anticipate, love, minister to, or compensate them perfectly enough. It is a devaluation intended to rob all women of metaphysical value.

The cruel, arrogant, and taunting depictions of women generated by Kenneth for Benn's benefit systematically implicate the narratee and the entire listening circle in misogynistic depictions of women at once crazy, scheming, chaotic, devouring, sexually rapacious, transvestite, and androgynous. Erotic teases, whores, rich bitches, or aged hospital inmates — each woman is passed around the listening circle for laughter, for horror, or for ratification as flagellating, physically abhorrent, or socially tyrannical. The critic Cixous explains why such formulas can only result in obstacles to the compassionate and truthful examination of the subject of love:

> in history, the first obstacle, always already there, is in the existence, the production of images, types, coded and suitable ways of behaving, and in society's identification with a scene in which the roles are fixed so that lovers are always initially trapped by the puppets with which they are assumed to merge.[4]

Clearly the gender club in the listening circle is scripted and cued by the text to see itself, Kenneth, and Benn as a community of unfortunate sexual victims of a droll mortality full of such contaminating women precisely because the roles are already fixed in stereotype. According to Kenneth, sex and women are cruel jokes nature has played on otherwise noble males, nurtured in "romantic" and even "chivalric" expectations. However compelling the erotic might be, for these men it is metaphysically devoid of value. Bachelorhood and celibacy are prized as morally and spiritually superior life-styles to be preserved, if necessary, by deception, abandonment, and flight. Even when Benn finally notes with amazement that "there *are* more deaths from heartbreak than from atomic radiation" (197), both men fail to see the role misogynous flight from women plays in such massive human misery.

Bellow is perfectly aware of these paradoxes of male gender ideologies. However, it is not women's gender sufferings or feminist readers' expectations that interest Bellow. He is attempting to measure a set of historically constructed romantic expectations and gender ideologies (male-authored ones) on contemporary men living through the last decade of this most American of centuries. Unfortunately, women characters are used only as objectified fictional creations of Kenneth, Benn, and the listening circle.

Everything builds from Bellow's use of Kenneth as the center of consciousness in the novel. Kenneth is carefully portrayed as a sexual "wraith" (40), a failed intellectual, an inept lover, and a disappointing son. Thus, Bellow casts him as the classic unreliable narrator, encased in several layers of persiflage and irony, whose many masks defy complete identification. The clues to Kenneth's unreliability, however, lie in his relationship with his father. He resents his father's cast iron good looks, success with women and ability to "strut" (24). He hates him for his flair on the dance floor, intimate knowledge of the erotic jungle, and "sex-intoxication" (37). He also envies Rudi's sure knowledge of who he is, avoidance of clumsiness, and unpunished debauchery. He further hates his father's estimate of him as "one of those continuing-education types" who, in Aristophanes terms, has "his head up his ass" (41). However, his greatest resentment is that his father, like a force of nature, "couldn't help jamming the broadcasts from other sources" (38). His final assessment: "Dad had all the definition, the finish, of a personage; I was still in metamorphosis" (38). His worst condemnation is his father's lack of family feeling:

> If my father had so much family feeling he wouldn't have been such a screwer of other men's wives. And didn't the wives adopt a similar outlook? The world crisis was everybody's cover for lasciviousness and libertinage (two little words you seldom see). (41)

Bellow's text suggests that Kenneth's belief that he himself is cut out for higher things than his father's mere creatureliness derives partly from compensatory mechanisms:

> I was determined to go beyond him. . . . [I am made] of finer clay, as they used to put it; smarter; in a different league. Where he outclassed me he outclassed me – tennis, war record (I had no such thing), in sex, in conversation, in looks. But there were spheres (and by this I mean higher spheres) where he had no standing, and I was way ahead of him. (12).

Rudi the roué must be rejected and the druidical metaphysical quester, Uncle Benn, substituted as a surrogate who does not jam transmissions from beyond the creaturely sphere. Benn is linked directly to Kenneth through their both being physically ungainly and somewhat Russian. Benn, the spiritual father, possesses a classic Russian face and ancestry, and a body like a Russian church. Like Kenneth, he is also single now, and mostly celibate. Kenneth is proud of their spiritual bond: "We were doubly, multiply, interlinked. Neither of us by now had other real friends" (15).

Benn's new interest in sex, however, proves to be a major drawback:

> Yet in the years before his second marriage he had his hands full, dealing with ladies: flirtations, courtships, longings, obsessions, desertions, insults, lacerations, sexual bondage – the whole bit from bliss to breakdown. (50)

While observing Benn's frequent farcical escapes via the airways, Kenneth wonderingly comments: "In an age when you have Eros on one side and Thanatos on the other in a jurisdictional dispute, you may as well pack up and head for the airport rather than stand and wait for the outcome. Better to be in motion?" (50). Kenneth's absurd gender model for this sort of behavior is Darwin, whose research he believes to have ruined him for larger emotions and directly caused his impotence.

Kenneth's response to Benn's secret marriage is that of a furious, domineering child: "I didn't take his marriage well; he should have given me advance notice" (50). Like a curious schoolboy he still wonders how Benn "made out" with Aunt Lena, who subscribed to Swedenborgian doctrines of human passion. Significantly, when he tries to visualize the druidical Benn in Eden contemplating his arcana, there is no Eve in Kenneth's picture, as opposed to Rousseau's famous painting of a forest clearing replete with a nude on a récamier sofa and surrounded by tigers of desire. When Benn confesses his attraction to Matilda Layamon, Kenneth is appalled at Benn's Poesque notions about the child love with "hyacinth hair" and "classic face." After a thunderstruck silence, he explodes: "Christ, what was I supposed to say! I can't bear to have this kind of stuff laid on me, and I was sore as hell" (17). And he notes: "I never dreamed that he might be so irresponsible, downright flaky" (17). He nastily compares Benn's comments about Poe's Helen to the equivalent of a Bing Crosby crooning, and he believes Benn could find no other way to take refuge from the demon of sexuality which inevitably reduces "the private life [to] . . . a bouquet of sores with a garnish of trivialities or downright trash" (39).

Small wonder that Kenneth's assessment of Benn's other women is so cruel. We sit trapped in the listening circle while he wickedly describes Caroline Bunge as "a big graceful (old style) lady, vampy, rich, ornate, slow-moving, a center-stage personality. Middle-aged, she still stood out like a goddess from a Zeigfeld extravaganza, the Venus de Oro type" (75). He laughs at the way she speaks through her nose, makes much of her use of make-up as heavy-handed and tasteless, her behavior distinctly predatory, and her general air, "somnambulistic." Since he will not gladly share his surrogate "father," he denigrates his rival as "a strange siren who took lithium or Elavil" (79).

Della Bedell he passes around the listening circle as an excessive weekend drinker who is inappropriately forward with his uncle and full of sexual predatoriness, belligerence, and shrillness. He delights in recounting to his audience the first of the bridegroom flight tales, about how Benn has high-tailed it to Brazil, causing Della Bedell to die of a heart attack brought on by sexual deprivation. His linking of Benn with the bridegroom flight in Gogol's *The Wedding* is quite explicit. Kenneth laughingly sums her up as "a fat little lady who hit the bottle" (88).

The climax of these misogynistic depictions comes in Dr. Layamon's sermon on the terrible contemporary vision of the literality of the female. While Benn's perception of women is initially a Poe-like idealization of the beloved, and while Kenneth's is that of the classic misogynist, Dr. Layamon sees women as aged hags. As Dr. Layamon takes the gagging Benn through the female surgical wards exposing him to the bald old privates of the elderly women patients, he carries the listeners with him on a journey calculated to alienate Benn from women. "When it becomes a matter of limbs, members and organs, Eros faces annihilation" (90), as the shocked Benn reports.

On the plane to Tokyo, the occasion of Benn's second bridegroom flight, Kenneth eagerly advances his project to deconstruct "Woman" and romantic love for Benn. He patronizingly explains that Benn's spiritual nature attracts educated women who are affected by such emanations. In his misogynistic discourse, he classifies a whole category of women he characterizes as being educated only enough to fear that they will bore important men. These women are girded up by the expectations of their stage mothers and live in outer metaphysical darkness "where their poor hearts are breaking." He tells Benn that "this feminine disappointment and sorrow is very hard on men [like Benn]. They often feel called upon to restore the self-esteem that's been lost" (93). This is a characterization of women as uneducable, metaphysically deficient, parasitic, and badly in need of repair.

Within this ideological framework, Kenneth then launches the main attack on the educated and powerful Matilda Layamon. He posits her as a Rappaccini's daughter who will inevitably bring death to her lover. Her hope chest, Kenneth notes, was probably full of cocaine. He nastily reminds Benn that Poe's child-lover was under-age and retarded, and he adds that he would prefer to think of Matilda in terms of William Blake's lines "And blights with plagues the Marriage hearse" (121).

He hadn't yet begun to understand that by marrying into the Layamon family he had carried me with him. Through my attachment to

Benn I had hoped for an enlargement of personality. We were moving
in the opposite direction instead. (126–27)

Kenneth imagines for his audience Matilda's morning moods as ferocious, her teeth as sharp, and her acquisition merely a consequence of
Benn's absent-mindedness. Once Matilda is resignified as bitch, he constructs Benn as "a Phoenix who runs after arsonists" – the lover who is
"Burnt to the ground, reincarnated from the ashes" (198–99).

Kenneth's intellectual agenda is the first clue to his gender hostilities. "Inner communion with the great human reality was my true occupation, after all," he confesses. "I did it out of a conviction that it was the
only worthwhile enterprise around" (188). His uncle's habitat was one he
had chosen over more attractive settings such as Paris because he hopes
that here human life was making essential advances.

However, it is a celibate male enterprise dependent on the exclusion
of the female erotic. For Kenneth and Benn, male/female relations must
remain metaphysically devoid of value.

"As Uncle's [Benn's] self-appointed guardian spirit, I, too, had to try
to interpret their motives and anticipate their plans" (188), he protests,
as Della Bedell, Caroline Bunge, and Matilda Layamon threaten to con-
taminate the joint quest with their neuroses, Elavil, and erotic powers.
But his quest is more absurdly grandiose than the comparatively modest
Benn's. He will do for human beings what Benn has done for botany: brilliant classification and mystic identification of rare states of Being.
Bellow is clearly making fun of Kenneth, whom he presents as a wraith
who can scarcely cope with ordinary life, love, parenting, sex, and everyday human relationships. Key to our understanding of this is Bellow's
careful depiction of him as son of a notorious womanizer and a sexually
deprived mother. Kenneth feels robbed of masculine identity by both parents. He calls himself skinny, diffident, passive, politically unambitious,
and sly looking. Treckie finds his French palate, talent for high-powered
conversation, middle-class sense of responsibility, and low libido inadequate for her sexual needs. He blames his much-abused mother for failing
to bolster his male ego and for becoming disenchanted with her female role
as a petted bourgeois Parisian subjected to habitual infidelity, so he denies
the validity of her protest by focusing only on his own abandonment.

Kenneth's gender hostilities are quite honestly come by, and they are
staged in his class, Russian 451 "The Meaning of Love." His curriculum is
an encoding of a long historical tradition of misogynous love-lore. Included
are such European commentators as Gogol, whose bridegroom-to-be in

The Wedding flees out the window before entrapment in marriage; Dostoyevsky, whose ill-starred lovers die unfulfilled; Rozanov, the critic-historian and Christian mystic who envied the Jews their fertility cult because he mistakenly thought their ritual baths to be sources of fertility; Rousseau, who argued human love a necessary social delusion; Yermelov, a childhood acquaintance who believed that, in the physical body, angelic love becomes mere carnality; Plato, who believed love between men the highest form of expression; Kojève, his own Russian teacher who taught of the small glaciers in the human breast which must be melted; Swedenborg, who believed nature, including sexuality, was mere hell; Stendhal, who thought more than one sexual experience was one too many; Freud, who believed that heterosexual love is merely "overvaluation" of the beloved; Kraft-Ebbing's theories of Victorian male sexual fetishism; Havelock Ellis's anti-romantic sociological model of human sexual behavior; Blake's dubious model of gender relations in *Marriage of Heaven and Hell* ("blight with plagues the Marriage hearse"); Poe's tragic attempt to defy rationalism and the industrial revolution with poetic myths of female perfection; Philip Larkin's theory of romantic love as a "deep sleep" which blots out reality; and Benjamin Franklin's cynical old saw: "Before marriage keep your eyes wide open, after marriage keep 'em half closed." It is an anti-feminist legacy the brutalizing effects of which on the primarily women students is metaphorically suggested in Dita's sadic mutilation at the hands of a dermatologist.

Apparently Kenneth's account of the "Meaning of Love" class, with its bizarre encoding of a tradition of male violence, is designed to finish off Benn's infatuation with Matilda. Romantic love, he tells Benn and the listening circle, has been debased by its accommodation within capitalism and merchandising: "natures that could love have become too unstable to do it" (219). Benn's counterthrust, "Through love you penetrate to the essence of a being" (225), panics Kenneth, who begins to despair over trying to resignify Benn's primitive, pre-industrial views on love. If Benn is questing for a classic beauty as the physical embodiment of his search for earthly perfection, Kenneth is superfluous, unqualified, and in short, powerless. He believes that he must reclaim Benn as the priestly celibate, druidical, charismatic, semi-mystical – a man who is destined to be one of the "Citizens of Eternity" (198). Not surprisingly, Benn seems instead to be obsessed not only by botany but by female sexuality:

> He couldn't leave the women alone. . . . Part of his Eros had been detached from plants and switched to girls. And what girls! A

phoenix who runs after arsonists! . . . Burnt to the ground, reincarnated from the ashes. And after all, every return of desire is a form of reincarnation. (198–99)

This vision of the sexual adventurer is a fearful index to Kenneth's ancient and outrageous gender ideologies. A soul such as Benn's "demands the abolition of such things as love and art . . . which it can tolerate intermittently [only] if they don't get in its way" (301). Poe and romantic ideology must be deposed. Blame rationalism and capitalism, he argues:

> Something was wrong here, off the wall with the classic face, the grandeur of Rome, the glory of Greece. Poe, this poor genius nitwit married to a moronic and forever prenubile girl . . . here was a poet who had run straight into a world rolled flat as a pizza by the rational intellect (and at a primal, crude stage of capitalist development – let's not leave out capitalism), and he fought back with whiskey and poetry, dreams, puzzles, perversions. Then also Baudelaire, Poe's successor, with his vicious madonnas, taking the field – sickness and sensibility against mechanization and vulgarity. (208–9)

Kenneth is identifying not only Poe's dilemma but also his own dilemma and Benn's dilemma as would-be-lovers in late capitalist, rationalistic, and mechanized America. In such a blasted world, the classic beauties of Rome have been deposed, chivalry is gone, and romance is impossible. In their places, only the tyranny of the literal or the biological now prevails, and heterosexual relationship built on courtship and romance has been deposed.

Kenneth's rhetorical use of the account of Cleopatra and Mark Antony is designed as the coup de grace in convincing Benn of the mutually exclusive nature of eros and the metaphysical quest. It serves as an interesting index to his views on human desire.

> Pondering it again, I began to consider that a man might either give women and love what time he had to spare from his major undertakings (for instance, the struggle for existence, or the demands of his profession; also vainglory, fanaticism, power – each person would have a list of his own) or else, released from work, enter a feminine sphere with its particular priorities and directed towards very different purposes. Here is an example everybody will understand. If you weren't at war like Marc Antony, you were in love like Marc Antony; in which case you left the battle and ran after Cleopatra when her galley fled at Actium. (210)

Entrapped in binary thought patterns which posit the existence of two mutually exclusive spheres symbolized by activities of war or love, Kenneth posits a falsely monistic system of desire which functions much like Deleuze and Guattari's Marxist and Freudian description of an economy of individual desires.[5] In such a system, there is only one libidinal economy of desiring because energy spent on sexuality is not available for higher intellectual tasks. This is a sexist, Freudian vision which reinscribes the kind of binary thinking which arbitrarily separates eros and intellect, body and spirit. Dr. Layamon's denunciation of his daughter enacts exactly the same binary gender ideology. To him and the other two men, she is an androgynous horror of gender unintelligibility. Dr. Layamon describes Matilda as "a mastermind" fit only for "the War College" (168) or a rich bitch with bohemian sexual tastes. His account is mediated through Benn and delightedly reported to the listening circle by Kenneth. Both Benn and Dr. Layamon represent her as moody, scheming, complaining, pot-smoking, ambitious, masculine, angry, controlling, devoid of consciousness, greedy, shallow, tormenting, too sexually adept, too intellectual, too beautiful, too educated, in short, too powerfully integrated. She is the "other," "lack," and "difference" in their economy.

Even Kenneth is shocked at his success with Benn, who savagely begins ritually to exorcise Matilda, until he jokingly calls Benn "a negative fetishist" (264). The beauty which has attracted Benn previously now appears to endanger his life's work. Suddenly Matilda's teeth and shoulders are unsatisfactory. Watching Tony Perkins' performance in *Psycho,* he transforms Matilda from desirable female to a perverted transvestite, bearing first Tony Perkins's masculine shoulders and then the shoulders of her dreadful father. Benn has obviously absorbed "motor-mouth Layamon's" ultimately contemptuous devaluation of the literal female body. When Kenneth wittily identifies Benn as the wicked Dr. Aylmer of Hawthorne's "The Birthmark" and Matilda as the unfortunately beautiful Georgiana with her one tragic defect, he also notes how similarly Benn dismantles his Poe "fantasy woman" bit by bit – tooth, shoulder, widely-spaced breasts – until she is transformed from classic, mythical beauty to vulgar rich bitch. Finally, she is a demiurge (in the Gnostic system and certain others a supernatural being imagined as creating the world in subordination to the Supreme being *RHD*). Now a scapegoat for the duplicity, corruption, and glitz Benn associates with the Electronic Tower of modern Babel, she is transmogrified from a Poe Madonna to a women's lib siren – a sexy, highly-educated career transvestite who wants to be the "tough broad in the brokerage world" (293). Matilda, the whore of high finance, has wasted and corrupted his powers to the point that he can no longer distinguish a silk plant from a real one.

Kenneth reports with shock Benn's final belief that Matilda has become a dangerous counterforce: "The case was built that there was a demiurge hidden just under the woman's skin – that while she was sleeping . . . there were exhalations of duplicity from that delicate, straight nose" (326). But even though Kenneth has watched Benn very wickedly transform Matilda into a demiurge, Kenneth characterizes Benn sympathetically for the listening circle as "the weary, wayworn wanderer in the Poe poem" (293). He actively encourages Benn's erroneous assessment that because of Matilda he has lost his special powers and has disobeyed the prophetic voice of warning sent via the psychopathic character played by Tony Perkins. "[A] man like me, trained in science, can't go by revelation" (298), rationalizes the well-tutored Benn as he enacts his third bridegroom flight into a sterile, perpetual night of polar ice, lichens, and an all-male research team.

Fortunately, Bellow's humor is generated by his awareness of the ironic gender ideologies involved. Hence, when Kenneth switches his desire from the ungrateful Treckie to the truly educated, mature, though facially-flawed Dita Schwartz, the resisting feminist reader has to note with amusement the timeliness of Kenneth's facile repentance over Dita. After all, Treckie has permanently rejected him, a beautiful woman seems unattainable, his baby daughter will need a temporary mother, Benn is lost to the Pole, his father is in Paris, his mother is away suffering with starving Ethiopians, and his metaphysical quest is on hold. Such a reader would also note how suddenly he becomes aware of how few women are capable of appreciating his fine palate, egocentric monologism, and low libido. From the image of an anonymous, scabbed-over face beneath the beehive of bandages, Kenneth suddenly presents us with Dita as a true friend, "Independent, complex, determined [and] imaginative" (173), "pale-faced, black-eyed, [with] . . . hair that grows with Indian force" (174), but a still flawed face.

> A woman with a well-developed figure, she had lips of the Moorish type, a nose perhaps fuller than my own criterion for noses could come to terms with and a solid face with nothing masculine in its solidity. Excepting some negligible defects, she was terribly handsome. (249)

Does this ambivalent aesthetic response to Dita's phyical aspect suggest he is now a repentant Dr. Aylmer, or has mere human necessity become transcendent?

For Kenneth and Benn, life remains possible only through sexual sublimation or transformation of the female into a repulsive, androgynous scapegoat. Eros and intellectual pursuit cancel one another out here as they do in the previous novels. The irony of the title now becomes fully apparent. Is Bellow saying that the quest for heterosexual love is probably more important than the quest for an end to radiation poisoning, or are both equally deadly? Is the book a witty exposé of the misogynous historical foundations of contemporary gender lore, or is it an elderly and bitter lament intended for a sympathetic male readership? Kenneth and Benn's misogyny remains an ethical problem for enlightened male readers as well as feminist readers, even when such readers are willing to concede what will inevitably be imported during Bellow's appropriation of a comic historical genre. The problem lies not only in the misogynous narrative strategy previously outlined but also in the fact that the text unabashedly coopts us to despise women and to forgive Benn and Kenneth's treatment at the hands of less-than-ideal women. We are scripted as readers to admire their idealism and conversational talents, and to believe with them that heterosexual love makes suckers of us all. Because of our cooptation into the sympathetic listening circle, we pass only a light sentence on such farcical misogynists; Kenneth and Benn are, according to the text, merely fallible but loveable types. It is a cooptation which defers what Kristeva calls the "dream of the undistorted relation to the other."[6]

Numerous Bellow fictions have lamented the failure of relations between the sexes and shamelessly invoked negative stereotypes of women, but none are quite so bitter as *More Die of Heartbreak*. Behind its comedy, intelligence, sophistication, good fun, and irony lies a virulent hostility to women which calls upon the sympathies of likeminded men. At the very time he appears to be conducting a serious investigation into the contemporary failure of heterosexual relations, Bellow fails to provide proper elucidation of his topic that could hold these male protagonists sufficiently accountable for their roles in the travesty of human relations. After all,

> gender is what gender *means*. It has no basis in anything other than the social reality its hegemony constructs. The process that gives sexuality its male supremacist meaning is therefore the process through which gender inequality becomes socially real.[7]

Barbara Johnson suggests that literature which is ultimately misogynist not only fails to illuminate the subject of gender relations, it also suc-

ceeds only too well in reinscribing all the old damaging stereotypes instead of a "newer choreography of sexual difference"[8]:

> If human beings were not divided into two biological sexes, there
> would probably be no need for literature. And if literature could truly
> say what the relations between the sexes are, we would doubtless not
> need much of it then, either. . . . It is not the life of sexuality that liter-
> ature cannot capture; it is literature that inhabits the very heart of
> what makes sexuality problematic. . . . Literature is not only a
> thwarted investigator but also an incorrigible perpetrator of the
> problem of sexuality.[9]

As in all androcentric texts, *MDH* functions politically as an "incorrigible
perpetrator." Its ideological and attitudinal collusion staged through the
sympathetic listening circle invokes sympathy and amusement at willfully
destructive male significations of "Woman." The woman reader is forced
to watch objectified women characters being handed around before her
very eyes, between male writer, male characters, and the male listening
circle as a medium of misogynous exchange at the very moment she is
being coerced textually into sympathetic identification with Kenneth
and Benn. It should be remembered that we are not just individual
readers. We cannot escape our acculturation as male and female readers
by maintaining the illusion that readers are just people. The woman
reader learns that the ontological status of women as readers is not anal-
ogous to that of the women in the text. "Man" equals mind, and "Woman"
equals sensory perception. The paradox here is that in any discourse of
misogyny, while misogyny desires to escape the senses, perception, the
corporeal medium for higher consciousness, being bound up in its very
desire for absolute totality, is its deathwish.

The very subject of misogyny makes visible some very obvious an-
tagonisms between female readers, male authors, misogynous texts, and
the female subjects of that very misogyny. It also points up the entire
problem with representation when there are oppositions between what
is perceived and what is endorsed. It demonstrates the limits of idealism,
and it highlights those conflicts between authors and readers which parallel the conflicts between misogynists and the women who are misrep-
resented by their pervasive, but often unrecognized, images. I suspect
that, when he chose to use the classic formulas of the misogynist text,
Bellow was only too well aware of these issues but valued the comic possibilities inherent in the formula over its drawbacks. However, the problem of authorial intention aside, a feminist critic is obliged to investigate

the effects of a discourse which simultaneously exerts such malign power against "woman" as a subjectivity. For the woman reader,

> the cultural reality is not the emasculation of men by women, but the *immasculation* of women by men. As readers and teachers and scholars, women are taught to think as men, to identify with a male point of view, and to accept as normal and legitimate a male system values, one of whose central principles is misogyny.[10]

It is a doubly disempowering strategy for female readers because, as Fetterly further suggests:

> powerlessness . . . derives from not only from seeing one's experience articulated, clarified, and legitimized in art, but more significantly, . . . [it] results from the endless division of self against self, the consequence of the invocation to identify as male while being reminded that to be male – to be universal – is to be *not female*.[11]

Annette Kolodny elaborates this intimate relationship between the androcentric text and androcentric methods of reading by explaining:

> insofar as we are taught how to read, what we engage are not texts but paradigms. . . . Insofar as literature is itself a social institution, so, too, reading is a highly socialized – or learned activity. . . . We read well, and with pleasure, what we already know how to read; and what we know how to read is to a large extent dependent upon what we have already read (works from which we've developed our expectations and learned our interpretive strategies). What we then choose to read – and, by extension, teach and thereby "canonize" – usually follows upon our previous reading.[12]

Patrocinio Schweikart has noted that androcentric literature is a particularly efficient "instrument of sexual politics because it does not allow the woman reader to take refuge in her difference." Instead, she argues, it "uses her against herself" by soliciting her complicity in the elevation of male difference into universality and, accordingly, the denigration of female difference into "otherness" with reciprocity. By this intricate means the "feminine" is being produced within a particular gender system. Schweikart reminds us that the power of male texts is the power of the false consciousness into which women are coopted.[13] In other words, men are women's material and symbolic conditions. The decentered subject, Woman, is precisely the subject who cannot within this textual economy escape the designations imposed by language. Perhaps Schweikart is right to suggest that feminist readers should also question their primary allegiance to the text and author-centered paradigms of critical reading and instead examine subject-object relations in the text with their possibly malign effects on readers.

As a classic misogynist text, *MDH* primarily stages the violation of women through its fictionally constructed male gaze. The text is scoptophilic because it engages in a humorous spectator sport for male readers who are invited to engage with Kenneth in humor based on visual narcissism and a sadistic, misogynist erotics. All of this culminates in one appalling nightclub scene depicting Japanese female prostitutes suspended in a cage above the heads of an exclusively male audience for whom they are displaying their genitals with their fingers. It is the companion scene to the hospital ward filled with wasted, asexual, elderly women. This scene invites a male conspiracy (writer, protagonists, and listening circle) against all the women inside the text and outside it who threaten the exclusivity of the male gender club with its political imperatives. It is the analogue for Kenneth's Russian 451 class and for the whole text.

Although I do tend to believe that any book is a rough analogue of what its author thought and felt, Wolfgang Iser reminds us that no text pops into the world as a neatly finished bundle of meaning. It has an effect upon the reader who must react upon the textual material in order to produce meaning. The reader collaborates by applying a code of meanings to match those offered by the text.[14] Applying feminist reading codes will produce a different reading result than Bellow perhaps intended when he chose as his ur-tale Gogol's "The Wedding" with its tale of the flight of the bridegroom. Just as a literary work refers to the outside world by selecting certain norms and value systems and world views, texts adopt repertoires of norms and then suspend their validity within their fictional world. Each norm asserts certain values at the expense of others, and each tends among other things to construct an image of men and women. What is preeminent in Bellow's unjust and cruel rendering is an overwhelming sympathy for women-hating men.

Jauss has theorized that as readers we intersect with the text along a "horizon of expectations" formulated by our own respective cultural environments as we try to discover the questions which the work itself was trying to answer in its own dialogue with history.[15] Small wonder that a reader who claims membership in a feminist interpretive community should fail to intersect with a misogynistic horizon of expectations. If Bleich[16] and Holland[17] are right in asserting that a reader's most urgent motivation is always to understand one's self, Bellow thwarts any female reader's expectation of an adequate representation. Gadamer articulates a justification for new reading paradigms: "every age has to understand a transmitted text in its own way, for the text is part of the whole tradition in which the age takes on objective interest, and in which it seeks to understand itself."[18] This assertion is doubly valid in an era one of whose primary concerns is gender and the status of women. Feminist readers of Bellow likewise have the right to rehabilitate the historical "significance" of *More Die of Heartbreak* for themselves. In doing so, they may well be rewriting the text of themselves as moral critics. Even if the material text remains untouched and unmoved by such an act, the reader may not. Our utopian hope for a better world freed from such ancient and violent gender ideologies is best expressed by Irigaray:

> A genesis of love between the sexes has yet to come about, in either the smallest or largest sense, or in the most intimate or political guise. It is a world to be created or recreated so that man and woman may once more finally live together, meet and sometimes inhabit the same place. . . . as Heidegger, among others, has written, this link must forge an alliance between the divine and the mortal, in which a sexual encounter would be a celebration, and not a disguised or polemic form of the master-slave relationship.[19]

Serious commentators on the subject of human love have an obligation to do more than rearticulate the old heterosexual impasses even in updated versions of old genres. What is needed is a thoughtful contribution to a new choreography of love. Saul Bellow has revealed some of the contemporary obstacles to love in enlightening, witty, and even sophisticated ways. *MDH* is a brilliant book. However, it fails to provide full vision of culpability and rehabilitation. Bellow fails to transcend traditional significations of "Woman."

NOTES

1. Saul Bellow, *More Die of Heartbreak* (New York: Morrow, 1987). Subsequent references will be made parenthetically by page number only.

2. Judith Butler, *Gender Trouble: Feminism and the Subversion of Identity* (New York: Routledge, 1990), p. 147.

3. Sandra Gilbert and Susan Gubar, *The War of the Words, No Man's Land: The Place of the Woman Writer in the Twentieth Century* (New Haven: Yale Univ. Press, 1988), I:5.

4. Hélène Cixous, "Sorties: Out and Out: Attacks/Ways out/Forays," in Hélène Cixous and Catherine Clement, *The Newly Born Woman*, trans. Betsy Wing (Minneapolis: Univ. of Minnesota Press, 1986), p. 113.

5. Gilles Deleuze and Felix Guattari, *Anti-Oedipus: Capitalism and Schizophrenia*, trans. Robert Hurley, Mark Seem, and Helen Lane (New York: Viking, 1977).

6. Naomi Schor, "This Essentialism Which Is Not One: Coming To Grips with Irigaray," in *differences*, 1.2 (1989): 54.

7. Catherine A. Mackinnon, *Toward a Feminist Theory of the State* (Cambridge: Harvard Univ. Press, 1989), p. 124.

8. Drucilla Cornell. *Beyond Accommodation* (London: Routledge, 1991), p. 35.

9. Barbara Johnson, *The Critical Difference: Essays in the Contemporary Rhetoric of Reading* (Baltimore: Johns Hopkins Univ. Press, 1981), p. 13.

10. Judith Fetterly, *The Resisting Reader: A Feminist Approach To American Fiction* (Bloomington: Indiana Univ. Press, 1977), p. xx.

11. Fetterly, p. xiii.

12. Annette Kolodny, "Dancing Through the Minefield," in *The New Feminist Criticism: Essays on Women; Literature and Theory.* (New York: Pantheon Books, 1985), p. 153.

13. Patrocinio Schweikart, "Reading Ourselves: Toward a Feminist Theory of Reading," in *Gender and Reading*, eds. Flynn and Schweikart, p. 42.

14. Wolfgang Iser, *The Act of Reading* (London: Munich, 1976).

15. Hans-Robert Jauss, *Toward an Aesthetic of Reception* (Brighton: Constance, 1967), p. xx.

16. David Bleich, *Subjective Criticism* (Baltimore: Johns Hopkins Univ. Press, 1978).

17. Norman Holland, *5 Reader's Reading* (New Haven: Yale Univ. Press, 1975).

18. Hans-George Gadamer, *Truth and Method* (London: Sheed and Ward, 1975), p. 263.

19. Luce Irigaray "Sexual Difference," in *French Feminist Thought: A Reader* (New York: Basil Blackwell, 1987), p. 127.

A Poet Looks at
Saul Bellow's Soul

Frederick Glaysher

I DO NOT presume to poke into the recesses of Saul Bellow's *soul*. What transpires there is between him and God. Rather, I propose to discuss what Bellow has called the "soul" throughout much of his fiction. I will, however, by way of approaching Bellow's understanding of the soul, reveal a little about my own soul. For it is the reverberations Bellow sets off in my deepest being that keeps me reading him and believing he has a more profound perception of contemporary experience than any other American novelist. Judging from my earliest recollection, I first became aware of my being a soul when I was eight years old. I had committed a childish sin and have a vivid memory of my owning up to my transgression within the confessional of Saint Anne's, in a dreary working-class suburb of Detroit, where my family on my mother's side, Croatian Catholics for generations, worshiped. Through the screen that separated us, the priest admonished me to recite the requisite number of Hail Marys at the altar. During their recitation, on my knees, I poured out my heart in penance and gazed in adoration at the crucifix, the icon of Mary, Mother of God, and the multicolored candles flickering at the side of the altar. The years went by. I grew up to read Stendhal and Nietzsche and to loathe the church. Often, though, I have wondered, especially as society continues to break down, whether there might not be something valuable in the old religions. Such reflections can also be found in Saul Bellow's books. For Bellow is one of the few writers to remember man is a soul, not a mere conglomeration of social conditioning. Bellow's soul is the modern soul — the soul set free from

43

its traditional Christian and Judaic past, even from its Buddhist, Islamic, or Hindu past, yet hungry, seeking, longing for its rightful home.

In Bellow's introduction to Allan Bloom's *Closing of the American Mind* (1987), he admits that, while still a young man reading widely, he was "quickly carried away from the ancient religion." There is no suggestion in his work that we ought to go back in that direction – back to Judaism or Christianity. For many, mutability has swept all that away forever. Having left that behind, as so many have, Bellow reveals in his Nobel lecture what remains, though most are afraid to say so: "'There is a spirit,' and that is taboo." From this spirit come "true impressions," "persistent intuitions," "hints" of another reality. The value of literature itself lies in such "hints." Bellow has been increasingly repudiating the taboo against the spirit. It is from the "glimpses" of the "essence of our real condition" that the sense of our "real powers" comes – "powers we seem to derive from the universe itself." I cannot help recalling how men and women, as the Roman Empire collapsed, turned fervently toward mysticism. The brutality, barbarism, confusion, and relativism of that thoroughly corrupt society drove thoughtful, sensitive people ever more toward transcendent understanding of the awful spectacle that surrounded them. Bellow has yet to answer convincingly how his soul differs from the soul in Mithraism, Manicheism, Neoplatonism, and other vaguely pantheistic mystery cults.

As one who has lived in Japan beyond the initial *gaijin* or foreigner stage, I know that the spectacle of modern upheaval extends to other than Western shores. We are witnessing not merely the decline of Western society but of all the traditional religions and the societies they supported. Though largely focused on Western society, Bellow realizes the worldwide scope of the crisis. In *More Die of Heartbreak* (1987), Uncle Benn and Kenneth Trachtenberg flee to Japan to escape their sordid sexual affairs only to be taken to a strip show in Kyoto, "one of the holy cities of Asia," by Uncle Benn's colleagues in the botany department of Kyoto University. Similarly, Trachtenberg, a specialist in Russian literature, observes the resemblance of St. Petersburg in 1913 to the Chicago of today: "By and by it became evident that the metaphysics that had long supported the ethical order had crumbled away." Whether in Russia, Europe, America, or the Far East, an unrelenting tidal wave of change has inundated and is obliterating all vestiges of the past. While the East, in the sense of the Soviet Union, "has the ordeal of privation, the West has the ordeal of desire," or sexual anarchy. In different ways, both ordeals are destroying the memory of the soul. Having a global view of sexual anarchy, Bellow writes, "whatever it is that snatches souls away by the hundred of millions has to be reckoned with." We are left, then, with the soul or spirit stripped of all orthodox accoutrements, encircled by a raging chaos, of which Beirut offers the "authentically contemporary" model.

Much earlier, *Mr. Sammler's Planet* (1970), perhaps Bellow's greatest novel, Sammler states that "very often, and almost daily, I have strong impressions of eternity" or "God adumbrations." Against the background of the collapsing of Western civilization in New York, Sammler remembers the cultural and religious past of Europe, his own Polish past in the Austro-Hungarian Empire, and his days in Bloomsbury, England, when it was at its cultural zenith. Thoroughly read in Freud, Marx, Weber, as well as such "worthless fellows" as Adorno, Marcuse, and Norman O. Brown, Sammler has reached the point where he wishes only to read "certain religious writers of the thirteenth century – Suso, Tauler, and Meister Eckhart." Sammler's character is firmly "on the side of the spiritual, Platonic, Augustinian." Early in the book, Sammler emphasizes that "the best and purest human beings, from the beginning of time, have understood that life is sacred." It is not so much that Sammler "literally believed" in Meister Eckhart but "that he cared to read nothing" else, finding there, by implication, food for the soul. The bestial violence of Raskolnikov, which he finds all around him in New York, inside as well as outside the university, appalls him and causes him to seek answers from deeper sources than fashionable, shallow intellectuals. Unsurprisingly, Sammler simply tells Walter Bruch, who comes to him seeking sophisticated rationalizations, by way of sincerely offering him the help he truly needs, "I'll pray for you." With the same purity of heart, Sammler admires Elya Gruner for his virtuous human qualities that reflect the best, the highest, in human nature. For despite all the misery and despair brought on by the malady of modern individualism, Sammler maintains "the spirit knows that its growth is the real aim of existence," which can be achieved only "by willing as God wills." And in this sense "the soul of Elya Gruner" meets "the terms of his contract," as each man knows his own contract in his inmost soul. For that truth, Sammler quietly counsels at the end of the book, is the truth each man inescapably knows.

Sammler observes that because "the sense of God persists," his "God adumbrations," the corresponding sense of the chaotic elements of modern life is heightened. The contradictions to his faith become all the more painful. His meditations on the mass murder of the Jews by the Nazis; his own killing of a Polish soldier during World War II; his perception of the increasing moral corruption of intellectuals; his recognition of the penchant for violence among New Left radicals; his awareness of the breakdown of civilized life in New York, "which makes one think about the collapse of civilization, about Sodom and Gomorrah, the end of the world"; the licentious sexuality of Gruner's daughter Angela and her brother Wallace's shiftless irresponsibility; the dire condition of many inner city blacks, as portrayed by the pickpocket – all these contradict Sammler's sense that God persists, for what truly merciful God, Sammler suggests, could permit such depravity and violence? Ultimately though, Sammler holds that "inability to explain is no ground for disbelief" and "all is not flatly knowable." One of the most common characteristics of the intellectuals Bellow so often loathes is that they imagine everything should indeed be "flatly knowable."

Instead of ignoring such contradictions, Bellow weaves them into the dialectical tapestry of his fiction. He juxtaposes them, even as early as in *Herzog* (1964), with the "potato love" of Moses Herzog, with all the weak, dreamy, and idealistic emotions to which so many of his characters are inclined. Herzog's wandering mind sums up this type of contradictory material in Bellow's work when he reflects:

> History is the history of cruelty, not love, as soft men think. . . . If the old God exists he must be a murderer. But the one true god is Death. This is how it is – without cowardly illusions.

Like Sammler, though, Moses Herzog dialectically dispenses with this view as merely accusing God of murder – putting him on trial for what we ourselves are guilty of. At the end of *Herzog,* God in a sense also persists. Herzog writes: "'Thou movest me.' . . . Something produces intensity, a holy feeling." He is satisfied "to be just as it is willed." Herzog returns to what Bellow calls Square One, to the "pri-mordial person" that "precedes social shaping," "to some primal point of balance." To "resume your first self" is qualitatively different from "potato love" that remains dialectically undeveloped. And it has a maturity of vision and, therefore, an affirmation far above the quotidian. At the end of his Nobel lecture, Bellow points out that it is the "true impressions" from "that other world" "which move us to believe that the good we hang on to so tenaciously – in the face of evil so obstinately – is no illusion." Far from living in a vacuum, Bellow fully faces the evil and contradictory material, boldly sees it for the reality that it is, and rightly values the good as having transcendent importance.

This becomes a settled if complex attitude. In an interview in *U.S. News and World Report,* after the publication of *The Dean's December*

(1982), Bellow discusses the pervasiveness of such contradictory material and locates its origin in the soul. Talking of the hundreds of millions of people who have been murdered in the twentieth century, Bellow laments, "We have become used to brutality and savagery":

> As a writer, I struggle with these facts. I'm preoccupied with the way in which value is – or is not – assigned to human life. A writer comes to feel that there is a way of grasping these horrors that is peculiar to poetry, drama and fiction. I don't admit the defeat of the humane tradition.

Far from turning away from these horrors, or buckling before them as so many writers of the last fifty years have done, Bellow's choice to grapple with the reality of what Emerson called the "odious facts" exemplifies the best in the humane tradition. Today, the work of very few writers shows, as does Bellow's, how much strength is still left in that tradition and how much ground can be reclaimed for it by assiduous labor and self-sacrifice. Bellow goes on to say that in the modern world "we are divested of the deeper human meaning that has traditionally been attached to human life." Emphatically, he states, "There's no sacred space around human beings anymore." In a November, 1990, interview on NBC, Bellow remarked that we are losing the sense of what it means to be a human being and to have a soul. "Our humanity is at risk," he warns, "because the feeling that life is sacred has died away in this century."

In *The Dean's December*, Albert Corde specifically confronts the breakdown of American democracy and Soviet totalitarianism and fathoms the nihilism of East and West. During a long December visit to Rumania, where his wife's mother is dying, he learns at first hand what life is like in a communist country. While there, he reflects on his involvement in a murder trial back in Chicago and on his two controversial articles in *Harper's* attacking the corruption of American society. Whether Corde meditates on the East, the West, or the Third World, he invariably discovers social oppression and decay. Bellow makes particularly brilliant use of Vico to bring out the decline of "human customs":

> Children born outside the law and abandoned by parents can be eaten by dogs. It must be happening in places like Uganda now. The army of liberators who chased out Idi made plenty of babies. Eaten by dogs. Or brought up without humanity. Nobody teaching the young language, human usages or religion, they will go back to the great ancient forest and be like the wild beasts of Orpheus. None of the great

compacts of the human race respected. Bestial venery, feral wanderings, incest, and the dead left unburied.

By implication this critique applies to the black ghetto in Chicago and elsewhere in America, though it is surely applicable as well in ways to white
America. Reading this book made me recall my own experience living in
Detroit where our failure to hand on human customs to the next generation
is so apparent. I also remembered studying with Robert Hayden and hear-
ing his confession that he had considered moving back to Detroit but the
fear of violence eventually dissuaded him. I can still hear his bemoaning to
me, "Blacks aren't any safer there than anybody else, you know." As Corde
puts it, "advanced modern consciousness" is "a reduced consciousness in-
asmuch as it contained only the minimum of the furniture that civilization
was able to install." Bellow's deepest insight resides in his recognition that
the collapse of civilization itself constitutes the most eloquent argument for
the reality of truly positive values – spiritual values, if you will. Like Vico,
who emphasizes the role the transcendent plays in maintaining the
customs of civilization, Bellow dramatizes throughout *The Dean's
December* that the progressive breakdown of society in Chicago and in the
Soviet Union is largely the result of the loss of the knowledge of the soul.
      Corde's purpose is "to recover the world that is buried under the
debris of false description or nonexistence." By passing "Chicago
through his own soul," Corde attempts to find the "underlying truth" of
reality. The false descriptions of psychology, sociology, economics, and
journalism merely exacerbate our plight. Corde's boyhood friend Dewey
Spangler, now a journalist with an international reputation, fails to convey anything of real substance in his writing. He is basically a media
hack pandering to the lowest common denominator. Corde, on the other
hand, has "the high intention to prevent the American idea from being
pounded into dust altogether." He has the inspired moral vision of the
artist that penetrates the layers of deception to look at what is actually
happening in America. In an interview in *Contemporary Literature,*
Bellow succinctly states his position: "the first step is to display the
facts. But, the facts, unless the imagination perceives them, are *not*
facts." Bellow goes on to say that "without art, it is impossible to interpret reality." Because the technicians, experts, and intellectuals lack the
"musical pitch" of the humanistic tradition, they merely add to the
cacophony of the "Great Noise." Spanning the modern world, both East
and West, *The Dean's December* meditates profoundly on the state of the
contemporary soul and concludes, "*Something* deadly is happening."

This vague "something" is more honest than an ostensibly precise word. In *Summations* (1987) Bellow mentions what writers should now pursue: "something lying behind the 'concepts' and the appearances." Earlier, in *Humboldt's Gift* (1975), Charlie Citrine brooded on a similar "something," fundamentally on the soul:

> I'm not a mystic. Anyway I don't know why mystic should be such a bad word. It doesn't mean much more than the word religion, which some people still speak of with respect. What does religion say? It says that there's something in human beings beyond the body and brain and that we have ways of knowing that go beyond the organism and its senses. I've always believed that. My misery comes, maybe, from ignoring my own metaphysical hunches. I've been to college so I know the educated answers. Test me on the scientific world-view and I'd score high. But it's just head stuff.

No one who has read much of Saul Bellow's work can doubt that he is a writer who in some hard-to-define way still regards mysticism and religion with respect. The way he attempts to restore such respect can clearly be seen in an exchange Citrine has with a collaborator on a proposed journal, the comically avant-garde Pierre Thaxter, who objects to Citrine, "For God's sake, we can't come out with all this stuff about the soul." Citrine observes, "Why not? People talk about the psyche, why not the soul?" Thaxter, submerged in all the dreck of modernism, all the "head stuff," retorts, "Psyche is scientific," adding "You have to accustom people gradually to these terms of yours." Wielding the knife of humor, Bellow undercuts the privileged position of modernism and exposes its unmitigated banality. Out of such intellectual play, he manages to bring truly serious reflections on the state of modern society and on the soul.

After observing that "the ideas of the last few centuries are used up," Charlie says,

> I *am* serious. The greatest things, the things most necessary for life, have recoiled and retreated. People are actually dying of this, losing all personal life, and the inner being of millions, many many millions, is missing. One can understand that in many parts of the world there is no hope for it because of famine or police dictatorships, but here in the free world what excuse have we? Under pressure of public crisis the private sphere is being surrendered. I admit this private sphere has become so repulsive that we are glad to get away from it. But we accept the disgrace ascribed to it and people have filled their lives

with so-called 'public questions.' What do we hear when these public questions are discussed? The failed ideas of three centuries. . . . Mankind must recover its imaginative powers, recover living thought and real being, no longer accept these insults to the soul, and do it soon. Or else! And this is where a man like Humboldt, faithful to failed ideas, lost his poetry and missed the boat.

Humboldt, Bellow's composite of Delmore Schwartz and Robert Lowell, remained faithful to the wornout ideas of symbolist poetry. Instead of "real being," Humboldt settled for the clichés of the prevailing modernist mentality. As Charlie Citrine writes early in the book, modern poets, unlike Homer or Dante, "didn't have a sane and steady idealization. To be Christian was impossible, to be pagan also. That left you know what" – the nihilism of the twentieth century. Hence, the soul receives nothing but insults, the failed ideas of disordered being. Like Sammler, Citrine has "incessant hints of immortality," and he is sickened that, for all our numerous, relativistic epistemologies, not one "speaks straight to the soul." With the demise of all the old ideas and the spread of disorder, Citrine argues that Humboldt's *poète maudit* "performance was conclusive" and "can't be continued." In a manner similar to Sammler, Herzog, Corde, and other characters in Bellow, Citrine has experienced all the vicissitudes of life, heard and studied all the rationalistic explanations, and has come to believe: "Now we must listen in secret to the sound of the truth that God puts into us."

Despite the obviously insincere use of Rudolf Steiner's anthroposophy, a use which indicates a spiritual failure of imagination on the part of Bellow, essentially the modern failure to find a true and satisfying way out of our predicament, Bellow argues broadly for the reality of the soul and opposes what he calls "the ruling premises":

> The question is this: why should we assume that the series ends with us? The fact is, I suspect, that we occupy a point within a great hierarchy that goes far far beyond ourselves. The ruling premises deny this. We feel suffocated and don't know why. The existence of a soul is beyond proof under the ruling premises, but people go on behaving as though they had souls, nevertheless. They behave as if they came from another place, another life, and they have impulses and desires that nothing in this world, none of our present premises, can account for. On the ruling premises the fate of humankind is a sporting event, most ingenious. Fascinating. When it doesn't become boring. The specter of boredom is haunting this sporting conception of history.

"The ruling premises," what Czeslaw Milosz calls the "fad of nihilism," have dogmatically repudiated any spiritual interpretation of reality throughout this century. Bellow's fiction increasingly opposes this dogmatism and asserts the reality of man's transcendent nature. "The ruling premises" are basically a catalog of failed ideas – three centuries' worth. Of intellectuals, Charlie earlier says, "I always said they were wasting their time and ours, and that I wanted to trample and clobber them." Citrine reflects that should the prevailing premise that nothing awaits us after death prove to be true, he would be astonished, "for the prevailing beliefs seldom satisfy my need for truth." He is unable to take stock in "respectable empiricism" because "too many fools subscribe to it." "Besides," Citrine argues, "people were not really surprised when you spoke to them about the soul and the spirit." In an interview in *Tri-Quarterly,* Bellow states, "To have a soul, to *be* one – that today is a revolutionary defiance of received opinion."

As late as in *The Theft* (1989), Clara, a country girl who becomes a successful executive in New York, has yet to be convinced that "no more mystical sacredness remained in the world." She can therefore say sincerely to Ithiel Regler, "I love you with my soul." Ithiel, a political operator in Washington, refers to her as "a strange case – a woman who hasn't been corrupted." When he suffers abandonment by his wife, Clara hastens to Washington, "for a human purpose," to console him in his time of grief. Many years earlier when their relationship was more promising, Ithiel had given her an emerald ring that becomes for her a "major symbol," "a life support," not only of their love but of much more. The novella revolves around the theft of this ring and the necessity of its recovery. At a time when all universals have been mechanically banished from the human realm, Clara holds to this ring as a symbol of the existence of love, however far "down in the catacombs" it might be. In fact, Clara knows "a lot and at first hand about decadence." Rather tired of the "collapsing culture bit," she prefers "to see it instead as the conduct of life without input from your soul" though she cannot give specific details. The ring becomes for her symbolic of all that is "the real thing," clear, perfect.

At the end of the novella, Clara describes Ithiel as a truthful, realistic observer who knows the big picture. One of Bellow's tough-minded characters, "he likes to look at the human family as it is." Ithiel concedes, though, that his idea of "what is real" is not as deep as hers. She possesses an understanding of the soul that goes beyond his worldly perception. Nevertheless, his realism gives him the advantage in his political world of international negotiations and intrigues. He remarks to her that

"Neither the Russians nor the Americans can manage the world. Not capable of organizing the future." Of the "new Soviet regime," Bellow puts into his mouth words that surely reflect Bellow's own assessment of Gorbachev and that to some extent have already proven their prescience:

> Some of the smartest émigrés are saying that the Russians didn't announce liberalization until they had crushed the dissidents. Then they co-opted the dissidents' ideas. After you've gotten rid of your enemies, you're ready to abolish capital punishment—that's how Alexander Zinoviev puts it. And it wasn't only the KGB that destroyed the dissident movement but the whole party organization, and the party was supported by the Soviet people. They strangled the opposition, and now they're pretending to be *it*. You have the Soviet leaders themselves criticizing Soviet society. When it has to be done, they take over. And the West is thrilled by all the reforms.

To this grimly realistic evaluation of East and West, Clara answers, "So we're going to be bamboozled again." This passage demonstrates that unlike many writers, Bellow does not live in a vacuum of Marxist clichés. His criticism of communism is one fully informed of the dialectical theories, actual history, and brutal reality of Soviet totalitarianism. Equally scathing is his critique of Western society, sunk in its own brand of decadence and, as Ithiel says later, craving "to be sold, deceived, if you prefer." Only Milosz and Solzhenitsyn have achieved such penetrating insight into the reality of East and West. Bellow's achievement may actually rank higher than theirs since it has not been forced upon him by catastrophe and exile but has resulted from the sheer struggle of his soul to resist the nihilism of modernity and to speak for what is noble and enduring.

In *The Bellarosa Connection* (1989), Bellow confronts in particular the condition of the Jewish soul. Sorella Fonstein says to the unnamed narrator of the novella, the founder of the Mnemosyne Institute:

> The Jews could survive everything that Europe threw at them. I mean the lucky remnant. But now comes the next test—America. Can they hold their ground, or will the U.S.A. be too much for them?

Harry Fonstein escapes the Nazis with the help of Billy Rose, a famous American Jew in the entertainment business. Fonstein wants to thank Rose in person for his help, but Rose, thoroughly Americanized and largely assimilated, wants nothing to do with him. The USA has proven too much for him. Fonstein resists assimilation and clings to the old world, to Mitteleuropa. Though the Fonsteins make a fortune in the thermostat business, they increasingly isolate themselves as a way of dealing with life in America. At the end of the novella, the narrator, "a Jew of an entirely different breed" from the Fonsteins, closer to Rose, attempts to reestablish contact with the Fonsteins after many years of having lost touch with them. He finally succeeds in reaching a Jewish friend of the Fonstein's son Gilbert. This friend, who is house sitting, reveals that they died six months earlier in an automobile accident. The narrator continues to talk to Gilbert's friend and discovers that Gilbert has become a professional gambler "more in the Billy Rose vein than in the Harry Fonstein vein" and is at that moment a pilgrim to America's holy city, Las Vegas. Although it occurs to the narrator that the Fonsteins avoided him for years to hide the truth about their son, it is the "low-grade cheap-shot nihilism" of Gilbert's young Jewish friend that disturbs him the most. Since even the narrator's own son has grown up to become "all administrator and executive," he ultimately learns that America has proven "too much" for everyone concerned. In a dream, his soul brings him the truth that he himself has become "half Jewish, half waspish." Yet he holds to "the roots of memory in feeling" and to the disclosure of his dream that he has "made a mistake, a lifelong mistake." His deepest answer to the nihilism of Gilbert's friend, who is thoroughly lost to the clichés of modernism, becomes his written "mnemosyne flourish," his account of the entire Bellarosa connection; in a sense, the novella itself, Bellow's own account of the Jewish soul in the modern world and in America. Holding to his dictum "Memory is life," the narrator establishes "at the very least that I am still able to keep up my struggle for existence."

It is this "struggle for existence" that is at the heart of Bellow's work. In his *Nobel Lecture* he states that neither science nor art is any longer at the center of human concern, but rather confusion and the individual struggling "with dehumanization for the possession of his soul." We seem to be in the "early stages of universal history" and are being "lavishly poured together," experiencing the "anguish of new states of consciousness." As Bellow remarks in an interview in *Salmagundi,* "we're in some sort of ideological or moral interregnum," "we're between epochs." The "central energies of man," as he states in his *Nobel Lecture,* are consumed with this crisis: "The decline and fall of everything is our daily bread." The Great Noise drowns out the small still voice of the soul. Leaving aside all nostalgia, all longing for a restoration of the Judaic or Christian past, Bellow asserts in *TriQuarterly,* "The modern age is our given, our crushing donnée." For a writer in the realist tradition, one who chooses to look at the facts, one capable of recognizing that the novel is "a sort of latter-day lean-to" for the shelter of the spirit, on a decidedly lower level than the epic, there is no escape into the kind of puerile fantasies of the self that have consumed the time of so many writers during the last fifty years or so. The only other American novel that approaches Bellow's confrontation with the modern soul is Isaac Bashevis Singer's *The Penitent.*

In 1987, in "The Civilized Barbarian Reader," an adaptation, published in *The New York Times Book Review,* of his introduction to Allan Bloom, Bellow identifies some important benefits of decline not mentioned in the version in the book itself:

> What no one was able to foresee was that all civilized countries were destined to descend to an inferior common cosmopolitanism, but that the lamentable weakening of the older, traditional branches of civilization might open fresh opportunities, force us to reassess the judgments of traditional culture and that we might be compelled – a concealed benefit of decline – to be independent. To interpret our circumstances as deeply as we can – isn't that what we human beings are here for? Quite simply, when the center does not hold and great structures fall down, one has an opportunity to see some of the truths that they obstructed. Longstanding premises then come in for revision and old books are read by a new light.

My own experience leads me to believe Bellow is quite right about "this concealed benefit of decline." The descent into "an inferior common cosmopolitanism," an emerging world culture constructed largely on the popular mass culture of the West, has indisputably weakened the traditional foundations of every country around the globe. For more than a century, certain modernizing and essentially Westernizing intellectuals have been at the forefront of social change in Russia, the Middle East, Japan, and elsewhere. The civilization of Western Europe and North America has spread over the entire earth. Much good has resulted from his long historical process, but much harm has also occurred to humane ways of life and thought.

The decline has reached such prodigious proportions, one cannot avoid wondering whether there might be something in the past still much needed, in an appropriate form to our changed condition. This reassessment of modernism is made possible by the very decline of modernism itself – its failure to produce a society worthy of its highest claims. All around us now, in the West as well as in the East, "great structures" are falling down, opening the way for a clear view of how bankrupt they have been all along. While we stand among their ruins, we know we cannot go backwards after having enjoyed their many benefits. We are forever changed. We need a "revision" of "longstanding premises," surely not a simple-minded return to the past, which we can all be glad is gone forever. As Bellow writes, "in the end a man must master his own experience," and we require a new mastery of our new circumstances, of our global, multicultural experience; a mastery that nevertheless does justice to the past – what our experience *has been* – and that yet rises above what Herzog calls "knee-jerk nihilism." Though we stand free of all traditional accoutrements, ever more free of all the clichés of modernism, we can find in the midst of such confusion "an open channel to the soul," an open channel "to the deepest part of ourselves."

Herzog's Divorce Grief

Andrew Gordon

"IF I'M out of my mind, it's all right with me, thought Moses Herzog."[1] Thus begins Saul Bellow's novel *Herzog*. But is Herzog really crazy? I would argue instead that he is temporarily crazed with grief over the breakup of his second marriage and that his apparently irrational thoughts and actions can be explained as normal for the process of grief. The psychiatrist Gerald F. Jacobson writes that "the divorce process requires a profound readjustment that in many instances produces a picture indistinguishable from that of more deep-seated pathology."[2] Although grief, including mourning the loss of a marriage, may resemble mental illness, it is a temporary healing process that usually follows predictable stages. The individual may even emerge strengthened at the end, as Herzog seems to do. Nevertheless, "bereaved people are so surprised by the unaccustomed feelings of grief that they often ask, 'Am I going mad?'"[3] – just as Herzog does.

I believe that, through his personal experience and intuition, Bellow has a profound understanding of the psychodynamics of mourning and of divorce grief. By referring to psychological and sociological studies of bereavement, marital separation, and divorce grief, we can better understand both the dynamics of Herzog's marriage and the process of his mourning.[4] Although Herzog is a unique fictional character, his thoughts and behavior are representative of those of many divorcing men.

Most of Bellow's heroes are mournful characters: Leventhal still mourns his mother; Tommy Wilhelm mourns his mother and ends up crying at a stranger's funeral; Henderson tries to commu-

57

nicate with his dead parents; Sammler lost his wife in the Holocaust and now is losing his nephew; Citrine mourns Humboldt; and Corde sadly waits while his mother-in-law is dying. Many of these melancholy heroes have also undergone painful separations or divorces, but none suffers as acutely from separation anxiety and divorce grief as Herzog.

I would rank *Herzog* with F. Scott Fitzgerald's *Tender is the Night* (1934) as one of the finest and most psychologically accurate portraits in American fiction of divorce and its aftermath. The difference is that Fitzgerald's Dick Diver goes into an irreversible decline (the 1930s were not called "The Depression" for nothing), whereas Herzog is apparently able to pull himself up by his psychic bootstraps. Bellow speculates that *Herzog* was a bestseller in 1965 because "it appeals to the unconscious sympathies of many people," including "those who had been divorced."[5] In fact, after stabilizing in the 1950s, the American divorce rate soared by seventy percent in the 1960s,[6] so *Herzog* was a timely novel with a hero representative of his decade. Significantly, Herzog's wife Madeleine chucks him out of the house in October, 1963, a month before John F. Kennedy was assassinated; thus Herzog's grief coincides with the nation's. (Indeed, Herzog feels as if he himself has been assassinated by his wife and best friend!)

However, as one critic points out, "it is not only the social and psychological ramifications of divorce with which Bellow is concerned. Bellow is interested in the components of Western suffering."[7] Nevertheless, we would not be interested in Bellow's abstract ideas on "Western suffering" unless they were grounded in the psychologically believable suffering of a fully realized fictional character.

Admittedly, Bellow is hostile to Freud and to the entire "modern vocabulary."[8] For Herzog (and for Bellow as well), psychoanalysis is too narrow and deterministic and explains away the mysteries of the human soul. For example, Herzog says of his behavior:

> It is, if you're looking for the psychological explanation, childish and classically depressive. But Herzog didn't believe that the harshest or most niggardly explanation . . . was necessarily the truest. (H, p. 231)

Bellow also satirizes psychoanalysis in the novel through the unflattering portrait of the psychiatrist Dr. Edvig.[9] Nevertheless, despite the resistance of both the author and his hero to psychoanalysis, numerous critics have argued that *Herzog* is a profoundly psychological novel that actually illustrates many Freudian ideas through the behavior of its hero.[10]

In part, Bellow was working out his private woes (two divorces), giving Herzog some of his own childhood memories and adult experiences (including a wife who has an affair with her husband's best friend) as well as his personal depression, rage, and intellectual egomania. Like Bellow, Herzog tends to intellectualize his personal misery into universal problems such as "Western suffering." But Bellow distances himself from his own emotional turmoil through art: form, style, and comedy. He makes fun of his defenses, including overintellectualization, by exaggerating them in his protagonist.

The activity in *Herzog* is largely mental; the hero is undergoing what Freud called "the work of mourning."[11] Herzog keeps sorting through his memories and emotions in a process of obsessive review. The crisis disrupts routine behavior and challenges the mourner to abandon old assumptions about the self and the world and to discover new ones.[12] The grieving person needs to "'make sense' of what has happened, to explain it, to classify it along with other comparable events, to make it fit into one's expectations of the world."[13] This is what Herzog is doing: "Late in spring, Herzog had been overcome by the need to explain, to have it out, to justify, to put in perspective, to clarify, to make amends" (H, p. 2).

The work of mourning that Herzog must do is to reinterpret his marriage and detach himself from his loved and hated objects: his ex-wife Madeleine and his ex-best-friend Gersbach, as well as past love objects (primarily his mother and father) with whom they are associated. He must make sense of his past before he can have a future. Appropriately, throughout most of the novel, Herzog is lying down, undergoing a talking cure in which he is both analysand and psychoanalyst.[14] Thus, the narrative shifts freely between the subjectivity of first person (Herzog as analysand) and the objectivity of third person (Herzog as analyst). He remembers and free associates until he arrives at the crucial moments of trauma. He ends the novel as he began, reclining on a couch. The grief crisis is over, and with it the need for obsessive review. Nevertheless, his neurotic conflicts remain; he is not cured but only temporarily at peace with himself.

To understand Herzog's divorce grief, we need first to understand his marriage. As a divorce therapist notes, most divorces occur because the marriages took place for the wrong reasons, such as "a need to parent someone, or . . . a need to be parented . . . a need for power and to be in control of someone, or to be controlled." Indeed, "sometimes we have to go through several relationships and divorces to rework our parental relationships."[15]

Herzog left his first wife Daisy because she was too conventional, a Jewish woman perhaps too much like his own mother. "Stability, symmetry, order, containment. . . . By my irregularity and turbulence of spirit I brought out the very worst in Daisy" (H, p. 126). In Madeleine, he finds the other extreme, a character more irregular and turbulent than his own. He marries her ostensibly because she is young, beautiful, and brilliant: "As long as Moses was married to Daisy, he had led the perfectly ordinary life of an assistant professor, respected and stable" (H, p. 5). But ordinary is not good enough for Herzog or for Madeleine either. Madeleine "hadn't wanted him to be an ordinary professor" (H, p. 6). She desires and offers glamor: "everyone drawn into the drama of her life became exceptional, deeply gifted, brilliant. It had happened also to him" (H, p. 38). Herzog doesn't realize until years later that in giving up his boring, ordinary life, he also lost respect and stability. He thought that, unlike Daisy, Madeleine could be his intellectual helpmate; she turned instead into his intellectual rival.

Madeleine is a harsh, angry, self-dramatizing spirit, more like Herzog's father than like his mother. John J. Clayton sees Herzog as a guilty masochist who wants to do penance to his father for his imagined sexual sins; "Mady the bitch is then a father substitute."[16]

After they are wed, Madeleine's disorder brings out the worst in Herzog, making him play Daisy's role as rulemaker and nag, constantly complaining about her sloppy housekeeping and spendthrift ways. He can't do scholarly work amid her chaos. As he becomes more critical of her, he grows to resemble his namesake, Moses the lawgiver. Finally, Madeleine commits adultery and dumps him, just as Herzog dumped Daisy.

There is a markedly sadomasochistic element in their relationship: Madeleine is the dominatrix Herzog secretly yearns for: "She seems to have served a special need" (H, p. 334). He refers to himself as "writhing" under her "elegant heel" (H, p. 76) and claims she wanted to bring him down and "kick out his brains with a murderous bitch foot" (H, p. 93). He admits that "there was a flavor of subjugation in his love for Madeleine. Since she was domineering and since he loved her, he had to accept the flavor that was given" (H, p. 8). But he will not admit that he loves her *because* she is domineering.

Herzog confesses, however, that he is "masochistic" and that "he had asked to be beaten too, and had lent his attackers strength" (H, p. 4). Herzog even believes in a morality of suffering, and claims "credit for his power to suffer" (H, p. 40). His lover Ramona tells him, "'Poor Moses— unless you're having a bad time with a woman you can't believe you're being serious'" (H, p. 157). Bernard J. Paris writes that Herzog chose Madeleine because he craved "a brilliant, domineering partner who will at once humble and exalt him," fulfilling his contradictory desires for suffering and for grandeur, or perhaps for grandeur through suffering.[17]

In addition to his grandiose and masochistic desires, Herzog is most erotically stimulated only when he is involved in a romantic triangle: with Madeleine and the Monsignor, with Madeleine and Gersbach, with Wanda and her husband, and with Ramona and her rejected lover, George Hoberly.[18] Herzog mimics the jealous Hoberly by spying on Madeleine and Gersbach, as if he wants to catch them in the act. In other words, Herzog keeps getting mixed up in oedipal triangles, and his guilt about his sex life and his desire for punishment may be closely connected to this complex.

Gersbach, a kind of double for Herzog, functions in two ways in the oedipal narrative: first, he is a stand-in for the avenging father, punishing Herzog by taking away Madeleine; and second, he acts out Herzog's own oedipal rebellion. In the former scenario, Gersbach is the father, "like a judge in Israel, a king" (H, p. 59); Herzog also calls his own father "a king" (H, p. 147). In the latter scenario, Gersbach is the rebellious son and Herzog the monarch Gersbach deposes. Herzog says that Gersbach reminds him of "the mobs breaking into the palaces and sacking Versailles" (H, p. 215). Paradoxically, Gersbach is both the potent son, cuckolding Herzog, and the castrated father (missing a leg).

Madeleine seems attracted to Herzog partly because she is playing out her own Electra complex. "Madeleine hated her father violently" (H, p. 8) and is determined not to repeat her mother's marriage. But in a sense she does, if only to get revenge against her egotistical father, the theatrical genius Pontritter, through the "genius" Herzog. Madeleine is in her twenties and Herzog in his forties, and "to her he was a fatherly, graying, patient seducer" (H, p. 112). She writes her mother that Herzog "resembled her father in too many ways." Herzog "was overbearing, infantile, demanding, sardonic, and a psychosomatic bully" (H, p. 191). He suspects she married him because "maybe she wouldn't make a father of anyone she liked" (H, p. 334). She punishes Herzog by doing to him what her father did to her mother Tennie: she enslaves Herzog and then rejects him.

Thus the union of Herzog and Madeleine provided a matching of neurotic needs. "Probably all of us marry, at least in part, to defend old solutions to old conflicts. The difficulty comes when two people so interlock their old conflicts and solutions that they cannot become aware of them, and hence cannot solve them."[19] Herzog and Madeleine stayed for years in an unhealthy and unhappy relationship, taking turns playing masochist or sadist, mother or father, to each other. Such a bad marriage can serve many needs, including discharging anger or relieving guilt through being punished by the partner.[20] And even a burdensome marriage may fend off anxiety.[21]

Nevertheless, their marriage began to disintegrate from the start. Madeleine displayed her discontent in many ways, both covert and overt, both financial and sexual. Marital conflict is often displaced into fights over money or sex, when the real difficulties "lie in unconscious or inadmissible areas."[22] The first signs of breakdown in communication are "the absence of knowledge about the other person's expenditures" and loss of sexual rapport, but these are symptoms, not the basic cause of the problem.[23]

Madeleine becomes a shopaholic, running up huge bills on purchases she claims she cannot recall. Herzog interprets this as a symptom of mental illness and feels "very tender toward her" (H, p. 57). He is not so tender, however, when she begins bouncing checks and spends five hundred dollars on a single maternity outfit. Herzog asks sarcastically, "'Who's going to be born – Louis Quatorze?'" (H, p. 123). However, if Herzog secretly thought of himself as a king, then it is not surprising he married a princess. Obviously her purchases are symptoms not of insanity but of discontent. After the divorce, he thinks, "A woman who squandered her husband's money, all psychiatric opinion agreed, was determined to castrate him" (H, p. 202).

This castration also takes place in the marriage bed. Their sex life becomes so bad that Herzog suffers from premature ejaculation and occasional impotence. These symptoms, as well as Madeleine's excruciatingly painful menstruation, may be physical expressions of their psychic pain: "the build-up of disappointment, hurt, and anger" over their first crisis of marital alienation.[24]

Worse yet, Madeleine complains to female friends and relatives about Herzog's sexual inadequacy, thus going public with her dissatisfaction and preparing for the dissolution of the marriage.[25] Public discontent marks the *second* crisis of marital alienation.[26]

Evidently, Herzog then tried to recoup his losses through extramarital affairs, of which Aunt Zelda accuses him. Herzog flushes but does not deny it, merely saying, "'She made it tough for me, too. Sexually'" (H, p. 39). But if Herzog was unfaithful to Madeleine (and we get no further information on this), she ups the ante by having a secret affair for years with his best friend. Even adultery "may be an attempt to communicate something, an unconscious effort to improve the marriage itself." Or else it may be "an attempt to humiliate the spouse into leaving."[27]

Gersbach began as a go-between, a friend to both partners in the troubled marriage; gradually his role changed to Madeleine's lover and Herzog's false friend. Such situations are not uncommon in real life.[28] Herzog begins to suspect them when he sees Gersbach retrieve Madeleine's diaphragm to bring it to her in Boston, where she had gone supposedly to save the marriage. But when he asks her if Gersbach is her lover, she vehemently denies it.

At this stage, Madeleine is playing hurtful games but is not secure enough to leave Herzog. According to the sociologist Diane Vaughan, "The initiator [the spouse who eventually initiates the divorce] will not risk losing the relationship until he or she has created what seems to be a secure niche elsewhere."[29] Madeleine and Gersbach keep their affair secret from their spouses for years (although not from selected friends and relatives) because it is still to their benefit to maintain their marriages. The secrecy gives her power "to create a separate world that the partner does not even know exists."[30] Perhaps she began the adultery to hurt or alarm Herzog, but gradually it provides her with what she needs to make the break: an identity independent of him and of their marriage. The decision to divorce is typically a slow, reluctant one, arrived at, on the average, over a period of two years, which is about how long it takes Madeleine to decide.[31]

During Madeleine's long affair, Herzog registered only those clues that fit his frame of reference and ignored or dismissed discordant ones. Writes John J. Clayton: "We must believe that he unconsciously needed to be the ground-under-heel cuckold."[32] Herzog's denial also preserved his sense of security, but it maintained an unhealthy status quo. "In deceiving ourselves . . . we keep secret from ourselves the truth we cannot face."[33] Thus Madeleine and Herzog collaborate in keeping up appearances, suppressing and denying the truth about her affair, a common phenomenon in troubled marriages.[34] But by Herzog's willful self-blinding, he victimizes and punishes himself.

He is so eager to misinterpret Madeleine's behavior that he urges her to see his psychiatrist. "Partners may attribute the negative signals . . . to a physical or mental affliction they think temporarily has beset the initiator. And this – not the relationship or themselves – is the source of the trouble."[35] When Madeleine accuses Herzog of hiring a private detective to tail her, Herzog, advised by Dr. Edvig, interprets this as a symptom of her paranoia, although Madeleine has good reason to worry about what a detective might uncover! Madeleine uses Edvig against Herzog; he also builds up her confidence so she can leave the marriage.[36]

Paradoxically, the more alienated and angry Madeleine becomes, the more meek and tender Herzog behaves in defense, conning himself into believing that she is mentally ill and that he will "cure" her. That is far more reassuring than to accept what is really happening. Even before the marriage, he had seen himself as her knight of rescue (just as the original Moses saved the Jews), and he clings to that notion to justify remaining in a marriage in which both are suffering.

> He still thought perhaps that he could win by the appeal of passivity, of personality, win on the grounds of being, after all, Moses – Moses Elkanah Herzog – a good man, and Madeleine's particular benefactor. He had done everything for her – everything! (H, p. 10)

He tells Zelda, "'She's sick. She's a diseased woman. I took care of her'" (H, p. 37).

His happiest memory of their entire relationship occurs when he nursed her after she injured herself. "He led her to the bed and lay down with her to warm and comfort her, just as she wanted him to" (H, p. 118). Memories of nursing others or of being nursed often evoke warm feelings in Bellow's heroes, including Joseph in *Dangling Man* and Tommy Wilhelm in *Seize the Day*; perhaps these are screen memories from the earliest mother-child bond.

Madeleine becomes enraged over Herzog's attempts to make her feel guilty about his sacrifices: "'Oh, balls! So now we're going to hear how you SAVED me. Let's hear it again'" (H, p. 124). In accepting Madeleine's abuse, Herzog adopts the role of the self-martyring Jewish mother – imitating, in fact, his own mother – while Madeleine plays an ungrateful, spoiled brat such as Herzog guiltily imagines himself to be towards his mother.

Finally, Madeleine carefully picks the moment to end the marriage. "The initiator's planning often culminates in a precise moment when, according to schedule, resources at hand, and with a well-rehearsed speech, the initiator confronts the partner about wanting to end the relationship."[37] When Madeleine confronts Herzog, he is stunned, regarding her calculation and her well-rehearsed speech as cruel. Madeleine and Herzog are simply out of synch, in different phases of the grief process: Madeleine has had years to grieve and put the marriage behind her; Herzog is just beginning.[38]

So much for the dynamics of Herzog's marriage. What about the process of his divorce grief?

Jacobson found two principal differences between bereavement and divorce: in divorce, the spouse is still alive, which complicates grief work, and there is much more *anger*.[39] The separated and divorced are also much more likely than the bereaved to think of suicide or to attempt it. To kill oneself, claims Jacobson, is to kill the introject of the hated spouse.[40] Herzog is consumed with anger toward Madeleine, Gersbach (to whom he telegrams a death threat), and himself and sometimes thinks of suicide. Studies also found that divorced or separated men fare worse than divorced or separated women in terms of numbers admitted to psychiatric hospitals and deaths from suicide and other causes.[41] And a spouse suddenly and unexpectedly dumped, like Herzog, is the most vulnerable to separation distress.[42] Murderous rage and homicidal fantasies are common among the separated and divorced, who sometimes actually murder their spouses.

One psychiatrist found the following behaviors characteristic of divorcing men: "violent behavior directed against their wives . . . ; violence toward their children and strangers; decreased work efficiency . . . ; compulsive and frenetic dating; indiscriminate sexual behavior . . . ; isolation from family and friends; limited and superficial relationships with other men; and early entry into new relationships with women."[43] Herzog exhibits all of these behaviors except violence toward children and strangers (although even that is arguable, considering his fascination with a murder trial, his auto accident that nearly injures his daughter, and his angry letters to people he has never met).

We see Herzog progress through various stages typical for those mourning a divorce[44]: first, *shock and denial* right after his wife suddenly throws him out; second, months of *depression,* which he defends against through restless travel and brief sexual flings; third, after he discovers his wife's adultery, a phase of homicidal *anger* mixed with nearly suicidal depression, culminating with an abortive plan to kill her and her lover; and fourth and last, after an accident and an arrest bring him down with a crash, a withdrawal to the country where he begins *recuperation and acceptance,* able to forgive others and, most of all, to forgive himself. Stages one and two are covered rather cursorily, through memories of his brief stay with the Himmelsteins after Madeleine asked him to leave and a few memories of his months of travel. In contrast, the narrative concentrates on the most acute and dramatic stage of divorce grief, covering in detail Herzog's rage and homicidal plans, followed by his retreat and the beginnings of his recovery in the country.

Many critics have wondered: if Madeleine is the heartless, castrating bitch Herzog portrays (the narrative offers no corrective to his distorted view), then why does he mourn so heavily her loss? Shouldn't he instead be celebrating his freedom from bondage? There is perhaps an element of masochism in Herzog's depression; he seems to enjoy making himself miserable. Now that Madeleine has stopped giving him grief, he will do it to himself.

Nevertheless, even if his naturally depressive and masochistic character were not complicating his grief, he would feel shattered anyway, given the circumstances. Mourning is inescapable, even for a lousy marriage, because so many years and so much of one's self-concept and psychic needs are invested in the relationship. In a sense, any marital partner is "an attachment figure, just as a parent is for a child."[45] In fact, the worst mourning occurs not after good marriages but after bad ones.[46] Moses was freed from bondage to Pharaoh but then had to wander the desert for years before finding the promised land. Something similar happens to Moses Herzog.

In fact, Herzog did not want the divorce; Madeleine did. He knew the marriage had problems, but he had assumed things were improving. Then, without warning, she kicked him out: he was unprepared for the loss.

There is also the fact that grief is personal, and "no one can say what constitutes a loss to another." Losses "are always phenomenological; that is, defined in terms of the meaning to the bereaved and not to the observer."[47] At age forty seven, Herzog mourns the wasted years, his second major failure as lover, husband, father, and Jewish son. He mourns his damaged career. But most of all, he mourns his lost self-concept.

He has lost not only a wife but also his beloved little daughter June, his best friend Gersbach, and his wife's relatives, some of whom he was fond of, particularly his mother-in-law Tennie and Madeleine's Aunt Zelda and Uncle Herman. He feels like a displaced person: he has lost family, friends, job, home and hometown – his entire secure existence, along with the stable identity that went with it.

He also mourns the loss to his scholarly career. During the marriage, he made no progress on the *magnum opus* that was to revolutionize intellectual history and tell everyone in the modern world how to live; he doesn't even know how *he* is supposed to live. The book was intended to vindicate him and justify his first divorce and his marriage to Madeleine. And he feels he has also failed as a Jewish son, failed to fulfill his parents' high moral and career expectations, which adds to his guilt.

Even his past has been stolen from him, with his belated discovery of Madeleine's adultery. Writes Vaughan: "The partner contemplates not only the loss of the future, but of the past, for the past was not what it seemed."[48] He begins to doubt his judgment: if for years he could so completely misinterpret those closest to him, then he may be wrong about *everything*. So much for his career as a brilliant intellectual!

Most of all, Herzog is mourning the loss of an idea of himself. A major stressor in divorce is "narcissistic injury": "the damage inflicted by the loss of the spouse to one's primitive fantasies of infantile greatness."[49] Herzog was attached to Madeleine in part because her youth, beauty, brilliance, and appearance of mastery affirmed his narcissism. Now that she has cruelly rejected him, certain childish and grandiose self-concepts that he had nourished for decades have utterly collapsed: he must rebuild his identity and restore his sense of self-worth.

He is angry at Madeleine but equally angry at himself for having played the fool. Herzog thinks everyone knew about the affair except him and were laughing at him behind his back or conspiring with Madeleine and Gersbach to cuckold him. He becomes bewildered, ashamed, self-loathing, and, in defense, enraged and vindictive as well. He has been injured not only in his masculine sexual pride but in his entire self-concept. This is his most severe loss, the one most difficult to recover from.

Divorce is a kind of psychic death. As Herzog tells his friends, "'Another divorce – out again, at my time of life. I can't take it. I don't know . . . it feels like death'" (H, p. 81). No wonder Herzog undergoes a nervous breakdown and is obsessed by thoughts of suicide and homicide; considering all the mental trauma he has suffered in a few months, it is surprising that he has not become physically ill as well. He is healthy but hypochondriacal (he thinks a urinary tract infection is gonorrhea, punishment for his promiscuity) and goes for a check-up, half wishing for a "real" illness, for care and sympathy of the kind that divorce never elicits.

Herzog's problems are compounded by the fact that he withdraws from people and defends against his own mourning. From his parents, he has "a great schooling in grief" (H, p. 148) and there is "much heavy love in Herzog; grief did not pass quickly with him" (H, p. 119). Nevertheless, he considers mourning to be idle, effeminate, or childish. He berates himself for grieving: "Grief, sir, is a species of idleness" (H, p. 3) and "'The busy bee has no time for sorrow'" (H, p. 276). He says, "I'm not even greatly impressed with my own tortured heart. It begins to seem another waste of time" (H, p. 17). He is ashamed of his feelings and ashamed to unburden himself before others.

Part of his problem lies in social attitudes toward grief, particularly toward divorce grief. "Mourning is treated as if it were a weakness, a self-indulgence, a reprehensible bad habit instead of a psychological necessity."[50] Grief is seen as idleness when it is really hard work. Divorce is stigmatized, and there are no socially acceptable rituals to cope with divorce grief. "Most divorced people in need of help do not seek it because, consciously or not, they have bought society's picture of them as failures. . . . They feel they *deserve* whatever suffering they are going through."[51] Herzog thinks, "what he was about to suffer, he deserved. He had sinned long and hard: he had earned it" (H, pp. 8–9).

People in mourning may isolate themselves, but just as often they are shunned by others, as if their loss might be catching. "It often happens that only those who share the grief or have themselves suffered a major loss remain at hand."[52] The only close male friend Herzog has left is Lucas Asphalter, who is grieving the death of his beloved laboratory monkey!

Herzog flees Chicago soon after the separation for a European lecture tour; he is embarrassed and afraid to see relatives or friends. He surrounds himself instead with strangers and tries to ignore his pain through restless movement and to reassure himself of his potency through a series of brief affairs. But he has avoided doing the work of grief, so he returns to Chicago, after months of travel, in worse shape than when he left. Then Asphalter reveals Madeleine and Gersbach's betrayal, a fresh blow which precipitates Herzog's crisis. In grief, the healing process is prolonged when "a further injury reopens a healing wound."[53]

Characteristic of Herzog's avoidance of mourning is the episode in which he flees New York City and his growing romantic involvement with Ramona to visit an old friend, Libbie Sissler, and her new husband in Martha's Vineyard. He spends the day on the train, only to flee the Sisslers' house less than an hour after he arrives, leaving a note and sneaking out the back door. He seems to feel ashamed to be seen by anyone in his condition. Touchy and contradictory, he approaches people only to avoid them, which makes it difficult for him to receive comfort and complicates his mourning.

Another complication in Herzog's grief is that even a minor loss can reactivate the emotions one felt (or failed to feel) at a major loss.[54] So in mourning the loss of Madeleine, Herzog is at the same time mourning again the two crucial losses of his life: the death first of his mother and second of his father, crises he remembers at critical points in the narrative. Herzog is re-experiencing separation anxiety, whose symptoms in adults are "similar to those exhibited by younger children who have lost attachment figures . . . reactions among children to loss of a parent include . . . rage and protest over desertion, maintenance of an intense fantasy relationship with the lost parent, persistent efforts at reunion, anxiety, and a strong sense of narcissistic injury."[55] Herzog thinks, "*This year I covered half the world, and saw people in such numbers—it seems to me I saw everybody but the dead.* Whom perhaps I was looking for" (H, p. 67). He mentions his fear of "desertion," "his childish disorder, that infantile terror of death that had bent and buckled his life into these curious shapes" (H, p. 266). Edvig tells him that "depressives tended to form frantic dependencies, and to become hysterical when cut off, when threatened with loss" (H, p. 53), which describes Herzog's situation.

In one case study, a woman compared her marital separation to being separated as a child from her mother: "When my husband left I had this panicky feeling which was out of proportion to what was really happening. I was afraid I was being abandoned. . . . I remembered later that the first time I had that feeling was when I had pneumonia and my mother left me in the hospital, in a private room, in the winter. . . . And I had such a feeling of panic and fear at being left."[56] A child in such a situation would connect abandonment with death. Herzog also remembers being left in the hospital in the wintertime as a child: "he had been eight years old, in the children's ward of the Royal Victoria Hospital, Montreal. . . . From the hospital roof hung icicles like the teeth of fish. . . ." (H, p. 22). This memory is bracketed by memories of his mother.

However, he associates the hospital mostly with the weekly visits there of a Christian lady who had him read the Bible. When Madeleine is a convert to Catholicism, Herzog associates her with this lady: both wear long skirts and a similar hat with a long hatpin (H, p. 112). Madeleine's face is "strained and grim" (H, p. 22) like the Christian lady's. This lady is an ambiguous figure: a substitute mother while Herzog's mother is absent, she seems to him a good person, but she is trying to convert him to her religion, she is grim, and she wears that dangerous-looking hatpin. By process of association, Madeleine is compared to the alien, repressive mother figure he childishly clings to out of fear of abandonment, castration, and death.

Herzog recalls his mother about two dozen times in the novel. She was a kind, dreamy, melancholy woman, and Herzog believes he has inherited her softness. She sacrificed for her family and spoiled Moses, her youngest child, whom she wanted to be a rabbi. Now he feels guilty for having failed her. And he still cannot forgive himself for ignoring her thirty years before, while she was dying, even though any young child would have great difficulty coping with such an event. At sixteen, he felt intense anger—"sick with rage" (H, p. 234)—but associated his anger with the book he was reading, not with her dying. Characteristically, Herzog displaces personal guilt and rage with a more impersonal, intellectual anger, which he finds easier to accept. Thus all his angry letter-writing and intellectual polemics. He remembers he could not cry at her funeral. He was unable to mourn, a problem that still plagues him, since he has been avoiding visiting her grave. (Perhaps, like Tommy Wilhelm, Herzog just needs a good cry.) The divorce reactivates all his ambivalent, unresolved feelings about his mother's death: guilt, anger, separation anxiety, fear of death, and inability to mourn.

In addition, since his separation crisis revives the feelings he has not worked through concerning his deceased parents, it precipitates a renewed oedipal crisis. The climax of the novel – Herzog's stealing his father's gun and spying on Madeleine and Gersbach with murder on his mind – replays the oedipal situation. In mourning his father, Herzog attempts to become the father. He usurps his father's role and his gun and spies on a "primal scene." Herzog's auto accident and arrest the following day constitute his punishment for oedipal rebellion.[57] Everything after this scene is decrescendo, for Herzog has passed through his oedipal crisis by acting it out.

Just as Herzog has inherited some of his mother's temperament, so he also resembles his father: angry, impulsive, self-dramatizing, and a frequent failure. Herzog recalls his father's being twice swindled and beaten by business partners who resemble Gersbach. When his father displayed his torn clothing and his wounds before the children, they cried along with him.

Finally, Herzog remembers how his father once waved his gun and threatened to kill him. When Herzog steals the gun but is unable to shoot Madeleine or Gersbach, he realizes he has been acting like his father, a "gilded little gentleman" who had never in his life "pulled the trigger of his gun. Only threatened" (H, p. 146). "But of course, thought Herzog, all of Papa's violence went into the drama of his life, into family strife, and sentiment" (H, p. 146). And, one might add, into self-victimization, just like Herzog. Early in the novel, Herzog had contemplated shooting Madeleine and Gersbach with his father's gun: "But I'm no criminal, don't have it in me; frightful to myself instead" (H, p. 41). He thereby foreshadows the climax of the novel.

In his violence, Herzog identifies with his father. Stealing the gun is an oedipal rebellion, but having his car rammed from behind by a truck (symbolic perhaps of spanking or homosexual rape) and being arrested with the gun in his possession is Herzog's punishment, the father's revenge.[58] Like his father's, Herzog's drama is self-defeating. Finally, when Herzog's little daughter June sees her father bloodied by the accident, he is reenacting yet another scene in his father's family drama.

Thus we see that, in his grief over the divorce, Herzog is mourning again the loss of his parents. As Freud suggested in "Mourning and Melancholia," the mourner resurrects the dead by in part *becoming* the lost person. Herzog both identifies with his parents and reenacts his anger and oedipal rebellion against them. His acting out with the gun is both cathartic and self-punishing. It momentarily relieves his mental anguish, his anger and his guilt, which had paralyzed him and blocked his mourning. Although his behavior is rash and bizarre, had he not partially acted out his homicidal impulses, he might have turned totally against himself, his rage combining with his guilt. Herzog frequently feels that he does not deserve to live and contemplates suicide as a solution.

Once we recognize that Herzog's grief crisis is both an identity crisis and an oedipal crisis, other incidents can be read differently. For example, Herzog's panic and flight during his visit to the Sisslers makes sense if we consider the couple as symbolic parents. The Sisslers are welcoming and emotionally reassuring: Libbie loves Herzog (the two had never been lovers, although they had once considered it), and her husband is a wise, kindly, older man who immediately senses that Herzog has a troubled soul. Nevertheless, Herzog feels like a third party intruding in a happy marriage. Because of his attraction to Libbie, living in their house represents for him being a Gersbach, coming between a married couple, a situation uncomfortably close to the oedipal arrangement he both desires and fears: thus he panics and flees.

Aside from Herzog's identification with his parents, his identification with his little daughter June plays a significant role in his grief work. When Herzog decides to take revenge, his justification is that he is not acting on his own behalf but as a father defending his daughter against two psychopathic child abusers. Actually, he is defending himself, not as a man but as a battered child.[59] There are many references to child abuse in the novel: Madeleine, Herzog, and the woman on trial were all sexually molested as children. That trial, which spurs Herzog's revenge, is of the woman and her lover accused of beating her son to death; the couple and the child are obvious counterparts to Madeleine, Gersbach, and June. But the boy, who was beaten around the genitals with the heel of a woman's shoe, represents Herzog as well.

Herzog, struggling against his frequently childish tendencies, could be said to be suffering in his divorce from the battered child syndrome. "Even when marriages turn bad and other components of love fade or turn into their opposites, attachment is likely to remain. The spouses resemble battered children in their feelings."[60] That is, they may be fearful and angry and desire revenge, yet they remain dependent and attached. One divorced woman, bothered by her continuing yearning for her husband, said, "You never find a battered child that does not want to be back with its parents, because they are the only parents it has. I just have very much this feeling."[61]

By the end of the novel, Herzog appears to have emerged successfully from the crisis. First, by partially acting out his rage and desire for revenge, he has released himself from the worst of it. Second, he finally sees Madeleine again and feels he gets the better of her; the fact that he was arrested for carrying a loaded gun seems to scare her! Third, he has begun the process of detaching himself from Madeleine and Gersbach by seeing them as ludicrous figures, unworthy of his attention. Freud writes, "It is possible for the [mourning] process in the unconscious to come to an end, either after the fury has spent itself or after the object has been abandoned as valueless."[62] Herzog has done both.

At the end, he is living alone in his old house in the country, refusing his brother's offer to send him to a psychiatric hospital for a rest. His temporary isolation has given him some peace of mind. When Ramona tracks him down, he offers her dinner but won't let her spend the night. Not yet fully healed, he is wary of relationships. Nevertheless, he has stopped his compulsive letter writing and obsessive thinking and begun both figuratively and literally to put his house in order. "For perhaps the first time he felt what it was like to be free from Madeleine. Joy! His servitude was ended, and his heart released from its grisly heaviness and encrustation" (H, p. 313).

Despite the positive signs, there are negative ones as well. He is so distracted that he loses track of the days and forgets to eat or sleep. When his brother Will pays a visit, Herzog appears to have lost ten pounds in less than a week; he seems agitated and overexcited.

Robert S. Weiss writes,

> Sometimes loss of attachment gives rise not to separation distress, but rather to its opposite, euphoria; or it may alternate with or be interrupted by euphoria. . . . Instead of needing the other, the individual feels that he or she needs only the self. Furthermore, removal of the other has made available to the self new opportunities for gratification and self-realization.
>
> This euphoria does not seem to be an integrated or lasting aspect of the separated individual's personality. . . . Most who experienced euphoria report that it proved fragile. When I have talked with individuals describing themselves as euphoric, it has seemed to me that they often displayed tension and anxiety without being aware of it.[63]

Thus Herzog's joy may only be fragile and temporary, perhaps a manic cycle countering his depression. John J. Clayton speculates that Herzog's cycle of guilt and masochism will return.[64] Bernard J. Paris believes that although Herzog has overcome the crisis, Herzog is as neurotic as ever, simply more detached for the moment.[65]

Although I agree with their skepticism about Herzog's psychic equilibrium, I wonder if they are demanding too much. First, recovery from grief does not necessarily constitute a transformation of personality. Those who were neurotic before the loss remain neurotic after recovery, although they may slightly reorganize their defenses. The crisis past, Herzog thinks, "Why must I be such a throb-hearted character. . . . But I am. I am, and you can't teach old dogs. Myself is thus and so, and will continue thus and so. And why fight it? My balance comes from instability" (H, p. 330).

Second, there are no miraculous cures in *any* Bellow novel; his heroes all go through a learning process, but at the end they have not undergone a change of character, merely a change of heart. We leave them after they have taken a first step toward becoming more fully human. Often at the end of the novel they are in a mood of temporary euphoria, just like Herzog's: think of Joseph, Augie, Henderson, or Corde.

Herzog may still be neurotic, but he has learned something from having survived his crisis of grief. Writes C. M. Parkes, "The pain of grief is just as much a part of life as the joy of love; it is, perhaps, the price we pay for love, the cost of commitment."[66] Herzog's ability to grieve deeply is testimony to his power to love deeply, the power that makes him and all of us human.

NOTES

1. Saul Bellow, *Herzog* (New York: Viking, 1964), p. 1. Further parenthetical page references will be preceded by H.

2. Gerald F. Jacobson, *The Multiple Crises of Marital Separation and Divorce* (New York: Grune and Stratton, 1983), p. 37.

3. Colin Murray Parkes, *Bereavement: Studies of Grief in Adult Life* (New York: International Universities Press, 1972), p. 164.

4. I want to thank two colleagues at the University of Florida for their suggestions: Dr. Maria Vera for aiding my research on the process of recovery from divorce and Dr. Bernard J. Paris for his helpful comments on *Herzog*.

5 .Gordon Lloyd Harper, "Saul Bellow: An Interview." *Herzog*, Viking Critical Edition, ed Irving Howe (New York: Viking, 1976), p. 354.

6. Robert S. Weiss, *Marital Separation* (New York: Basic Books, 1975), p. 5.

7. Jonathan Wilson, *Herzog: The Limits of Ideas* (Boston: Twayne, 1990), p. 6.

8. Daniel Fuchs, "Bellow and Freud," *Saul Bellow in the 1980s,* Ed. Gloria L. Cronin and L. H. Goldman (East Lansing: Michigan State Univ. Press, 1989), p. 27.

9. Wilson, p. 51.

10. See in particular John J. Clayton, *Saul Bellow: In Defense of Man,* 2nd edition (Bloomington: Indiana Univ. Press, 1979); Fuchs; Claude Lévy, *Les Romans de Saul Bellow: Tactiques Narratives et Stratégies Oedipiennes* (Paris: Klincksieck, 1983); Mark Shechner, *After the Revolution: Studies in the Contemporary Jewish-American Imagination* (Bloomington: Indiana Univ. Press, 1987); and Wilson.

11. Sigmund Freud, "Mourning and Melancholia," *The Standard Edition of the Complete Psychological Works of Sigmund Freud,* Vol. 14, trans. and ed. James Strachey (London: Hogarth, 1957), pp. 244–45.

12. Parkes, p. 35.

13. Parkes, p. 75.

14. See Robert R. Dutton, *Saul Bellow* (New York: Twayne, 1971), p. 121–22.

15. Bruce Fisher, *When Your Relationship Ends* (Boulder, CO: Family Relations Learning Center, 1984), p. 88.

16. Clayton, p. 197.

17. Bernard J. Paris, "Herzog the Man: An Analytic View of a Literary Figure," *The American Journal of Psychoanalysis,* 36 (1976): p. 253.

18. Lévy, pp. 182–83.

19. Paul Bohannon, "The Six Stations of Divorce," *Divorce and After: An Analysis of the Emotional and Social Problems of Divorce,* ed. Paul Bohannon (Garden City, New York: Doubleday, 1971), p. 61.

20. Jacobson, pp. 72–74.

21. Robert S. Weiss, "The Emotional Impact of Marital Separation," *Journal of Social Issues,* 32.1 (1976): 137.

22. Bohannon, p. 38.

23. Bohannon, p. 39.

24. John F. Crosby, Bruce A. Gage, and Marsha Croy Raymond, "The Grief Resolution Process in Divorce," *Journal of Divorce,* 7.1 (1983): 5.

25. Diane Vaughan, *Uncoupling: Turning Points in Intimate Relationships* (New York: Oxford Univ. Press, 1986), pp. 42–43.

26. Crosby, p. 5.

27. Bohannon, p. 40.

28. Weiss, p. 150.

29. Vaughan, p. 78.

30. Vaughan, p. 26.

31. William J. Goode, *Women in Divorce* (New York: Free Press, 1965), p. 137.

32. Clayton, p. 194.

33. Sissela Bok, *Secrets: On the Ethics of Concealment and Revelation* (New York: Pantheon, 1982), p. 20.

34. Vaughan, p. 64.

35. Vaughan, p. 75.

36. Vaughan, p. 76.

37. Vaughan, p. 85.

38. Vaughan, p. 135.

39. Jacobson, pp. 66–67.

40. Jacobson, pp. 68–70.

41. B. L. Bloom, S. W. White, and S. J. Asher, "Marital disruption as a stressful life event," *Divorce and Separation: Contexts, Causes and Consequences,* ed. G. Levinger and O. Moles (New York: Basic Books, 1979), pp. 184–200.

42. Michael Myers, *Men and Divorce* (New York: Guilford, 1989), p. 8.

43. Myers, p. 13.

44. Kenneth Kressel, "Patterns of Coping in Divorce and Some Implications for Clinical Practice," *Family Relations,* 29 (1980): 236.

45. Colin Murray Parkes and Robert S. Weiss, *Recovery from Bereavement* (New York: Basic Books, 1983), p. 72.

46. Parkes and Weiss, p. 97.

47. Bertha G. Simos, "Grief therapy to facilitate healthy restitution," *Social Casework,* 58 (June 1977): 339.

48. Vaughan, p. 149.

49. Kressel, p. 235.

50. Geoffrey Gorer, *Death, Grief and Mourning in Contemporary Britain* (London: Cresset, 1965). Quoted by Parkes, *Bereavement,* p. 9.

51. Mel Krantzler, *Creative Divorce: A New Opportunity for Personal Growth* (New York: Evans, 1974), p. 44.

52. Parkes, p. 8.

53. Parkes, p. 5.

54. John Bowlby, *Attachment and Loss,* Vol. III. *Loss* (New York: Basic Books, 1980), p. 160.

55. Weiss, "Emotional Impact," p. 140.

56. Weiss, p. 140.

57. Clayton, p. 222.

58. Clayton, p. 122, and Shechner, p. 144.

59. Shechner, p. 144.

60. Weiss, "Emotional Impact," p. 44.

61. Weiss, p. 137.

62. Freud, p. 257.

63. Weiss, *Marital Separation,* pp. 53–55.

64. Clayton, p. 229.

65. Paris, p. 260.

66. Parkes, *Bereavement,* pp. 5–6.

Bellow's Hand Writing: The Tactile Imagination

Michael Greenstein

Three times the concentred self takes hold, three times
The thrice concentred self, having possessed

The object, grips it in savage scrutiny.

> – Wallace Stevens, "Credences of Summer"

I N SAUL BELLOW'S world, one way of seizing the day is to grab the body, for as Dr. Adler tells his beleaguered son Wilhelm, "the massage does a world of good."[1] Whereupon the doctor opens his "small hand on the table in a gesture so old and so typical that Wilhelm felt it like an actual touch upon the foundations of his life." The contiguity between table and personality adumbrates a Bellovian connection between touching and metaphysics, or between massage and the transcendental. Towards the middle of *To Jerusalem and Back,* Bellow follows Dr. Adler's advice and takes time off for the here-and-now of a sublime rubdown: "Moshe the masseur is delicate in person; his hands, however, have the strength that purity of purpose can give. . . . He seems untouched by life."[2] And while the author immediately explains the phrase "untouched by life" as pertaining to someone who has lived without cynicism, the reader should also note the contrast between delicacy and strength in the person of the masseur whose hands fulfill the carpe diem of the flesh. Moshe's delicate strength not only enables him to relieve people of their muscular tensions, but his oxymoronic quality and purity of purpose also transcend the anatomical aspects of his vocation: "For me, massage is a personal relationship and kind of an act of love" (p. 65). If there is any doubt about Bellow's metaphysics of massage in its approximating Buber's

I-Thou relationship and Wilhelm Reich's orgone therapy, we need only turn the page of *To Jerusalem and Back,* for the next chapter begins with a reference to Israel's losing touch with reality. In Bellow's vocabulary, "touch" is a loaded term connecting physical sensation to other realms of the imagination and a world of good.

While most of Bellow's fiction celebrates the therapeutic value of the steam bath, "Him with His Foot in His Mouth" reveals the hazards of excessive handling. In a long epistle to Miss Rose, Dr. Harry Shawmut— musicologist, ironist, and metaphysician—explains to the retired librarian why he had insulted her thirty-five years earlier. Having wounded her a generation ago, he now suffers not only from remorse but from hypertension, cardiac disorders, cracked dental roots, a hemorrhoid the size of a walnut, and a creeping arthritis of the hands. Exiled in British Columbia, Shawmut discovers that something has gone wrong with the middle finger of his right hand: "The hinge had stopped working and the finger was curled like a snail—a painful new affliction. Quite a joke on me. . . . I have been served with papers."[3] After sixty years of writing or serving papers, wiping himself twice daily, and combing his mustache downward with his fingernails, the curled finger appears as some kind of retribution: he who has inflicted so many verbal practical jokes on others, now becomes the suffering joker with the additional twist of writer's cramp. Like a comma in his writing, the finger's snail forces him to pause and review his past; like a character with his foot in his mouth or curvature of the spine, the curled finger indicates a degree of ironic self-reflexiveness in the process of aging. Dr. Shawmut's list of afflictions extends through the length of his writing career, until the reader protests—metaphysician, heal thyself. Through the physicality of writing and the writing of physicality, Bellow draws attention not so much to any postmodern notion of textuality as to more old-fashioned demands of humor, feeling, connection, and metaphysics.

And if Shawmut's hands aren't crippled from writing letters and a book on Pergolesi, then perhaps his effort at conducting both his life and music has gone from hypertrophy of the limbs to atrophy. "By waving my long arms, conducting Mozart's *Great Mass* or Handel's *Solomon,* I wafted myself away into the sublime" (p. 51). The aging of Shawmut's active limbs reaching for the heights forms an integral part of the story that begins with his palpable offense to Miss Rose and ends with his "private resistance to the giant public hand of the law (that hand will be withdrawn only when I am dead)" (p. 58). The long arm of the law extends from Seattle to Florida, from private to public spheres, from person to person, and from Eddie Walish's limping foot to the mouth of Mrs. Gracewell's Swedenborgian metaphysics. If "fiction is only the jittery act of reaching," then reading Bellow forces us to pay attention to this jittery reach.[4] With tongue in cheek, foot in mouth, and hands all over the place, the tactile imagination is Bellow's *Fatum*. If Shawmut is a reverberator and if his letter to Miss Rose is a communion, then Bellow keeps the ironic hinge on the middle finger working, for he adheres to one of his favorite epigraphs – "Whatsoever thy hand findeth to do, do it with thy might."[5] In other words, seize the day.

One early example in *Dangling Man* sets the tone for much of the fiction to follow. On the afternoon of January 5, Joseph sits on the floor and polishes shoes. Chicago's feeling of tranquility recalls childhood shoe-shining in Montreal when Joseph thrust his arm above the elbow into Aunt Dina's shoes, "and I could feel the brush against my arm through the soft leather."[6] This hedonistic "brush" with experience creates a heightened sense of reality for Bellow, who exploits the palpability of the mundane as a means of bridging any kind of mind-body dualism. If the novelist dangles not merely to wait but to transcend, he nevertheless knows when to keep both feet on the ground so as to keep in touch with the pavement's teachings. According to Robert Alter, Bellow's tactile mode, or rite of massage, defeats modernist alienation by celebrating instead the connective tissue of ordinary life: "The present object – here part of a ritual reenactment and not an adventitious discovery as in Proust – launches the narrator upon a journey into himself which reveals to us much of what had made him the particular moral and psychological individual he is."[7]

This soft touch contrasts with the novel's opening era of "hardboiled-dom" (p. 9) where one is supposed to strangle the emotions, to grapple with them silently. Rejecting that kind of Hemingwayesque doctrine, Joseph intends to talk about his feelings with as many mouths as Siva has arms. So this polyphonic journalist touches his books that surround, if not hold, him. If Joseph has a close grasp on himself, he nevertheless extends his tight hold when he rubs down with alcohol his father-in-law who grunts with pleasure during the massage. By the end of the novel, Joseph announces that he is relieved to be "in other hands," (p. 191) for those hands are not only a synecdoche for the rest of his body but also for his relationship to the larger body of mankind beyond the four walls of his room. While one hand keeps a journal, the other reaches out to society and to history to encompass humanity in the broadest possible sense. In all of Bellow's ten-finger exercises, hands serve as conduits between the inner life and a transcendent shove against wider horizons.

The *Doppelgänger* relationship between Asa Leventhal and Kirby Allbee in Bellow's next novel, *The Victim,* hinges on a sense of touch. In Leventhal's neighborhood park the "benches formed a dense, double human wheel," as if to emphasize the intertwined fates of victim and victimizer.[8] "There was an overwhelming human closeness and thickness, and Leventhal was penetrated by a sense not merely of the crowd in this park but of innumerable millions, crossing, touching, pressing" (pp. 183–84). Any Dostoyevskian symbiosis between Jew and anti-Semite carries universal implications. Allbee "fingered Leventhal's hair, and Leventhal found himself caught under his touch and felt incapable of doing anything" (p. 225). An electromagnetic current flows between the two, for "attach" and "attack" form two psychological sides of touch. Copy editor and hand writer, Leventhal turns palm reader toward the end of the novel: "he diverted himself by observing the hands, shuffling, dealing, manipulating the money, the variety of knuckles and fingers. . . . he might be a printer. The flesh of his palm was red and brutally crosshatched" (p. 248). To Mark Shechner's anatomical list, one should add Bellow's hands: "an acute observer of necks, throats, chests, mouths, teeth, and the inflected corners of the eyes, tiny fortresses in which defenses of the entire system may be read."[9] Conversely, one may read a partial system of offense in the knocks and knuckles of Bellow's protagonists.

The Adventures of Augie March opens brashly with an insistence on American anteriority: "first to knock, first admitted; sometimes an innocent knock, sometimes a not so innocent. . . . [a]nd in the end there isn't any way to disguise the nature of the knocks by acoustical work on the door or gloving the knuckles."[10] A graduate of the school of hard knocks, Augie never dons kid gloves nor does his mother whose hands are work-reddened "to heed the knocks as they come" (p. 4). That Bellow favors this metaphor may be seen from his comment about rationalists who think that they have all the answers to life's mysteries in contrast to Augie's intuitive knowledge: "The mystery is too great. So when they knock at the door of mystery with the knuckles of cognition it is quite right that the door should open and some mysterious power should squirt them in the eye."[11] In his metaphysician's manual, Bellow shifts effortlessly between Groucho Marx's slapstick and Karl Marx's dialectical materialism.

While Augie worries that he is "an easy touch for friendships" (p. 12), Grandma Lausch complains about her dentist's heavy hands: "The touch is everything to a dentist" (p. 7). But she herself can be heavy-handed with indelible punishments inflicted on Augie: "She shook the crabbed unit of her hand at me with the fierceness of the words. . . . And the fall-

ing hand landed on my arm; it was accidental, but the effect was frightful, for I yelled as if this tap had tenfold hit my soul" (pp. 36–37). This
play of hands and arms reverberates to the extent that Augie becomes
Einhorn's arms and legs, not just his metaphorical right hand (p. 60).
Since Einhorn has to be in touch with everything, Augie arranges a little
screwdriver convenient for touching off the telephone and raises his
arms to his desk in several stages. Bellow taps the soul tenfold.

Augie describes his apprenticeship among the Einhorns of the world:
in one direction, those who read whopping books in German or French and
knew their (meta)physics and botany manuals; in another direction, the
criminals. "I touched all sides, and nobody knew where I belonged" (p.
113). Augie and most of Bellow's other characters touch too many sides,
their elusiveness defies simple categorization, and their charm derives
from their deft juggling of lower limbs and higher spheres of thought from
narcotics to Nietzsche. Augie's intellect craves "to have the reach to grasp
both ends of the frame and turn the big image-taking glass to any scene in
the world" (p. 252). Bellow's encyclopedic mirror reflects life and art, for
he is the arch realist who transcends mimesis by adding history's axial line
to this three-dimensional portrayals. Augie learns equally from Mimi's
abortion, Caligula's claw on his hand, Georgie's shoemaking, Mintouchian's
Turkish bath, Basteshaw's blow, or any stolen text.

No sooner does Augie light out from Chicago with Thea than he drags
with him his all-encompassing memory, not precisely Wordsworthian
recollection in tranquility: "Some things I have an ability to see without
feeling much previous history. . . . I can fix my memory down to an ant in
the folds of bark. . . . Or such discriminations as where, on a bush of
roses, you see variations in heats that make your breast and bowel draw
at various places from your trying to correspond; when even the rose of
rot and wrong makes you attempt to answer and want to stir. . . . So
there are burning roses, there are sores, and there are busted circuits"
(p. 327). In the anagram of sores and roses lies the key to Augie's nature:
the polarity of pain and beauty, the amalgam of epic knocking about and
lyric tenderness, and the correspondence of bowel and brain in Midwestern rot. In his picaresque march through America and beyond, Augie experiences his share of burning roses and sores from a myriad of women
and reality instructors. When Augie returns from the plucks and pulls of
Mexico, the sores fester: "I wasn't getting any younger myself. . . . I
smiled minus a couple of teeth of the lower line and was somewhat
smeared, or knocked, kissed by the rocky face of clasping experience" (p.
447). The first to knock undergoes his rite of passage throughout America

and Europe until he grasps his inner nature, the carnivalesque *animal
ridens* to emerge as a Columbus of those near-at-hand.

By contrast, where Augie March comes of age in America and Europe,
Eugene Henderson belatedly lights out for darkest Africa to explore
tribal rituals among the Arnewi and Wariri. From the opening pressure
in Henderson's chest until the final tingling over the pure white lining of
a gray Arctic silence, we are in the presence of Bellow's tactile imagination. Henderson's fingers wipe his enormous nose before he shakes
hands with his wife's guests, but they are equally capable of tenderness
when he rubs his wife's pregnant belly with baby oil. What binds Henderson to his wife Lily is their mutual suffering with their teeth: they both
wear bridges. Whereas his first wife Frances has white teeth that cannot
be seen in her dark open mouth, Lily possesses new porcelain teeth. In
Africa Mtalba licks his hand with her small tongue. "There was this happy
agitation in me, which made me fix my teeth together. Certain emotions
make my teeth itch. Esthetic appreciation especially does it to me. Yes,
when I admire beauty I get these tooth pangs, and my gums are on
edge."[12] An anthropological edgeman undergoing his rite of passage,
Henderson expresses his emotions through his teeth and hands that
taste and tell. Comedy and esthetics converge around teeth, nose, hands,
chest, and facial gestures. What Gabriel Josipovici says about Henderson's pectoral burden applies equally to other sensory and anatomical
organs: "the words acquire weight, a tangible quality, and it is the weight
of the words that removes the weight on the chest."[13]

Despite all of these pressures on his mind and body, Henderson com-
municates with such counterparts as an octopus (a multiple *Doppelgänger*) with its eightfold touch: "I looked in at an octopus, and the creature seemed also to look at me and press its soft head to the glass. . . .
The eyes spoke to me coldly. But even more speaking, even more cold,
was the soft head with its speckles, and the Brownian motion in those
speckles, a cosmic coldness in which I felt I was dying. The tentacles
throbbed" (p. 19). Between microcosmic and macrocosmic forces, Bellow
opts for an ironic apocalypse in this anti-hero, Henderson. Highbrow,
lowbrow, comic, skeptic, and ironist – Bellow makes touching faces in his
anthropological panorama or anatomy of witticism. Sharpened sensory
impressions enter his protagonists' brains through their eyebrows, fingertips, nosetips, mouths, chests, or other organs before passing out as
verbal messages to the rest of the world. This whole complex network of
nerves lies at the heart of his fiction. King Dahfu's gripping coversation
stimulates Henderson in a similar octopal manner as he grips his legs

through the Sungo's green silk trousers: his face stretches to the length of a city block and he sees things not merely double or triple but in countless outlines of wavering color. Henderson's bulk is almost an extension of himself, a way of going beyond the personal toward interpersonal relationships between noumenal and phenomenal spheres. Amidst huge numbers, every thumb and fingerprint is a mystery; accordingly, Henderson tries to feel as if with his fingers the characteristics of his African situation with King Dahfu.

The lion and Henderson confront each other: "I felt her muzzle touch upward first at my armpits, and then between my legs. . . . Clasping me and holding me up, the king still talked softly and calmingly to her while her breath blew out the green silk of the Sungo trousers. I was gripping the inside of my cheek with my teeth, including the broken bridgework" (p. 222). The Bellovian body, so accustomed to massage, accepts this frisking between king of the beasts and rain king who confesses to having the Midas touch in reverse. With tongue in cheek and participle dangling to indicate mutual exchange for the ménage à trois and also to reflect Henderson's shrinking member, Bellow humors his reader in the lion's den. The king takes the rain king by the wrist and presses his hand on Atti's flank. "Slowly her fur passed under my fingertip and the nails became like five burning tapers. The bones of the hand became incandescent" (227). Although Henderson refuses the amazons' "joxi" or trample massage, he does engage in touching in extremis: like Harry Shawmut, his "hands have lost shape a good deal as a result of the abuses they have been subjected to" (pp. 249–50). Nimble, flexible Henderson instructs Romilayu in life's rhythm where the left hand shakes with the right hand while both hands play in the give-and-take of patty cake.

Henderson fiddles around while Africa burns. Having declared that "to be untouched by madness is a form of madness," (p. 25) he takes up his father's violin: "It was like a feeling creature" (p. 25). His manual training encompasses many experiences, for he is octopal as well as oedipal in his goal of reaching his father by playing on his violin. "And with these hands I've pushed around the pigs; I've thrown down boars and pinned them and gelded them. So now these same fingers are courting the music of the violin and gripping its neck and toiling up and down on the Sevcik" (p. 30). The steel E string wounds Henderson's gargantuan fingers that clutch continents, wrestle with Itelo, and touch Mtalba's breast or the secrets of life. Seated with Dahfu, who has thrown his father's skull, Henderson thinks in French of a "luth suspendu . . . sitôt qu'on le touche il résonne" (p. 210)—a dangling lute resounding to a correspondent touch. The pun on "raisonne" (reason) matches the instrumental play of music with its universal overtones; that is, Bellow moves in his five-finger exercise from the particular to the universal, from the phenomenal to the noumenal, from touch to harmony of the spheres, from bear hug to barbaric yawp.

Skeptical, precocious Moses Herzog asks his mother how Adam was created from the dust of the ground. Sarah Herzog then rubs the palm of her hand with her finger until something dark appears on her deep-lined skin, a particle of what looks to her son like earth.[14] Many years later, outside Magistrate's Court, Moses repeats the experiment successfully in a spirit of comedy. Having done justice to this ironic palm-reading, Moses is able to reanimate Adam, revise the Bible, exorcise his dybbuk, revive the golem of inertia, and face the future. When Mrs. Tuttle's broom raises too much dust at the very end of the novel, he instructs her to "damp it down," for he has learned to damp down the particles of his own dissemination.

Moses Herzog writes on scraps of paper with a great pressure of eagerness in his hand, the sheer physicality of his hand-writing mirroring J. S. Bach's putting on black gloves to compose a requiem mass. Eventually, Moses' hand rebels, and he suffers from writer's cramp when commenting on monographs from university presses; or, he fears a hernia from dragging Shapiro's heavy volume all over Europe. A virtuoso of manual dexterity, Moses as a child rubbed his patent-leather shoes with butter so that when Madeline announces that she wants a divorce, Moses does not smash any tablets but instead takes a firm grip on the storm windows (objective correlatives for his inner tempest) because he can't allow himself to feel crippled (like Valentine Gersbach). But the handyman of Ludeyville mishandles much of his life. The first chapter of *Herzog* ends with Moses writing to Wanda and wondering how to translate "blond little cushioned knuckles in French" (p. 26). Herzog's writer's cramp is both synecdoche for larger bodily pains (heartaches and headaches) and also his paralysis of the will where letters never seem to get finished. Where *Ulysses* ends with "Yes," *Herzog* achieves its affirmative through a double or quadruple negative in the concluding sentences.

Herzog's opponent, Valentine Gersbach, has the thick grip of a monarch all the while he holds the upper hand of any I-Thou relationship he shares with Herzog. Dragging his shoelaces, his past, and Pratt's short history of the Civil War, Herzog boards a train and immediately weighs his thoughts, "If . . . Yes . . . No . . . on the other hand" (p. 105). Burdened by syllogisms, alternatives, and all the other hands, he "let his head fall into his hands, almost silently laughing" (p. 105), for only comedy can

relieve him of his excess Kierkegaardian baggage. If Moses suffers as a
writer, he also agonizes as a painter with his taut hand trying to achieve
finesse in Ludeyville, building Versailles as well as Jerusalem. An ironic,
unskilled naif rather than the Michelangelo of *Moses,* his artistry contrasts
with Madeleine's painterly skills which Bellow outlines in Popean detail.
Like Belinda in *The Rape of the Lock,* Madeleine applies makeup and cos-
metics deftly, "bracing at the mirror, holding her hands as if to support her
bust but not actually touching it" (p. 111). The mirror's reflection, Moses'
sideway glance, and his retrospective narrative yield a double perspective
of satire and affection, the systole and diastole of marriage and divorce.

"Solitary as a stone / With my ten fingers—alone" (p. 135). Ravitch's
drunken refrain epitomizes *veritas:* Moses uses his ten fingers on his oboe
to bind others to his feelings, for his head, heart, and hands strive to overcome solipsism and enter society, to go beyond monologues towards dia-
logic wholeness. Interaction with Ramona takes an odd form: "A free foot
on a summer night eases the heart" (p. 156). With Sono, there is the
mutual massage or the imprint of his touch on her eyelid. Moses palpates
heartaches and rubs palms to extend lifelines and dampen the spirit's dust.

In *Humboldt's Gift* the massage receives even fuller treatment at the
hands of the Bellow-Citrine who reminisces about Chicago's steam bath:

> As a kid I went to the Russian Bath with my own father. This old
> establishment has been there forever, hotter than the tropics and rot-
> ting sweetly. Down in the cellar men moaned on the steam-softened
> planks while they were massaged abrasively with oak-leaf besoms
> lathered in pickle-buckets. The wooden posts were slowly consumed
> by a wonderful decay that made them soft brown. They looked like
> beaver's fur in the golden vapor.[15]

With an ironic and nostalgic Midas touch that turns almost everything to
realms of gold, Bellow conveys the sensuality of steam baths through
their oxymoronic richness: sweet rot, soft abrasiveness, wonderful
decay, and a gradual eternity "slowly consumed . . . forever." Accordingly,
Division Street is the appropriate address for the Russian Bath: not simply
a division within Chicago, but a more cosmopolitan division between old
and new worlds, past and present.

Old-timers like Citrine's father and Mr. Sweibel believe in the therapeutic value of being scrubbed with lathered oak leaves. "Such retrograde people still exist, resisting modernity, dragging their feet. . . . the
old guys at the Bath do seem to be unconsciously engaged in a collective

attempt to buck history" (pp. 77–78). Whether bucking or bucketing history, Bellow is attracted to this tension between the primitive and the modern, and he goes on to list their antique form of swelling buttocks and fatty breasts. After steaming, these old fellows eat salt herring or salami and drink schnapps. "You feel that these people are almost conscious of obsolescence, of a line of evolution abandoned by nature and culture. So down in the super-heated subcellars all these Slavonic cavemen and wood demons with hanging laps of fat and legs of stone and lichen boil themselves and splash ice water on their heads by the bucket" (p. 78). The "you feel" serves as a universal acknowledgment of the visceral reality of this primitive scene, so hot to the touch, and the paragraph's concluding sentence reiterates the universal quality of the baths by speculating that there may be no village in the Carpathians where such practices still prevail.

Still in the Bath, Cantabile forces Citrine to the toilet where Charlie thinks about the human condition over-all and distracts himself with his past reading of ape behavior – "visceral-emotional sensitivities in the anthropoid branch" (p. 83). Even thinking such improving thoughts ironically reinforces evolutionary speculation not only about Cantabile's simian deportment but about all the retrograde denizens pickled in the Russian Bath. Furthermore, the episode recapitulates Charlie's "weakness for ontogeny and phylogeny" (p. 72). And the bucket seats in Cantabile's T-bird – "so soft, so crimson" (p. 88) – contrast with the hard toilet seat upon which he has just relieved himself, and the pickle buckets for scrubbing the body. Bellow's tactile imagination thrives in the tropical Bath, combining his excremental vision with higher levels of intellection.

The day after this brutal encounter, Charlie Citrine relaxes by lying down on his goose-down sofa and pulling off his shoes. Under his head he places a needlepoint cushion embroidered by an anthroposophist who "was a little *noli me tangerine.* She did and did not wish to be touched" (p. 111). As a member of the citrus family, this "tangerine" connects her to Citrine who meditates extensively (pp. 110–68), basing his exercises on Rudolf Steiner's *Knowledge of the Higher Worlds and Its Attainment.* Charlie's meditation reveals much about Bellow's technique in fiction, for it serves as a narrative frame, bracketing long stretches of flashback and reminiscence about Humboldt. Interruptions to the lengthy meditation such as the hall-buzzer going off and the hammering of the brass door-knocker return the meditation to the everyday world of felt experience. If on the one hand these framing devices for higher thought function somewhat like Browning's dramatic monologues, the entire meditative process reverts two centuries earlier to metaphysical poetry where meditation served as a crucial element.

At the outset of *The Poetry of Meditation,* Louis Martz discusses a painting by Georges de la Tour: "This person's thoughts are not abstract: the left hand, with its sensitive, tapered fingers, probes. . . ; the arm, so delicately clothed, conveys a rude sensation to the brain. . . . Sight and touch, then, meet to form these thoughts, meditative, piercing, looking through the mirror, probing whatever lies beyond."[16] Like some of the religious poetry of the seventeenth century, Bellow-Citrine's meditation emphasizes the composition of place, the concrete, dramatic scene firmly established and graphically imaged via a tactile imagination. For all the distance separating the poetry of John Donne and Von Humboldt Fleisher, Bellow's narrative frequently acts as an extended metaphysical conceit, yoking together disparate elements from Chicago's or New York's violence. Indeed, the longest paragraph in *Humboldt's Gift* recounts the poet's metaphysical wit in conversation: "he moved easily from the tabloids to General Rommel and from Rommel to John Donne" (p. 31). And Humboldt's ballads, favorably noticed by T. S. Eliot, are pure, musical, witty, radiant, humane, and Platonic – terms applicable to seventeenth-century poetry and Bellow's fiction. If seventeenth-century lyrics and Bellow's novels display introspective narratives, they both likewise touch base with reality, and their combination of physics and metaphysics gives rise to the ironies and ambiguities of *noli me tangerine* – to touch or not to touch, to pin down the elusive Bellow or to allow the drumlin woodchuck to burrow further.

After the opening sequence of Humboldtism, Bellow shifts abruptly to Citrine's problems: "And now the present. A different side of life – entirely contemporary" (p. 34). These sudden transitions coupled with an encyclopedic inclusiveness give rise to a kind of *discordia concors* in Bellow's prose that requires an adjustment comparable to Citrine's apprehension of his battered Mercedes: "difficult to grasp – to grasp, I mean, even in an esthetic sense" (p. 35). The esthetic, sociological, and psychological combine with the physical grasp as a means of apprehending the connection between American baseball bat and German machine – seize the day, the bat, and the silver steering wheel. If baseball is Cantabile's game, racquet ball is Citrine's, but he is not a good player because he is "too tangled about the heart, overdriven" (68). Where others die of heart attacks on the court, Charlie loses a front tooth. "I tell myself that when I achieve mental and spiritual clarity and translate these into play nobody will be able to touch me" (68). In and on Chicago's courts, nobody and everybody touches Bellow-Citrine in the process of achieving mental and spiritual *claritas*. Another flashback parodies Citrine's return to the womb as he seeks his birthplace in Appleton, Wisconsin, where he beholds a fat old woman in underpants in the room where he was born. The woman's husband, a gas station attendant with oily hands, nabs Citrine in his exquisite grey suit. Citrine's explanation, which includes Houdini and hints at the riddle of man, suffices: "These matters of the spirit are widely and instantly grasped" (p. 91). Once again, Bellow's reach exceeds his grasp, the husband's oily hands or Houdini's prestidigitations, in the magic of narrative connection.

Whether dancing on racquet ball courts or meditating in cashmere socks, Citrine pays close attention to his feet as something more than pedestrian: "for an atypical foot you need an atypical shoe. . . . And is there still any typical foot? I mean by this that such emphasis has fallen on the erotic that all the eccentricity of the soul pours into the foot" (p. 190). A foot-and-hand fetishist, Saul Bellow maneuvers cunningly between sole and soul. Just as eccentricities fall to man's foot, so Citrine after fingerprinting longs for his barber not for a haircut but "for the sake of the touch" (p. 290). Where the masseur's motto is *me tangerine*, Citrine uses his fingers for penning transcendent music: "My very fingertips rehearsed how they would work the keys of the trumpet, imagination's trumpet, when I got ready to blow it at last" (p. 396). No matter what instrument Bellow chooses, his fingers find the keys to register meaning.

Touching plays a vital role in *Mr. Sammler's Planet*. Dr. Gruner probes mysteries: "Gruner was a toucher. His habit, even in passing through a room, was to touch."[17] His uncle, Artur Sammler, opens the novel by examining with his finger tips the satin binding of his electric blanket as well as its internal sinews and lumps. Just as these internal sinews and lumps connect to the Polish refugee's damaged tissues or nerve-spaghetti, so his finger tips relate to those of the pickpocket: "with the touch of a doctor on a patient's belly the Negro moved back the slope leather" (p. 10). On lunar metaphysics Sammler speculates: "Finite is still feeling through the veil, examining the naked inner reality with a gloved hand" (p. 53). Bellow handles his galaxy *ad astra* with kid gloves that fondle *kulturny* or jab at creatureliness. Sammler's daughter Shula, a pickpocket of manuscripts, "touched things and claimed them. As property" (p. 194). Bellow's magical touch claims property, not in any anti-Marxist sense but as both the *terra firma* and *terra incognita* of fiction. Sammler connects horticulture and culture when Shula wanders through the garden: "All visible and almost palpable" (p. 258). By the end of the of the novel Sammler, who "had remained touchable, vulnerable to trifles" (p. 197), manages to think things through: "Still in touch. With reality, that is" (p. 299).

Bellow's *nervosa* connection integrates all of his characters who stay in touch with reality. Fingers work overtime to tap the imagination tenfold from sublimation in the steambath to the feel of upholstery, for, in the complex web of words – touch, taste, tact, text, textile, tactile – ambidextrous Bellow weaves a seamless pattern. Whatever embroidery his hand finds to do, he does it with might, holding his thought tight and turning the pages of his metaphysician's manual. All of his dangling bipeds balance with their hands, the *via media* between upper and lower, inner and outer. A member of the Hart, Schaffner, and Marx outfit, a teller and tailor, Saul Bellow nimbly stitches the very fabric and texture of fiction where the first to knock on second thought has the last laugh. Touching Bellow resonates.

NOTES

1. Saul Bellow, *Seize the Day* (New York: Viking, 1956), p. 44. Further references are to this edition.

2. Saul Bellow, *To Jerusalem and Back* (New York: Viking, 1976), p. 64. Further references are to this edition.

3. Saul Bellow, *Him with His Foot in His Mouth and Other Stories* (New York: Harper & Row, 1984), p. 4. Further references are to this edition.

4. Saul Bellow, quoted in Jeanne Braham, *A Sort of Columbus: The American Voyages of Saul Bellow's Fiction* (Athens: Univ. of Georgia Press, 1984), p. 6.

5. This quotation from *Ecclesiastes* appears as epigraph to "Looking for Mr. Green," in *Mosby's Memoirs and Other Stories* (New York: Viking, 1968), p. 85.

6. Saul Bellow, *Dangling Man* (New York: Vanguard, 1944), p. 85. Further references are to this edition.

7. Robert Alter, *After the Tradition: Essays on Modern Jewish Writing* (New York: Dutton, 1969), p. 100.

8. Saul Bellow, *The Victim* (New York: Vanguard, 1947), p. 183. Further references are to this edition.

9. Mark Shechner, *After the Revolution: Studies in the Contemporary Jewish-American Imagination* (Bloomington: Indiana Univ. Press, 1987), p. 123.

10. Saul Bellow, *The Adventures of Augie March* (New York: Viking, 1953), p. 3. Further references are to this edition.

11. Saul Bellow, quoted in an interview in *Paris Review* 37 (Winter 1965), reprinted in Ellen Pifer, *Saul Bellow Against the Grain* (Philadelphia: Univ. of Pennsylvania Press, 1990), p. 18.

12. Saul Bellow, *Henderson the Rain King* (New York: Viking, 1959), p. 79. Further references are to this edition.

13. Gabriel Josipovici, "Introduction," *The Portable Saul Bellow* (New York: Viking, 1974), p. xxxii.

14. Saul Bellow, *Herzog* (New York: Viking, 1964), p. 232. Further references are to this edition.

15. Saul Bellow, *Humboldt's Gift* (New York: Viking, 1975), pp. 58–9. Further references are to this edition.

16. Louis Martz, *The Poetry of Meditation: A Study in English Religious Literature of the Seventeenth Century* (New Haven: Yale Univ. Press, 1962), p. 1.

17. Saul Bellow, *Mr. Sammler's Planet* (New York: Viking, 1970), p. 151. Further references are to this edition.

The Styles of Saul Bellow

Robert F. Kiernan

B ECAUSE OF the density of allusion in a novel like *Herzog* and the esoteric terms in which characters like Eugene Henderson and Artur Sammler conceptualize their experience, commentators on the Bellovian oeuvre have attended primarily to its ideational extravagance. Indeed, that ideational extravagance is commonly understood as Bellow's mature style. The taut, somewhat crabbed mode of *Dangling Man* and *The Victim* is thought to reflect the fumbling of a young writer who had not yet found his style; the expansive mode of *The Adventures of Augie March,* to constitute a breakthrough into his authentic voice; that authentic voice, to culminate in such masterpieces of the expansive style as *Herzog* and *Humboldt's Gift.*

There can be little question that Bellow has written in at least two different styles, but it is the view of most critics that he moved decisively in the early 1950s from the pronunciative style of the French Existentialists to a more ample and rhetorically indulgent nineteenth-century style. Such a view fails to grasp the persistence of both styles in his oeuvre, from the early work to the most recent. As early as *Dangling Man,* an interaction of the one style with the other is evident:

> The quest, I am beginning to think, whether it be for money, for notoriety, reputation, increase of pride, whether it leads us to thievery, slaughter, sacrifice, the quest is one and the same. All the striving is for one end. I do not entirely understand this impulse. But it seems to me that its final end is the desire for pure freedom. We are all drawn toward the same craters of the

spirit – to know what we are and what we are for, to know our purpose, to seek grace. And, if the quest is the same, the differences in
our personal histories, which hitherto meant so much to us, become of
little importance.[1]

In this attempt of the Dangling Man to aver that "the quest . . . is one and
the same," one catches immediately the tone of the Existential novelists
and behind it the tone of a modernist like Hemingway. It amounts to a
pronunciative, *ipse dixit* tone, based on a reductive use of syntax and on a
chiaroscuric interplay of philosophical abstractions with vernacular
speech. Typically, the Dangling Man's use of that tone is undercut by a
subjective interjection ("I am beginning to think") and then dissipated in
a clutter of subordinate clauses, themselves cluttered with lists of conceptually striking composition. He attempts to recover the tone of pro-
nouncement by repeating "the quest" in juxtaposition with its deferred
verb, but the ungrammatical repetition is inadequate to the solemnity of
"thievery, slaughter, sacrifice" and seems patchwork – merely a nervous
iteration. The immediately succeeding sentences are pared almost to the
bone both syntactically and rhetorically in apparent compensation for
this *crise de nerfs*. Only in the fifth sentence does the syntax erupt into a
clutter of phrases once again ("to know what we are and what we are for,
to know our purpose, to seek grace") as if the narrator could not repress
some amplificational imperative at odds with the pronunciative austerity
that he affects. The final sentence attempts to regain a measure of control
by repeating the key word "quest" still once again, but the initial "and" is
weakly additive, and the scattered subordinate clauses debilitate its pro-
nouncement. The net effect is a struggle of the two styles for dominance.

This confrontation of a pronunciative, essentially modernist style
with a more ample, nineteenth-century style is equally evident in *The
Adventures of Augie March,* although that novel is generally thought to
constitute Bellow's rejection of modernist aesthetics. Appropriately, the
narrator affects therein the hard-boiled version of pronunciative style to
which modernism gave birth in Chicago:

I am an American, Chicago born – Chicago, that somber city – and go
at things as I have taught myself, free-style, and will make the record
in my own way: first to knock, first admitted; sometimes an innocent
knock, sometimes a not so innocent. But a man's character is his fate,
says Heraclitus, and in the end there isn't any way to disguise the
nature of the knocks by acoustical work on the door or gloving the
knuckles.[2]

The famous first line of this paragraph begins on a richly assertive note, and "I am an American" carries the crisply phrased if syntactically weaker "Chicago born" very well. But "Chicago, that somber city" stretches the sequence of appositional constructions too far, and the sentence never recovers the vigor with which it begins and for which it continues to strain via its parallelisms and measured rhythms. Gradually, the failures of its pronunciative impulse mount: the second and third main verbs are far removed from their common subject and lose their potency to a significant degree; "first to knock, first admitted" is not the clarification of "my own way" that the colon promises; and the four-way parallelism that clusters around the semicolon is improperly balanced. The coyness of the terminal "not so innocent" fails terribly the robust standard of the initial "I am an American," measuring thereby the rout of the hard-boiled style. The second sentence barely attempts a recovery: its initial "but" defers argumentatively to the first sentence; it proceeds to hand over to Heraclitus its pronunciative authority; it degenerates finally into metaphorical playfulness.

Even Moses Herzog, the most uncontrolledly verbose of Bellow's protagonists, strives for the pronunciative style. That striving is especially evident when he is masking his narration of the novel with a pretense of third-person objectivity and employing an economical, no-nonsense syntax. So powerful is the amplificational instinct in him, however, that his obsessive rethinkings and abrupt questions are able to make that style of syntax a vehicle of isocolonic iteration – a vehicle, ultimately, of amplification:

> His indignation rose, and he tried to check it. Ramona was being considerate, giving him a chance to sound off to release spleen. This was not what he had come for. And anyway he was growing tired of his obsession. Besides, she had troubles of her own. And the poet said that indignation was a kind of joy, but was he right? There is a time to speak and a time to shut up. The only truly interesting side of the matter was the intimate design of the injury, the fact that it was so penetrating, custom-made exactly to your measure. It's fascinating that hatred should be so personal as to be almost loving. The knife and the wound aching for each other. Much of course depends upon the vulnerability of the intended. Some cry out, and some swallow the thrust in silence. About the latter you could write the inner history of mankind. How did Papa feel when he found that Voplonsky was in cahoots with the hijackers? He never said.[3]

A similar point about style can be made for Woody Selbst, the effaced narrator of the 1978 story "A Silver Dish." Like Augie March, Eugene

Henderson, and Moses Herzog before him, Woody feels so strongly the pull of hyperbole that his pronunciative style slips into isocolonic and finally catalogual iteration as if into orgasmic release:

> Woody was moved when things were *honest*. Bearing beams were honest, undisguised concrete pillars inside highrise apartments were honest. It was bad to cover up anything. He hated faking. Stone was honest. Metal was honest. These Sunday bells were very straight. They broke loose, they wagged and rocked, and the vibrations and the banging did something for him – cleansed his insides, purified his blood. A bell was a one-way throat, had only one thing to tell you and simply told it. He listened.[4]

The commonplace that Bellow rejected modernism once and for all with the publication of *Augie March* needs to be qualified, then, by a recognition that at least one important aspect of his early modernism – the pronunciative style – survives in an ongoing tension with the amplified style. Some other aspects of his early modernism, such as autotelic plotting, seem largely and permanently to have been jettisoned in the rapture of writing for the first time in what seemed to him his own mode. "The great pleasure of [*The Adventures of Augie March*] was that it came easily," Bellow told Harvey Breit upon the novel's first publication; "All I had to do was be there with buckets to catch it. That's why the form is loose."[5] Indeed, it appears that so thoroughly did the experience of writing *Augie March* liberate Bellow from a modernist notion (art must reject realism and practice high aesthetic self-consciousness) that several of his mature novels seem specifically to mock the notion that plot must have an end in and not apart from its own realization. One thinks especially of the cavalier manner in which *Henderson the Rain King* teases the rubrics of the quest novel – held in almost religious esteem by the modernists – and how different that teasing is from the ritualistic dance of ego and alter ego in *The Victim*. The difference between the two is the difference between two tasks of art: one, the task of annotating and explicating a stipulated reality; the other, the task of plumbing reality itself through the artifact's unique self-realization, outside and beyond established orders, in a world of eccentrically drawn perspectives.

The tension between the pronunciative and amplified styles of discourse seems to have survived Bellow's otherwise general rejection of modernism because it had proven itself in *Dangling Man* a viable technique of characterization. It had proven itself a technique, in particular, of characterizing the divergent impulses of Bellow's narrator-

protagonists, all of whom tend to dangle between identities, like the protagonist of *Dangling Man*. The technique is, of course, endemic in first-
person narratives such as *Augie March* and *Henderson the Rain King*
and in speciously third-person narratives that are really first-person narratives, such as *Herzog*,[6] but it is also a technique of characterization in
fully third-person narratives such as *Mr. Sammler's Planet* and "The Old
System," wherein it is an intermittent function of the omniscient narra-
tors' adopting the protagonists' angles of vision – and adopting also, by
extension, their styles. Thus, the syntax in passages such as the two
quoted below is elaborately pronunciative in covert reminder that Mr.
Sammler was a Bloomsbury aesthete and that Dr. Braun disdains all
messiness of emotion in a thoroughly modernist way. But classical techniques of amplification like *isocolon* (repetition of phrases of equal length
and usually corresponding structure), *pleonasmus* (needless repetition of
what has already been said or understood), and *exergasia* (repeating the
same thought in multiple figures)[7] overlie the reductive syntax and
cause it to strain for feverish effects in apparent suggestion that Mr.
Sammler and Dr. Braun are caught up in a riot of suprasensible awarenesses. The tension between the two stylistic impulses serves effectively
to deepen the two "Dangling Man" characterizations, dramatizing the
pressure under which both Mr. Sammler and Dr. Braun strive to maintain a modernist point of view:

(1) Unfortunately, Bruch was obliged to repeat, and Sammler was
sorry. He was annoyed and he was sorry. And with Walter, as with so
many others, it was always, it was ever and again, it was still, inter-
minably, the sex business. Bruch fell in love with women's arms. They
had to be youngish, plump women. Dark as a rule. Often they were
Puerto Ricans. And in the summer, above all in the summer, without
coats, when women's arms were exposed. He saw them in the subway. He went along to Spanish Harlem. He pressed himself against a
metal rod. Way up in Harlem, he was the only white passenger. And
the whole thing – the adoration, the disgrace, the danger of swooning
when he came! Here, telling this, he began to finger the hairy base of
that thick throat of his. Clinical! At the same time, as a rule, he was
having a highly idealistic and refined relationship with some lady.
Classical! Capable of sympathy, of sacrifice, of love. Even of fidelity,
in his own Cynara-Dowson fashion.[8]

(2) It was a thoughtful day for Dr. Braun. Winter. Saturday. The
short end of December. He was alone in his apartment and woke late,

lying in bed until noon, in the room kept very dark, working with a thought—a feeling: Now you see it, now you don't. Now a content, now a vacancy. Now an important individual, a force, a necessary existence; suddenly nothing. A frame without a picture, a mirror with missing glass. The feeling of necessary existence might be the aggressive, instinctive vitality we share with a dog or an ape. The difference being in the power of the mind or spirit to declare *I am*. Plus the inevitable inference *I am not*. Dr. Braun was no more pleased with being than with its opposite.[9]

It could be argued that the varying success of Bellow's novels is linked to this ongoing confrontation of styles, for readers generally prefer the novels of tempest-tossed styles to the novels of more gently interactive styles: on the one hand, *The Adventures of Augie March, Henderson the Rain King, Seize the Day, Herzog, Humboldt's Gift;* on the other hand, *Mr. Sammler's Planet, The Dean's December,* and *More Die of Heartbreak.* Indeed, if Henderson and Herzog are Bellow's most memorable characters, Bellow's best subject would seem to be the mind overburdened by too many ideas, all its endeavors to conceptualize reality brought to nothing. I have suggested elsewhere that Bellow renders the overburdened mind as a Symphonie Fantastique, majestic in scope and power;[10] I should point out that the orchestration is sometimes as delicate as lute song, too, notably when it is meant to convey intellectual catharsis. Alex Corde's climactic vision at the Mount Palomar observatory is especially fine in the latter mode, for it is distinguished by a drift of the pronunciative style into easy amplifications that stretch gently both outward to the universe and inward to the self:

> And what he saw with his eyes was not even the real heavens. No, only white marks, bright vibrations, clouds of sky roe, tokens of the real thing, only as much as could be taken in through the distortions of the atmosphere. Through these distortions you saw objects, forms, partial realities. The rest was to be felt. And it wasn't only that you felt, but that you were drawn to feel and to penetrate further, as if you were being informed that what was spread over you had to do with your existence, down to the very blood and the crystal forms inside your bones. Rocks, trees, animals, men and women, these also drew you to penetrate further, under the distortions (comparable to the atmospheric ones, shadows within shadows), to find their real being with your own. This was the sense in which you were drawn.[11]

Probably the finest instance in Bellow's oeuvre of a restrained interplay of the pronunciative and the amplified styles is Herzog's decision at the end of his otherwise turbulent narrative to write no more of the letters that symptomize his mania:

> Perhaps he'd stop writing letters. Yes, that was what was coming, in fact. The knowledge that he was done with these letters. Whatever had come over him during these last months, the spell, really seemed to be passing, really going. He set down his hat, with the roses and day lilies, on the half-painted piano, and went into his study, carrying the wine bottles in one hand like a pair of Indian clubs. Walking over notes and papers, he lay down on his Récamier couch. As he stretched out, he took a long breath, and then he lay, looking at the mesh of the screen, pulled loose by vines, and listening to the steady scratching of Mrs. Tuttle's broom. He wanted to tell her to sprinkle the floor. She was raising too much dust. In a few minutes he would call down to her, "Damp it down, Mrs. Tuttle. There's water in the sink." But not just yet. At this time he had no messages for anyone. Nothing. Not a single word.[12]

The pronunciative style may seem quietly regnant here, at least upon first impression. A reductive syntax that generally disaccommodates qualifying clauses, the speciously assured "in fact," the reiterated "really," the thick-coming negatives ("not just yet," "no messages," "nothing," "not a single word") that seem at the end an incantation – all repress the tentativeness of locutions like "perhaps" and "seemed to be passing." But an amplificational impulse is also a part of the rhetorical gestalt. As in hundreds of pages beforehand, it generates anew Herzog's compulsion to rename and reassert what has already been said. It inspires his measured, somewhat too-methodical attention to each step of his recumbency, first of body, then of mind. It explains his serendipitous awareness of the roses and the lilies, the notes and the papers scattered beneath his feet, the loosened mesh of the screens and the scratching of Mrs. Tuttle's broom – all such awarenesses indulged both because they stake their individual claims to attention and because they forestall larger awarenesses. In effect, the very great tension between the two modes of discourse until this point in the novel is muted but not resolved.

And that mutedness is both aesthetically and rhetorically what it should be. An unambiguous resolution would suggest that Herzog's terrible agitation of spirit had been simply a kind of fever, finally broken, rather than an unresolvable agon. It would suggest that Herzog's pronunciative and amplified styles were only symptoms of fever rather than ongoing vehicles of his entirely estimable passions both to simplify reality in some ultimate figure of understanding and to be faithful to his multiform understandings of the moment. Artfully, several aspects of the scene reinforce the mutedness of stylistic interplay by qualifying the catharsis in their own ways. One notes the sweet absurdity of such a man as Herzog taking his rest on a Récamier couch; the suggestion that the wine bottles are a set of Indian clubs and that whatever release Herzog will find in the wine is only a juggling act; the irony of Herzog's "Damp it down" being addressed ostensibly to Mrs. Tuttle but surely, therapeutically, to himself.

Indeed, to recognize that an ongoing contention of the pronunciative and amplified styles shapes the effects of Bellow's fiction is not to forge a tool by which to discriminate among the novels and stories but to perceive how much it is a technique of characterization in the less popular narratives as well as in the more popular. A novel like *Mr. Sammler's Planet* has suffered in its reputation primarily from a distaste for Mr. Sammler himself, who is thought to be offensively disengaged from life, too drily intellectual, and something of a curmudgeon – altogether too much like Bellow himself as he was perceived in the late 1960s and early 1970s. Temperamentally more decorous than madcaps like Augie March and Moses Herzog, Sammler does not often rush headlong into great follies, and he expresses little patience with theater of the soul. "The luxury of nonintimidation by doom – that might describe his state," the reader is instructed.[13] But Sammler is haunted as much as any other Bellovian protagonist by existential contradictions: "Once take a stand," he expostulates, "once draw a baseline, and contraries will assail you. Declare for normalcy, and you will be stormed by aberrancies. All postures are mocked by their opposites."[14] Even in so brief a statement of Sammler's irritation with the nature of things, the pronunciative style contends with the amplified: the one, an agent of Sammler's disdain for contraries; the other, an agent of his anxiety that contraries should nevertheless exist. And it is the contention of the two styles that continually humanizes Sammler, providing basis for understanding him as still another Dangling Man however much he would disdain the label. What is the eloquence of his final prayer for the soul of Elya Gruner but the climax of a book-length wrangle between his Bloomsbury self and his Polish-Jewish self? Which is to say: between a pronunciative tone, adopted at the end even with God, and a wracked, circinate syntax that unrolls itself as tentatively as a butterfly's tongue en route to its desperate, final averment?

Remember, God, the soul of Elya Gruner, who, as willingly as possible and as well as he was able, and even to an intolerable point, and even in suffocation and even as death was coming was eager, even childishly perhaps (may I be forgiven for this), even with a certain servility, to do what was required of him. . . . He was aware that he must meet, and he did meet – through all the confusion and degraded clowning of this life through which we are speeding – he did meet the terms of his contract. The terms which, in his inmost heart, each man knows. As I know mine. As all know. For that is the truth of it – that we all know, God, that we know, that we know, we know, we know.[15]

To recognize in Bellow's oeuvre this ongoing contention of the two aspects of modernist and nineteenth-century styles that I have termed *pronunciative* and *amplified* is finally to perceive what is implicit throughout the foregoing argument: that the styles belong less to the man than to the tales. The notion that Bellow decisively turned his back on modernism in the early 1950s fails to credit him with an experimental impulse vis-à-vis matters of style and voice that has in fact produced notable variations upon at least one aspect of modernist style by playing it against an older, more amply rhetorical style. As constant as Bellow's interest in dramatizing the mind overburdened with problems of history and selfhood is his interest in dramatizing the multiple, discordant awarenesses that threaten to unbalance such a mind. No device of characterization has transformed those awarenesses into felt experience more strategically than the stylistic variations that are their symbol and cipher.

NOTES

1. Saul Bellow, *Dangling Man* (New York: Vanguard, 1944), p. 154.

2. Saul Bellow, *The Adventures of Augie March* (New York: Viking, 1953), p. 3.

3. Saul Bellow, *Herzog* (New York: Viking, 1964), p. 189–90.

4. Saul Bellow, "A Silver Dish," *Him with His Foot in His Mouth* (New York: Harper & Row, 1984), p. 195.

5. Harvey Breit, "Talk with Saul Bellow," *New York Times Book Review,* 20 September 1953, p. 12.

6. For an argument in defense of this understanding of the point of view in *Herzog,* see my *Saul Bellow* (New York: Continuum, 1989), pp. 103–05.

7. The definitions are Richard A. Lanham's in *A Handlist of Rhetorical Terms* (Berkeley: Univ. of California Press, 1969), p. 125.

8. Saul Bellow, *Mr. Sammler's Planet* (New York: Viking, 1970), p. 58–59.

9. Saul Bellow, "The Old System," *Mosby's Memoirs and Other Stories* (New York: Viking, 1968), p. 43.

10. Kiernan, *Saul Bellow,* p. 234.

11. Saul Bellow, *The Dean's December* (New York: Harper and Row, 1982), p. 311.

12. *Herzog,* p. 341.

13. *Mr. Sammler's Planet,* p. 134.

14. *Mr. Sammler's Planet,* p. 118.

15. *Mr. Sammler's Planet,* p. 313.

Saul Bellow's Remembrance of Jewish Times Past: *Herzog* and "The Old System"

S. Lillian Kremer

I

WRITERS WHOSE work evidences deep understanding of their own ethnic, cultural, and religious backgrounds are often acclaimed for their universal appeal. Dante speaks for the human condition while focusing on Catholic Florence; Dostoevsky and Tolstoy address all people through the prism of czarist Russian life; and Joyce reveals universal perceptions in narrative imbued with Irish ethnicity.

Saul Bellow's fiction, emanating from the core of Jewish thought and history, is similarly universal. The Bellow canon reveals the influence of Jewish thought, language, and history on theme, character constructs, and literary style. The novelist's tone, imagery, allusions, and character types affirmatively demonstrate the influence of Hebrew and Yiddish literatures. Bellow's protagonists rely on biblical and talmudic ethical injunctions as they struggle to understand the human condition and to live as good men. Although the ethical values of Bellovian characters are shared by the non-Jewish world, their Judaic origin is manifest. Most Bellow characters are assimilated Jews; yet, they consider themselves a part of an identifiable group; they observe selected commandments and traditions; they maintain social relationships with fellow Jews; they voice loathing of anti-Semitism, horror of the Holocaust, and support for the survival and well-being of Israel; they express themselves in language marked by inclusion of Yiddish diction and idiom, Hebrew liturgy and biblical allusion. Critics attest to the centrality of Jewish culture in Bellow's work, arguing that Judaism is vital to Bellow's

101

belief in humanity, his veneration of life, and his pervasive concern for morality. In commentary and interviews Bellow has acknowledged the significance of Jewish thought and experience during his formative years and has identified the Jewish view that the world is sanctified and man is capable of moral dignity and holiness as the source of his own objection to twentieth-century apocalyptic romanticism.[1]

II

"The Old System,"[2] published in 1967, and largely ignored in the wake of the enormous critical attention lavished on *Herzog*,[3] offers fertile ground for study of Judaic matter and manner in Saul Bellow's fiction. This long short story is significant as a companion piece to the Montreal Jewish memoir of *Herzog* which appears to be its germ. The Montreal recollection and the short story share commonalities of subject and approach. Each is a narrated remembrance of Jewish times past by an intellectual protagonist, the historian of ideas, Moses Herzog and the biochemist, Samuel Braun. The works exhibit parallel development of the Jewish immigrant experience through families who escape Russian persecution, emigrate to the New World, and reside in Canada before resettling in the United States. Thematic parallels and corresponding minor characters are evident in *Herzog* in the Aunt Zipporah /Uncle Yaffe interlude and "The Old System" in the Aunt Rose /Uncle Braun chronicle.

Secular success and assimilation fail to fulfill emotional and spiritual needs of Herzog and Braun, who are revitalized by memories of Jewish social and religious values. Historian Herzog "with clouded eyes" concludes that he is compelled to recall "these cries of the soul. . . . These personal histories, old tales from old times" (p. 184). A post-Holocaust consciousness, Herzog is sustained, in troubled times, by Jewish prayer, by the implications of the historic duration of Judaism, and the knowledge of the continuum of that liturgical tradition, despite many attempts to annihilate Jewish life and civilization. The secular scholar discovers emotional and intellectual satisfaction in recollection of a story of his starving grandfather seeking a prayer quorum in the Winter Palace after the Revolution and in his own childhood recitation of *Ma Tovu*, a prayer celebrating Jewish communal worship:

> The children of the race, by a never failing miracle, opened their eyes on one strange world after another, age after age, and uttered the same prayer in each, eagerly loving what they found. (p. 174)

Memory of his own prayer in the company of orthodox Jews leads Herzog to understand: "Here was a wider range of human feelings than he had ever again been able to find" (p. 174). Bio-chemist Braun, too, realizes that Jewish life is central to his comprehension of the human drama: "Oh! these Jews—these Jews! Their feelings, their hearts! . . . And these tears! When you wept from the heart, you felt you justified something, understood something" (p. 83).

The growing significance of Judaic themes is suggested in comparison of the content and stylistic complexities Bellow employs to introduce and sustain the crucial remembrance construction in each fiction. Remembrance is activated in *Herzog* by the protagonist's chance glimpse of a former playmate from Napoleon Street, the Jewish immigrant section of a Montreal slum. In the novel, Bellow employs simple flashback presented through the narrator's consciousness to disclose Herzog's Jewish past. In the short story, Bellow introduces a more sophisticated and symbolic approach to counterpoint past and present cultures. Time and juxtaposition of the Hebrew and Gregorian calendars[4] are the keys to Bellow's complex vision, to his structural schema, and to his thematic concerns. The frame story, set in December of the Gregorian calendar, is controlled by the consciousness of the scientist-narrator Dr. Samuel Braun, whose feelings of inability to love lead him to meditate on "the old system." The inner tale, set in the Hebrew New Year season of *Rosh-Hashanah* and *Yom Kippur*,[5] chronicles the Braun family history with emphasis on the spiritual life of Samuel's cousin, Isaac. The vital connection between the outer and inner tales is found and sustained in the calendar references. Each is a period of reflection as the year draws to a close and in anticipation of the next. Samuel Braun's December meditation is the catalyst for recollection of his cousin Isaac's high holiday week spiritual renewal. The religious essence of the holy period is *t'shuva,* a return to God through repentance and spiritual renewal. The drama of the inner tale focuses on Isaac Braun's *Yom Kippur* introspection and spiritual redemption. Its connection to the frame story lies in the narrator's spiritual stocktaking and reflection on the old system's ethical and ethnic value systems.

Saturday, another calendar reference, provides further direction for the reader. Bellow sets the frame story on the Sabbath, a day in Jewish life devoted to prayer, study, and celebration. A secular Jew, Dr. Braun neglects traditional Sabbath synagogue worship, fails to listen to the week's Torah portion, and ignores the commentaries. Instead, he meditates at home on the problems which the traditional worshiper ponders: the nature and quality of the human condition, human relationships and passions, and ancestral history. Braun's reflection, like Herzog's, yields the uncomfortable realization that the old system of Jewish life embraced a dimension of love absent from his assimilated lifestyle.

Just as eating a bit of cake begins the journey back in time for Marcel Proust's central consciousness, for Braun the simple act of washing initiates remembrance of times past. As he washes, Braun recognizes the contrast between his morning toilet, a simple act of physical hygiene and the ablutions of his ancestors, to whom every act was religious, "for whom bathing was a solemnity" (48).[6] The juxtaposition is the catalyst for Braun's spontaneous recollection, the emergence of thoughts and feelings about his Jewish past.

III

Herzog's Montreal reverie illuminates religious and cultural ties between generations of Herzogs, between Old and New World religious and cultural authenticity. Samuel Braun's remembrance, revealed in the interior tale, unfolds a family saga of love and hate played against the backdrop of religious commitment and disavowal. Like Jonah Herzog, who escaped from the anti-Jewish restrictions of the infamous May laws during the Pobedonostsev era of Czarist Russia, the patriarch of the Braun family escaped Czarist persecution and fled to the New World via Manchuria. In *Herzog,* Bellow delineates the Jewish attitude toward Czarist military service through Aunt Zipporah's volatile voice. Using diction and syntax that will later characterize the speech of Aunt Rose, Zipporah comments on her husband's military experience: "'A *finsternish,*'" (a darkness) she exclaims, envisioning injustices perpetrated against Jews in the Russian army. She describes his imagined depravity in terms of sexual and dietary transgressions: "'I can't say what else he was doing with Tartars, gypsies, whores, eating horsemeat, and God only knows what abominations went on'" (p. 179). Three years later, when Bellow returns to the theme of Jewish resistance to Russian military service in "The Old System," he intensifies the response. He introduces an expository passage deftly crafted in Yiddish idiom to convey the religious basis for Jewish opposition in terms of Jewish reverence for life and abhorrence for violence. Resistance to the czarist goal of extinction and Russification of the Jewish population is evident in the association of military service with forced transgression of the dietary laws.

> How those old-time Jews despised the goy wars, their vainglory and obstinate *Dummheit.* Conscription, mustering, marching, shooting,

leaving the corpses everywhere. Buried, unburied. . . . So by irrational decree, as in the *Arabian Nights,* Uncle Braun . . . left wife and
child to eat maggoty pork. (p. 50)

This passage is typical of Bellow's evocation of a period in Russian-Jewish
relations when a third of the Jewish population was to be encouraged to
leave Russia and another third was to be absorbed into Russian society via
an intensive program of Russification through educational and military in-
doctrination. Jewish schools were criminalized, and mandatory Russian
education for Jews was imposed. Twelve-year-old Jewish boys (one year
prior to religious maturity of the *Bar Mitzvah*) were conscripted for a
twenty-five year tour of military duty in an effort to assure their lapse
from Judaism or an early death. The final third of the Russian-Jewish
population was more expeditiously dispatched through state sponsored
anti-Semitic pogroms systematically annihilating Jewish communities.

Following this brief reference to the family's past, Bellow sketches
the Brauns' North American immigrant experience in poignant, albeit
brief, narrator recollections. Like Herzog's Uncle Yaffe, who labored as
a construction worker and then operated a junk yard in St. Anne, Canada, Samuel's Uncle Braun worked on the Canadian railroads before
opening a second-hand furniture shop. Jewish upward mobility in American society is evident in the economic progress of the Herzogs and
Brauns from poverty-level working class to small business entrepreneur-
ship, to lucrative real-estate business, and finally, to the professions.

Biblical rhetoric heralds the arrival of Isaac Braun in America, the
secular promised land of the Jew seeking refuge from European persecution. Isaac's 1910 arrival is rendered in cadence, tone, and imagery
reminiscent of the journeys of Hebrew patriarchs. Like his biblical namesake, the young Isaac enters a strange land, not as a defeated refugee,
but proud and dignified, aware of his own worth.

Born to be a man, in the direct Old Testament sense . . . Isaac, when
he had come to America, was still a child. Nevertheless his old country Jewish dignity was very firm and strong. He had the outlook of
ancient generations on the New World. Tents and kine and wives and
maidservants and manservants. (p. 50)

The narrator recalls a childhood scene in which Cousin Isaac, with
one of his "archaic looks" (p. 52), informs Samuel that the family is
descended from the tribe of Naphtali and cautions him to remember this.

The allusion, while enigmatic in its immediate context, assumes its proper prophetic dimension when viewed from the perspective of Isaac's wealth and Samuel's professional success. Twenty-four pages after Bellow's initial reference to the tribe of Naphtali, during an interview with an Orthodox rabbi, Isaac declares that he was destined to be rich. He thereby clarifies the biblical allusion to Naphtali, the tribe that was to inherit one of the most fertile sections of Canaan.[7]

Bellow further authenticates the cultural milieu by acknowledging the Yiddish press as a political and social index in the lives of Immigrant Jews. The Jewish newspaper provided a vital link between Old and New Worlds, registering the reactions of the newcomers to American life, their enthusiasm for personal liberty and economic opportunity, their political concerns and aspirations, and their religious conflicts centering on the disputes between adherents of orthodoxy and non-traditional Judaism. The Herzogs read *Der Kanader Adler* to locate European relatives and friends, and the Brauns enjoy the "melodramas of the Yiddish press" (p. 56) laughing at the matrimonial advertisements.

The East-European *shtetl* attitudes and distinctive Jewish humor which characterize the Braun family's domestic scenes demonstrate Bellow's organic use of religious and ethnic material. During a comic interlude, Bellow yields to grotesque humor in creating the officiating *mohel,* the man licensed to perform ritual circumcision, the ceremony that inducts the male child into the covenant with God: "Bearded, nearsighted old Krieger, fingers stained with chicken slaughter, cut away the foreskin" (p. 51). Thus Bellow combines two respected occupations of the *shtetl,* the *mohel* and the *shokhet,* a skilled and learned ritual animal slaughterer, who performs a religious function for the community and is not to be confused with the commercial butcher. While it is not unusual for the functions of *mohel* and *shokhet* to be performed by the same person in *shtetl* society, Bellow's suggestion that Krieger performs a circumcision with hands still stained with the blood of a chicken is ludicrous. Comic interpretation of the scene is supported by the unlikely role acted by Aunt Rose. In addition to the customary role of godmother, Rose usurps the male position of *sandek* by holding the child during circumcision. Aunt Rose's behavior offends tradition and adds to the comic tone of the passage. Through the occasional comic rendition of sacred events, Bellow avoids the sentimentality which has plagued some American Jewish writers as they depict holiday and religious events.

Character parallels in *Herzog* and "The Old System" are nowhere more dramatically evident than in the two formidable matriarchs, Herzog's

Aunt Zipporah and Braun's Aunt Rose. Bellow enriches his humorous portrait of Rose in much the same manner he earlier used for Zipporah. Each woman is bitter, has a shrew-like tongue, and expresses frustration in colorful Yiddish curses. The insults Zipporah hurls at her brother, Jonah Herzog, are marked by irony and inconsistency. She reverses the honorific epithet "edel mensch" (p. 179) signifying traits such as honesty, nobility, and refinement of character to comment sarcastically on her brother's failure to engage in common labor. She continues to reproach him as a *gazlan,* a robber, a bandit, for his Prohibition Era bootlegging. When recalling the family experience with Russian anti-Semitism, Zipporah accuses the Bolsheviks of wanting "to make the world *horav*" (p. 178), to destroy world, to make it desolate; she resorts to a traditional impotent curse: "May their hands and feet wither" (p. 178). Comedy reigns in "The Old System" as the redoubtable Aunt Rose, in the role of tyrannical Jewish mother, conducts a genealogical investigation of her son's fiancee in language reminiscent of Zipporah. Rose's denunciations of women who want to marry Isaac are characterized by comic hyperbole. "A false dog." "Candied poison." "An open ditch." "A sewer." "A born whore" (p. 55). When Isaac finally marries, Rose concentrates her scorn on the bride's father, hurling conventional Jewish insults his way. She condemns him as ignorant and common. To Isaac's rejoinder that his father-in-law is hard working, honest, and pious, the matron expresses her disbelief: "'A son of Ham like that. A cattle dealer'" (p. 55). The overbearing mother thus expresses her doubts alluding to the biblical legend of Ham, father of the Canaanites, cursed by Noah to be a servile nation.

Class consciousness within the Jewish immigrant community provides Bellow another vehicle for comic parallels. Each woman regularly comments on Jewish social structure, which Bellow identifies by its Yiddish nomenclature, *yichus,* in *Herzog.* The upper social class, *sheyneh yiden* or *fayneh yiden,* is characterized by scholarship and piety, by lives exemplifying Jewish law. Identification with either upper class or lower class Jews includes educational, financial, behavioral, and ancestral criteria. Historically and ideally, learning is regarded as the prime value and wealth is secondary. Consequently, a person of great learning belongs to the *sheyneh* regardless of income and a person of little learning and significant wealth who does not use his money according to Judaic laws of charity is lower class, *prost.* A scene of mock kitchen *krieg* between the Herzog sisters-in-law, Zipporah and Sarah, focuses on educational and social aspirations for their children and alludes to the historic *Hasidic-mitnagdic*[8] feud between the mystical and rational factions

of Orthodox Judaism. Zipporah underscores her arguments in favor of
sending her children out to work by attacking Sarah's *mitnagdic* heritage and tries to undermine Sarah's pretentions by citing her own Hasidic
pedigree, claiming descent from "the greatest Hasidic rabbis" (p. 177).
Defending her sons' honor, she insists: "'They know a page of Gemara
too'" (p. 177).[9] Although their argument is about secular education, Zipporah introduces the *hasidic* apologist's avowal of Hebraic competence
and the polarities of *hasidic* veneration of common labor in contrast to
the *mitnagdic* emphasis on intellectualism.

"The Old System" examines the relationship of marriage and social
standing. Rose is identified as a commoner by her language and manners, yet she is socially pretentious about marriage. In derogating
Isaac's father-in-law, Rose mistakenly emphasizes occupation in her
assignment of social status, neglecting the attributes of decorum, charity,
and piety so crucial to social identification among Jewish people. Her contempt for the cattle dealer based solely on his occupation reveals her distortion of traditional Jewish values as did her usurpation of the traditional
male role during the circumcision ceremony. Isaac's respect and admiration for the pious cattle dealer and pride in his scholarly cousin's research
conform to the traditional value system. Bellow's treatment of the respect
Isaac shows for sacred and secular learning astutely charts the transfer of
esteem from sacred to secular knowledge among secular Jews. Cultural
authenticity is established, as it was in *Herzog,* through realistic and
allusive treatment of the Jewish experience. Illustrative of Bellow's historic perspective is his attention to the emigration of Russian Jews to
America and his skillful portrayal of the retention of Jewish ways despite
assimilation to other cultures. Unlike the ersatz Jewish milieu and characters created in the work of American Jewish writers void of Jewish education, Bellow's writing reveals his rich understanding of Jewish thought,
history, literature, and language and his proficiency in integrating the
tone, inflection, idiom, and syntax of Yiddish in English prose.

IV

Paralleling the sociological similarities of *Herzog* and "The Old System"
is the resolution of the protagonists' spiritual crises through scenes of
redemptive intimation or achievement. *Herzog* shifts between past and
present so that the reader experiences Herzog's evolving religious consciousness in the sequence that Herzog remembers and writes about.
Pivotal recognition scenes are rendered through retrospective visions of

childhood and adult encounters, as well as in analytical letters to friends, enemies, philosophers, clergy, and God. At the nadir of his despair, contemplating the murder of those who betrayed him, the sight of a dim entry hall light reminds Herzog of the *ner tamid,* the synagogue vigil light. An image of eternal Judaism and eternal truth, the *ner tamid* prompts Herzog's self rebuke for straying from the Judaic code. Like Samuel Braun's remembrance of ancestral piety, Herzog concludes: "Ancient Herzogs with their psalms and their shawls and beards would never have touched a revolver" (p. 350). Like his own ancestors and Isaac Braun, Herzog petitions God for mercy by employing a traditional Hebrew construct: "*Dear God! Mercy! My God! Rachaim olenu . . . melekh maimis Thou King of Death and Life*" (p. 370). Herzog's letter to God, declares the necessity for selfless devotion and, like Bellow's protagonists from Joseph of *Dangling Man* to Sammler, affirms the individual's moral commitment to Divine Law, "*How my mind has struggled to make coherent sense. I have not been too good at it. But have desired to do your unknowable will, taking it, and you, without symbols*" (pp. 396–97). Moses Elkanah Herzog, named for the first prophet and Jewish lawgiver (Moses) and the state of being possessed of God (Elkanah) is a man of feeling, loving God, as is written in Hebraic liturgy, with all his heart (Herzog). His faith tested, Herzog proclaims his allegiance in the Hebrew of the biblical patriarchs, ". . . here I am. *Hineni*" (p. 377).

A chronicle of an intellectual's attempt to understand the modern condition, *Herzog* traces the protagonist's self-analysis, his considerations of contemporary pessimism and nihilism, and his exploration of alternatives to despair. Because he knows the void, Herzog refutes the apostles of alienation, disputing the philosophies of Nietzsche, Heidegger, and Kierkegaard. His sharpest invective is reserved for intellectuals "playing at crisis, alienation, apocalypse, and desperation" (pp. 385–86). As a Jew of post-Holocaust consciousness, Herzog rejects Nietzsche's view of history, his philosophy of self-mastery, his claim that God is dead; he repudiates Kierkegaard's advocacy and praise of suffering as essential to the religious experience, the view that "*truth has lost its force with us and horrible pain and evil must teach it to us again*" (p. 385). Embracing a philosophy older than German Romanticism and French Existentialism, Herzog posits Judaic veneration for life and ethical precepts as central to his insistence on human community. He argues in the Jewish manner for "the strength of a man's virtue or spiritual capacity measured by his ordinary life" (p. 133). True to the Judaic tradition, he asserts a direct connection between humanity's covenant with God and responsibility to mankind. Employing rabbinic tone, Talmudic logic, and Hasidic affirmation of divinely sanctioned human brotherhood, he condemns the asceticism, monastic withdrawal, and indulgent self-absorption characteristic of existential heroes; positing instead that

> brotherhood is what makes a man human. . . . 'Man liveth not by Self alone but in his brother's face. . . . Each shall behold the Eternal Father and love and joy abound.'. . . The real and essential question is one of our employment by other human beings and their employment by us (p. 333).

Herzog's insistence on ethical and charitable behavior reflects the Judaic teaching that the way to God is through the world.

Bellow sustains the sociologically authentic rendition of the immigrant experience in "The Old System" by incorporating Jewish ethical and religious allusions to inform the story's moral crisis. The tale, whose title is a direct reference to Orthodox Judaism, explores the spiritual crisis of the twentieth-century American Jew by paralleling the situations of Samuel Braun, a secular scientist who has abandoned Jewish ritual observance but experiences nostalgic longing for traditional Judaism, and that of Isaac Braun, a believer whose sense of perdition is dramatized in terms of religious and economic conflict between Jew and Philistine.

America presents moral problems to the Old World Jew. The corruption of the marketplace snares Isaac. He is troubled by an unethical real-estate transaction with an aristocratic Gentile who demands a $100,000 tribute for selling an exclusive country club to a Jew. The commonplace business practice of bribing zoning inspectors presents further cause for ethical trial. Succumbing to the conventional business norm, Isaac believes he is now spiritually lost, "lost to his people, his family, lost to God, lost in the void of America" (p. 61).

The moral drama of the inner tale centers on religious conflict and sibling rivalry between Isaac and Tina Braun; it stems from Tina's unsubstantiated allegation that Isaac has damaged the family's investment opportunities. A thoroughgoing materialist, Tina accuses her brother of denying the rest of the family any opportunity to invest in his lucrative real-estate business. Yet it was she and another brother, Aaron, who reneged on their investment and left Isaac in a precarious financial position. Convinced of his innocence, Isaac strives to restore family harmony by taking on the role of penitent. Tina repeatedly rejects his conciliatory efforts, responds with harassment, and seizes every opportunity to reiterate her false charge and ill-conceived grievance.

Bellow elevates the Braun financial quarrel from the economic to the moral/ethical realm by introducing a complex biblical schema evoking discord between the Israelites (Isaac) and the Philistines (Tina) and setting the contemporary conflict in the *Yom Kippur* period of moral judgment, a period of fasting, atonement, and prayer, a time when observant Jews first seek forgiveness of people they have offended and then petition God's forgiveness for transgressions against divine law. After the customary pre-holiday visit to his parents' graves, Isaac appears at Tina's home seeking reconciliation. Innocent of any misconduct toward Tina, Isaac nonetheless pleads with her, in the name of God, to forgive him and make peace. Dismissing Isaac with a vulgar insult, Tina violates Jewish ethics and the *Yom Kippur* spirit of forgiveness. The timing of Isaac's reconciliation effort with Tina's rejection underscores the ethical and spiritual dimensions of their quarrel.

The spiritual conflict between philistine and Jew is expressed in Tina's intolerance of Isaac's piety and Bellow's sustained association of Isaac with fidelity to Judaism's traditions and values. Tina mocks her brother's "Orthodox cringe" (p. 69), charging that his prayer is insincere and opportunistic: "'He reads *Tehillim* aloud in his air-conditioned Caddy when there's a long freight train at the crossing. That crook! He'd pick God's pocket'" (p. 58). Signaling the error of Tina's slanderous remarks, Bellow allusively connects the fictional Isaac to legendary historic Jews of the same name, the second patriarch and a Hasidic leader celebrated for their devotion to prayer.

Contrary to Tina's slander, prayer is an integral part of Isaac's life. He worships as the spirit moves him and wherever he happens to be. While touring a construction site, he observes: "'When I consider the heavens, the work of Thy fingers. . . . What is Man that Thou art mindful of him?'" (p. 67) In the company of non-Jews, during his first airplane flight, Isaac intones *Shema Yisrael,* Hebrew liturgy's central monotheistic declaration and the traditional final words of a dying Jew. Tina's emphatic denigration of Isaac's predilection for psalm reading in his automobile is juxtaposed with Isaac's defense of his father-in-law's recitation of "'psalms even when he's driving. He keeps them under his wagon seat'" (p. 55). Thereby, Bellow allusively associates the fictional Isaac with the legendary Hasid, Isaac of Berdichev, who reportedly experienced great joy in witnessing a coachman, clad in prayer shawl and phylacteries, reciting psalms as he tended to the maintenance of his wagon. This sight moved the rabbi to exclaim: "How noble is this people You have chosen. Even when they oil the wheels of their wagons, they are mindful of You and commune with You." [10] Like his rabbinic name-sake, Isaac Braun embraces the Hasidic value of spontaneous prayer rather than limiting devotion to prescribed form, time, and context of tra-ditional settings of home and temple. Like the Hasid, Isaac Braun cares for the intent of prayer, the spirit of prayer. Bellow often juxtaposes Isaac's defense of praying in unconventional settings with condemnation by the immoral women of the inner tale, thereby casting Isaac in a favor-able light. Devotion to the Book of Psalms reflects Isaac's affirmative view of God and the universe and confirms his role as peacemaker. The psalm-ist's tone is positive, stressing the need for unity and peace among men. This is consistent with Isaac's peace-loving nature, dramatically evidenced in his repeated attempts to unite the family Tina has divided.

Characteristic of the import of Jewish textual influence in Bellow's fiction is the novelist's appropriation of the biblical Israelite/Philistine antagonism and its three major components (the judge Samuel, Isaac representing the ancient Israelites, and Tina typifying the Philistines) to reinforce the thematic interest and buttress the structural connections between the frame and inner tales of "The Old System." In contrast to the brief esoteric link between Isaac and Berdichev, Bellow offers sustained parallels between the fictional Isaac and his biblical namesake. Isaac Braun bears the name of the second patriarch who is credited with insti-tuting the daily afternoon service of the Hebrew liturgy.[11] The parallel is objectified by Bellow's decision to render Isaac Braun's arrival in the New World in biblical imagery and cadence and to dramatize the devotional and economic correspondences of the two men. The patriarch settled among the Philistines at Gerar, devoted himself to husbandry and suc-ceeded so well as to incur the envy and wrath of his neighbors. The fic-tional Isaac settles among American philistines, worshipers of mammon, and prospers in their midst. Each man suffers harassment and submits patiently to economic conflict. Despite a gentle, loving nature, each wit-nesses family conflict centering on the distribution of wealth. The patri-arch's sons, Jacob and Esau, were engaged in a bitter birthright and inheritance quarrel, and Isaac Braun is a central figure in his familial financial and inheritance disputes.

Within the context of the contemporary morality drama, Tina plays the Philistine role, her name signaling the novelist's allusive intent to evoke the historic antagonism between the biblical Israelites and Phil-istines. The name *Tina* is emblematic of the character's dramatic func-tion, her early sexual promiscuity, her relentless campaign to denigrate Isaac and turn their brothers against him, her contempt for the praying

Jew, and her immoral denial of "the old system," marked by her rejection of *Yom Kippur* atonement and forgiveness. Allegoric naming, a conventional device of Bellow's characterization, evidences the novelist's capacity to use the historic context of the Jewish-Philistine enmity to inform the contemporary conflict of religious devotee and non-believer.

Bellow uses religious devotion both as a means of delineating character and as a means of exploring the divisions within the American Jewish community and the meaning of Jewish identity in contemporary secular society. "The Old System" parallels Isaac's private spiritual quest with the internal divisions of American Judaism. Differences between German Jewish Americans and East European Jewish Americans have emerged as a leitmotif in Bellow's fiction; overtly in the Grandma Lausch section of *The Adventures of Augie March,* allusively in the Adler/Tamkin dichotomy of *Seize the Day,* and prominently in Isaac's ambivalence regarding his denominational affiliation and his Jewish identity. Bellow contrasts the passions expressed in the East European Orthodox synagogue of Isaac's childhood with the suppression of emotion in the German Reform Temple of his prosperous maturity. Unlike the small synagogue, where physical beauty was unimportant and where Uncle Braun was respected for his learning, Isaac's Madison Avenue Reform Temple is "like a World's Fair pavilion" (p. 62), its "worldly rabbi with his trained voice and tailored suits, like a Christian minister except for the play of Jewish cleverness in his face" (p. 62). Isaac's dissatisfaction with the Reform Movement and its manners is evident in his satiric reference to its female congregants: "If you wanted the young women to bless the Sabbath candles, you had to start their rabbi at $20,000 and add a house and a Jaguar" (p. 63). Even the most sacred of services, the *Yom Kippur* worship, suffers change from the historic format in the Reform service and displeases Isaac. For him, the restrained Reform style is un-Jewish, a denial, inexpressive of feelings. The Madison Avenue Temple meets the aesthetic sensibilities of its membership, but it fails Isaac's religious and emotional needs.

He . . . walked to the temple . . . with an injured heart. A leader of the congregation, weighted with grief. Striking breasts with fists in old-fashioned penitence. The new way was the way of understatement. Anglo-Saxon restraint. The rabbi, with his Madison Avenue public relations airs, did not go for these European Judaic, operatic fist-clenchings. . . . He made the cantor tone it down. But Isaac Braun, covered by his father's prayer shawl with its black stripes and shedding fringes, ground his teeth and wept near the ark. (p. 69)

Isaac's discomfort with his congregation suggests that social or business considerations led him to join a Reform Temple. As American Jews prospered and became culturally assimilated, many abandoned eastern, parochial, and Orthodox Judaism to affiliate with other Jewish denominations such as the German-originated Reform Movement, a western, assimilationist, progressive denomination. But for others, who like Isaac Braun were children of east-European immigrants, the ties and preference for Orthodox Judaism lingered. Isaac is dissatisfied with the Reform Movement's style and its diminished Jewish ethnicity. Thus, in the time of his moral crisis, he seeks counsel, not from his fashionable American Reform rabbi, but from an Old World Hasidic rabbi who leads an Orthodox congregation of Holocaust survivors. The unnamed Williamsburg rabbi of the inner tale is the counterpart of the frame story's narrator, Samuel Braun. Before he answered the religious calling, the rabbi too was a practicing bio-chemist in France. Samuel Braun and the rabbi correspond in their scientific professions and in their roles as judges. The rabbi judges as spiritual leader, performing the traditional rabbinic offices of settling disputes between opponents; Braun judges as commenting narrator.

Bellow's decision to locate the rabbi to whom Isaac turns in Williamsburg places him in a well-known Orthodox community, and his description of the rabbi surrounded by bearded men in gabardines implies a Hasidic community. The portrait of Isaac waiting in the anteroom among "followers" also evokes the vision of the Hasidic court in which the disciple seeks an audience with his spiritual leader. Like the Hasidim, the Williamsburg rabbi speaks vernacular Yiddish to Isaac, explaining that although Tina has no cause for complaint against her brother, her deathbed request should be honored since Isaac can afford to meet her terms and doing so may achieve the desired reconciliation. The sterile environment of the Madison Avenue Temple can offer Isaac no solace. He finds consolation and strength in the Hasidic rabbi's counsel. Although the rabbi does not quote Talmud, Hebraic law and commentary, Isaac knows he has "old laws and wisdom on his side" (p. 79) for he "had the old tones, the manner, the burly poise, the universal calm judgment of the Jewish moral genius" (p. 78). Compliance with the rabbi's instruction leads to religious acts of mutual forgiveness, purgative tears signifying the resolution of the family quarrel, expressions of love, and moral rejuvenation. *T'shuva,* redemption, which is at the heart of the story, is dramatically achieved for brother and sister when Isaac follows the rabbi's advice.

In "The Old System," biblical allusions organically link the narrative frame with its inner tale and contribute to the novella's structural and thematic unity. By selecting the Hebrew name "Samuel," the novelist evokes the judicial function of the biblical Samuel who lived during the period of the Israelite-Philistine wars and thus solidifies the link between outer and inner tales. Biblical naming unites the moral crisis and ideas of the inner tale with Samuel Braun's spiritual quest. In addition, biblical analogue is relevant to interpretation of Samuel Braun's character, suggesting his reliability as narrator-judge. During several interjections and the concluding frame, Braun meditates on the philosophical and ethical implications of his reverie. Like his namesake, Samuel Braun appraises both the private morality drama of the inner tale and also public morality as evidenced in his judgment that "in America the abuses of the Old World were righted. It was appointed to be the land of historical redress" (p. 67). Like his biblical counterpart and rabbinic counterpart of the inner tale, Samuel Braun evaluates the motives and behavior of his ancestors and proclaims their guilt or innocence. Furthermore, like the biblical antecedent, the scientist-moralist enlarges his judgment, convinced that "Mankind was in a confusing, uncomfortable, disagreeable stage in the evolution of its consciousness" (p. 48). An authentic Bellovian critic, Braun is saddened that "thought, art, belief of great traditions should be . . . misemployed" (p. 48).

The Jews of Bellow's fiction are enriched by historic memory. A child of Russian-Jewish immigrants, Saul Bellow demonstrates sensitivity to the perplexities and conflicts of first generation Jewish Americans who value ethnic existence within the larger framework of American society. His delineations of immigrant and native-born American Jews evidence the distinction Josephine Knopp recognizes between the east-European Jews who neither considered themselves assimilated nor were granted full citizenship by their countrymen and the American Jews who perceive themselves as acculturated citizens.[12] Educated as a sociologist-anthropologist, Bellow is sensitive to the ambivalence accompanying Jewish adaptation to American life. Living securely, enjoying personal freedom and a high standard of living, Bellow's American Jews are threatened by hollow materialism. They often experience a crisis of belief and cultural identity produced by assimilation into American society. In some characters, like Dr. Adler of *Seize the Day*, Bellow depicts the erosion of observance; in others like Herzog, Isaac, and Samuel Braun, he traces the metamorphosis from estrangement to renewal of Jewish selfhood and commitment to Jewish values. Samuel Braun's Saturday reverie of Jewish times past, dramatizing the spiritual redemption of Isaac and Tina, transports the scientist-narrator beyond skepticism to knowledge of life and death, to affirmation of "the old system," to comprehension of "A promise that mankind might – might, mind you – eventually, through its gift which might – might again! – be a divine gift, comprehend why it lived" (p. 83). Like Bernard Malamud, I. B. Singer, Cynthia Ozick, and other Jewish-American authors who write in the redemptive mode of spiritual return, Saul Bellow consistently affirms humankind's spiritual capacity and ethical potential, and nowhere more forcefully than in "The Old System," which he identifies as a favorite among his works.[13]

NOTES

1. See the interviews, Nina Steers, "Successor to Faulkner?" *Show*, 4 (September 1964): p. 38 and "Saul Bellow: An Autobiography in Ideas," *Bostonia*, November/December 1990: 37–47.

2. Saul Bellow, "The Old System," *Mosby's Memoirs and Other Stories* (Greenwich, Connecticut: Fawcett Publications, 1968), p. 83. Subsequent citations will be from this edition and appear in the text in parentheses.

3. Saul Bellow, *Herzog* (Greenwich, Connecticut: Fawcett Publications, 1965), p. 184. Subsequent citations will be from this edition and appear in the text in parentheses.

4. The Hebrew calendar is both solar and lunar, the years reckoned by the sun and the months by the moon. For a thorough explanation of the Hebrew calendar see Philip Birnbaum, *A Book of Jewish Concepts* (New York: Hebrew Publishing, 1965), pp. 306–10.

5. Repentance and reconciliation with fellow humans and God mark the holiday spirit. *Rosh Hashanah* is designated by two biblical and two liturgical names. Biblically, it is identified as a day of Sabbath observance and *shofar* (ram's horn) blasts. Liturgically, *Rosh Hashanah* is called *Yom ha-Din* (Day of Judgment) and *Yom ha-Zikkaron* (Day of Remembrance) when mankind is believed to be judged by the Divine. *Rosh Hashanah* and *Yom Kippur* are known collectively as *Yamim Nora'im* (Days of Awe).

6. Observant Jews partake in various ritual cleansings to symbolize acts of spiritual purification. The religious discipline of Judaism requires washing of the hands on such occasions as arising from sleep, before offering prayers, before eating, and after the elimination of bodily wastes. At other occasions complete immersion in the *mikveh*, the ritual bath, is prescribed.

7. According to Joshua 19, during the period of land division among the tribes of Israel, the tribe of Naphtali was one of the last to receive its share. Nevertheless, its portion was one of the most fertile sections of Canaan.

8. *Hasidim* constitute a Jewish sect, founded in Poland in the eighteenth century by Israel Baal Shem-Tov and characterized by its emphasis on mysticism, religious zeal, and joy. *Mitnagdim,* orthodox Jewish critics of the *Hasidim,* objected to early attitudes and practices of *Hasidic* exaltation of their leaders, whose authority stemmed from personal charisma irrespective of rabbinic ordination and scholarship; emphasis on the doctrine of immanence rather than the traditional Judaic balance between immanence and transcendence of God; establishment of separate synagogues; and dominant use of Lurianic worship.

9. *Gemara* refers to the second part of the Talmud consisting of discussions and amplifications of the *Mishnah* which is the first part covering Jewish legislation and religious and ethical teachings. The *Gemara* interprets the *Mishnah* by the Amoraim, active in Palestine and Babylonia from the time of the completion of the *Mishnah* until the redaction of the Babylonian Talmud.

10. Harry Rabinowicz, *The World of Hasidim* (Hartford: Hartmore House, 1970), p. 51.

11. Genesis 24:63. A. Z. Idelsohn, *Jewish Liturgy and Its Development* (New York: Schocken Books, 1975), p. 27.

12. Josephine Zadovsky Knopp, *The Trial of Judaism in Contemporary Jewish Writing* (Urbana: Univ. of Illinois Press, 1975), p. 19.

13. "Literature and Culture: An Interview with Saul Bellow," *Salmagundi,* 30 (1975): 21.

From Breakdown to Bliss: Wasteland Themes in *More Die of Heartbreak*

G. Neelakantan

I T IS intriguing to note that Saul Bellow, for all his vehement out-
bursts against the wasteland outlook of most modern literature,
himself makes operative a palpable wasteland metaphor in all his
novels. Critics have, in general, shown sufficient awareness of this
aspect in Bellow's fiction.[1] However, no critic has effectively analyzed how Bellow employs the whole configuration of the wasteland metaphor to arrive at a balanced and positive vision of life. To
this end, I propose to study Bellow's *More Die of Heartbreak*[2] and
show how wasteland as theme and metaphor in fact reinforce the
author's insistently melioristic vision of life.

Set in the Midwest of America, *More Die of Heartbreak* attempts to capture the collective reality that manifests itself through
the impersonal nature of the city. The Bellow city projects a vision of
a titanic entity that ruthlessly cancels out all clarity of perception.
The city is represented as a "cauldron of modern consciousness" (p.
93), one in which a multitude of human passions seethe, annihilating
all human values. The driving force behind this novel remains, as
Alfred Kazin puts it, "the exultantly sordid views of modernity, sexuality, women, the local and international scene, by the smartly om-
nipresent narrator, Kenneth Trachtenberg."[3] To the extent that the
Bellovian city serves as the context of the wasteland, the artistic
treatment of lust, death, the destructive power of money, sterility,
and a fragmented consciousness become inevitable. Being a veritable contemporary version of the "Holy Knight of Faith," and living
amidst the welter brought by the wasteland virus, the Bellow hero
seeks to bring some remedy to the ailing human community.

I shall show how Bellow employs the whole configuration of the wasteland metaphor – the motifs of decay and death and its antidotal counterparts in renewal and life – to reject the wasteland vision of life and assert instead a more balanced view of life.

In *More Die of Heartbreak*, Bellow projects a wasteland that revels in wild sex. Holding humanity in thrall, the "demon of sexuality" (p. 23) is a contemporary reality in Bellow's city. Bellow characterizes it as one of "contemporary democratized-plus-Third World erotic mixture" (p. 215). In the Bellovian universe, sex comes to exercise the consciousness of the high-minded and the low-minded alike, the difference being that the former are vaguely aware that the proper end of human existence is love, while the latter, given to carnal jamboree, have become impervious to the pain of mortality. Aiming to make his life something of a "turning-point" (p. 68), Kenneth Trachtenberg describes the "sexual fireworks" (p. 110) of his father:

> The premise of his eroticism was mortality. The sex embrace was death-flavored. He translated Eternity as Death. I checked repeatedly with my soul, which always answered, "Your father is not it, and if you resembled him exactly you'd go no further than he has gone." (p. 69)

Harrowing in its absence of love, the modern world has found recourse in the rites of "human carnality."

In its role as an "analgesic" (p. 86), sex seems almost to have replaced religion in the contemporary world. Sex, however, comes to us mixed with many a human motive in Bellow. To such as the senior Trachtenberg, Treckie, and Caroline Bunge, it is an end in itself. Matilda Layamon and her father Dr. Layamon use it as a power to manipulate others to serve their personal ends. Della Bedell, Benn's hysterical neighbour, seeks sex as a palliative for the loneliness that tears at her heart. Pilgrims in the cause of love, Kenneth and his uncle Benn Crader, themselves, fall victims to this malady. They are aware of the illusory nature of the sexual game though, and they continue to search for human love and understanding.

Sex is often associated in Bellow's novels with a willful perversion of higher love. Commenting on *More Die of Heartbreak*, Stephen L. Tanner observes that the relationship between sex and love is a key issue in this novel.[4] In devitalizing the power of human love, sex becomes the cause of a dull pain in the recesses of man's soul, adding to the "pain schedule" (p. 11) he is cursed with. Kenneth ascribes the painful search for love to the "immortal longings" (p. 11) of the human heart. This moral commentator, much unlike the wastelanders, believes in the Larkinian concept that "'in everyone there sleeps a sense of life according to love'" (p. 44). Though guided by motions of love, Benn and Kenneth are often "unstable" under the chaotic influences of the present. Finding themselves defenseless before the depredations of sex, they become forgiving of others who have been overwhelmed by it. Karl F. Knight points out rightly: "When things go wrong, both Kenneth and Benn see themselves as sinners."[5] But his argument that their "movement from innocence to experience" does not bring "clarification but ironic confusions"[6] is not in keeping with the spirit of the novel. Sinners though they are, it is only they who undertake the task of melting the "glacier" in the human heart so as to experience what love is.

Benn, for instance, realizes in the depths of his soul that it is only "through love you penetrate to the essence of a being" (p. 225). For the most part, however, he is no more than "fighting the humiliation of not being in love" (p. 278). Surrendering himself to the beauty of Matilda, Benn believes that he has found the ideal woman, but he only deceives himself. Bellow pits Benn, his priest of love, against a powerful set of people who celebrate death and nihilism. The Layamons and Harold Vilitzer, uncle of Benn, constitute the votaries at the pantheon of "Thanatos." To cite an example, Matilda's unnatural sleeping habits and certain physical deformities testify to a phantasmagoric quality about her. Similarly, the artificial azaleas of Layamon's house which Benn mistakes for the real ones assume the force of symbol in that they substantiate the Layamons' disrespect for life-forces. Likewise, Uncle Vilitzer remains thoroughly alien to love. Even at his death-bed, he is unforgiving and dies without ever reconciling with his son Fishl or his cousin Benn. Ellen Pifer aptly observes: "Uncle Vilitzer occupies the unusual, and paradoxical, position of denying the reality of love while being its recipient."[7] Recognizably similar to the death-bed situation in *More Die of Heartbreak,* Bellow's short story "The Old System"[8] shows how Tina forgets in her last moments the lifelong grudge she bore her brother by truly opening her heart and accepting and returning his "tender love." In contrast to the Layamons and Vilitzer, Benn has a reverential attitude to life; he resents death's carrying his loved ones beyond life and even longs to see them restored to life.

No less a *malaise* than sex and death, money also wreaks destruction in the contemporary American waste land. The power of money in the modern world – a deep distraction of the modern consciousness – is a motif that is brilliantly developed in *More Die of Heartbreak.* Vilitzer, uncle of both Benn and Kenneth's mother, defrauds them of millions of dollars by betraying the trust conferred on him by Grandma Crader, who made him the executor of her will. Aware of Vilitzer's cheating of Benn, the Layamons concoct a plot to have their daughter marry Benn so that he can be pressured to retrieve his loss; this way Matilda will be assured both social respectability and money. Bellow captures vividly the power of politics in the modern world and shows that often politics and money are mutually complementary. Amador Chetnik, the judge whom the Republican administration is investigating, was once a confidant of Vilitzer, the Democrat. Alienated from Vilitzer and fearing attack from the Republicans, Chetnik turns against Vilitzer. Exploiting the situation, the politically shrewd Layamons bring Chetnik under their control to strengthen their blitz against Vilitzer. Bellow also presses into service certain symbols to evoke the ominously overwhelming ambience of the modern wasteland. The Electronic Tower, described as the tallest skyscraper in the city, is a recurring symbol in *More Die of Heartbreak*. It stands at the place where previously stood the Jewish household of the Craders, and it is on this property that Vilitzer cheated Benn and his sister of millions of dollars. Overshadowing the Layamon's residence, this Electronic Tower brings to Benn's mind the sense of cruel power that broods over it. In short, the Tower is everything bad that the modern city represents. In such a world of power and riches, Kenneth and Benn are misfits, but it is only through them that the modern wasteland could regain its fertility.

The Bellovian city, clearly in the grip of sex, money, death, and politics, seems to have exorcized both thought and feeling. Preyed on by "city-vexations," the masses seek solace in less enervating surroundings.

> I silently followed uncle [Benn] as he inspected his native city with that cobalt gaze of his – empty factories, stilled freight yards, upended streets, stretches of river where the water was still as a fish tank; and then the countryside, prairies liberated from the darkness of the city, farmlands under white icing, and skies suggesting freedom and eliciting ideas of flight or escape. (p. 201)

The horrid sense of waste derives both from the monstrous force that perverts order, thought, and feeling and also the menacing emptiness which pervades the city. Under the crushing influence of such a force, nobody, including Kenneth, is in full control of his or her faculties. Benn, a prospective "Citizen of Eternity" (p. 69) according to Kenneth, himself remains confused for the most part. His misalliance with Matilda and his paranoiac infatuation with her attest to the fragmented nature of his consciousness. The feeling of strangeness that registers on his consciousness stems from his unconscious knowledge of this malefic force. Sensitive as he is to Benn's deep ruminations, Kenneth accurately focusses on this notion of the monstrous force:

> There seems to be a huge force that advocates, propels, and this pro-pellant increases its power by drawing value away from personal life and fitting us for its colossal purpose. It demands the abolition of such things as love and art. . . . of gifts like uncle's which it can toler-ate intermittently if they don't get in its way. (p. 301)

The wasteland which Kenneth sees at the core of modern life, though universal, peculiarly concerns Russia and America. While preoccupied with the American wasteland, he also shows an awareness of the anal-ogous situation obtaining in the East. Bellow's bold statement in one of his interviews on the eve of his receiving the Nobel Prize ("I feel it is time to write about people who make a more spirited resistance to the forces of our time") is demonstrated in both *The Dean's December* and *More Die of Heartbreak,* novels published subsequent to the award. As Kenneth views it: "the ordeal of privation" and "the ordeal of desire" (p. 100) operating at the psychic level of the Russians and Americans explain the preposterous condition in which humanity finds itself. Russia and America are alike in that the evil they manifest is similar. The massive political systems of both these superpowers have hounded out even the most basic human values from the public. Kenneth bemoans this phenomenon:

> In the U.S.A. you had, instead, a population confined to the lowest of human interests – the emphasis in Russia being on the abolition of the higher, in America on indulgence of the lower. (p. 99)

A sense of primitivism and hopelessness pervade both these super-powers. Kenneth draws attention to this aspect:

> Moreover, this American metropolis on the prairies was rich in resemblances to St. Petersburg, 1913. Here, too, there was a mixture of barbarism and worn-out humanist culture (granting that the latter had never had much of a chance to flower in these parts). (p. 187)

Even more striking parallels, however, are to be seen in the arena of sex and in the creation of inauthentic worlds. Kenneth observes:

Sexually, too, there were parallels. For instance, a cerebral animalism or primitivism; crazy drug cultists pursuing visionary ecstasies
once experienced only by mystics; sadomasochism (raging abuse inflicted or endured, and identified with love and pleasure). A further
similarity was the proliferation of a multitude of false worlds to
whose rules people were earnestly committed. (p. 187)

Attributing the "death-in-life" mentality in modern man to the
smothering effect of false consciousness, Kenneth believes a "full wake-
fulness" (p. 101) of consciousness to the present soul-atrophy would be an
experience akin to "purgatory."

A professor of botany and something of a "plant mystic" (p. 52),
Benn is the holy redeemer who undertakes the perilous journey to bring
home the secret of fertility. This "communicant in a green universal
church" (p. 305) is not disturbed by "the oscillations of desire or memory"
(p. 253), so long as he stays in the domain of nature. But, in time, Benn
realizes that unless he brings his wisdom to bear on the business of life,
his own existence will eventually lack purpose. Addressing himself to
this "crucial project" (p. 33), he shifts his consciousness from the remote
world of plants to the imperatives of the "present moment" (p. 79).
Benn, however, undergoes a phase of uncertainty before he learns to
comprehend what actually ails the modern consciousness. Confused
though he is, Benn never gives in to this "reality-fantasy" (p. 279) of contemporary reality, and through all "preposterousness" and clownery constantly pushes his "gifts" toward "human completion" (p. 54). His journey is fraught with every conceivable risk, but his heart, resolute with
the knowledge of his mission, guides him through.

The death of Vilitzer proves to be a cathartic experience for Benn. It
dawns on him that it is futile to seek the meaning of life in material
things. In mulling over his past, Benn realizes that he had been untrue to
his deeper instincts. Ellen Pifer is perceptive in observing that "Benn's
failure also derives from his refusal to heed the promptings of his inmost
self."[10] Keen though his insights are into the plant world, they are not
aglow with the warmth of love. Society also disappoints Benn with its
celebration of death and its unmindful rejection of all his offers of love.
Still worse, it even tries to kill his appetite for love. Unable to find any
therapy, Benn decides to go to the chilly wastes of the North Pole so as
to observe how lichens survive against all odds. Surely, this expedition
will brace him to face the nihilistic onslaughts of his society and regain
his faith in the power of love. The survival of lichens at sub-zero temper-

atures is symbolic of the continued force of love in human life. Karl F. Knight reads only "defeat" and "withdrawal" into this scene: "Benn wants to hide from himself in the darkness, having lost confidence in his perceptions."[11] However, Stephen L. Tanner and Richard F. Kiernan have viewed this scene in a positive light. Seeing in Benn a "visionary," Tanner argues that Antarctica, being the "boundary of boundaries," Benn will experience there "a foretaste of eternity."[12] Reading the relationship between the humanist and the scientist to be one of the important thematic concerns of the novel, Kiernan appropriately argues: "His final decision to join the Arctic expedition is at once an affirmation of his scientific commitment, an exercise in scientific purification, and an intuitive exercise in self-therapy."[13] In referring to Benn's "extra tenacity about love," Kenneth alludes to certain religious writers who posit "that there is no old age of the soul" (p. 326). This testifies to the religous nature of Benn's enterprise. Both Tanner and Pifer emphasize the religious concerns of this novel. While Tanner argues that Bellow "brings us to a sense of religion" by his "eloquence and strong images,"[14] Pifer points out that Bellow's religious vision consists in "unfolding" the "'hidden design' behind the appearances of modern life."[15] Thus the affirmation of *More Die of Heartbreak* is truly earned, and in underscoring the "perils" of life the novel also brings into relief the principle of immortality and harmony underlying human existence.

The novel registers a shift from indecisiveness to resolve, from confusion to clarity, and from breakdown to a kind of bliss. The recurring image of the phoenix employed in connection with Benn suggests his role as the agent of resurrection. While conceding to the unmistakable pressures of modern existence, Bellow never wholly subscribes to a wasteland outlook on life. The schism between life and death inherent in the wasteland world view, not wholly unfelt in Bellow, is often replaced by a comprehensive perspective that encompasses this polarity and points to things that lie beyond it. In most of Bellow's novels, there are certain images which suggest such a vision. In telescoping the twin aspects of life and death in an appropriate image, Bellow rises above the wasteland world view of corruption, death, and decay. Benn cries out:

> "Well, you know what the old books say – Dionysus and Hades are one and the same, the god of life and the god of death are one and the same god, meaning that life for the species demands the death of the individual." (p. 255)

A similar expression, "King of Death and Life," used in addressing the Jewish God in *Herzog,* brings out the same idea. Shifting his faith from the gods of the world to the "God of Mercy," Benn realizes that mortality applies only to the body and not to the soul. It is this new-born conviction which makes him undertake the spiritual journey at the end.

The title of the novel, echoed at several places in *More Die of Heartbreak,* helps to give it a thematic direction. Bellow suggests that "the queerness of existence" bewilders many to death. Swollen with longings, Della Bedell dies of sheer heartbreak. Vilitzer dies ignominiously, untouched by love, as he had lived. It is through Benn, who has experienced the "immortal longings" of the spirit, that the mysterious sources of life would make themselves felt. It is in this "yea-saying" to the endless possibilities of life that *More Die of Heartbreak* counteracts successfully the pessimism of the wasteland world view.

NOTES

1. Raymond M. Olderman, John Clayton, Sanford Pinsker, Malcolm Bradbury and Dan Vogel, among others, have particularly highlighted this aspect. See Raymond M. Olderman, *Beyond the Waste Land: The American Novel in the Nineteen-Sixties* (New Haven: Yale Univ. Press, 1972); John J. Clayton, *Saul Bellow: In Defense of Man,* 2nd ed. (Bloomington: Indiana Univ. Press, 1979); Sanford Pinsker, "Moses Herzog and the Modern Wasteland," *Reconstructionist,* 34 (December 1968): 20–26; Malcolm Bradbury, *Saul Bellow* (London: Methuen, 1982): Dan Vogel, "Bellow, Herzog, and The Waste Land," *Saul Bellow Journal,* 8, No. 1 (1989): 44–50.

2. Saul Bellow, *More Die of Heartbreak* (London: Alison Press/Secker & Warburg, 1987; rpt. New York: Penguin Books, 1988). Subsequent page numbers for references to the novel will be given in parentheses in the text.

3. Alfred Kazin, "Trachtenberg the Brain King," *New York Times Book Review,* 16 July 1987: 3.

4. Stephen L. Tanner, "Religious Vision of *More Die of Heartbreak,*" in *Saul Bellow in the 1980s: A Collection of Critical Essays,* ed. L. H. Goldman and Gloria Cronin (East Lansing: Michigan State Univ. Press, 1989), p. 291.

5. Karl F. Knight, "Saul Bellow's *More Die of Heartbreak:* Point of View and Irony," in *Saul Bellow Journal,* 9, No. 2 (1990): 18.

6. Knight, p. 20.

7. Ellen Pifer, *Saul Bellow: Against the Grain* (Philadelphia: Univ. of Pennsylvania Press, 1990), p. 157.

8. Saul Bellow, "The Old System" in *Mosby's Memoirs and Other Stories* (New York: Viking Press, 1968; rpt. New York: Penguin Books, 1977).

9. See interview with W. J. Weatherby, *The Guardian,* 10 November 1976.

10. Pifer, p. 155.

11. Knight, p. 19.

12. Tanner, p. 163.

13. Richard F. Kiernan, *Saul Bellow* (New York: Continuum, 1988), pp. 220–21.

14. Stephen L. Tanner, "Rev. of *More Die of Heartbreak,*" in *Saul Bellow Journal,* 7, No. 1 (1988): 76.

15. Pifer, pp. 161–62.

Winners and Losers:
Bellow's Dim View of Success

Ellen Pifer

IN A CAREER spanning half a century, Saul Bellow has gained a greater national and international reputation than any other living American writer. Certainly he has won more awards and prizes than virtually any novelist we can remember. In addition to the Nobel Prize in Literature in 1976, Bellow has claimed everything from the Pulitzer Prize to the French *Croix de Chevalier;* and he has won the National Book Award three times. By any standard we care to apply, the seventy-five-year-old novelist has proved himself a "winner." Confronted with his worldly success, on the other hand, Bellow might well reject the label. I take as evidence his comments, some years ago, during a lengthy interview with Jo Brans. Discussing his then recently published novel, *Humboldt's Gift* (1975), Bellow was told that the novel's protagonist, Charlie Citrine, is clearly a "successful writer." The Nobel Prize winner flatly denied the charge, saying, "Charlie is not really successful. Charlie is a man who, by having success, has excused himself from success."[1]

What Bellow meant, I think, is that Charlie Citrine, like his author, is unwilling to *identify* with success or to accept it as an adequate measure of the human being. One of the themes of *Humboldt's Gift* is, in fact, Citrine's attempt to disengage himself from "the American dollar-drive." In the novelist's own case, this act of disengagement—of excusing oneself from the codes, values, and assumptions that fuel America's obsession with making it—has been raised to the level of an art: the art of fiction. From *Henderson the Rain King* to *Humboldt's Gift* to *More Die of Heartbreak,*

129

Bellow's seekers cast off the creature comforts as they take up a quest for meaning, value, and truth.

The dim view that Bellow takes of worldly success is linked to the reductive vision of the human being that it fosters. In *The Dean's December* (1982), the novelist compares the worlds of Bucharest and Chicago, balancing the "cast-iron gloom" of totalitarian bureaucracy against the degradation of America's inner-city slums. In the race for material power, he suggests, the avatar of capitalism does not differ as much as he thinks from the totalitarian bureaucrat: both kinds of materialists exhibit, in Bellow's view, a sinister belief in the human being's "earthenness." "The view we hold of the material world," says Albert Corde, the Dean of Bellow's novel, "may put us into a case as heavy as lead."[2] Our worship of things and our tendency to view ourselves *as* things may turn out to be fatal. Morally, spiritually, and perhaps even physically, we may end up dying of our devotion. The crushing weight of matter – its worship by the scientist, bureaucrat, and consumer – bears down on the consciousness of Bellow's protagonists as they struggle to lift the lid, break open the case, and discover a fresh vision of the world and what it means to be a human being.

No wonder, then, that a character like Charlie Citrine must "excuse himself" from the claims of worldly success. The same may be said of other Bellow protagonists – most of whom are educated, productive members of society. Virtually all of these accomplished people are engaged, like Citrine, in the process of "excusing" themselves from the codes, values, and assumptions that fuel America's faith in success. In *Henderson the Rain King* (1959), Bellow's protagonist is a Connecticut millionaire who has, materially speaking, everything going for him: money, health, wealth, and plenty of women. All the same, Henderson abandons the comfort and security of his estate for the dark continent of Africa. Suffocating beneath the weight of all his *stuff,* he flees to Africa because, as he later says, "I wouldn't agree to the death of my soul."[3]

Henderson's crisis is hardly the kind of ordeal for which American life prepares us – our nation's business being, as Calvin Coolidge once said, business. In Bellow's view, America's obsession with business has tended to swallow up that other essential "business" that should concern each and every one of us: the business of achieving a meaningful life. To discover that meaning or purpose, his characters leave home either literally, like Henderson, or figuratively, like Herzog, in search of new territory. After considerable hardship and internal discomfort, they begin to discover strange new continents of thought and feeling. And some even arrive at a new and liberating vision of reality.

In *The Victim* (1947), published when Bellow's career was still in its early stages, we find the young novelist already examining the shadow-side of America's faith in material success – the dark side of what is often called healthy ambition. Through the eyes of Asa Leventhal, a New York Jew, Bellow depicts the psychological and spiritual hazards attending our national obsession with making it. A victim of this way of thinking, Asa Leventhal is also a victim of his own worst fears. Although he enjoys a modest degree of professional success and security, Leventhal is haunted by the possibility that in the future he may yet fail, may yet tumble back among the ranks of the losers. The world, after all, is an unstable and threatening place; beneath every success looms the possibility – the abyss – of failure. Insecure in his identity as a "winner," Leventhal is filled with dread of becoming a "loser." For him, existence is a mined field; and as he cautiously picks his way through this mined field, he tries to avoid any situation that looks explosive, any encounter that might unsettle his precarious equilibrium. Hoping to spare himself and avert disaster, Leventhal works hard at staying aloof from others.

Sometimes, however, in rare moments of tranquility and confidence, Leventhal glimpses the absurdity of his efforts to seal himself off from the frightening "depths of life." Then, in passages like the following one, he thinks to himself: "We were all the time taking care of ourselves . . . laying up, storing up, watching out on this side and that side, and at the same time running, running desperately, running as if in an egg race with the egg in a spoon. . . . Man is weak and breakable, . . . has to keep his bones from breaking and his fat from melting. . . . Hoards sugar and potatoes, hides money in his mattress, spares his feelings whenever he can, and takes pains and precautions. That, you might say, was for the sake of the egg."[4]

Here Leventhal temporarily breaks through the wall of his defenses to contemplate a larger vision of reality. Picturing the drive for success as an egg race, he sees it as doomed from the start by the conditions of mortality. Even if the "egg" or precious ego were carried safely through to the finish line – its shell intact – no one could keep it from spoiling. Engaged in a futile attempt to protect himself, Asa Leventhal has developed a shell of indifference to life and other people. He has tried, we might say, to "hardboil" that tender egg, the ego. But "hardboiling" the egg, to extend the metaphor, is only a temporary defense against the forces of disaster and decay – as Leventhal appears to recognize when he asks himself, "Dying is spoiling, then?" (p. 99). Faced with the ultimate terms of existence, Bellow suggests, human beings must admit that winning and losing are only relative terms: some of us may run faster and win the race, but eventually we all wind up in the same place.

To the reductive view of life as an "egg race," Bellow opposes a more authentic vision of reality – a vision of the journey shared by and uniting all human beings. Dramatizing this perspective throughout his fiction, he also reveals how an obsession with winning can prove more dangerous than the perils of losing. In the great rush to achieve success, we may fail to honor, in ourselves as well as in others, the special dignity and obligations of being human. To assume the privilege and the burden of being "exactly human" – that is what *The Victim* and all of Bellow's subsequent novels are about. To the degree that his characters fulfill this difficult task, they are *true* successes or failures.

The paradoxical nature of human success and its worldly double – the tension between palpable profits and inner loss or between life's material demands and its spiritual requirements – underlies virtually all of Bellow's fiction. Nowhere is the paradox more radically drawn than in his early short novel *Seize the Day* (1956). Here the protagonist, Wilhelm Adler, is by all obvious standards a miserable failure. At the age of forty-four, Wilhelm has lost his job, his wife and his family. On the "day of reckoning" during which the novel takes place, he even loses his last seven hundred dollars. As he stands in front of a hotel vending machine, Wilhelm cuts a pathetic figure – that of a man bent and nearly broken by the harsh winds of misfortune: "He swallowed hard at the Coke bottle and coughed over it. . . . By a peculiar twist of habit he wore his coat collar turned up always, as though there were a wind. It never lay flat. But on his broad back, stooped with its own weight, its strength warped almost into deformity, the collar of his sports coat appeared anyway to be no wider than a ribbon."[5]

Wilhelm not only looks like a loser, he feels like one. Viewing himself as a failure, he often behaves self-destructively. So much has been said about his guilt, self-hatred, and need to fail that Wilhelm's peculiar strength of spirit – sickened as that spirit may be – is often overlooked.[6] What I should like to emphasize, therefore, is the way that this sloppy, inept "loser" turns out to be, in a deeper sense, a profoundly "successful" human being. Down on his luck and down on himself, Wilhelm Adler proves, all the same, to have a special talent, a real gift, for feeling. Graced with intuition and profound sympathy for others, he has the capacity to experience what Bellow elsewhere calls "an emotion of truth."[7] To feel from the heart – to feel not just intensely but generously, humanely, even self-lessly – such capacity for feeling is not, as the novel's other characters at-test by default, a trifling matter.

In the practical world, Wilhelm's gift for feeling makes him seem more bumbling, more stupid, than he is. Time after time his "soft heart" and "sensitive feelings" confuse him – and prevent him from making the right decision (p. 25). At the same time, Wilhelm's generous emotions lend him his special "dignity" as a human being. And to this dignity Bellow deliberately calls attention. He does so in a strategically located passage that occurs right after Wilhelm's father – the cold, fastidious and highly "successful" Dr. Adler – observes to himself, "What a dirty devil this son of mine is. Why can't he try to sweeten his appearance a lit-tle?" Bellow's narrator then comments: "Wilhelm sat, mountainous. He was not really so slovenly as his father found him to be. In some aspects he even had a certain delicacy. His mouth, though broad, had a fine out-line, and his brow and his gradually incurved nose, dignity" (p. 42).

Wilhelm's "dignity," Bellow suggests, derives from something other than worldly success or status. It springs from his nature rather than his achievements – from the state of his soul rather than the state of his ap-pearance. This distinction is clarified when we turn, for purposes of com-parison, to the title story of Bellow's 1968 collection. In "Mosby's Mem-oirs," Willis Mosby is quite literally Wilhelm Adler's opposite. While Wilhelm is sloppy, clumsy and undisciplined, Mosby is fastidious, agile, adroit. A political thinker, noted author and former high-ranking government of-ficial, Dr. Mosby is a "master" of logic, "merciless" in debate. While Wil-helm has drifted through life making mistakes, Mosby has carried out "imperative tasks" with rigorous discipline.[8] And while Wilhelm, destitute at forty-four, faces personal and professional failure, elderly Dr. Mosby – who has spent his successful career in American universities and the leading circles of government – has been awarded a Guggenheim grant to write his memoirs.

In conduct and appearance, Mosby is as trim, elegant, and self-possessed as Wilhelm's own father. Dr. Adler's cool disdain for his son is more than matched by Dr. Mosby's heartless treatment of his bumbling friend Lustgarten – a man whose physical, emotional, and mental inepti-tude bears a striking resemblance to Wilhelm's own. When Lustgarten, "down on his luck," goes to his friend for solace, Dr. Mosby, like Dr. Adler, feels only disgust. "Mosby," we are told, "had no wish to see a man in tears. He did not care to sit through these moments of suffering" (pp. 172–73).

Wilhelm Adler's "sensitive feelings" place him at an obvious disadvantage, in every worldly sense, with "dry" men like his father or Mosby. These "dry" types (Bellow borrows the term from the French "*un type sec*") are never unsettled by deep feeling or concern for others (MM, p. 159). Admittedly, Wilhelm is responsible for the disasters that befall him: the loss of his job, the failure of his marriage, and his imminent bankruptcy at the hands of the charlatan Dr. Tamkin. Yet Bellow also reveals the way in which Wilhelm's receptivity to life and to other people contributes to his vulnerability and lack of worldly success. Dr. Tamkin, for one, takes full advantage of Wilhelm's sympathetic nature, preying on his emotional neediness and his compassion for others. A telling example of the way Tamkin takes advantage of Wilhelm's sympathy occurs near the end of *Seize the Day*. Wilhelm has just demanded that Tamkin accompany him to the brokerage office in order to sell the shares that Tamkin has talked Wilhelm into buying. Outside the office door, the two men are waylaid by an old man named Rappaport who lives in their hotel. Nearly blind, Rappaport is afraid to cross the busy street alone.

As Wilhelm and Tamkin approach the door where Rappaport is standing, it is Wilhelm whom Rappaport "somehow recognize[s]" and asks for help (p. 100). Tamkin, eager to get rid of Wilhelm, urges him to do as the old man asks. Wilhelm kindly agrees to help Rappaport – even though the rich old man hoards his "information" about the commodities market and has refused to give Wilhelm the slightest bit of financial advice (pp. 86–87).

Clearly Rappaport is a man who lives his life as though it were, in Asa Leventhal's phrase, an "egg race." Feeble, nearly blind and at death's door, he is still running, still competing, still hoarding the precious "egg" that makes him a "winner." (With ironic appropriateness, Rappaport has made his fortune in the chicken business – burning electric bulbs at night in the coops in order to "cheat the poor hens into laying" [p. 86]). Even after Wilhelm leads the blind man across the street and into a store, Rappaport does not give his helper any word or sign of gratitude. By the time Wilhelm completes his thankless task and returns to the brokerage office, his shares have plummeted. He has lost his "chance to sell," and Tamkin has disappeared without a trace (pp. 102–03).

By helping old Rappaport across the street, Wilhelm proves the kind of "loser" that Willis Mosby scorns. Unhampered by generous emotions, Mosby himself has cut a narrow swath through the world – eliminating all obstacles, including other people, with his razor-sharp intellect. Wilhelm's susceptibility to feeling, on the other hand, hampers his progress: where Mosby is brutally decisive, Wilhelm is easily "confused under pressure." As the specter of financial failure looms ever larger for Wilhelm, the pressure mounts – until he cannot find "enough air in his lungs" to breathe (p. 114). Interestingly, Willis Mosby also experiences the dread of suffocation. But for Mosby, the experience comes as an unpleasant surprise, or twist, at the end of the story.

While visiting the ruins of a stone temple at Mitla, Mosby descends to an underground tomb. There the detached and erudite thinker suddenly panics, terrified by the thought that he might die: "The vault was close. [Mosby] was oppressed. He was afraid. It was very damp. . . . His heart was paralyzed. His lungs would not draw. Jesus! I cannot catch my breath! To be shut in here! To be dead here! Suppose one were! . . . *Dead-dead*. Stooping, he looked for daylight. Yes, it was there. The light was there. The grace of life still there. Or, if not grace, air" (p. 184, Bellow's italics). All at once "stone-hearted" Dr. Mosby is brought, by recognition of the "end," to a surprising discovery (pp. 158, 167–68). For a brief moment he glimpses what Bellow calls "the grace of life." He sees life, in other words, as a sacred gift rather than a contest to win, a condition to exploit. By pursuing the implications of this vision, Mosby might conceivably overcome his terror of death. But in his urgency to escape from the tomb, he fails to confront his own mortality.

The panic that grips Mosby in the underground tomb provides a striking contrast to Wilhelm Adler's calm recognition that, as he says to his father, "everyone on this side of the grave is the same distance from death" (p. 45). Timid and confused, Wilhelm exhibits remarkable steadfastness before the mystery that reduces clever Dr. Mosby to a state of abject terror. As Wilhelm walks through the crowds thronging a subway corridor beneath Times Square, he is struck not by fear but by sympathy for others. And "all of a sudden," Bellow writes, "a general love for all these imperfect and lurid-looking people burst out in Wilhelm's breast. . . . They were his brothers and sisters. He was imperfect and disfigured himself, but what difference did that make if he was united with them by this blaze of love? And as he walked he began . . . blessing them all as well as himself" (pp. 84–85). Here in this tomblike corridor, Wilhelm realizes that he is not alone – that even his suffering and his failures unite him with other human beings.

At the close of *Seize the Day*, Wilhelm has a more sustained experience of this shared plight. And at this crucial moment he assumes that very figure of a man despised by Mosby: "a man in tears." Having wandered into the funeral of a stranger, Wilhelm weeps "at first softly and from sentiment, but soon from deeper feeling." This "deeper feeling,"

Bellow's language clearly indicates, is something more than self-pity or despair. Here, as in the earlier scene in the underground, Wilhelm grieves not just for himself but for each and every "human creature" whose final destiny is "the end of all distractions" (pp. 117–18). As a flood of tears unties "the great knot of ill and grief," loosening the "clutch" of despairing "thoughts" that have paralyzed his will and spirit, Wilhelm, sinking "deeper than sorrow," may well be on his way to "a different life." Faint though it may be, this promise of renewal is unavailable to Dr. Mosby, who rejects the shared burden of humanity as he deplores the very sight of "a man in tears." Mosby's detachment from others proves not a sign of strength but of failure: heart-failure.

The nature of Wilhelm's strength is admittedly obscure, even paradoxical. Yet as Robert Alter points out in *The Pleasures of Reading,* literary language – by "superimposing significant images" and "establishing unlooked-for connections" – lends itself to the creation of such "paradoxical perceptions."[9] As *Seize the Day* and Bellow's other fiction amply testify, the novelist's verbal and visual resources for exposing the paradoxes of American "success" are infinitely rich. In his novella *A Theft* (1989), Bellow deftly creates still other unlikely and "unlooked-for connections" between America's winners and losers. The story's heroine, Clara Velde, appears in every apparent way, including gender, the polar opposite of Wilhelm Adler: a formidable success. A highly paid executive in a New York publishing firm, Clara is a tall, good-looking blonde who wears designer clothes and lives in a "vast Park Avenue co-op apartment."[10] Still, Clara is no Mosby. The mother of three young daughters, she is a generous, hardworking, compassionate human being for whom the author has obvious affection.

Far luckier at life than Wilhelm Adler, Clara Velde does not lose anything at the end of her story. She manages, instead, to recover a stolen ring, set with a rare emerald. For Clara, the emerald is more than valuable; it is irreplaceable – the symbol of her lifelong bond with the man who gave it to her. Having recovered the ring at the end of the story, Clara is overwhelmed by a flood of feelings: feelings of relief, gratitude and renewed faith in the power of love. And how does she give vent to all these sublime feelings? By crying! At the end of *A Theft,* we see this handsome, successful, essentially *happy* woman weeping uncontrollably as she stumbles, in her fashionable high heels, down Madison Avenue:

> She hurried, crying, down Madison Avenue, not like a person who belonged there but like one of the homeless, doing grotesque things

in public, one of those street people turned loose from an institution. The main source of tears came open. She found a handkerchief and held it to her face in her ringed hand, striding in an awkward hurry. She might have been treading water in New York harbor – it felt that way, more a sea than a pavement, and for all the effort and the motions that she made, she wasn't getting anywhere, she was still in the same place. (p. 109)

In this passage, Bellow's reference to Clara's "ringed hand" is all that reminds us that the end of this story is a *happy* one. After all her worry and distress, Clara has recovered her precious emerald and can return to her life with a renewed sense of accomplishment and well being. What Bellow leaves us with, however, is not a radiant image of success – but of a woman *drowning* in tears: an image that oddly recalls Wilhelm Adler weeping, in the closing lines of his story, at the funeral of a stranger. In Clara's case, as in Wilhelm's, tears symbolically dissolve the social signposts that separate her from others. Just as Wilhelm sinks "deeper than sorrow" as he weeps for himself and for every other mortal being, so Clara is absorbed by her tears into the community of human suffering. And just as Wilhelm's heart is paradoxically strengthened by his sorrow, Clara Velde's happiness paradoxically leads her to identify with all the "homeless" and destitute. At this moment of personal victory, Clara understands that, contrary to all appearances, she really isn't "getting anywhere" – that she is, in Bellow's words, "still in the same place," or the same boat, with the humblest of her fellow creatures.

Bellow's latest novella takes its name from a rich and famous American, the Broadway producer Billy Rose. But *The Bellarosa Connection* (1989) is hardly a celebration of celebrity. What it does celebrate, once again, is the extraordinary intelligence, warmth and wit of a woman. Unlike Clara Velde, however, Sorella Fonstein is no fashionable beauty. Weighing in at two-hundred-pounds-plus, Sorella is so fat that, as Bellow's narrator puts it, "she made you look twice at a doorway. When she came to it, she filled the space like a freighter in a canal lock."[11] But Sorella is larger than life in a more telling sense, her enormous heft being the outward "sign" of a prodigious humanity. By the sheer weight of her intelligence and insight, Sorella has transformed the social "disgrace" of obesity into the design of greatness (32). "Greatness," the narrator avows, is the only word for Sorella's special honesty or "candor." "In this world of liars and cowards," he adds, "there *are* people like Sorella. One waits for them in the blind faith that they *do* exist" (p. 56, Bellow's italics).

The narrator pays homage to Sorella's "greatness" by recounting events that transpired thirty years earlier – when, for the sake of her husband, Harry, she confronted the famous producer, Billy Rose, and put his humanity to the test – a test he unambiguously fails. During the war, Rose had financed the escape of Harry Fonstein and other Jews from the Nazi Gestapo in Italy; but in the years following, Rose repeatedly rejected Fonstein's request for a personal interview. Having staged Fonstein's escape, the producer would not grant him the opportunity to thank Rose and, in this way, to grant closure to the brutal and arbitrary experience Fonstein had survived. "Something is due from every man to every man," the narrator of *The Bellarosa Connection* tells us. "But Billy [Rose] hadn't heard and didn't want to hear about such [things]" (p. 57).

Preoccupied with being a "big-name" celebrity, Rose avoided human "entanglements" in his relentless drive for success: "Billy had to reserve himself for his deals, devote himself body and soul to his superpublicized bad marriages"; his "squalid, rich residences"; and an array of "provocative" young "chicks whom he couldn't do a thing with when they . . . stripped and waited for him" (pp. 59, 56–57). Rose's impotence, the narrator implies, goes far beyond the sexual; stunted by his worship of fame and fortune, he is, despite his multi-millions, a man *poor* in spirit – a "squalid" failure.

Rose's human failure is manifestly demonstrated in the novel when the narrator relates the famous producer's confrontation with Sorella in Jerusalem in 1959. Rose has arrived in Israel to donate an expensive sculpture garden intended to buy him a permanent place in Jewish history. That Rose refuses to assume the full burden of the Jews' history is revealed, however, by his brutal reaction to Sorella's simple request: she asks him to grant her husband, a Holocaust survivor, fifteen minutes of his time. Flying into a fury at Mrs. Fonstein's dogged persistence, Rose hurls unspeakable insults at her in "a screaming fit," and ends by calling her "a heap of fat filth!" Before she quits him forever, Sorella not only tells Rose off but tells him she has changed her mind. "I don't *want* my husband to talk to the likes of you. You're not fit," she says (pp. 62–63, Bellow's italics).

Recounted by a professional memory-man, the retired founder of "the Mnemosyne Institute in Philadelphia," *The Bellarosa Connection* pays homage to an obscure woman who, he avows, occupies a much more meaningful place in Jewish history than the "legendary personality" and millionaire, Billy Rose. And as he reflects upon his admiration for and old friendship with Sorella Fonstein, the narrator comes to recognize the hollow nature not only of Rose's "worldly success" but of his own (p. 2). Thus by the time he begins to relate his story, Bellow's narrator is detached, even cynical, about his success. The "innate gift of memory," he tells us, "became the foundation of [my] commercial success – an income of X millions soundly invested and an antebellum house in Philadelphia furnished by my late wife" with costly antiques (p. 2). With his Jewish inheritance – the ancient gift of memory passed down by a people who "ask even God to remember, '*Yiskor Elohim*'" – he has bought his American success (p. 102). "There is nothing in this country," he says, "that you can't sell, nothing too weird to bring to market and found a fortune on" (p. 25).

The narrator finds, however, that he has paid a high "price for being a child of the New World" (89). Waking up one morning to a sense of isolation and confusion about his American life and his Jewish history, he has the sudden urge to get in contact with Sorella Fonstein and her husband, whom he has not seen in thirty years. Somehow they had been forgotten or set aside during the busy decades devoted, ironically, to building his memory-business. As the narrator now says with regret, "My time then was unusually valuable. Horribly value, as I now judge it" (p. 66). To his dismay he learns that the Fonsteins have died, only six months earlier, in an accident on the New Jersey Turnpike. The narrator must now face the grim fact not only of death but of personal failure: "I had abandoned two extraordinary people whom I had always said I valued and held dear" (p. 96).

In remorse and humility, the elderly narrator of Bellow's novella sets out to make the only reparation he can: to exercise his gift not for profit but in homage to the dead. As he tells the reader, "I am preoccupied with feelings and longings, and emotional memory is nothing like rocketry or gross national products" (p. 3). His story celebrates not only Sorella and Harry Fonstein but the human power of memory as it performs its rescue operation against the forces of oblivion. This, he concludes, is "what retention of the past really means" (p. 102). Thus, through a process of recollection that taps his author's own invaluable resources of memory, imagination and language, Bellow's narrator undermines the material signposts of success to unearth buried treasure.

In this, his most recent novella, as well as in his previous fiction, Bellow plays with appearances in order to delve beneath them – testing conventional assumptions and giving the lie to facile categories. Exposing his characters' success and failure to the searchlight of imaginative language and moral vision, his fiction creates paradoxical perspectives that unsettle our reductive, if convenient, notions about ourselves and the world. To the members of a society obsessed with memory banks, data pools and statistical graphs that measure every conceivable form of

performance, every kind of financial, professional or political success –
the language of Bellow's fiction brings more ancient knowledge to light:
knowledge of the winner's hidden losses and the loser's secret gains.

NOTES

1. Jo Brans, "Common Needs, Common Preoccupations: An Interview with
   Saul Bellow," *Southwest Review,* 62 (1977): 1–19; rpt. *Critical Essays on Saul
   Bellow,* ed. Stanley Trachtenberg (Boston: G. K. Hall, 1979), p. 66.

2. Saul Bellow, *The Dean's December* (New York: Harper & Row, 1982), p. 227.

3. Saul Bellow, *Henderson the Rain King* (New York: Viking, 1959), p. 277.

4. Saul Bellow, *The Victim* (New York: Vanguard, 1947), p. 99. Subsequent references are in the text.

5. Saul Bellow, *Seize the Day* (New York: Viking, 1956), pp. 15–16. Subsequent
   references are in the text.

6. See the discussion of Wilhelm's alleged masochism in my *Saul Bellow Against
   the Grain* (Philadelphia: Univ. of Pennsylvania Press, 1990), p. 79 and attending notes.

7. *The Adventures of Augie March* (New York: Viking, 1953), p. 384.

8. Saul Bellow, *Mosby's Memoirs and Other Stories* (New York: Viking, 1968),
   pp. 176, 184. Subsequent references are in the text.

9. Robert Alter, *The Pleasures of Reading in an Ideological Age* (New York:
   Simon and Schuster, 1989), p. 96.

10. Saul Bellow, *A Theft* (New York: Penguin Books, 1989), p. 12. Subsequent ref-
    erences are in the text.

11. Saul Bellow, *The Bellarosa Connection* (New York: Penguin, 1989), p. 48. Sub-
    sequent references are in the text.

Aesthetic Intoxication and Tutelary Spirits: Russian Connections in Saul Bellow's *More Die of Heartbreak*

David Rampton

> An arcanum is more than a mere secret; it's what you have to know in order to be fertile in a creative pursuit, to make discoveries, to prepare for the communication of a spiritual mystery.[1]

THUS KENNETH Trachtenberg describes his Uncle Benn's subject of study in Saul Bellow's novel *More Die of Heartbreak*, in a passage that attempts to define what makes certain people especially gifted and how variously their gifts can be applied. In retelling the history of Benn Crader's marital woes, *More Die of Heartbreak* clearly suggests that extensive taxonomic knowledge in the world of plants is no guarantee against one's guessing wrong about human relations. Even though he is extraordinarily percipient about all sorts of non-scientific matters, Benn Crader is at a bit of a loss with Eros. His arcanum, in other words, is limited. But, as so often in the novel, the narrator might well be speaking about himself here. For, despite his repeated denials, Trachtenberg is telling us his story as well as his Uncle Benn's, and he has his own "arcanum," his own secret knowledge bound up with creative pursuits, revealing discoveries, and spiritual mysteries. What plant science is to Benn Crader, Russian literature is to his nephew, and he alludes to it repeatedly in the course of the story he relates. In this essay I shall discuss why Bellow chooses Russian literary history as the background for *More Die of Heartbreak*, how its essential traits, as he conveys them, can extend our understanding of this novel, and how the allusions to Russian literature form part of a chorus of voices which compete for the reader's ear. Not only does

Bellow's peculiarly Russian sensibility, so often commented upon, express itself most fully in *More Die of Heartbreak;* but also his interest in the usefulness of literary and historical analogies makes the novel a stimulating compendium of his concerns as he enters his eighth decade, that is, as he reaches an age when most novelists have either long since quit writing or made even their most fervent supporters wish they had.

The narrator explains early on that he works as an assistant professor of Russian literature, but for most of the novel he is on a de facto sabbatical. This is important, for his principal task is not teaching his students: the one seminar he does give in the course of the novel he arrives for ill-prepared and confesses that its subject is a puzzle to him. Like Moses Herzog, he needs to use both the time available to him and the literature he knows so well to put his own house in order. Thus Trachtenberg's seemingly light-hearted approach to his academic responsibilities is actually occasioned by a sense of deep moral obligation to them. He is, in effect, the most serious of teachers, in the sense that he is intrigued by the question of whether literature can teach us something not just about human life in general but about the way that we should conduct ourselves; and every time he starts talking about literature, he ends up talking about actual people. In his mind, for example, even the sort of scholarship one pursues carries with it its own moral connotations. Matilda Layamon stands revealed at the end of the novel as something of a moral nullity, but in a sense we have known all along what sort of person she would turn out to be, because as a Ph.D. student her subject was French culture under the Nazi occupation, which was, according to Trachtenberg, a blend of "pornography, heartfelt *douleur,* corrupt love, patriotism, and a fine literary style," that was "[r]otten through and through" (p. 114).

There is, of course, something decidedly old-fashioned about this stance. But Bellow's choice of Russian literature as subject matter is particularly apposite in this regard. From the time that Belinsky wrote his famous letter to Gogol, excoriating him for betraying the progressive cause and abasing himself before the reactionary forces of church and state, *the* great tradition in Russian literary criticism, despite the impressive brilliance of the formalist critics from Eikhenbaum and Shklovsky to Levin and Lotman, has been comprised of the stern Platonic rather than the cool Aristotelian critics, those who have involved themselves less with questions of structure and plot than with the ethical stance of authors and the task of informing and educating readers about a range of vital questions that affected their lives. Because censorship in the nineteenth century made literature the primary means of articulating political or social ideas, the great novelists – Gogol, Tolstoy, Dostoevsky, Turgenev, Goncharov, Saltykov-Shchedrin – used their medium to comment on social and political questions. Radical critics like Dobrolyubov and Pisarev, as well as more esthetically-minded ones like Druzhinin and Botkin, and conservatives like Strakhov and Grigoriev elucidated for readers the implications of arguments made, ideas presented, and positions taken in whatever literary work they happened to be discussing. All the writers mentioned above, indeed almost all nineteenth-century Russian writers, shared an attitude towards the events of their time, a seriousness that made them accept, in varying degrees to be sure, the didactic function of literature, and to pose for themselves the important questions on the minds of all Russians. And each one of them believed, like Kenneth Trachtenberg, that writing itself could hardly be discussed as a thing existing independently of the life that informed it.

Kenneth Trachtenberg's particular area of interest is Russian literature of the fin de siècle and the Silver Age in the first decades of the twentieth century, so he naturally uses the writers from this period, figures like Soloviev, Rozanov, Blok, Bely, and Mandelstam, to illustrate the various ideas he wants to examine. During this era the problems of Russian society caused by the liberation of the serfs in 1861, the consequences of the rapid growth of industrialization, the debate between Westerners and Slavophiles about the course Russia should pursue, the battle between the Orthodox church and its most famous dissenter, Tolstoy, the political activities of the anarchists and a wide range of left wing radicals – all these made Russia's situation that much more unstable and the obligations of the writer that much more urgent. For Trachtenberg, a teacher committed to committed literature, and both intrigued by and somewhat skeptical about the idea that books can actually change individual lives as well as the course of history, no national literature and historical period could be more appropriate. For Bellow, a novelist similarly committed, such an arcanum seems to have stimulated his own creativity, as he wrote a novel about the problems of laying claim to any knowledge in the face of a spiritual mystery, and about how that knowledge might best be communicated.

Trachtenberg's interest in Russian literature is of course part of his fascination with ideas generally, and his ambivalent attitude towards the subjects which so intrigue him is part of what makes the book so tricky to deal with. He says fairly early on:

> I take very little pleasure in theories and I'm not going to dump ideas on you. I used to be sold on them, but I discovered that they were noth-

ing but trouble if you entertained them indiscriminately. We are looking at matters for which theorizing brings no remedy. Still, you don't
want to miss what's happening under your very eyes, failing to recognize how disappointing the familiar forms of experience have
become. (p. 19)

The flood of theories which follows should not be taken to indicate a simple
inconsistency that Bellow wants to ironize. The lack of coherence in the
novel on this point is anticipated by the uncertainties in the passage itself:
there is the reservation expressed rather hazily in the last sentence, for
example; and the pejorative implications of "dump" and "indiscriminately"
suggest that there are other, more acceptable, ways of introducing ideas
into the subsequent account. And yet, despite Trachtenberg's ambivalent
attitude to them, these ideas eventually become the most interesting thing
in *More Die of Heartbreak*. For those who know Bellow's earlier work, the
story that links the various parts together is quite familiar, and the recycled
characters in the smaller rôles – Fishl, Vilitzer, Matilda Layamon, Dita –
would seem to indicate a certain imaginative flagging in this regard. The
reader is ultimately left in the position of someone who has discovered an
extraordinarily rich collection of lecture notes, strung together by a narrative line and animated by the presence of some old friends. Like any nervous, over-eager lecturer, Trachtenberg tends to jump around a lot, to
wing it with free associations, to leave allusions unexplained, to grow impatient with his imagined listeners. But out of all this peripatetic erudi-
tion, some central occupations do emerge, and in exploring them one can
usefully comment, without being excessively mandarin, upon the
narrator's expert knowledge and its applications.

The most extensive network of references to Russian literature in
the novel involves the Russian Symbolists, the poets and novelists who
dominated Russian literature at the turn of the century in a way that
even their French counterparts did not. Bellow's narrator invokes them
as often as he does because they responded to the chaos they witnessed
in their own age in ways that he finds attractive himself: by getting a
sort of contact high from it; by attempting to understand and build upon
its patterns; and, failing that, by musing about an escape to a world in
which their most profound aspirations can be realized.

Let us consider two of these figures more closely. First there is Alex-
ander Blok, a lyric poet who tried to hear the music of the Revolution in
a time that was manifestly not his own. Blok also wrote poems about the
cataclysms awaiting Russian culture that Kenneth Trachtenberg finds

particularly evocative, poems like "The Scythians" which Trachtenberg discusses with his mother while visiting her at a refugee camp in Somalia. Like Trachtenberg, Blok was intrigued by the idea of the existence of a spiritual world that tries to influence our own in inscrutable ways, ways that sometimes go disastrously wrong, and by the notion that life on the planet had reached a turning point, visible to those possessed of the gift for perceiving the pattern of history as it unfolded. In 1911 he wrote in his diary: "It is very probable that our time is great, and that it is namely we who stand at the centre of life, that is in that place where all the spiritual threads come together, where all the sounds are audible."[2] Like Bellow's narrator, Blok was profoundly influenced by and attracted to European culture, yet for all its charm, Europe was a symbol of decay for him, and Russia's own decadence was a symbol of the European infection. In another journal entry he blames this decay on "*tartarshchina,*" a yearning for destruction and violence that was rooted in Russian culture. The life of the mind, the capacity to feel passion, the existence of the individual soul, all would be swept away if the Russians give in to the "Asian" side of their character. Blok goes on: "The sense of tragedy is in the *hopelessness* of the conflict; but here is no despair, no listlessness, no folding of the hands. An exalted dedication is essential."[3] If we ignore the rather unsavoury racist implications of the "yellow peril" argument lurking here, and think of it as a metaphorical expression of a self-destructive urge, then the relevance of the allusions to Blok's poetry start to become clearer. From Trachtenberg's perspective at the end of the century, surrounded by starving masses – what he calls the old suffering – and soul-starved masses – the new – he can see the same challenge, the same hopelessness, and the high dedication required if a new acquiescence in the face of death is to be fought and mastered.

Blok's sympathy with and feelings of repulsion for benighted humanity are germane here as well. Gorky saw in Blok's "Scythianism" simple despair and "a concession to the instinctive antipathy to state authority of the Russian masses," for if one really considered them to be uneducable, Gorky contended, then one simply acquiesced in one's own destruction.[4] But Blok's position vis-à-vis the working class was born in part of the aristocratic hauteur that he considered his birthright and an index of his status as a poet. Trachtenberg relates with considerable sympathy the story of how Blok "lost his temper at a public meeting because he had had to stand in line to get a piece of fish" (p. 54). He can sympathize because he feels a similar distinction and a concomitant contempt for the uneducated mass. Here he is on the same subject:

> We human creatures should be at play before the Lord – the higher
> the play, the more pleasing to God. I doubt that it can interest Him
> much to watch the shits at their play. I don't refer now to the Iago
> type but to people of ordinary stunted imaginative powers. The work
> of psychology is to explain and excuse these shits. (p. 116)

The biblical reference is to Proverbs 9: 30–32, the passage in which Solomon advises his son about the appropriate conduct for those sensitive to
all the joys of God's creation, and concludes with the admonition, "Hear instruction, and be wise, and refuse it not." If the mass of humanity will not
or simply cannot learn enough from literature and history to save its soul –
and this is after all a central question posed by the novel – then Bellow,
whose acerbic voice seems to be speaking through his narrator here, can
have the satisfaction of having said what he thought about his species.

Blok functions in *More Die of Heartbreak*, then, as one possibility for
Bellow's narrator in his attempt to make sense of history and human
potential at a time of spiritual crisis. The Russian poet is a seeker of
other realms who fails, an idealist who proposes a truce between passion
and reason but is driven in the end to fear the former and give up on the
latter altogether. (Gorky reports him as saying in one conversation: "If
we could only completely stop thinking, for at least ten years. To extin-
guish that deceptive little swamp-light which draws us deeper and
deeper into the world's night, and listen with our hearts to the harmony
of the universe."[5]) He is also a figure who comes to see the raw material
of the world as profoundly recalcitrant in the face of any attempt to
transform it. Blok's interest in the ideas that characterize an epoch
makes him a kindred spirit for Trachtenberg; his conviction that his life
and his era were important turning points for the human spirit makes
him a useful guide; his sense of impotence and frustration in the end
make him a warning for those who come after.

Andrei Bely will serve as the other representative of the Symbolist
movement which intrigues Bellow in *More Die of Heartbreak*. Both
writers are troubled by the incipient weakness of humanism in the face
of the various apocalyptic threats to it, and both are therefore particularly
attuned to the noise of history, its music and its cacophonous discords. In
choosing Bely, Bellow clearly wanted an example of ideas in action, an
instance of how the doctrine of the Symbolist "other world" might manifest itself in the life of someone who actually lived it, for Bely's belief in
the multiple worlds his art posited amounted to an all-encompassing cer-
tainty for him. (He was convinced at one point that the First World War

was the product of his thoughts about European destruction.) Bely was impatient with what he took to be the arid theoretical stance of the French symbolists and dismissed them as "a narrow little school."[6] When he embraced Steinerian anthroposophy and advocated the regeneration of the whole man, he fervently believed it could happen and never wavered from this view. Admittedly the references in Bellow's novel to the mediating rôle of the spiritual world are more skeptical, more tinged with irony and hedged in by qualification, than they are in Bely's fiction, but the parallels are nevertheless illuminating.

In *More Die of Heartbreak,* Bely's fiction is discussed in a long passage that lists some of the points of comparison between Russia at the turn of the century and contemporary America. Trachtenberg refers to the "mixture of barbarism and worn-out humanist culture," in both eras, the fascination with "a cerebral animalism or primitivism," the drug cults, the interest in sadomasochism, and concludes:

> A further similarity was the proliferation of a multitude of false worlds to whose rules people were earnestly committed. They could draw you along because they seemed to know what they were doing. All the while they were in a deep trance but still spoke authoritatively for the "real." A man like Bely's Ableukov, for instance, under the influence of a group of conspirators, agreed to plant a bomb in his father's bedroom. He didn't really want to be a parricide. An apparent ethical logic drew him on. But by and by it became evident that the metaphysics that had long supported the ethical order had crumbled away (p. 187).[7]

The allusion to Ableukov, the principal character in *Petersburg,* Bely's great examination of the question of Russia's national identity, directs our attention to what is most important in the passage. In that novel, too, the conflict between "west" and "east" as posed by Russia's history and culture is seen as a conflict between reason and order on the one hand, the irrational and the intuitive on the other. These elements are parts of both human and national consciousness in *Petersburg,* and their conflict reflects the need for a new ethical and metaphysical order. Steinerian anthroposophy suggests that Christ will function as the mediator between the opposing tendencies, but the general sense of gloom and disaster is much more prominent in the novel than are the signs of miraculous redemption. For Bellow's narrator, *Petersburg* is relevant because he constantly finds himself musing, in a lower, more meditative key, about similar sorts of questions: national identity, for example, and what the idea can mean to a Jew raised in Paris who teaches Russian in the

American midwest; the conflict between the rational and the irrational, particularly as it manifests itself in the sexual proclivities of his uncle and the other wandering souls of late twentieth-century America; the ordeals of "privation" and "desire" respectively that have resulted from this conflict; and the spiritual apocalypse that threatens his world just as surely as idealistic revolutionaries and anarchists threatened Russia at the beginning of the century. In addition, Bely uses Ableukov's rebellion against his father to suggest a revolt against Peter the Great himself, the father-figure who westernized his country and built the capital where the new revolution against his legacy of patriarchal authority threatens to break out. For Trachtenberg, this rebellion is an "intoxicating analogy" (p. 187) because of its "Oedipal" implications; that is, it combines the personal and the historical in a way that he finds compelling, given his own attempt to work himself out from under the influence of his father, and given the larger historical implications of the sexual battle between father and son. (This point will be discussed in more detail below.)

One of the things that makes *More Die of Heartbreak* so intriguing is the comprehensive quality of the Russian connection. Given his interest in Steiner, it is easy to see how Bellow would be drawn to figures like Blok and Bely. But Symbolism represents just one of a number of literary movements discussed in the novel. While visiting his mother at the refugee camp in Somalia, Trachtenberg also summarizes one of his articles called "The Morning of Acmeism," the title of which he has borrowed from an essay by Osip Mandelstam, the most important of the poets who reacted against the technical slackness and the general fuzziness implicit in the Symbolist schema. Mandelstam's brief essay is the best known manifesto for the poetic movement that came to be known as Acmeism. It stood for precision, equilibrium, immediacy, toughness, in contradistinction to the Symbolists' ethereal flights of fancy. As Clarence Brown has argued, "The 'logic' of the Acmeist aesthetic, and world view, rests upon a fairly unassailable basis, the Law of Identity itself, A is A. This is meant of course to strike at the root of the Symbolist method, the 'correspondences' themselves, which might be most simply expressed as A is Something Else."[8] Or as Mandelstam himself put it, in language that makes clear why Bellow would consider him a crucial literary antecedent for his own preoccupations: "We do not wish to divert ourselves with a stroll in the 'forest of symbols,' because we have a more virgin, a denser forest – divine physiology, the boundless complexity of our dark organism."[9]

Mandelstam reiterates this argument in the sentences from "The Morning of Acmeism" quoted in *More Die of Heartbreak:* "To be – that is the artist's greatest pride. He desires no other paradise than existence" (p. 98). This selection from the essay is noteworthy because it leaves out the rest of the second sentence, which continues: "and when he hears talk of reality he only smiles bitterly, for he knows the endlessly more convincing reality of art." Such a blanket assertion was no doubt deemed inappropriate for a novel in which Bellow insists on "the incompleteness of the art garment" (p. 119) and describes the humanities as "nursery games" (p. 247). But the excerpt from Mandelstam does enunciate in brief the law of identity that, for the Acmeists, binds together the poem, the world, and the universe itself. In articulating this identity, he implicitly rejects the Symbolists' notion of getting to some "more real reality," and rejects as well their egocentricity at a time when Russia most needed something other than a strictly individualistic view of human potential. So how are we to square this with all the references to all the versions of the Symbolist world just discussed?

No doubt it is Mandelstam's skepticism that appeals to Professor Trachtenberg, for as soon as the mystical tradition is introduced, the problem of pretense arises. As Bellow knows perfectly well, the mere mention of a spiritual world that exists alongside everyday reality invites a rush of imposters who pretend to have exclusive access to what the searcher is so earnestly investigating. Mandelstam's preoccupation with the precise detail and his acute sense of the individual as part of a larger community joined together by language and its ethical imperatives also allow him to serve in the novel as a counterweight to the Symbolists, and make him an appropriate alternative reference point for a novelist as immersed as Bellow is in the "complexities of our own dark organism." But beyond that, presumably, Mandelstam's links with European literature and culture, his Jewishness, his belief in the poet's obligation to educate not merely citizens, but "men," that is, citizens of a world culture – it is these qualities that make him such a significant figure in the book. Mandelstam's fate also hovers over *More Die of Heartbreak* in another way, since in this novel Bellow alludes a number of times to the crudity and brutality of the political regime that eventually condemned millions of Soviet citizens (including writers like Mandelstam) to concentration camps and death, and to "the ordeal of privation" that resulted from the ill-fated attempt to remake a whole country. Like Bellow, Mandelstam argues that the only way forward, the only way that will assure our survival as potentially compassionate, creative individuals, is some revitalized form of humanistic values. In 1923 he wrote:

That the values of humanism have now become rare, as if taken out of circulation and hidden, is by no means a bad sign. Humanistic values have merely withdrawn, concealed themselves, like gold currency, but like the gold reserves they secure the entire circulation in ideas of modern Europe, and their control is all the more powerful for being hidden.[10]

In all its variety, Russian literature for two centuries has circled around assumptions like this. What has happened since Mandelstam penned these desperately optimistic words has shaken the faith of those who share his assumptions, and in *More Die of Heartbreak* Bellow pits his humanities professor against the world to ask if such beliefs are still tenable.

Another strain in Russian literature of this period that finds all sorts of echoes in the novel is the preoccupation with sexuality. When, as a student in Paris, young Kenneth learns Russian and Russian mysticism at the feet of M. Yermelov, he hears all about "angelic love" and "human carnality," about how angels seeking to instill the warmth of love in us inadvertently do their work on the flesh and the instincts instead of the sentient soul, with catastrophic results: "Pure love is overcome by perversity. We become fixated on the sexual members. The angels failing, the physicians take over, as Plato foretold in the *Symposium*" (p. 73). Like most cultured Russians of his generation, M. Yermelov developed these ideas after reading Soloviev, the Russian philosopher and religious thinker who published his influential study of Plato in 1898. And we are told in the novel that Benn Crader is, at the instigation of his nephew, a great reader of Soloviev, particularly this book (p. 143).[11]

Soloviev devotes the concluding sections of his *Plato* to a study of Eros, which he sees as a Daemon that functions on two distinct levels:

The lower soul desires an infinite creation on the physical plane only – a negative, evil infinity, accessible solely to victorious matter; a constant repetition of the same fugitive phenomena, an eternal hunger and thirst without satiation . . . But what will the infinite power of Eros give to the higher intelligent soul? Will it direct it to the contemplation of the truly existent, ideal, cosmos? . . . [Plato] reaches the logically clear and very promising thought that the work of Eros, even in the best souls, is a substantial task, just as real as generation in animals, but immeasurably higher in its significance, in correspondence with the true dignity of man as an intelligent, wise and upright being. Having reached this point, Plato loses his way, as it were, and begins to wander in obscure paths without issue.[12]

The attempt to complete what Plato left undefined occupies Soloviev for the rest of the book, but he does not come up with much, and in the end contents himself with noting Plato's human fallibility in regard to Eros, and allowing for either "a reasonable measure of animal impulse"[13] or, failing that, asceticism (his choice in his own life), and, ultimately, the androgynous state that will attend the transformation of the human into the divine. It should not be surprising that, educated on speculations like these, Trachtenberg's uncle proves incapable of dealing with Della Bedell or Matilda Layamon. The gap that Plato was unable to bridge in his own life, and the gap that Soloviev chose not to bridge, except as a form of words, is the same one that separates Benn Crader from the world of desire into which his eager body keeps dragging him.

But, like the Symbolists, Soloviev has a philosophic counterpart in the novel, Vasilii Rozanov, one of the "sexual mystics" Trachtenberg teaches in a graduate seminar, the man who wrote that "The soul is passion"[14] and who scandalized family, friends, and acquaintances with the frankness of his treatment of sex. Andrei Sinyavsky, another Russian writer referred to in *More Die of Heartbreak,* characterizes Rozanov this way:

> No one before Rosanov wrote about sex in such an exalted and chaste manner, with so much of what I would call a believer's religiosity, with such piety. And that is precisely why – because of his respect for sex – Rozanov allowed himself to speak out on the theme of sex *so* openly and freely, including an attempt to understand the metaphysics of the sexual organs.[15]

Rozanov also insisted that man's desire to break taboos and his fascination with perversions were part of something incomprehensible to those who merely wanted to study it from the outside.

More Die of Heartbreak brings up to date this interest in sex, this frankness, this musing about its implications. The crucial scene occurs when Kenneth and his uncle go to a strip show in Tokyo. After performing the customary antics of their trade,

> each of the girls in turn stood, opened her knees, and dilated herself with her fingers. Dead silence. A kind of static insanity descended on the house. You could have drawn the lines of force straight from the eyes of the men into the center of desire, the chaste treasure fully opened. Everybody had to see, to see, to see the thing of things, the small organ red as a satin pincushion. . . . Miss Osaka and Miss Nara put it in front of you, as literal as it was possible to be, and the more literal it was, the more mystery there seemed to be in it. (pp. 107–08)

In effect, the strip show dramatizes Rozanov's metaphysics. By forcing the participants to focus on the female sex organs in such a blatant way, it demonstrates what any religion of sex must ultimately arrive at, the depersonalized worship of the object of desire, which is irrational self-abasement at the shrine of rational (i.e., profit-minded) self-abasement. Benn Crader is distinctly upset by this version of desire, because it implies for him an impossibly limited version of human potential. Steeped in Rozanov, his nephew is more willing to entertain it as a possibility, just as he is prepared to confront the various minimalist conceptions of the species he mentions in the novel: Freud's view of love as overvaluation, or Admiral Byrd's dismissal of man as poor, bare, forked animal, revealed in the Antarctic cold for the crude mechanism he is. If "to be seen literally dries out one's humanity" (p. 89), then here everyone is seen, both as they are and as sex reduces them metonymically. The oxymoronic language of the passage ("the more literal it was, the more mystery there seemed to be in it") suggests that here is the ultimate arcanum: that is, here is the symbol that stands for nothing but itself, that enables the viewers to see the truth about themselves and their desires, about the irrational self-abasement at the heart of this particular spiritual mystery. Rozanov on the washing of the genitals in the Jewish ritual bath, also alluded to in *More Die of Heartbreak,* sounds remarkably similar. He breathlessly discusses the *mikvah* for several pages in *Solitaria* and concludes: "Hence there is already a direct deduction concerning the 'secret sacred' that exists in the world; 'the sacred that *must be hidden*' and 'which *must never be named*'; the mysteries, *mysterium.* There is disclosed the origin of the very name, and there is cleared up the very 'body' of the mystery."[16] Rozanov is talking about a secret ritual, not a public show, but his subject is the same, the power that accompanies the mystery of desire.

Rozanov also figures prominently in the novel because he represents the one figure among all of Trachtenberg's "sexual mystics" who, in a sense, never does go beyond the sexual. Soloviev became an ascetic; Blok told his new bride that they would not need to be physically close, that that sort of thing was all darkness; Bely fled the temptations of earthly love with Nina Petrovskaya so as not to become a sullied prophet. But, unlike them, Rozanov did not flee women because he had no desires to create a new world or to remake those who inhabit this one. For him, to accept the nature of physical desire meant to accept one's quintessential humanity. One of his most perceptive critics, Renato Poggioli, discussing the fundamentally anti-utopian strain in Rozanov, remarks:

> Like Dostoevsky before him, he tried to show that any philosophy of
> social change is vain when it does not take into account, along with
> what can be changed, what can never be changed in man. In this
> sense, Dostoevski and Rozanov showed, better than anybody else,
> the factors of permanence and inertia, the ahistorical element of the
> human soul.[17]

This prognosis has proved to be one of their most troubling legacies.

The last author to be considered in this sampling of allusions to Russian writers is Alexandre Kojève, the émigré intellectual whose life and work represent a sort of synthesis of all the points of view examined thus far. He began as a young student by attempting to bring together Western philosophy and Buddhism, wrote a thesis in Germany on Soloviev, became one of the century's most important commentators on Hegel, and, having announced "the end of philosophy," retired to public life where he wrote a number of very perceptive reports as an expert on economic affairs for the French government. Kojève is also an appropriate choice for a crucial rôle in the novel because of his early interest in Russian mysticism, his Gallic taste for abstract reasoning, and a magnetic personality that brought his ideas alive for his listeners and made him by all accounts enormously attractive to women.[18] In *More Die of Heartbreak,* we are told that Trachtenberg got to know Kojève personally in Paris, where the Russian thinker would expound his neo-Heideggerian reading of Hegel and eat *rognon de veau.* Of particular interest is Kojève's commentary on Hegel's *Phenomenology,* parts of which Trachtenberg paraphrases to give us a flavor of the dinnertime conversation. The relevant section of the commentary he alludes to is a long "Note to the Second Edition" in which Kojève writes about his understanding of the "end of history."[19] In 1946, he had glossed Hegel's claim that "Nature is independent of Man" by denying that man's disappearance at the end of history was a cosmic or a biological catastrophe, since "man remains alive as animal in *harmony* with nature or given Being." The free, historical Individual" is annihilated, but Kojève insists that "art, love, play," everything that makes Man happy, remains unchanged and can be preserved indefinitely. But in a subsequent note, he disputes his own earlier conclusions. Now he sees man the animal as enjoying a very different art, love, and play, since these facets of his life would be as natural as birdsong, the copulation of adult beasts, and the frolicking of young animals. Man's language would become not the creative instrument that makes literature and philosophy but something analogous to the language of bees. Kojève then goes on to say that the end of history so conceived is not some Wellsian dystopia scheduled to arrive after many millenia but one that is already here:

> Observing what was taking place around me and reflecting on what had taken place in the world since the Battle of Jena, I understood that Hegel was right to see in this battle the end of History properly so-called. In and by this battle the vanguard of humanity virtually attained the limit and the aim, that is, the *end,* of Man's historical evolution. What has happened since then was but an extension in space of the universal revolutionary force actualized in France by Robespierre-Napoleon.

But Kojève also saw Japan as having evolved very differently from the west. Its life at the end of History, its three centuries devoid of wars, are in no sense characterized by an "animal existence," and this makes him revise his conclusions about post-historical man. The Japanese have disciplines that negate the natural man; they live according to formalized values, that is "values completely empty of all 'human' in the 'historical' sense."

Kojève's name is introduced during a discusion of Trachtenberg's father and his amatory exploits, and Bellow's narrator is clearly trying to bring together the metaphysical intricacies of the philosophy of history Kojève expounded with the flesh and blood characters playing out their rôles in his own personal history. This comes out in his attempt to see his Casanova-father as a World Historical Individual, who is to intercourse what Napoleon is to modern history:

> Now suppose that instead of Napoleonic armies you have women, instead of Jena you have bedrooms, instead of cannon you have you-know-what – then you begin to see Papa's life in a truer light. The historical thing which millions of sex-intoxicated men were trying to do and botching, he did with the ease of a natural winner. (pp. 36–37)

In the Hegelian scheme of things, taking all those women to bed is presumably Rudi Trachtenberg's unconscious acting out of Reason's great plan for men, his acquiescence to being an instrument of the World Spirit and an articulation of what History portends, an anticipation of what all men unconsciously aspire to. Bellow seizes on the comic implications of the analogy, but he does use it to insist on the importance of a "historical compass" of which "Eros is the fixed pole" (p. 37), and to suggest that "more die of heartbreak" because they are unable to orient themselves with such a compass. The experience in Japan at the strip show suggests that even Kojève's great exception needs serious qualification in this regard. And thus we come back to the truth that Rozanov in his very different way articulated. In the end, Kojève and his analysis of history must contend with the same obstacles that get in the way of all the other theories in the novel. If the ideals of liberal democracy triumph, thus freeing human beings to become acquisitive animals, there will still be Bellow's sort of history to live and to write. The need for love, the search for something other than happiness as an ideal, and the confrontation with one's own mortality remain the same.[20]

Of course, such a conclusion draws on traditional assumptions about language and values that Bellow has long defended and that most of his readers share. Those involved in the more austere kinds of formalistic criticism that have recently become popular in North American universities might well argue that all this is entirely too cosy, that *More Die of Heartbreak* is not so easily recuperated, that Trachtenberg's attempt to use literature as an arcanum ultimately reveals itself as mere emptiness and chaos. And if all the arcana turn out to be so many gaps that only seemed to offer a plenitude, then the cool, analytical approach that highlights precisely those empty, non-qualities of the text might well provide the most suitable vocabulary for describing its character. For example, the effect of the revolution that has taken place in regard to how literary texts should be read has been to "undermine the referential status of language,"[21] a problem that is repeatedly raised in a novel which muses about the problematic status of all literary texts in a world in which science and violence constantly threaten to reduce literature to the status of a plaything for the very naïve. The new new criticism has attempted to undo "the very comforts of mastery and consensus that underlie the illusion that objectivity is situated somewhere outside the self,"[22] which is something that Bellow's narrator also ponders in the course of assessing the nature of his involvement in the events he relates. Part of the novel's subversion bears upon the mechanistic or atomistic or homogenizing view of man that gives rise to such notions as objectivity in the first place. Those who contend that any text refuses "to offer any privileged reading,"[23] that it refuses to subscribe to "traditional values and concepts,"[24] that it instead reveals the gaps or silences in the middle of a cacophony of warring discourses, will similarly find much in *More Die of Heartbreak* to serve as grist for their mill. For such readers the novel will be the perfect example of an incoherent, self-contradictory text in which love is discussed as a panacea and dismissed as an illusion, marriage is seen as the inevitable outcome of a natural desire and a closed circle that isolates and destroys its victims, the mass of humanity is disdained as a collection of imaginatively stunted individuals and exalted as a group with infinite potential, each of whom is eminently capable of possessing absolute significance, and ideas are touted as essential for anyone hoping to function in the modern world and scorned as the quasi-random free association of intoxicated consciousness that gambols in a plethora of ideas that seem to lead nowhere. So, too, with the tendency to operate with tendentious and implicitly hierarchical dichotomies in which there is always a prioritized term: masculine/feminine, culture/nature, consciousness/unconsciousness. Every one of these paradigms is treated at considerable length in this extraordinarily wide-ranging novel. Think of all the opprobrium heaped on Matilda Layamon for her "masculine" qualities, the fake azalea as an index of Benn's failing perspicuity, and the contrast between the hyper self-consciousness of the narrator and the unreflective mental lives of the great unwashed masses he discusses. There is clearly a great deal in *More Die of Heartbreak* that would lend itself to this sort of discussion.

Yet the simpler, more traditional, explanation can deal with many of these questions as well. The congenial pluralist is happy to admit not only that the novel requires us to re-examine the set of critical assumptions we bring to it but also that it serves as its own auto-commentary. According to this view, an author called Bellow is still in control of his material, including the allusions to the literature(s) he knows so well. Too faithful to the complexities of the century he has chronicled so meticulously to trust in any kind of totalizing explanation, whether it be Symbolist, Acmeist or Hegelian, he thus makes *More Die of Heartbreak* his own wry commentary on the ultimate futility of the attempt to arrive at such an explanation. And despite the confusion, the self-contradiction, the emptiness at the center, the novel does dramatize the notion that ideas about the world remain crucial for simple survival. For Benn Crader, specialized knowledge saves him in the end because it allows him to retreat from the world and head off on a sensory-deprivation excursion to the Arctic. His nephew had not done particularly well in managing his own human relations, but his arcanum has provided a set of feelings that are at least cognate with those offered by more immediate human contact. He quotes Kojève on the "transfiguring intoxication" (p. 256) of loving someone, but he uses the same lexical register when thinking about the literary antecedents that comment instructively on the barbarous mind/body split that is his subject:

> It was esthetically intoxicating to entertain [all the associations]. Furthermore, it was characteristic – it was me: me as it excited me to be, fully experiencing the fantastic, the bizarre facts of contemporary reality, making no particular effort to impose my cognitions on them. (p. 253)

He has learned something about Eros both from his encounters with women *and* from his esthetic intoxications. His arcanum has also helped him to understand that, self-conscious about being at the end of an era, we compare ourselves to others who have felt the same, as for example the Russian writers he so avidly cites, only to realize that the great end or beginning or equilibrium or chain of being that their chiliastic inclinations made them see on the apocalyptic horizon can never exactly be ours. Yet we can learn from them, notwithstanding. A sense of reality that is adequate to our own time and place depends on believing that our irrational self-abasements, our confusions, our inability to see are only part of the truth, that the world's arcana can still intoxicate and teach those who care about the world of the spirit.

NOTES

1. *More Die of Heartbreak* (London: Penguin, 1988), p. 27. All subsequent references are to this edition and will be included in the text.

2. *Sobranie Sochinenii,* ed. V. N. Orlov et al., 8 vols. (Moscow and Leningrad: Gosudarstvennoe Izdatel'stov Khudozhestvennoi Literatury, 1963), 7: 69. All translations are my own unless otherwise indicated.

3. Blok, 7: 89.

4. "A. A. Blok," *Aleksandr Blok v vospominaniiakh sovremennikov,* ed. V. N. Orlov, 2 vols. (Moscow: Khudozhestvennaya Literatura, 1980), 2: 328.

5. Gorky, 2:331.

6. *Mezhdu dvukh revolyutsii* (Leningrad: Izdatel'stvo Pisatelei, 1934), p. 181.

7. Such a list serves to remind us that the differences between the two eras are at least as striking as the similarities. American culture in the eighties can

hardly be considered as brilliant and innovative as its pre-revolutionary Russian counterpart. America's current problems with potentially massive unemployment and the brutalization of the ghettos may well lead to the kind of revolt against civil authority that manifested itself in the strikes, assassinations and uprisings of the earlier era, but to posit an exact parallel would seem gratuitously apocalyptic at the moment. Even the "cerebral animalism" Trachtenberg refers to seems more typical of the late sixties than the eighties.

8. *Mandelstam* (Cambridge: Cambridge Univ. Press, 1973), p. 149.

9. *Sobranie Sochinenii,* ed. Gleb Struve and Boris Filippov, 4 vols. (New York: Interlanguage Literary Associates, 1971), 2: 323. Clarence Brown's translation, which I have used here, is included in *Mandelstam,* p. 145. Gumilyov, another of the Acmeists who figures in Trachtenberg's essay, puts it this way: "To revolt in the name of other conditions of existence here, where death exists, is as strange as for a prisoner to break down a wall when there is an open door in front of him. Here ethics becomes aesthetics, spreading to the last sphere. Here individualism in its highest strain creates community. Here God becomes the Living God, because man has felt himself worthy of such a God. Here death is a curtain dividing us, the actors, from the spectators, and inspired by our performance we despise the cowardly peeping to see what will come next." ("Acmeism and the Heritage of Symbolism," *Sobranie Sochinenii,* ed. Gleb Struve and Boris Filippov, 4 vols. [Washington: Victor Kamkin, 1968], 4: 174).

10. "Humanism and the Present," 2: 354.

11. Blok and Bely were both profoundly influenced by Soloviev, particularly his ideas about the conflict in the Russian soul between Europe and Asia. Soloviev was as disappointed as they were in the spiritual emptiness of his generation, and believed that a new man would be born of the coming crisis, a man who, Christ-like, had been purified through suffering.

12. *Plato,* trans. Richard Gill (London: Stanley Nott, 1935), pp. 64–66.

13. Soloviev, p. 71.

14. *Uedinennoe* (Petrograd: Novoe Vremya, 1916), p. 49.

15. *"Opavshie list'ya" V. V. Rozanova* (Paris: Sintaxis, 1982), p. 29.

16. Rozanov, p. 76.

17. *The Phoenix and the Spider: A Book of Essays about Some Russian Writers and Their View of the Self* (Cambridge: Harvard Univ. Press, 1957), p. 205.

18. A recent biography of Kojève tells of how he seduced and carried off the sister-in-law of Alexandre Koyré, distinguished émigré historian, who promptly set off to get her back. Yet once he had met and talked with the seducer, Koyré re-

linquished his objective, saying "The girl is right: he's much better than my brother" (Dominique Auffret, *Alexandre Kojève: La philosophie, l'état, la fin de l'histoire* (Paris: Grasset, 1990), p. 154.

19. *Introduction to the Reading of Hegel,* ed. Allan Bloom, trans. James H. Nichols, Jr. (New York and London: Basic Books, 1969), pp. 159–62.

20. In this regard, it is interesting to contrast the Hegel/Kojève view of Napoleon's victory at Jena with Rozanov's: "Humiliation always changes in a few days into a radiance of soul that cannot be compared with anything. It is not impossible to say that certain, indeed the very highest, spiritual illuminations are unattainable without preliminary abasement; that certain spiritual absolutes thus remain forever hidden from those who have perpetually triumphed, conquered, been on top. [new paragraph] How crude, *and hence also how unhappy* was Napoleon. . . . After Jena he was more pitiable than the holy beggar to whom those in a wealthy house say: God bless you" (*Uedinennoe,* 92).

21. J. Hillis Miller, "Deconstructing the Deconstructors," *Diacritics,* 5 (1975), p. 30.

22. Barbara Johnson, "Nothing Fails Like Success," *SCE Reports,* 8.4 (1980), p. 11.

23. Vincent B. Leitch, "The Book of Deconstructive Criticism," *Studies in the Literary Imagination,* 12 (1979), pp. 24–25.

24. Christopher Norris, *Deconstruction: Theory and Practice* (London and New York: Methuen, 1982), p. vii.

Beyond All Philosophies:
The Dynamic Vision of Saul Bellow

Eusebio L. Rodrigues

B Y 1975, the year *Humboldt's Gift* was published, Bellow had dis-
carded the great ideas and ruling orthodoxies of modern western
man. "I've had it," Charles Citrine asserts, "with most contemporary ways of philosophizing."[1] In the Nobel address (1976) Bellow
calmly announced, "With increasing frequency I dismiss as merely
respectable opinions I have long held – or thought I had – and try
to discern what I have really lived by and what others live by."[2]
This dismissal of established ways of looking at man and his
world, together with Bellow's gradual acceptance of other modes
of grasping the human mystery, led to a change of fictional direction. In *Humboldt's Gift,* Bellow throws off the modern belief that
man has a single existence that ends with death, the basic
assumption of the scientific and rational world-view. Charles Citrine comes to realize that death is not the final reality, that we are
not natural but supernatural beings who continue to live on in
mysterious ways that the Cartesian mind fails to understand.

Bellow's protagonists are terrified of death. Joseph, Augie
March, Henderson, and Herzog suffer from acute death anxieties.
Joseph, the first Bellow protagonist, suffers the most. For him,
death is *the* murderer who suddenly, inexplicably, snatches man
into nonexistence. His reading of Hobbes, of Diderot and the phil-
osophes of the Enlightenment, does not provide him with any
answer to the question of death.

The later protagonists, frantically wanting to escape from, but
forced to confront the brutal reality of death, reconcile themselves
to "the final fact of the material world" (*HG,* 436) by relying on their

161

intuitions and insights, guided by the Bible, and directed by western philosophical idealists and poets. Augie March rejects Machiavellian systems of power and instead derives from Emerson, Whitman, and Wordsworth a belief in the axial lines of truth, love, and harmony (the embrace of true people) that enables him to set aside his dread of fast change and short life. Tommy Wilhelm and Eugene Henderson come face to face with death, but they are consoled by Blakean and Romantic intimations that lead them to experience a feeling of human brotherhood and to sense the continuing vitality of mankind that death does not end. Herzog realizes that all his life he has been avoiding the stern reality of death. He gradually rejects the rational philosophers (Hobbes, Locke, and Bacon), throws off the prescriptions of Heidegger and the German existentialists, sweeps aside the wasteland outlook, and, taught by William Blake, accepts the need for love and human brotherhood, reconciling himself to the fact that he is a human being more or less. Herzog and Mr. Sammler both believe in God. Turning away from the great world systematizers (Toynbee, Freud, Burckhardt, Spengler, and Max Weber), Mr. Sammler seeks sustenance in the Bible and in the religious writers of the thirteenth century (Suso, Tauler, and, above all, Meister Eckhart). The awareness that there is in every human being a splash of God's own spirit allows Mr. Sammler to recognize the psychic unity of mankind, to accept the death of Elya Gruner, and to resist giving in to a sense of imminent apocalypse.

The Bellow protagonist, slowly questing for the truly human condition, desiring answers to fundamental questions about life and death, finds himself compelled, inexorably, to modify his view of human nature: he has to abandon the profane and reach out to the sacred.[3] In the profane world of *Dangling Man* (1944), *The Victim* (1947), and *Augie March* (1953), human nature has an animal base which the protagonist has to recognize and accept. This view of the animal core of human nature springs from Bellow's training in anthropology.[4] Man is, to adapt the title of the literary journal Bellow edited with Keith Botsford in 1960–62, a "noble savage." In the fourth issue of *The Noble Savage,* the editorial (unsigned) set forth its view of mankind: "not gods, not beasts, but savages of somewhat damaged but not extinguished nobility."[5] That is why Eugene Henderson goes to Africa, the original home of mankind, seeking a cure for sick humanity. King Dahfu, who has read William James's *Psychology* which states that "man is the most ruthlessly ferocious of beasts,"[6] reconciles Henderson to the animal in man and leads him to a Blakean truth about the human imagination, that it is the source of all human accomplishment, an endowment that can sustain, alter, and redeem mankind.

Similarly, undisturbed by the recent discoveries from the Olduvai Gorge in East Africa that man has descended from fierce carnivorous apes, Herzog believes that it is possible for mankind *"to live in an inspired condition, to know truth, to be free, to love another, to consummate existence, to abide with death in clarity of consciousness"* (*H*, 165). Before Mr. Sammler can reach out to the sacred by acknowledging the truth that there is in the heart of every human being a splash of God's own spirit, he accepts the criminality of our crazy species which mankind has managed to overcome. "'We are an animal of genius,'" proclaims Mr. Sammler (*MSP*, 305).

After 1970, Bellow abandons the view that man is merely a noble animal. The core element of his belief is now no longer man's animal base but that mysterious entity, the soul, an imperishable, deathless element. Rejecting the Greek term "psyche," Bellow uses the word "soul" for the immortal spirit in man. In the essay "A World Too Much With Us" (1975), Bellow puts his faith in an inadmissible resource for a writer, "something we all hesitate to mention though we all know it intimately – the soul."[7] Also, it is taboo, avers Bellow in the Nobel lecture, to talk about the spirit in our day ("NL," 325). But Charles Citrine cannot stop talking about the soul. Echoing Mr. Sammler, he refers to the need today "to listen to the sound of the truth that God puts into us" (*HG*, 477). It is "the core of the eternal in every human being" (*HG*, 438). Most people according to Citrine, are aware that the soul exists despite the prevailing scientific world-view: "The existence of the soul is beyond proof under the ruling premises, but people go on behaving as though they had souls, nevertheless" (*HG*, 479).

Bellow's protagonists are born with an intuitive knowledge of the soul which they forget but which their ordeals force them to remember. Augie March recovers the thrilling axial lines that had passed through his soul when he was a kid. In *Arnewi* land Henderson sees the pink light that had soothed his five-year-old soul in America, and he senses that he "might find things here which were of old, which I saw when I was still innocent and have longed for ever since, for all my life – and without which *I could not make it*" (*HRK*, 92).

Charles Citrine writes his account only after he has recovered his child's soul, his early and peculiar sense of existence (*HG*, 3). "I speak," he says confidently, "as a person who has lately received light" (*HG*, 177). Citrine had received this light in his eighth year in a sanatorium: "Owing to the TB I connected breathing with joy, and owing to the gloom of the ward I connected joy with light, and, owing to my irrationality I related light on the walls to light inside me" (*HG*, 65).[8] Light, in Bellow's later fiction, is a metaphor for the soul.[9] Bellow also uses the metaphor of a persistent voice that cries out from the very depths of one's being. In *Seize the Day*, Tommy Wilhelm listens to the promptings that arise from his soul telling him about the highest, the real business of life. Likewise, Henderson is driven to Africa by a voice that tortures him with its insistent demand, "I want, I want," but which will not tell him what it wants. Moses Herzog, too, is plagued by a voice within, one that demands order (*H*, 11). The ordeals Citrine goes through compel him to reject the intellectual route to a higher life which his friend, Richard Durnwald, places before him. Instead, Citrine decides "to listen to the voice of my own mind speaking from within, from my own depths" (*HG*, 186).

Listening to this voice within him, listening also to Humboldt's voice from beyond the grave which tells him we are supernatural beings, Citrine discovers that his world has become more spacious, that the topography of his universe is quite different from that of his brother protagonists. No longer is Africa the original home of mankind. Humboldt had sung about a home-world of glorious origin, believing that this earth was a "thrilling but insufficiently humanized imitation of that home-world" (*HG*, 24). Charles Citrine is convinced about the spiritual origins of man from which we have been exiled and to which we have to return.

Bellow presents both versions of man's origins in *Humboldt's Gift*. George Swiebel's trip to Africa is an affectionate parody, a dismissal of Henderson's journey. Like Henderson, Swiebel believes that Africa is "the place where the human species got its start" (*HG*, 447). He has visited the Olduvai Gorge and met Professor Leakey who has told him that Africa is where man came from. The letter to Citrine strongly, if ironically, contradicts this belief. It is not Africa but twentieth-century Chicago that is far removed from man's home-world: twenty-five murders occur here during a weekend; here also live mafia sharks and cannibals, like lawyer Pinsker. Things have changed for the worse as Africa plods along toward modern civilization: Atti is now a lioness jumping on wild pigs in Nairobi's game park; the naked Arnewi wear nightgown- and pajama-type costumes made on old foot-pedal Singer sewing machines found in every village; the primitive virtues of Romilayu have degenerated into the smooth cunning of Theo and Ezekiel (the names are highly ironic). *Humboldt's Gift* inverts the premise on which *Henderson the Rain King* is based: mankind, originally noble and good, now inhabits a fallen world and has to seek the home-world it has lost.

This supersensible spiritual world is invisible, but it can be sensed by those who are half blind: Queen Willatale and Mr. Sammler look inward into themselves to discover it with their damaged eye. That Bellow himself senses the existence of this mysterious world is clear in the interviews he has given and the statements he has made after 1975. In a 1979 interview, Bellow states that he is in the process of revising his view of the world and suggests that "we receive epistemological guidance of which we are unaware and that we actually have infinitely deeper and better ways of knowing than those we've been 'educated' in."[10] In the *Salmagundi* interview (1975), Bellow claims: "We think now that we are mortal and that we have only one life; we've given up all belief in an afterlife, and our time has become more valuable because of this."[11] In the Nobel lecture he maintains that "for every human being there is a diversity of existences, that the single existence is itself an illusion in part, that these many existences signify something, tend to something, fulfill something; it promises us meaning, harmony, and even justice" ("NL," 325).

Bellow faced the difficult problem of dramatizing in fiction his changed view of the world with its new belief in the soul, in man's home-world, and in the diversity of human existences. He felt drawn to the anthroposophical writings of Rudolf Steiner, who claimed to employ a spiritual-scientific method so as to achieve knowledge of the higher worlds. Steiner based his dynamic model of the universe on sources that include the writings of Goethe, the profound insights of the Vedic and Upanishadic seers, and, above all, the doctrines of the Sankhya system. Anthroposophy is an amplification of the three features of the Sankhya system, the primary system created by Indic thought.[12] The first is its pulsating, evolutive cosmology; the second, the proof it offers for the existence of the spirit by means of the *cogito* (one of the meanings of *sankhya* is reasoning); the third, according to Schweitzer, "the relation of the soul to the world of the senses in such a way that its imprisonment within that world and liberation from it will become comprehensible" (Schweitzer, 67). Bellow was apparently led to Steiner by his reading of Owen Barfield's *Saving the Appearances: A Study in Idolatry.*[13] He may have been drawn to anthroposophy by his own familiarity with some elements of Indic thought.

It is impossible to determine precisely where Bellow, who contributed to the *Syntopicon* of the great books of the western world, obtained his insights into Indic thought. He probably read Max Weber's book on the Indian religion (references to Max Weber abound in his writings), or else he may have absorbed some Indic ideas from his random dipping into *The Encyclopaedia of Religion and Ethics.*[14] Precipitations of his awareness of things Indian are found in his fiction. In the second paragraph of *Dangling Man* is a witty reference to Siva Nataraj, the king of dancers dancing his cosmic dance. Joseph comically laments: "If I had as many mouths as Siva has arms and kept them going all the time . . ." (*DM*, 9). Twice Bellow uses "Buddha" for purely descriptive purposes: Wilhelm has a "Buddha's head" (*Portable SB*, 75), while Humboldt's face is "Buddhistic," but not tranquil (*HG*, 20). The first talk session between King Dahfu and Henderson, after the Wariri rain festival, has many parallels to the scene in *The Bhagavad Gita* between Lord Krishna and Arjuna, just before the great battle of Kurukshetra.[15] Henderson sees King Dahfu against the background of concentric many-colored haloes; Lord Krishna deigns to manifest himself to Arjuna as a mass of radiating splendor. Both are guided by teacher figures, without whom, in Indic tradition, one cannot acquire spiritual wisdom, and without whose help, in Bellow's fiction, the protagonist cannot proceed on his quest. The Lord of the Universe teaches Arjuna, the human soul, a true philosophical wisdom, and thus he arouses the soul from deep spiritual despondency; King Dahfu bestows on Henderson his own deep faith in mankind and in the human imagination.

Bellow's later fiction, especially *Mr. Sammler's Planet* and *Humboldt's Gift*, contains terms like *purdah* (literally "curtain," seclusion of women), *chandala* (outcaste), *guru* (spiritual teacher, initiatory master), and *mandala* (literally "circle," a complex design manifesting an image of the universe and a theophany) (Eliade, 220). The later fiction refers to *karma*, *maya*, *nirvana*, and *yoga*, four basic and interdependent concepts that form the essence of Indian spirituality (Eliade, 3). Bellow uses three of these terms in a colloquial or popular sense. Henderson compares the pink light he sees in Arnewiland to "the fringe of Nirwana" (*HRK*, 92). Citrine is not familiar with the philosophy of *yoga* (which is the same as that of *sankhya*), but he does perform a *Hatha Yoga* physical exercise: he stands on his head, at one time to recover calm and stability (*HG*, 47), at another, merely to relieve his arthritic neck (*HG*, 9). His definition of *karma* is simple: paying for the evil of a past life in this one (*HG*, 171).

It is the concept of *maya* that has had perhaps the most significant impact on Bellow, whose Citrine is "perfectly sure that *this* could not be *it*" (*HG*, 89). One of Augie March's friends, Kayo Obermark, talks knowingly about it: "*Moha* – a Navajo word, and also Sanskrit, meaning opposition of the finite. It is the Bronx cheer of the conditioning forces. Love is the only answer to *moha*, being infinite. I mean all the forms of love, eros, agape, libido, philia, and ecstasy" (*AM*, 450). Citrine frequently mentions the painted veil of *maya* and refers to "the deluded human scene" (*HG*, 373). The full force of the concept of *maya* comes through in *Mr. Sammler's Planet*. Mr. Sammler, who considers himself an Asian (*MSP*, 116), and who knows that "Jews, after all, are Orientals" (*MSP*,

184), is fascinated by the philosophy of Schopenhauer, who often used *maya* for the illusory phenomenal world of individuality and multiplicity. In *The World as Will and Idea,* which Mr. Sammler read when he was 16, Schopenhauer writes about the all-supreme Unitary Will, that unseeable cosmic force. Whatever is manifest is, according to "Hindu philosophy – Maya, the veil of appearances that hangs over all human experience" (*MSP*, 209).

Bellow deliberately bypassed the rigorous Indic faiths and speculative systems with their deep disillusionment with human existence, and chose instead anthroposophy, a lightweight system created by Rudolf Steiner who amplified its Sankhya-base into an elaborate and dynamic spiritual cosmos and expounded a doctrine both "ethical and world and life affirming" (Schweitzer, 74). Bellow had read a number of Rudolf Steiner's writings. *Humboldt's Gift* mentions *Knowledge of the Higher Worlds: How it is Achieved?, Between Death and Rebirth,* the pamphlet "The Driving Force of Spiritual Powers in World History," and other Steinerian "texts." In the Epstein interview, Bellow states first that Rudolf Steiner "had a great *vision* and was a powerful *poet*" and goes on to add, "as well as philosopher and scientist."[16] In the same interview, Bellow admits that he is intrigued with Steiner but does not know enough "to call myself a Steinerian" (Epstein, 93). Citrine confesses that "in the learned world anthroposophy was not respectable" (*HG*, 276). We must remember that Citrine's Steiner must not be simply equated with Saul Bellow's Steiner, just as Citrine the narrator is not Saul Bellow the novelist.

Charles Citrine has been drawn to Steiner in two odd ways: first, through his affair with Doris Scheldt, whose father is an anthroposophist (she considers him a crank) from whom Citrine gets instruction; secondly, through his rationalist friend, Richard Durnwald, who jokingly suggested that Steiner had much to offer on the deeper implications of sleep. Steiner enters his life at a time when Citrine is on the verge of utter collapse: he is slowly being drained of his money by his lawyers, the IRS, his ex-wife, and his friends; his lovelife is in shambles, but he cannot break away from his current mistress, Renata; he is in a state of intellectual torpor and turns out books that do not sell and are remaindered; above all, he is terrified of the finality of death. He mistakenly thinks his love involvement with Renata will enable him to get rid of his death anxieties. It is the reading of Steiner that has a calming effect on Citrine: "Under the recent influence of Steiner I seldom thought of death in the horrendous old way. I wasn't experiencing the suffocating grave or dreading an eternity of boredom, nowadays" (*HG*, 220–21).

Citrine's reading of Steiner's views on spiritual-scientific knowledge, on death, immortality, and sleep, also stirs up some of the childhood intuitions that Citrine had forgotten under the pressure of his rational and scientific education. He had forgotten what he had always believed, that "we have ways of knowing that go beyond the organism and its senses" (*HG*, 228). Another opposing belief that Citrine has never held is that death is the end: he maintains that he has always "challenged and disputed the oblivion view" (*HG*, 347). He has never doubted he had an immortal spirit (*HG*, 109), a belief, he says comically, he had kept under his hat. His mother had inadvertently told him a Steinerian truth when he was a young boy, to the effect that the soul leaves the body when we sleep. "Mother was right," he claims (*HG*, 350).

Steiner reinforces many of the lifelong intimations of Citrine, who has read several books on anthroposophy given to him by Professor Scheldt, whom he (mistakenly) hails as his guru (*HG*, 261). He is deeply impressed when the professor talks to him about the evolution of the cosmos and of man. He appreciates the anthroposophical claim that "thinking makes it obvious that the spirit exists" (*HG*, 262).[17] He makes use of some of the meditative techniques recommended by Steiner in *Knowledge of the Higher Worlds,* which has become his "manual" (*HG*, 416).

Though fascinated by the doctrines of Steiner, Citrine realizes that his own knowledge is limited: "I was a beginner in theosophical kindergarten" (*HG*, 356); "I hadn't done my homework" (*HG*, 391). He goes to Dr. Scheldt for reassurance but knows he is not a completely believing Steinerian. He cannot shed the scepticism that his rational and scientific training has fostered in him. He dismisses certain esoteric mysteries as "spiritual hokum" (*HG*, 288) and then hails others as "poetry, a great vision" (*HG*, 439).

The anthroposophy of Rudolf Steiner is an essential constituent of the epic comedy that is *Humboldt's Gift* in that it provides Citrine, who rejects the prevailing scientific world-view, with some faith to which he can cling, but it does not provide the novel with a structure or a framework. Bellow has always felt a healthy distrust of theoretical programs. He refuses to allow his creative imagination to be imprisoned by any system: "Once you've given yourself over to one of these systems, you've lost your freedom in a very significant way" ("*Salmagundi,*" 19). "Writers are not cast in the role of philosophers," states Bellow ("*Salmagundi,*" 17). The artist, says Bellow, echoing Conrad, descends into his own self and discovers there what Proust terms "his true impressions," and what Bellow calls "persistent intuitions" ("NL," 321). Bellow's intuitions have been nourished by his reading of the Bible when he was a child, and by his later reading of Plato, St. Augustine, and Dante (Epstein, 93). Emerson, Whitman and the transcendentalists, Wordsworth, Blake and the romantics, the Jewish tradition, the poetry of Rilke, some elements of Indic thought – all these tributaries have fed and sustained the inner depths out of which Bellow's vision of life and his fiction spring.

Beyond all philosophies, western and eastern, Bellow's vision consists of charged insights and intuitions that he does not define (for that would be reductionist) but embodies in his fiction. His later fiction still seeks answers to fundamental questions but demands a "more comprehensive account of what we human beings are, who we are, and what this life is for" ("NL," 325). His vision has widened its spectrum to take in the full mystery of human life. The two essential elements of his dynamic vision are the powerful forces of love and the human imagination.

Even Joseph, the most defenseless of Bellow's protagonists, has a faint inkling that he would not seek the true human condition by himself for himself, but should discover it "in the company of other men, attended by love" (*DM*, 92). Asa Leventhal is aware that love exists, but he does not trust its power: "Would we have to be told 'Love!' if we loved as we breathed?" (*V*, 81). Kayo Obermark reinforces Augie March's belief in the axial lines by telling him that love can oppose the negative forces of *maya*.

Bellow's increasing faith in love as a dynamic power projects itself in *Seize the Day* and, more confidently, in *Henderson the Rain King*. In both novels, Bellow introduces the ideas and therapeutic methods of Wilhelm Reich as a form of structural camouflage to conceal what really happens to his protagonists.[18] Tommy Wilhelm does not know how he has achieved the "consummation of his heart's ultimate need" (*Portable SB*, 109). His heart needs love. Because of the demands of the world of business and success, money, having displaced love in his heart, "circulates" within his system. That is why he complains about hemorrhaging money (*Portable SB*, 36). It is only after all his money has been drained from him by his wife and by Tamkin that the healing power of love asserts itself.

Wilhelm has always been aware of this power (he senses it as energy) within him. "'A man is only as good as what he loves'," he tells Tamkin (*Portable SB*, 9). What he wants from his father is not money but love. The mere touch of his father's hand thrills "the foundations of his life" (*Portable SB*, 41). Dr. Tamkin stirs up the inner depths of Tommy Wilhelm. When the doctor asks him if he loves his father, Wilhelm feels "a great pull at the very center of his soul" (*Portable SB*, 85). The Reichian insights appeal greatly to Wilhelm, but what makes a greater impact are lines from poems by Shakespeare, Milton, Keats, and Shelley, lines that he recalls under the influence of Tamkin. These lines voice the needs of his soul and speak of natural human experiences, suffering, love, death, and the healing influences of nature. Even more profound and subterranean are the intimations about love that con man Tamkin casually tosses out. "I am at my most efficient," claims Tamkin, "when I only love" (*Portable SB*, 60). Tamkin's intimations percolate into Wilhelm's being, and he suddenly experiences in the subway a "blaze of love" and an "onrush of loving kindness" for his brothers and sisters (*Portable SB*, 78). The explosion deep within him that occurs when he sees the corpse in the funeral chapel, besides being a Reichian throat spasm, is also a realization of his heart's ultimate need, a gush of love that cleanses his system as he experiences a sense of communion with all mankind.

Henderson, too, experiences a throat spasm in the form of a sob as he starts to climb up the ladder of the hopo platform. More than just the dissolution of his chest armor, it is a release of all the bitterness and rage against his father that he had suppressed on the day of his brother's funeral. On another level, that of Henderson as mankind, it is a freeing of the despair about death and the terror of nuclear annihilation that modern man has locked within himself. The process of this release had begun in America with Lily's love. Lily had asked Henderson whether he knew what love *could* do? (*HRK*, 14) Henderson discovers the answer in Africa: "It's love that makes reality reality" (*HRK*, 259). In the plane on the way back to America, Henderson makes an astounding discovery: "Once more. Whatever gains I *ever* made were *always* due to love and *nothing else*" (*HRK*, 307, italics added). It is not the shot in the arm from animal nature or the Reichian therapy that has changed Henderson but the spirit of love that King Dahfu instilled in him that has cleansed his heart and calmed that all-demanding voice. The "something of the highest importance" that Henderson bears back for his fellow men is the message of love and of human brotherhood (*HRK*, 18).[19]

Citrine, too, has a message of the utmost importance for mankind. He is in a hurry to tell the whole world about the tremendous change in his life. He narrates his account almost immediately after his experiences, so that he has not had the time to reflect on or distance them. As narrator, Citrine knows he has changed but does not know how the change happened.

The profound change in Citrine appears to be the result of his involvement with anthroposophy but really has been wrought by love, that powerful force that works in mysterious ways. A favorite Bellow quotation is from Simone Weil: those whom we love, exist. In *Humboldt's Gift* those who love and those whom we love not only exist but help each other in ways that go beyond ordinary understanding. The anthroposophical framework of Rudolf Steiner with its cosmic hierarchies, like the elaborate character armor system of Wilhelm Reich, proves to be a smokescreen that hides the operation of a real spiritual force, love.

Citrine ends the first paragraph of *Humboldt's Gift* with the statement, "I always loved him," a declaration repeated two or three times in his account. So powerful is the "ecstatic connection" (*HG*, 477) between the two friends (Citrine and Humboldt) that, despite their disagreements, it sets in motion certain forces that change Citrine's life. In December, 1973, when Citrine is on the verge of collapse, help arrives in the form of Rinaldo Cantabile, a manic manifestation of Humboldt. Cantabile is *not* a reincarnation of Humboldt, for, according to both Indic tradition and Steiner, a vast stretch of time is needed for the return to earth.[20] Bellow adapts and transforms the idea of metempsychosis, daringly linking it with love, for his own fictional purposes. "Be sure if there is a hereafter I will be pulling for you," Humboldt had written in his letter (*HG*, 347). Cantabile, a strange emanation of Humboldt's love, rescues Citrine from complete disaster.

Bellow establishes the connection between Humboldt and Cantabile — difficult for the western mind to accept, easier for the Jewish and oriental sensibilities to acknowledge — in many ways. Citrine is powerfully drawn to Cantabile. At their very first meeting he becomes aware that a "natural connection" exists between them (*HG*, 91). He senses that they are united by a "near mystical bond" (*HG*, 287). The parallels between Humboldt and Cantabile are many. Like Humboldt, Cantabile is a fanatical schemer. Both drive elegant cars, and their driving habits are similar: Humboldt tailgated other drivers; Cantabile rides the bumpers of the car ahead, forcing the motorist to chicken out. Both carry guns to exercise threats of vengeance. Both celebrate their triumphs by spending the night with girls. Cantabile hails Citrine as his "pal," a term used by Citrine for Humboldt.

What happens to Citrine after December, 1973, has to be understood in the context of his earlier involvement with Humboldt. Citrine was Humboldt's protegé, and they had both exchanged blank signed checks which, according to Humboldt, had interknitted them as blood brothers. Citrine did not understand the significance of this ritual-like covenant because he did not understand that money has assumed a demonic power in the modern world, usurping the place of blood and love in the human heart. Both friends break their covenants: Humboldt cashed Citrine's check for over $6000 at a time when Citrine was grieving the death of

Demmie; Citrine doesn't go to see Humboldt at Bellevue and avoids speaking to him two months before Humboldt's death.

Humboldt/Cantabile forces Citrine to undergo symbolic shock treatments that make him realize the truth about himself. Cantabile has to awaken Citrine from the slumber that has sealed his spirit. Citrine at first cannot understand what Cantabile hurls at him: "I'm not sleeping, why should you be?" (HG, 37); "You don't know what you're into. Or who I am. Wake up!" (HG, 86). Cantabile then proceeds to bash in an extension of Citrine's false sleeping self, the Mercedes Citrine had bought under the influence of Renata. He forces Citrine to experience in the Russian Bath the same stink Humboldt had to smell when he had diarrhea on the way to Bellevue. His stratagem of passing Citrine off to Stronson as his hit man parodies Humboldt's absurd scheme of sending Citrine to Ricketts as his emissary, a scheme to which Citrine had agreed with great reluctance. Cantabile sends Denise a death-threat note, causing Judge Urbanovich to have Citrine post a bond of two hundred thousand dollars, thus draining the money-poison from Citrine's system and hastening the process of his separation from Renata. By sailing away Citrine's fifty-dollar bills, Cantabile demonstrates in action what Humboldt warns Citrine about in words: "Don't get frenzied about money" (HG, 247).

Cantabile also stirs up and sets in motion the forces of love in Citrine's past that help in the rescue. The rendezvous at the Russian Bath (where Citrine used to go with his father as a kid) and the events of the "day of atonement" (HG, 103) compel Citrine, who knows that Plato links recollection with love, not merely to meditate in Steinerian fashion, but to recall and re-evaluate his past. He realizes that he has sinned against Humboldt. The talks and meetings with Naomi Lutz, Menasha and Julius allow Citrine to recapture the world of childhood he had forgotten. Naomi Lutz was his first love: "I loved you with my soul," he tells her (HG, 213). Menasha, who had loved and protected Citrine as a child, urges Uncle Waldemar, who had looked after Humboldt, to give Citrine Humboldt's papers. "Love made these things unforgettable," claims Citrine (HG, 330). The visit to his brother, Julius, brings back "the conditions of childhood under which my heart had been inspired" (HG, 396). It awakens in him the "love fever" for the whole family that he had experienced in the sanatorium as a child.

Humboldt's representatives gather around Citrine. Huggins, Humboldt's friend, sets in motion another set of events that lead to Citrine's getting Humboldt's gift. His message is conveyed by Kathleen, Humboldt's wife. Thaxter, Citrine's own protegé and friend, whose "eccentricities would eventually reveal a special spiritual purpose" (*HG*, 247), cons Cit-rine into going to the Ritz in Madrid, thus tearing him away from Renata and Milan. The trip to Corpus Christi to visit Julius also separates Citrine from Renata. She acknowledges that Citrine's "passion for Von Humboldt Fleisher speeded the deterioration of our relationship" (*HG*, 432).

Love, generated by Humboldt and his representatives who appear whenever Citrine needs them, swirls through his inner being. He realizes that "love is a power that can't let us alone. It can't because we owe our existence to acts of love performed before us, because love is a standing debt of the soul" (*HG*, 190). But he has no need, after the Paris visit, for Cantabile, who reverts to being a mafia hoodlum. For Humboldt's letter, "an act of love" (*HG*, 351), pierces Citrine's soul. The postcard-poem had alerted Citrine to the savior-faculty of the imagination. The letter, the gift of a poet, restores "the early talent or gift or inspiration" (*HG*, 178) of a brother poet who had lost faith in the imagination. Humboldt quotes from Blake to make Citrine aware of a "World of Imagination and Vision" (*HG*, 347). The infusion of love and inspiration awakens Citrine's Orphic powers and will allow him to fulfill his true mission. He had to use his imaginative soul to "recover living thought and real being" (*HG*, 250). He can now blow imagination's trumpet to rouse mankind from its slum-ber. Citrine sets about his task by first writing this account.

Bellow's faith in the soul and in the imagination as a way of knowl-edge continues in *The Dean's December,* yet another experimental novel like *Mr. Sammler's Planet,* one that widens Bellow's fictional world in that it seeks to present and explore great public, not merely personal, matters. Death is still the problem of problems, the death of human be-ings, and also the death of cities. Dean Corde knows that at the moment of death the soul is loosened, ready to be set free. His response is a dec-laration: "I also love you, Valeria" (*DD*, 128). The use of "also" implies a form of bonding: Corde enters into the love-relationship between mother and daughter and continues it. The death and anarchy of Chicago, Corde comes to realize, cannot be analyzed and explained as he had tried to do in the two sociological articles he wrote for *Harper's.* It can only be understood and accepted after it has passed through a soul that had been strengthened by the vision of poets who have always seen beyond this world of shadows. Leaving Hell, Dante saw the stars again (*DD*, 78). Corde, at Mount Palomar, can see only distortions, like the ones he saw in the Chicago slums, not stars. But the wartime letters of Rilke, who was aware of human doom, reassure Corde of the presence of stars and of hope. That will pass, wrote Rilke, who knew that behind fate and a sense of impending disaster lay "the all-surviving stars."[21]

Bellow's vision, even at this stage of his career, cannot be circumscribed, for he is continually widening its range even as he extends his fictional universe. Four elements, soul, heart, love, imagination, melt and flow into each other to form a glowing, pulsing center that seeks to throw light on the human mystery. Philosophers, intellectually arrogant, impose a pattern on the universe man lives in, attempting to make all things blindingly clear. Bellow, sure of the gift of poetry he has been endowed with, accepts the mystery of existence and, with his protagonist Citrine, calmly proclaims (*HG,* 52): "Humanity divine incomprehensible!"

NOTES

1. Saul Bellow, *Humboldt's Gift* (New York: Viking, 1975), p. 356. Hereafter, page numbers will be cited in the text with the abbreviation *HG.* The following abbreviations will be cited in the text for other novels by Saul Bellow: *DM* for *Dangling Man* (New York: Vanguard, 1944), ; *AM* for *The Adventures of Augie March* (New York: Viking, 1953); *Portable SB* for *The Portable Saul Bellow,* introduced by Gabriel Josipovici (New York: Penguin, 1977), which contains the complete text of *Seize the Day* with minor text corrections by Saul Bellow; *HRK* for *Henderson the Rain King* (New York: Viking, 1959); *H* for *Herzog* (New York: Viking, 1964); *MSP* for *Mr. Sammler's Planet* (New York: Viking, 1970); *DD* for *The Dean's December* (New York: Harper and Row, 1982).

2. Saul Bellow, "The Nobel Lecture," *American Scholar,* 46 (Summer 1977): 324. Hereafter page numbers will be cited in the text with the abbreviation "NL."

3. The terms "sacred" and "profane" are taken from Mircea Eliade's book on the nature of religion, *The Sacred and the Profane,* trans. from the French by Willard R. Trask (New York: Harcourt Brace & Jovanovich, 1959).

4. Bellow graduated from Northwestern University with honors in anthropology and sociology in 1937.

5. "Arias," *The Noble Savage,* 4 (Chicago, 1960), p. 5.

6. William James, *The Principles of Psychology* (Chicago: Encyclopaedia Brittanica, 1952), p. 717.

7. Saul Bellow, "A World Too Much With Us," *Critical Inquiry, No. 1 (Autumn, 1975): 8.*

8. Herzog is eight years old when he is in the children's ward of a hospital in Montreal where a Christian lady had come once a week and had had him read aloud from the Bible (*H*, 22).

9. In *To Jerusalem and Back* (New York: Viking, 1976), Bellow refers to the filtering and purifying powers of the light of Jerusalem: "I don't forbid myself the reflection that light may be the outer garment of God" (p. 93).

10. Maggie Simmons, "Free to Feel," *Quest* (February/March 1979): 34.

11. "Literature and Culture: An Interview with Saul Bellow," *Salmagundi* (Summer 1975), p. 11. Hereafter cited in the text as "*Salmagundi*."

12. For a good introduction to Sankhya, see *Hindu Theology: A Reader*, edited with an Introduction and Notes by José Pereira (New York: Image Books, 1976). For *karma* and rebirth, see *Karma and Rebirth in Classical Indian Tradition*, ed. Wendy Doniger O'Flaherty (Berkeley: Univ. of California Press, 1980). For *yoga* see *Yoga: Immortality and Freedom* by Mircea Eliade (New Jersey: Princeton Univ. Press, 1970), hereafter cited as Eliade. For the Indian influence on Rudolf Steiner, see Albert Schweitzer, *Indian Thought and its Development* (Boston: Beacon, 1957), cited in the text as "Schweitzer."

13. (London: Faber and Faber, 1965). The book refers cursorily to Steiner on pp. 140–141, 147. Barfield has written extensively on anthroposophy and on Rudolf Steiner. See "A Bibliography of the Works of Owen Barfield," in *Evolution of Consciousness*, ed. Shirley Sugerman (Connecticut: Wesleyan Univ. Press, 1976). Saul Bellow has recently written a foreword to *The Boundaries of Natural Science* (New York: Anthroposophic Press, 1983), a collection of eight lectures Rudolf Steiner had given in Switzerland in 1920.

14. Max Weber, *The Religion of India* (Glencoe, Illinois: Free Press, 1958). Mr. Sammler and Citrine occasionally read *The Encyclopaedia of Religion and Ethics*, ed. James Hastings (New York: Scribner's, 1908). Also, see *MSP*, 229, and *HG*, 175. In the *Salmagundi* interview (p. 9), Bellow jests that he opens this "strange set of books" when he wants to discover what people are doing on the west coast.

15. Wm. Theodore de Bary, ed., *Sources of Indian Tradition* (New York: Columbia Univ. Press, 1969), I, 288–89.

16. Joseph Epstein, "A Talk with Saul Bellow," *New York Times Book Review*, (December 5, 1976): 93, cited in the text as "Epstein." Herbert J. Smith, in "*Humboldt's Gift* and Rudolf Steiner" (*Centennial Review*, 22 (1979): 479–89), summarizes the basic tenets of anthroposophy and tries to show that Citrine's character is altered but not transformed by his anthroposophical experiences.

17. Pereira (p. 70) quotes from Vijnana Bhiksu: "The experience 'I know' is a general proof of the existence of Spirit, as no means of knowledge contradicts it."

18. For Reichianism in *Seize the Day* and in *Henderson the Rain King,* see my articles, "Reichianism in *Seize the Day,*" in *Critical Essays on Saul Bellow,* ed. Stanley Trachtenberg (Boston: G. K. Hall, 1979), pp. 89–100; and "Reichianism in *Henderson the Rain King,*" *Criticism,* 15 (1972): 212–33.

19. For a detailed account of Henderson's transformation by love, see my article, "Saul Bellow's Henderson as Mankind and Messiah," *Renascence,* 25 (Summer 1983), pp. 235–46.

20. Steiner speculates that the period of time between death and a new birth takes approximately 2100 years. See Rudolf Steiner, *An Outline of Occult Science* (Spring Valley, New York: Anthroposophic Press, 1972), p. 373.

21. Rainer Maria Rilke, *Wartime Letters 1914–1921,* trans. M. D. Herter (New York: Norton, 1964), pp. 21–22.

Disconnectedness in
The Bellarosa Connection

Marilyn R. Satlof

A RTHUR HERTZBERG, in his latest book *The Jews in America: Four Generations of an Uneasy Encounter,* poses this question: "How will American Jews affirm their Jewishness?"[1] Sorella Fonstein, a character in Saul Bellow's book *The Bellarosa Connection,* poses the question more starkly: "The Jews could survive everything Europe threw at them. . . . But now comes the next test — America. Can they hold their ground, or will the U.S.A. be too much for them?"[2] In this novella Bellow depicts several dangling men who, through a loss of communal memory, have become alienated from the Jewish people. Judaism itself stresses memory with both Biblical and rabbinic injunctions. According to Yosef Hayim Yerushalmi, the Hebrew word *zakhar* "remember," reverberates throughout the Bible "no less than one hundred and sixty-nine times, usually with either Israel or God as the subject — for memory is incumbent upon both."[3] Judaism and its collective memory are inexorably bound by the covenant, which God insists binds not only those who stood before Him on that momentous day at Sinai but also all succeeding generations. In post-Biblical literature Rabbi Akiba warns his fellow Jews not to separate themselves from their community, from the sense of their past.

Gullette speculates that Bellow's protagonists often match his own chronological age and concerns.[4] In *The Bellarosa Connection* Bellow, now seventy-five, presents the reader with a seventy-two year old nameless narrator whose isolation is exacerbated by his loss of group memory. Bellow himself recalls wearing the ritual *tallith* under his clothes as a child (a remembrance of God's 613

177

commandments) and describes Hassidic Jews still wearing *tallisim* 4,000 years after Sinai. He writes movingly of the bond forged among Jews through their communal prayers. He even feels momentarily guilty eating his *traif* chicken when seated next to a fervent Hassid. But when the British Airways plane lands in Tel Aviv, Bellow acknowledges a seemingly unbridgeable gap as the Hassid sees in Bellow "what deformities the modern age can produce in the seed of Abraham" and Bellow views the Hassid as "a piece of history, an antiquity."[5]

The narrator's plight in *The Bellarosa Connection* is immediately made ironic since his personal fortune was based on his "innate gift of memory" (p. 2). He has trained business executives and government officials to transform their minds into memory banks at his Mnemosyne Institute. Now at the end of a sterile use of his gift, he becomes aware of "feelings," "longings," "emotional memory" (p. 3). A widower, he is ensconced in a twenty-room museum of a house replete with eighteenth-century furnishings selected by his Christian wife. In an attempt to enter more deeply into his late wife's thoughts and world, he reads books left on her night table. He compares his wife's readings in her last years with the mystical readings absorbed by Poe's Morella, who was obsessively concerned whether the *principium individuationis* was irretrievably lost with one's death and who predicted her own resurrection: "I am dying yet shall live."[6] "Kore Kosmu," one of his wife's bedside readings, is an excerpt found in *Hermetica,* a collection of writings allegedly based on the teachings of the Egyptian Hermes Trismegistus. In "Kore Kosmu" Isis reveals to her son Horus the Egyptian story of creation, death, and resurrection. Guilty souls become incarcerated in bodily forms from which they are released to the ether upon death if they have led blameless lives on earth. The now cleansed souls have the potential of becoming star gods or gods themselves.[7] The *Zohar,* also found on her night table, is a mystical attempt at connecting the individual soul with the Godhead after death.

In each of these cases the concentration is on the individual, not the community. In contrast, the narrator's allusion to the equally mystical Book of Ezekiel evokes a horrifying picture of the dry bones of a people followed by the hope of their collective redemption and rebirth. While trying to reconnect with his emotional memory, and thus his group memory, the narrator retrieves a photograph of the Fonsteins posed against a Judaean desert backdrop, "the burning stones of Ezekiel, not yet (even today) entirely cooled, those stones of fire among which the cherubim walked" (p. 79). After wondering if the trip to Israel has been memorable to the Fonsteins – Harry, the Holocaust survivor, and

Sorella, its messenger – the narrator further wonders if there is anything worth remembering. Elie Wiesel, reflecting on the Book of Ezekiel, feels that the messenger Ezekiel has enabled each succeeding generation of Jews to have hope. Ezekiel's vision of Israel's resurrection as a people is indeed probably more relevant to Wiesel's generation than to Ezekiel's own generation in that his generation has itself seen the valley of dry bones and yet has held fast to the consolation that the dry bones will be resurrected.[8] The narrator, in recalling the Fonsteins, must differentiate between "literal and affective" memory; he must erase the Fonsteins as mere data and reconstitute them as connectors to their mutual heritage.

Earlier in his life his father had sought to wean him from his American rootlessness through listening to refugee Fonstein's story. In a seemingly convoluted relationship, Fonstein is the nephew of the narrator's stepmother and thus part of the Jewish family unit, *mishpocha.* And family member Fonstein had, after all, "survived the greatest ordeal of Jewish history" (p. 7). In an echo of Bellow's imagined personal summation by the Hassid on British Airways, the narrator imagines that Fonstein sees him as "an immature unstable American . . . something new in the way of human types" (p. 7). Later the narrator ponders the Americanization of Jews. Eight inches taller than his father, he feels his father views this additional height negatively. After all, King Saul, who was taller than the average Israelite, did not find favor in God's eyes. The narrator, however, glories not only in his size but in the quick Americanization realized by Jews. Another assimilated Jew, Gertrude Stein, had philosophized: "It has always seemed to me a rare privilege, this, of being an American, a real American, one whose tradition it has taken scarcely sixty years to create. We need only realise our parents, remember our grandparents and know ourselves and our history is complete."[9] But short, gimpy, Mitteleuropean Fonstein occasionally relates his stories in Yiddish, the appropriate language for their transmission. In "My Friend Saul Bellow," Alfred Kazin defines Yiddish as the "life thread of a cultural and religious tradition," and Bellow, he asserts, is "lovingly connected with the religious and cultural tradition of his East European grandfathers."[10] At the end of listening to the serialized account of Fonstein's wanderings in Nazi Europe and his rescue from death in Italy through the efforts of Broadway Billy Rose (the Bellarosa Connection), the narrator's unspoken advice to Fonstein is "Forget it. Go American" (p. 29). The narrator thus becomes the prototype of the "reality" commentators about whom Elie Wiesel writes, friends who berate survivors for retaining their memories.

Ten years later the narrator and the Fonsteins meet by accident in Jerusalem. The narrator, by now a successful memory trainer and husband of a Philadelphia Main Liner, is considering opening a branch of his Mnemosyne Institute in Israel. With the father-son quarrel engendered by his inter-marriage, followed by his father's death, the narrator has severed all tenuous ties to his family in New Jersey. "I was a Philadelphian now, without contacts in New Jersey. New Jersey to me was only . . . psychic darkness" (p. 38). Symbolically, while he has established outposts in Taiwan and Tokyo, "Mnemosyne didn't take root" (p. 50) in Israel. Jerusalem, however, recalls him momentarily to his own roots as he speaks of the mystery evoked by Jerusalem. Elie Wiesel calls Jerusalem "a miraculous city reaching into heaven,"[11] and Bellow autobiographically reflects that the light of Jerusalem "may be the outer garment of God."[12] Taking an uncharacteristic moment out for ethnic reflection, the narrator traces the Jewish people from their inception as a people under Moses through Judges to Prophets to Rabbis to the "end of the line" in "secular America (a diaspora within a diaspora)" (p. 37). John Clayton traces this diaspora, providing points of reference from *Herzog:* "The *diaspora* – the scattering of the Jews into exile – is threefold: from the promised land to the shtetl, from the shtetl to the Jewish slum (Napoleon Street in *Herzog*), from the ghetto to the modern world (Chicago in *Herzog*)."[13] The modern-world narrator in *The Bellarosa Connection* has been disconnected in the process, dislocated, "he couldn't say what place he held in this great historical procession" (p. 37).

While Rosh Hashanah marks the birth of the world to traditional Jews, Passover marks their beginning as a people. At each Seder since the exodus, Jews in collective remembrance have intoned their gratitude to God for delivering them from Egyptian bondage "with a mighty hand." The narrator alludes to this holiday on two occasions. In Jerusalem, where Sorella has come to force Billy Rose to accept her husband's gratitude for his deliverance, the narrator sarcastically compares the unsavory Rose with God. Although he recalls the Hebrew wording, *byad hazzakah* ("with a mighty hand") from his youth, he does not seek to restore his connection with Jewish history. After his encounter with the Fonsteins in Jerusalem, he does not attempt to communicate with them for thirty years. While he had sometimes thought of inviting them for Passover, the Seder is no longer part of his life: "But that's what the Passover phenomenon is now – it never comes to pass" (p. 67). The word "pass" in this sentence is more than a Bellovian play on words. The Hebrew expression *vayehi* ("and it came to pass") is a repetitive, almost formulaic one which serves as a transition for the reader of Torah as he moves from one Biblical narrative to another. The allusion is thus a significant one: with the loss of transition, American Jews have lost their communal memory; they have severed their ties with their beginnings. To quote Milan Kundera, another post-Holocaust expert in memory, "The first step in liquidating a people . . . is to erase its memory."[14] Interestingly, the narrator blames his photogenic memory for his failure to contact the Fonsteins. Like his early lessons in religious school, they are frozen in his memory. He has no real need to bring them to life; they have been safely consigned.

Bellow moves the narrator from Passovers no longer observed and frozen relations to a spring thaw and a reconnection with Judaism via a modern medium—the telephone. Ironically he is recalled to Judaism while searching for a poem by George Herbert, "The Flower," which Christologically allies spring renewal with Jesus's resurrection. In conversation the narrator learns that a rabbi whose "ministry" is Jerusalem has been approached by another Fonstein Holocaust survivor who wants to locate Harry Fonstein. The modern rabbi, perhaps Reform, perhaps Conservative, uses a trite motivator when he assures the narrator that finding Harry would be a *mitzvah,* an observance of the commandment concerning good deeds. In a beautiful amalgamation, the narrator interiorizes an oath: "Christ, spare me these *mitzvahs*" (p. 69). He delays attempts to find the Fonsteins, however, as he grapples with a temporary loss of memory—he had been unable to recall the river in Stephen Foster's song. "A bridge was broken: I could not cross the ——————— River" (p. 71). "Swanee River" lyrically depicts the longing to return home. The narrator will not only recall the name of the river; he will eventually repair the bridge and cross the river.

Since the rabbi had suggested that the Fonsteins had moved, the narrator begins his search by recalling old family names and then calling various members. Rejected by them for his thirty-year neglect, he feels completely isolated, albeit his isolation was self-imposed: "At times I feel like a socket that remembers its tooth" (p. 79). While in conversation with equally isolated Hyman Swerdlow, the narrator pictures Swerdlow's correct Brooks Brothers attire and understated Wasp manner: "One could assimilate now *without* converting. You didn't have to choose between Jehovah and Jesus" (p. 81). Swerdlow has managed to exorcise his Jewishness. "Your history, too, became one of your options. Whether or not having a history was a 'consideration' was entirely up to you" (p. 82). Swerdlow, however, serves as a link to the Fonsteins when he suggests they may still be found in the directory.

Bellow now introduces a wonderful digression, a dream sequence which serves as a communication to the narrator. His whole life had been predicated on a false assumption, "a lifelong mistake: something wrong, false, [was] now fully manifest" (p. 87). Although he musters every strength he possesses, in the dream the narrator finds himself unable to escape from a pit, a trap dug by an unknown person. He equates his unsuccessful struggle with Harry Fonstein's struggle to escape from Nazi Europe, a struggle from which he had previously divorced himself. After all, he was not a Mitteleuropean Jew, he was an American Jew and thus invincible, "a Jew of an entirely new breed" (p. 89). In *To Jerusalem and Back* Bellow boldly states that "Jews, because they are Jews, have never been able to take the right to live as a natural right . . . not even in the liberal West."[15] The narrator awakens to the burning lights of his night table lamps. At an earlier point he had noted the unusual shape of the lamps, like thorn bushes, but as long as he perceived them as his wife's lamps flanking the sides of their Wasp-Jewish bed, they had merely been objects of art which cast insufficient reading light. After the dream he is struck by their Biblical association. He is reminded of the near sacrifice of Isaac by Abraham, whom he now refers to with the traditional phrase "Abraham *avinu*," our patriarch Abraham, and of the substitution of the ram caught in the thicket. The allusion to God revealing Himself to Moses through a burning bush floats through the air. While fragments of Jewish history assail him, the totality and his connection still elude him. The need to reestablish contact with the Fonsteins, "where my heart apparently was yearning ever" (p. 91), becomes more urgent.

A friend of the Fonsteins' son, and Gilbert, their own promising son, are two minor dangling men in the novella. The friend, who answers the narrator's call to the Fonstein house, agrees with the narrator that there is nothing unusual about disconnectedness as practiced in America. People are able to isolate themselves from family members and fantasize a sustained relationship. Concentrating solely on developing his American persona, the friend sees no need to concern himself with his Jewish heritage. Gilbert Fonstein himself has become a warped version of his parents' hopes. His is the last station in the diaspora as outlined by Clayton— "from the ghetto to the modern world." His mother Sorella dreamed that her prodigy son would become a physicist with growth potential higher than that of her generation's. Instead he became interested in probability theory and attempted to capitalize on his "innate gift of memory" at the blackjack tables in Atlantic City – an antiphony of the narrator's hollow use of his gift of memory. Harry and Sorella are killed driving to Atlantic City to rescue their "American son" from gambling problems. The friend circumvents answering the narrator's probing question: "Does Gilbert take any interest in his Jewish background – for instance, in his father's history?" (p. 99). Gilbert is now in Las Vegas, a twentieth-century "holy-city" (p. 100), entertainment capital of the world as defined by his friend who is housesitting for him. Broadway Billy Rose's vision of America has obviated Gilbert's need for Jewish connectedness through Jewish history.

Billy Rose, or Bellarosa as pronounced by his Italian connections, "on a spurt of feeling for his fellow Jews" (p. 13), had mounted a one-man rescue effort resulting in Harry Fonstein's liberation from an Italian prison and certain death. Bellow liberally details Billy's multi-faceted personality: "business partner of Prohibition hoodlums . . . multi-millionaire . . . producer . . . consort of Eleanor Holm . . . collector of Matisse, Seurat" (p. 12). His rescue operation is a whim on the same level as another day's desire for a baked potato or a hot dog. His remembrance of the "God of his fathers" is viewed as a temporary spasm. When Harry attempts to remind Billy of his role in Jewish history, to connect with him through an expression of his gratitude, he is rebuffed both in letter and in person. The narrator speculates that Billy's refusal is based on his fear of being associated with Jewishness and thus appearing less American, while Harry, according to Sorella, feels Billy's refusal is based on a genetic change found in all second generation Americans. Later the narrator realizes: "You pay a price for being a child of the New World" (p. 89).

In the late 1950s the American Sorella, "tiger wife" of Harry, and self-appointed bearer of the Holocaust burden, anticipates Billy Rose's arrival in Jerusalem. Fortified with a diary revealing Billy's sexual inadequacies and unsavory business dealings, as recorded by his deceased, disgruntled secretary and left to Sorella, Sorella then engages in blackmail. Her husband must be allowed to acknowledge his indebtedness to Billy and Billy must accept his gratitude – all to be accomplished in only fifteen minutes of Billy's time. But Billy will not contribute to meeting Harry's needs. Billy's connection with the Holocaust episode in Jewish history has already been erased from his memory. The confrontation between the generic Jew, Sorella, and the American sometimes Jew, Billy Rose, serves as the crux of the book, and the narrator, to whom Sorella relates this confrontation, stores the data in his memory bank but has no reason to access it for thirty years. Initially he views her account with "an American mind" (p. 50).

Hiding behind the safety of her girth and gender, Sorella begins her sortie by mentioning her name – Fonstein. When Billy refuses to parry, to acknowledge his rescue of Fonstein, she taunts him: "I can't believe you don't remember" (p. 53). Billy's cavalier answer is symptomatic of his disconnectedness from Jewish communal memory, and thus Jewish history: "Remember, forget – what's the difference to me?" (p. 53) According to Robert McAfee Brown, when Elie Wiesel visited Babi Yar where 85,000 Jews had been slaughtered in 1943, Wiesel posed a question to the mayor of Kiev, a question which he continues to answer through his own writings: "Mr. Mayor, the problem for all of us . . . is: what do we do with our memories? We must deal with them."[16] Brown poses a follow-up question: "How does one deal with memory?" His answer: "One becomes a messenger, a transmitter."[17] In refusing to acknowledge the messenger, Harry Fonstein, Rose refuses to become a transmitter of the message. His next connection with Jewish history will be death related. He will bequeath to Israel a Rose Garden of Sculpture, situated within a few miles of the Dead Sea, as a splendid memorial to himself. Years later, when Billy Rose's body awaits burial while lawyers battle over a legal provision for a million-dollar tomb in the United States, the Fonsteins will quizzically discuss this flagrant disregard of Jewish law which mandates a burial within twenty-four hours after death.

As the narrator listens to Sorella's continuation of the confrontation story, he mentally compares disengaged Billy's refusal to become entangled – "I don't need entanglements" (p. 56) – with Washington's warning against European entanglements in his Farewell Address. Sorella's insistence on Billy's seeing Harry founders against Billy's Americanism which discounts what is past. "What's it got to do with now – 1959? If your husband has a nice story, that's his good luck. Let him tell it to people who go for stories. I don't care for them" (p. 58). Mark Harris quotes Bellow's own plaint against anti-history post-modernists: "Common to them all is a certain historical outlook. All that is not *now,* they say, is obsolete and dead . . . they find sanction in the Contemporaneous. For whatever is not Contemporaneous is worthless."[18]

Stories as a means of transmitting history and lessons to be learned have always been paramount in Judaism. The quintessential messenger Elie Wiesel's use of stories is legendary. In *A Jew Today* he explains with deliberate pacing, "Jewish tales are useful . . . and important . . . and timeless. . . . Just as all Jews in history are related, so are the events in it interdependent."[19] Elie Wiesel's stories thus serve as binding links. *Midrashim,* which are parables, sometimes even poetic fictions, in fact, date back to Biblical times. The word *midrash* itself is derived from *d'rash*, meaning explanation. But dangling Billy, who becomes a symbol of second generation, fast-moving, success-ridden American Jews, has no time for stories and explanations. Connections serve no function; they are no longer pertinent. Jeffrey Hart's question thus becomes more than rhetorical: "Was Hitler, as compared with freedom and pluralism, really not much?"[20] Fonstein's assimilated American cousin Swerdlow tells the narrator he himself had severed his connection with the Fonsteins because of Sorella's insistence on retelling her tale. He justifies Billy Rose's refusal to meet with Fonstein. Since Swerdlow had been unable to understand Sorella's motives (to him Sorella and Harry are only celebrity hungry), he saw no reason for Billy to capitulate to their whimsical demands.

When Gilbert's house-sitting friend responds with a non-answer to the narrator's question concerning Gilbert's association with his Jewish roots, the narrator surmises the friend is also a dissociated Jew. It wasn't that the American Jew disowned being Jewish but that being Jewish was no longer relevant, particularly when matched against his overwhelming Americanness. Relieved of the burden of proving itself through successful competition in the marketplace, the third generation could dawdle indefinitely, dressed, in the narrator's imagination, in adaptations of clothing worn by an earlier American working class – blue jeans, boots, with the stereotypical unshaven face – all the while mouthing nihilistic platitudes and scorning Jewish emotions as being outmoded. The housesitter hangs up after accurately commenting on the narrator's poor timing.

The principals, Harry and Sorella, are dead, Gilbert has refused his Jewish inheritance while eagerly accepting the American fortune left him, the young friend is reduced to anonymity through thoughtless broken connections which characterize modern American Jewry. The narrator's need to reconnect seems destined to be unfulfilled. With whom can he reconnect? In a master stroke Bellow moves from Mnemosyne and the many ramifications the Greek word holds to the narrator's return to his own ancient heritage. According to instructions engraved on gold plates which were buried with the dead in Magna Graecia, the pure soul after death will find two fountains, the fountains of Lethe and Mnemosyne. He is enjoined to avoid the fountain of forgetfulness but instead to drink from the spring of Mnemosyne, memory, so that he can continue life in the world below in the company of "the other heroes."[21] The aged narrator will remember and record "with a Mnemosyne flourish" (p. 102). But through the act of recording that is in fact this very book, the narrator reconnects himself with Jewish history. He becomes its messenger to future generations.

Perhaps the most horrifying curse in the Jewish vocabulary is the one which negates a person's history as well as the potential for his recollection by future generations: "May your name be blotted out for all eternity." Mourners' *Kaddish* is the prayer children traditionally recite on the anniversary of a parent's death so that the name will not be blotted out. Herzog nostalgically recalls the rabbi's frustrated warning to a young Hebrew school friend who incorrectly translates a word in the Torah: "I'm sorry for your father. Some heir he's got! Some Kaddish! Ham and pork you'll be eating before his body is in the grave."²² Procreation, Judaism's first commandment, thus becomes essential both to remembering and transmitting. In *The Bellarosa Connection* there are no children to remember and transmit. Billy Rose dies childless. Gilbert Fonstein and the housesitter choose not to remember. The narrator is already nameless, and his Christian son can neither resurrect his father's name nor transmit his father's heritage.

Arthur Hertzberg closes his last chapter, "The End of Immigrant Memory," by warning that the memory of memory, which is all that Jews in America really possess, must be strengthened through a spiritual revival if particularistic Jewish memory is not to meld into general American memory. Bellow's answer to the question of Jewish survival in America seems more equivocal. One the one hand, his dangling men in *The Bellarosa Connection* have paid the price for being children of the New World. They have become disconnected amnesiacs. And yet, and yet – the the nameless narrator upon learning of the Fonsteins' death will now both remember and record. He moves from the sterility of the Mnemosyne Institute with its emphasis on memory as data collector to the warmth of memory which is rooted in feelings. In a sense he becomes a *baal teshuvah,* a returner to the faith, when he now recalls the *Yizkor* prayer which is recited on the four most significant Jewish holy days. When reciting this prayer one goes from petitioning God to remember one's own dead family members to invoking God's recollection of all the Jewish dead. In Eastern European Jewish tradition there is even a belief that when God remembers these dead He will bless their descendants in memory of their merits. Again the movement from the present to remembering the past in order to ensure the future. Thus, while the now introspective narrator realizes the futility of attempting to reconnect the alienated, admittedly narcissistic, young Jewish housesitter with his communal past, he places himself once more firmly in the continuum of

Jewish history. Although denied communication with the Fonsteins through their death, his preserving their memories by writing this book becomes an affirmation of belief in a Jewish future.

The novel begins with the narrator's fervent desire "to forget about remembering" (pp. 1–2), although he realizes that release from memory comes only with death; the book concludes with his choosing to remember: "I chose instead to record everything I could remember of the Bellarosa Connection" (p. 102). In the Book of Deuteronomy, God offers the Jews this intriguing choice: "I have set before thee life and death, the blessing and the curse; therefore choose life, that thou mayest live, thou and thy seed" (30:19 Masoretic Text). The narrator, who had once motivated clients with his clever but unfelt statement "Memory is life" (p. 2), now consciously chooses memory and through memory, life.

NOTES

1. Arthur Hertzberg, *The Jews in America: Four Centuries of an Uneasy Encounter* (New York: Simon and Schuster, 1989), p. 6.

2. Saul Bellow, *The Bellarosa Connection* (New York: Penguin Books, 1989), p. 65. Subsequent references to the novel appear parenthetically in the text.

3. Yosef Hayim Yerushalmi, *Zahkor: Jewish History and Jewish Memory* (Seattle: Univ. of Washington Press, 1982), p. 5.

4. Margaret Morganroth Gullette, "Saul Bellow: Inward and Upward, Past Distraction," *Safe at Last in the Middle Years* (Berkeley: Univ. of California Press, 1988), p. 121.

5. Saul Bellow, *To Jerusalem and Back: A Personal Account* (New York: Viking Press, 1976), p. 5.

6. Edgar Allan Poe, "Morella," *The Works of Edgar Allan Poe,* ed. Hervey Allen (New York: P. F. Collier, 1927), p. 337.

7. Hermes Trismegistus, "Kore Kosmu," *Hermetica,* vol. 1, ed. and trans. Walter Scott (1924; rpt. London: Dawsons of Pall Mall, 1968), pp. 457–81.

8. Elie Wiesel, "Ezekiel," *Congregation: Contemporary Writers Read the Jewish Bible,* ed. David Rosenberg (New York: Harcourt Brace Jovanovich, 1987), pp. 186, 169.

9. Gertrude Stein, *The Making of Americans: The Hersland Family* (New York: Harcourt, Brace, and World, 1934), p. 3.

10. Alfred Kazin, "My Friend Saul Bellow," *The Atlantic Monthly,* January 1965, pp. 52, 53.

11. Elie Wiesel, *A Jew Today,* trans. Marion Wiesel (New York: Vintage Books, 1979), p. 25.

12. Bellow, *To Jerusalem and Back,* p. 93.

13. John Jacob Clayton, *Saul Bellow: In Defense of Man* (Bloomington: Indiana Univ. Press, 1968), p. 51.

14. Milan Kundera, *The Book of Laughter and Forgetting,* trans. Michael Heim (New York: Alfred A. Knopf, 1980), p. 159.

15. Bellow, *To Jerusalem and Back,* p. 26.

16. Robert McAfee Brown, *Elie Wiesel: Messenger to All Humanity* (Notre Dame: Univ. of Notre Dame Press, 1983), p. 20.

17. Brown, p. 20.

18. Mark Harris, *Saul Bellow: Drumlin Woodchuck* (Athens: Univ. of Georgia Press, 1980), pp. 168, 170.

19. Wiesel, p. 185.

20. Jeffrey Hart, "Review of *The Bellarosa Connection*," *National Review,* March 5, 1990, p. 52.

21. William Keith Chambers Guthrie, *The Greeks and Their Gods* (Boston: Beacon Press, 1950), pp. 229–30.

22. Saul Bellow, *Herzog* (New York: Penguin Books, 1964), p. 131.

Bellow's Fictional Rhetoric: The Voice of the Other

Walter Shear

Let me hear a sound
Truly not my own;
The voice of another,
Truly other . . .

— "The Gonzaga Manuscripts"

"TRUTH COMES with blows," according to Eugene Henderson, Bellow's Rain King and erstwhile quester for enlightenment. But the truth that descends upon Saul Bellow's protagonists, at least until the early 1960s, does not often come literally in blows (violence in Bellow almost invariably taking place off-stage) and is in fact not always the whole truth, certainly not the complete story about their lives. Although Bellow is one of the most intellectual of American novelists, a writer who in fiction after fiction forces his characters to examine their lives, to come to conclusions about what they have done and what they are doing, he is oddly frustrating, not simply about ultimate wisdom, but about the value of ideas as vital components in contemporary living. Truth for his characters may seem to come in blows because it is often judgmental and objective rather than sympathetically subjective and because it seems absolute in its retrospective tendencies. The future for his characters is always the necessary possibility in their visions, but its promises seem to depend on their laying hold of that totality which has been their existence.

One reason for their predicament is Bellow's liberal notion of the intellect, its hopeful openness, its simultaneous faith in external validities and existential authenticities, its sympathetic, vulnerable sensitivity to a world of otherness and its struggle against

despair in its negotiation with such a world. According to Malcolm Bradbury, Bellow's books reflect the tradition of the liberal novel, "where
there is some community of need between self and society, where individuals may reach out into the world of exterior relationships for reality,
civility, and maturity, where the possibility of moral enlargement and
discovery resides."[1]

It is liberal ideals that impel his early fiction toward a base in humanistic individualism, with the picaresque adventures of *Augie March*
marking his "revolt against classical form" and *Herzog* the final break
from "victim literature," "the end of a literary sensibility, . . . [one] which
implies a certain attitude toward civilization – anomaly, estrangement,
the outsider, the collapse of humanism."[2] As the last quotation suggests,
it is a base which struggles with the last vestiges of Naturalism, that
stage of Modernism where humanism emerges chiefly in the heroic suffering of an individual periodically haunted by his/her own animalism but
also by recurrent transcendent impulses. In Bellow's transformation of
Naturalism, it is the terms of the self's involvement with the external, its
sense of a "natural" relationship to the world in its open tolerance and
commitment to authenticity of being, which causes the investigation of
the environment of the nonself to exude consistently a tension that
becomes the sense of an otherness for the self.

Although on the surface the social encounters of Bellow's characters
and the earnest tolerance of their voiced thoughts reveal an attractive
acceptance of reality, a quickening curiosity that seems evidence of an
idealism about social life, the notion of otherness is ultimately evidence
of the self as its own barrier to coming to terms with one's identity and
one's position in the world. Tony Tanner has noted that while Bellow in
the early 1960s was worrying over "the single Self in the midst of the
mass," his fictions had tended to focus on individuals: "Where the novels
are not actual first-person autobiography by the major character, they
remain almost exclusively within a single consciousness," and in Tanner's
view this meant the main subject of these books was consistently
"solitary self-communing."[3]

The gamut of the frustrations for the self are suggested in Bellow's
"progress" through the 1950s, a development which is framed by the distance between Asa Leventhal's anxious, naturalistic question to Allbee,
"What's your idea of who runs things?" and Herzog's expressive existentialism – part resignation, part blatant performance – "I reject your definitions of me;"[4] "I am Herzog. I have to be that man. There is no one
else to do it" (p. 67). Bellow's protagonists move from a concern with

becoming, most explicitly manifested in Augie March's peculiar declaration, "I have always tried to become what I am,"[5] and to Eugene Henderson's defiant challenge to his world: *"Being.* Others were taken up with *becoming. . . .* Enough! Time to have Become. Time to Be! Burst the spirit's sleep. Wake up, America."[6] But to be – that is, to act and express oneself – within the context of liberalism implies a preliminary sorting out of obligations and personal possibilities, a process which, in the fiction, occurs in a social dimension that cannot fully contain a religious and/or transcendent source of value.

One barrier is thus simply the sense that the world is not some divinely-created home for the self. As early as *The Victim,* Bellow's environments seem prone to bizarre, alien moments in which the ordinary is endowed with a tantalizing sense of an unrevealed significance, one sensed in this novel as oddly embedded in familiar situations that both encourage and deny Asa's search for a social morality. A basic strangeness is structured in the book through violation of contemporary norms, Bellow's reversal of the terms of prejudice in making the Jewish sensibility to be not some departure from the normative but the conventional perspective for viewing the peculiar in the American scene. An exotic note is struck in the first sentence: "On some nights, New York is as hot as Bangok," and the subsequent antics of Allbee, as gadfly and as alterego, create an appropriately unpredictable atmosphere, one that continually verges on the surreal. While Asa tries to rationally measure his social responsibilities in the case of Allbee and to manifest his personal responsibilities to his brother's family in the absence of the brother, the objects of his concern are consistently unsettling.

At one extreme a dark naturalistic psychology creates a paranoiac vision of the world. Elena's mother with her "old-country ways" is a silent, foreboding figure evoking all the possible hostility of the strange. Allbee himself as the grotesquely pushy, performing self appears and disappears in mysterious ways which make Asa wonder over the man's reality. And there is a feeling that obligations are not simply being accepted but are forced, almost physically, into Asa's being. At one time in one of the images of weight which Irving Malin notes as recurrent motifs in Bellow's fiction,[7] Asa has "the strange feeling that there was not a single part of him on which the whole world did not press with full weight, on his body, on his soul, pushing upward in his breast and downward in his bowels."[8]

In the ideological context of the book, the psychological release represented by one of Asa's Allbee-inspired conclusions, "everybody wanted to be what he was to the limit" (p. 92), is played as counterpoint to Schlossberg's classical mean. "It's bad to be less than human and it's bad to be more than human" (p. 121). In the interaction, the other instructs the norm. Whatever Allbee's overreaching incivilities, they must be squared with his cry for fundamental justice. For Asa, Allbee's outrages ultimately become in large measure manifestations of the vital self's refusal to be suppressed. In this respect, Allbee anticipates Herzog. By contrast, Clarence Feiler, the rather timid central character of "The Gonzaga Manuscripts," utilizes the same terms of individual élan to perceive an ultimate hopelessness in the encounter with the alien in the world.

> "I used to welcome all
> And now I fear all.
> If it rained, it was comforting,
> And if it shone, comforting,
> But now my very weight is dreadful. . . .

When I read that, Gonzaga made me understand how we lose everything by trying to become everything."[9] For Clarence, who wants a world that answers to his vision, the weight of otherness comes to mean that life can be constantly discomforting through the very thirst for life.

In Bellow's work in the 1950s, the sense of a disconcerting otherness becomes the basis for the essential rhythm of the narrative movement. For example, in *Seize the Day* the structuring of the sporadic movement of puzzlement and insight in Wilhelm's relationships forms the desperate drama of his place in the world. The concern for hiding the self from others which is present in the very first sentence – "When it came to concealing his troubles, Tommy Wilhelm was not less capable than the next fellow" – projects that cultural barrier to one's sharing one's existence and receiving sympathetic advice and help from one's fellows which is the central puzzle of the story. It is a human tendency perhaps, one Tamkin would universalize into a global vision: "If you were to believe [him], most of the world was like this. Everybody in the hotel had a mental disorder, a secret history, a concealed disease."[10]

Wilhelm's involvements with others are worked out as a series of insights, immediate and delayed, which seem continually on the verge of unlocking the prosaic mystery of his life, but which for him constantly fade to mere collections of moments of knowing and not knowing. In his session with Maurice Venice, for instance, Wilhelm moves from being initially ready to take the man at his word, to being made suddenly suspicious by Venice's emphasis on his credentials. While Wilhelm is slow to understand Venice's hint that he and Nita Christenberry are engaged (for it has no clear relevance to him), he is immediately full of insight and understanding at the information that Maurice is related to the producer Martial Venice: "poor guy. He was the obscure failure of an aggressive and powerful clan. As such he had the greatest sympathy from Wilhelm" (p. 22). In retrospect, Tommy realizes that the failure in understanding results from the fact that he and Venice were each trying to make a good impression on the other, each in his own way desperate, fearful of failure. The recommendation Wilhelm pleads for turns out to be "the kiss of death," and the final irony for Wilhelm's hopes comes years later when Venice is indicted for pandering. Down on his luck and feeling the failure of his movie-career decision, Wilhelm is left wondering, "what did he want with me?" but is still "unwilling to believe anything very bad about Venice" (p. 25).

Tommy's relationship to Tamkin, the fradulent psychologist, illustrates how ideas themselves exist in ambiguous externality to the self. In working on Tommy, Tamkin explains: "The spiritual compensation is what I look for. Bringing people into the here-and-now. The future is full of anxiety. Only the present is real – the here-and-now. . . . Seize the day" (pp. 61–62). Wilhelm does need to become more the dynamic realist, to lay hold of his life and to perceive the truth which he senses about the man giving him advice. But, as Tamkin may be aware, only part of the advice is good. If Wilhelm's involvement in the here-and-now means giving up his knowledge of past mistakes and ignoring future consequences, he will simply be trapped in someone else's willful scheme. Thus the idea of the here-and-now functions as both critical comment and challenge in a narrative that intends to strip and expose Wilhelm's vulnerabilities. Wilhelm's dilemma is aptly described by Eusebio L. Rodrigues: "The Bellow protagonist cannot accept such abstract truths unless they are inscribed on his being by sorrow and genuine suffering."[11]

The pattern of life's proffering a series of possible answers but ultimately no final answer is the substitute for conventional plotting in Bellow. It is this promise of some answer in otherness, in the foreign and the exotic, that Bellow's characters come to seek. Often his characters seem to search out the most alien environment in their world: Henderson to Africa, Augie and Clarence to Europe, Hattie to the American West – even Tommy and Asa come to regard New York City as not so much home but some weird country they have just entered. Henderson seems attracted to the foreign for its own sake; indeed, he often demands to be involved, to participate in strange beliefs, to come to terms with strange gods. Even on the literal level, the journey is the entry into a cultural otherness.

Bellow's account of the writing of *Augie March* defines its essential problem in similar terms: "We are called upon to preserve our humanity in circumstances of rapid change and movement."[12] His explanation further stresses how composing in different places seemed to transform alienation into a form of inspiration: in the quotation Bellow borrows from Robert Penn Warren, you become inspired in places "where the language is not your own and you are forced into yourself in a special way" (p. 17). The result, Bellow claims, was that in the writing "Chicago itself had grown exotic to me" (p. 3).

Although a character's journey to strange lands manifests the belief that one can discover through the other one's essential, hidden self, what these worlds really offer, for all their strangeness and apparent irrelevancies, are the terms of a possible settlement for the self. Even as Henderson tries to make his aim explicit to Itelo, "Your majesty, I am really kind of on a quest" (p. 65), his is ultimately a quest to end questing, to rid himself of the impulse to become. His aim is in one sense a shedding of his own otherness, his own feeling of being strange to social normality. His salvation will come from the Goethian side of his character, the social side of the existential self, but with the sense of mission for a deep self. Thus spiritual possibility here takes the form of the clumsy, bull-in-the-China-shop American, inspired by good intentions but blundering through social values others hold sacrosanct.

For other Bellow characters the idea of settlement can only imply some sacrifice of essential being, often configured as a kind of temptation. At one extreme, as Mintouchian points out to Augie, the self can virtually eliminate itself—as in marriage the husband or wife gets the spouse (as the other) to murder them: "'Kind spouse, you will make me my fate'" (p. 484). Tommy Wilhelm is the one Bellow character who seems to make a career of self-destruction: "Ten such decisions made up the history of his life. He had decided it would be a bad mistake to go to Hollywood, and then he went. He had made up his mind not to marry his wife, but ran off and got married. He had resolved not to invest money with Tamkin, and then had given him a check" (p. 24).

In the light of such character tendencies, the sense of the surviving self, Augie's own bright voice, is perhaps the most refreshing effect in *Augie March*. Bellow's early tentative title for the book, "Life Among the Machiavellians," emphasizes the basic structure. Augie's encounters with a parade of strong figures—Grandma Lausch, Einhorn, Mrs. Renling, Thea,

Mintouchian. In each case these interactions create paradigmatic versions of the other, whose power for Augie is attested by his confession: "In the most personal acts of your life you carry the presence and power of another. You extend his being in your thoughts, where he inhabits" (p. 335).

Through Augie, Bellow indicates that greatness of being lies not simply in coping with but in experiencing others, coming to terms with their ideas as these are manifested in their lives. On the level of what might be called visionary intuition, these others are the ones who, for Augie, "persistently arise before me with life counsels and illumination throughout my entire earthly pilgrimage" (p. 478). But accumulated experiences make him wary. His relationship with Mrs. Renling is representative. Even as she swears to make him perfect and does all his "choosing," he is aware that his new and better appearance can be only that—the surface of the self. As he realizes and the sheer number of his close relationships suggest, his being has grown firm and deep with the wide variety of its external nourishments.

When Augie confesses to Thea that "I had looked all my life for the right thing to do, for a fate good enough" (p. 318), she warns him of the self-defeating danger in his quest: "I see how much you care about the way people look at you. It matters too much to you. . . . you don't really matter to them. You only matter when someone loves you" (p. 318). Love, mattering, and being all seem key components of the self that functions in the public arena in some genuine fashion, and Bellow's existential "I" is a complex of willing, caring, and being truly expressive of the self. But love in Bellow's fiction also features risks, always. Augie comes to see in his love for Stella that otherness is the pervasive complication of his desire for simplicity. To his generalization about people, Stella shouts, "'People! But I am not other people. . . . This is happening to *me*'" (518). The other's demand for recognition is the necessary reminder that authentic existence will discover need and vulnerability to be fused. Being's search for significance is not for any image or appearance but for an interaction guided by valuing and caring.

The intimate risks of the self are paralleled in Bellow's views of public roles and civil duties. He claims: "This society with its titanic products conditions us but cannot absolutely denature us."[13] However, Bellow's natural beings need society for their growth. The soul dimension of the self wants some reassurance of its nobility.

In one of his journeys into the strange tribes of Africa, Henderson encounters a burning bush, a phenomenon at once familiar as Biblical allusion to God's appearance to Moses, but which in this case is not produced by God but by Henderson himself. Even though it comes, as it were, from within, it is still a sign – in this instance a sign of a sign. What Bellow's characters need is not the symbol, the indicator of a truth beyond or some absolute truth. Symbols, some firm tie between meaning and thing, seem to have broken down, so that as Grebe surveys the ruins of 1930s Chicago, things "only stood for themselves by agreement, and were natural and not unnatural by agreement, and when things themselves collapsed the agreement became visible" (*MM,* p. 103). That is, the idea of culture as the cement of meaning becomes an evident vulnerability in an era of rapid sociological change. As Bellow makes clear in his warning to symbol hunters: "Meanings themselves are a dime a dozen. . . . We need to see how human beings act after they have appropriated or assimilated meanings."[14] The characters want that sense of words described by Ludwig Wittgenstein:

> Someone may for instance say it's a grave matter that such and such a man should have died before he could complete a certain piece of work, and yet, in another sense, this is not what matters. At this point one uses the words 'in a deeper sense.' Actually I should like to say that in this case too the *words* you utter or what you think as you utter them are not what matters so much as the difference they make at various periods in your life.[15]

Bellow's characters need signs of personal significance, signs, actions that bring out their significance – for themselves as well as for others – and signs that act as conduits between the private and the public. As Grebe begins the task of searching for Mr. Green, he feels that he "needed experience in interpreting looks and signs and, even more, the will not be to be put off or denied and even the force to bully if need be" (*MM,* p. 88), for he feels himself laboring "in the fallen world of appearances" (*MM,* p. 95). That there are satisfactions where one might expect them, in the working out of some task in the public world, is suggested by the prominence of gerunds in the titles of at least two stories of the period, "Looking for Mr. Green" and "Leaving the Yellow House." Indeed "The Gonzaga Manuscripts" might have been titled "Searching for the Gonzaga Manuscripts." Grebe, the main character of "Looking," wants "to do well, simply for doing-well's sake," for the chance to use his "energy" in a coherent and constructive fashion (*MM,* p. 86).

At this time Bellow is bothered by the make-up of the public world. In "The Sealed Treasure," an essay published in 1960, he argued that vital human qualities, even the potential for greatness, was still present in American society but had been forced into hiding by the avalanche of "things":

> A modern mass society has no open place for [the greatest human] qualities, no vocabulary for them and no ceremony (except in churches) which makes them public. So they remain private and are mingled with other private things which vex us or of which we feel ashamed. But they are not lost.[16]

The situation is clearly, if tentatively, defined in a later essay – "We seem to have come to a time when the main problem for culture is to make it personally applicable."[17]

One manifestation of the search for the personal in the public is the prominence of documents of various kinds in several of the 1950s stories. As potential signs, the documents set in motion anxieties over relationships between the self and the other, chiefly emphasizing the way social assumptions about a person become demands for clarifying, articulating, and purifying the self. In each story the situation of the character involves a public mission and thus the necessity to reach out, to seek social cooperation.

The mission of Grebe in "Looking for Mr. Green," the delivering of a welfare check, is partly a generous act – and Bellow has provided a humanities background for Grebe which may well be designed to emphasize notions of service and humane obligation – but the time is the Depression, and Grebe is obviously glad to have this job. He too is one of the needy, but he is also one of the lucky ones. However similar he may be to Mr. Green, the recipient of the check – and the likeness in names calls attention to a parallel – the story stresses that as white man, he is in strange territory, the black section of the city where people, though poor and needy, are frequently suspicious of the white world, even when it appears in the form of welfare.

Grebe's goal is a human answer to his sense of social order, a confirmation in the seemingly chaotic other-world of an identity resembling his own. In this context, the welfare check is both link and barrier to such a humane vision. It serves to inspire personal dedication within him, manifested both in the search and in the growing awareness of need which emerges from his encounter with the hostile environment. There is some satisfaction simply in the doing: "To be compelled to feel this energy and no task to do – that was horrible: that was suffering" (*MM*, p. 103). But it also forces upon him a raw, confused otherness he can only cope with in a fumbling manner and which makes him feel "a faltering of organization that set free a huge energy, an escaped, unattached, unregulated power from some giant raw place" (*MM*, p. 102). The social and philosophic problem is the breakdown of an essential semantic linkage: "The same man might not have the same name twice" (*MM*, p. 99). And in this "fallen world of appearances" there is no ultimate reality: "everything stands for something else, and that thing for another thing, and that thing for a still further thing" (*MM*, p. 95). Appropriately the story ends with a kind of pragmatic philosophic compromise, a wryly ironic settlement as Grebe finally turns the check over to a naked, drunken woman who curses him. As he concludes by assuring himself about Green's existence, ". . . after all . . . he *could* be found" (*MM*, p. 108), he bizarrely discovers himself in the other. The angry contempt and ridicule make him aware of himself as "an emissary from hostile appearances," and in a "service like this, which no one visible asked for, and probably flesh and blood could not even perform," he sees not Mr. Green but the alienating power of all public roles in a period of rapid social change (*MM*, pp. 108, 102).

By contrast, "The Gonzaga Manuscript" focuses on a rather personal mission in a post-World War II environment. Although the outward calm of the pax Americana is apparent in the Europe which Clarence Feiler searches, he also discovers that to be an American in such an environment is to set off the nervous anxiety which the atomic age and its bombs have engendered. The story plays on such paradoxes: amid the gracious living of Feiler's Spanish environment and the backdrops of an ancient civilization, people respond to one another with secret suspicions, fears, and misunderstandings. Clarence's idealistic quest for Gonzaga's lost poems is haunted by recurrent reminders of the way art is intransigently mixed with the demands of money, the flesh, and the violence of war.

Though Clarence feels his attraction to Gonzaga's poetry to be based on the poet's concern for a creaturely existence, the narrative almost obsessively reveals his distaste for the physical in the people he encounters. Their hair, their bellies, even the odd shapes of their heads run like a motif through Clarence's mind. The man who finally reveals the location of the manuscript—one Alvarez-Polva—is described as one whose "face seemed to have been worked by three or four diseases and then abandoned" (*MM*, p. 133). Indeed, it is appropriate finally to discover that the poems have been buried with the Countess; linked to her fleshly existence in life, they are now tied forever to her decaying body.

"The Gonzaga Manuscripts" may be too dominated by the personality of the finicky Clarence to be entirely successful. Nevertheless, the narrative plays a rich variety of cultural attitudes against Clarence's narrowing vision of high culture. His reverence for Gonzaga's poetry and the dedication this inspires seem genuine. Often, he is the contemporary secular knight on his own sacred mission, reminding himself at moments of frustration that he should seek the poems in a manner that would not discredit the spirit in which they were written. While he believes he has prepared himself for the contamination of his mission by the actual, arranging, for example, to purchase the manuscripts with black-market currency, his fussy disgust with the varied reactions of others to the idea of culture demonstrates his longing for the pure and uncontaminated. He is bothered by Guzman del Nido's social dinner and the man's meandering if cultivated conversation, by the wild Napoleonic charades of the nephews of Don Francisco Polvo, and he is stunned by Alvarez-Polvo's uranium stock. Ironically, what he wants is his own encounter with the poems rather than the world the poems describe and respond to. As a critic, he finds great beauty in the lines: "Let me hear a sound / Truly not my own; / The voice of another / Truly other . . ." (*MM*, p. 116). But as to experiencing being itself, he is repulsed precisely by the otherness of the world, its irreverence, its creaturely qualities. The very sensitivity that leads Clarence to respond to the other as conceived in art impels him impatiently to reject the otherness of actuality. In this case, only the religious dimension of his dedication steels his defensive ego for an emersion in experience; indeed, it supplies the broad terms that make deep experience possible.

Bellow's other notable short story of the decade, "Leaving the Yellow House," features Hattie Waggoner as one who is increasingly vulnerable physically. Now old, given to drinking too much, Hattie seems not able to recover from a car accident and its aftermath. Her broken arm, her general physical incapacity, is her goad to self-analysis, ultimately to her efforts at spiritual revision. Fearfully and resentfully, she senses herself alone and isolated, a person whose life is littered with weaknesses and mistakes. She imagines that the incredible "objective" technology of modernism exists to indict her: she "saw her own life as though, from birth to the present, every moment had been filmed. Her fancy was that when she died, she would see the film shown" (*MM*, p. 17). Slowly though, as she reels from both self-analysis and the criticism of her neighbors, she gathers a hidden strength. What is self-criticism becomes self-sustaining as she emerges from weakness to confront death itself. Moments of humiliation – with Wicks, with India – become the modes of a truly existential pride, an essential rugged individualism that survives and saves. She is in this respect like those Biblical characters described by Erich Auerbach: "There is hardly one of them who does not, like Adam, undergo the deepest humiliation – and hardly one who is not deemed worthy of God's personal intervention and personal inspiration."[18]

In Bellow's story, of course, God does not personally intervene. But there is a sense in which the legal will with which Hattie valiantly struggles – brooding over the question of who deserves the only value she owns, her house – is the will that is at the essence of her personhood and which, in bizarrely transcending her own fate, exists as the frustrated human impulse toward an after-life perspective, simultaneously condemning, expiating, and forgiving – the undeveloped negative of the photo of the transcending will. The arrogant greatness of the story, if one reads it this way, is its hubristic grasp at the ultimate Other and its vision of a plight simultaneously comic and tragic. The vision of the other in "Leaving the Yellow House" is ultimately in the eye of God.

During the 1950s, Saul Bellow's fiction moved to an American agenda. The European tradition (Frenchified Dostoyevsky) of *Dangling Man* was early in the decade superseded by a modernized *Huckleberry Finn*, i.e., *Augie March*. "The Gonzaga Manuscripts" is an updated "Aspern Papers," examining the contemporary American in cold war Europe. "Looking for Mr. Green," set in Depression Chicago, broods over the welfare problem. *Seize the Day* features Tommy Wilhelm as a Willy Loman type, the failure in the land of success. "Leaving the Yellow House" presents Bellow's version of the American West with Hattie Waggoner making a last stand for rugged individualism.

Augie March is not merely the revolt from classical form but the movement of the American self from the confines of naturalistic assumptions to the spatial openness of a global perspective. The major tension plaguing this transformation of national identity is the dialectic between becoming and being. On the one hand, the American feels the obligation in the land of opportunity to improve the terms of his/her existence and to be accepted by one's fellow citizens who would serve to confirm and reassure. But there is also a deep fear in the increasingly mobile self that an erosion is taking place – that roots are being lost, some fundamental betrayal of identity is occurring, that one is simply becoming a phony, even breaking some sort of social law.

The classic modern examnation of these national tensions is Scott Fitzgerald's characterization of Jay Gatsby, a man who tries to invent himself socially. Twenty-five years later, the issue is more nearly how to preserve a personal self in whatever social situation one finds oneself. In this context, otherness emerges both as a complex of fears, chiefly the extremes of being swallowed up or rejected by society, and as the need to learn and grow, to see one's mistakes and profit from them. Even though the simple truth Henderson discovers, "man want to live," forms a clarifying core for the American quest, the erratic shifts in a multidimensional cultural situation require that values themselves generate elasticities. As Henderson's experience demonstrates, the interaction between self and world is complicated by the fact that the power which self brings is both posititve and negative and that the meaning now floating in that cultural otherness surrounding the self can only be sporadically, in most cases only painfully, absorbed.

NOTES

1. Malcolm Bradbury, *Saul Bellow* (London: Methuen, 1982), p. 29.

2. "Saul Bellow of Chicago," *New York Times Book Review,* May 9, 1971: 12; David Boroff, "The Author," *Saturday Review,* Sept. 19, 1964: 39.

3. *Saul Bellow* (Edinburgh: Oliver and Boyd, 1965), pp. 103, 104.

4. *Herzog* (New York: Viking, 1964), p. 229. All subsequent references to this text will be placed in parentheses. Among others who would argue that Bellow's characters have always reflected "the Sartrian view of man as a free, indeterminate being who is thrust into a variety of situations, but who can control them and model himself into whatever he wants to be" (p. 43) is Ada Aharoni, one of the most insistent in arguing for Bellow's existentialism. See "Saul Bellow and Existentialism." *Saul Bellow Journal,* 2, No. 2 (1983): 42–54.

5. *The Adventures of Augie March* (New York: Viking, 1953), p. 485. All subsequent references to this text will be placed in parentheses.

6. *Henderson the Rain King* (New York: Penguin, 1966), p. 160. All subsequent references to this text will be placed in parentheses.

7. *Saul Bellow's Fiction* (Carbondale: Southern Illinois Univ. Press, 1969), p. 86.

8. *The Victim* (New York: Vanguard-Signet, 1965), p. 226. All subsequent references to this text will be placed in parentheses.

9. *Mosby's Memoirs and Other Stories* (New York: Fawcett, 1969), p. 111. All subsequent references to the stories in this volume will be placed in parentheses with the designation *MM.*

10. *Seize the Day* (New York: Popular Library, 1958), p. 59. All subsequent references to this text will be placed in parentheses.

11. *Quest for the Human: An Exploration of Saul Bellow's Fiction* (Lewisburg, Pa: Bucknell Univ. Press, 1981), p. 12.

12. "How I Wrote Augie March's Story," *New York Times Book Review,* Jan. 31, 1954: 3, 17.

13. "The Sealed Treasure," *Times Literary Supplement,* July 1, 1960: 414.

14. "Deep Readers of the World, Beware!" *New York Times Book Review,* Feb. 15, 1954: 34.

15. Ray Monk, *Ludwig Wittgenstein: The Duty of Genius* (New York: Free Press, 1990), p. 573.

16. "Sealed Treasure," p. 414.

17. "Skepticism and the Depth of Life," in *The Arts and the Public,* ed. James E. Miller, Jr., and Paul D. Herring (Chicago: Univ. of Chicago Press, 1967), p. 21.

18. *Mimesis,* trans. Willard Trask (Garden City, New York: Anchor Doubleday, 1957), p. 15.

Still Not Satisfied:
Saul Bellow on Art and Artists
in America

Ben Siegel

F OR MANY years Saul Bellow has been unhappy with America's
"cultural condition." He is dissatisfied primarily with the country's
deflation of humanistic standards and values and its disdain for the
creative artist, especially the writer. His culprits are many and
varied. But the creative artist himself is for Bellow not without
fault, for, if serious poets and fiction writers are viewed by many of
their countrymen as mere entertainers and buffoons, they cannot
blame solely the corporate or business – or, as he still puts it on occasion, the Philistine – mentality. Much of the problem, as he made
clear in *Humboldt's Gift,* derives from the posturings and ambitions of the poets and writers themselves. Still, he finds it ironic
and sad that institutions and groups that should contribute to the
well-being and general appreciation of the artist in America often
act in a contrary fashion.

1. The Media Intellectuals

High on Bellow's list of malefactors here are the American university and, of all people, its humanities professors. These entrenched
academics do not champion or nurture the creative young. Instead, they often prove envious, bureaucratic corruptors of the truly
gifted entrusted to their care. Part of Bellow's quarrel with the
university stems from his conviction that the American intellectual and American writer are poorly educated. "Intellectuals have
not become a new class of art patrons," he charges. "This means
that the universities have failed painfully. They have not educated

viewers, readers and audiences as they should have done, and philistinism emerges as a new negative force in all countries. As a result, the learned are farther from art and taste than they were even a generation ago."[1] American writers have fared no better, suffering as they do "from lack of mind, or at least of learning," declares Bellow. They do not know "the literary past very well." Hence this country's writers are strongly "inclined to repeat things that we are thoroughly familiar with already. Certain rebellious, radical or bohemian attitudes, certain vanguard attitudes, certain postures that they discover for the first time [they treat] as though they were new." Rather than being fresh or original, these positions have been pushed "again and again *ad nauseam*."[2]

To make matters worse, professors have failed to inform their literature and writing students that cultural conditions have changed drastically. Today, serious writers and writing have much less social significance. The old masters may be followed slavishly in the classroom, but modern writers exert little cultural influence. Indeed, "I don't know that they really do influence the public," Bellow states. "Some of them may, depending on whether they strike a significant vein. Occasionally this happens. I know that there was a great Hemingway influence. I don't know that that would be all to the good either."[3] Bellow's unhappiness with America's arts and artists extends far beyond the university. He repeatedly, almost obsessively, targets those individuals who move from the campus into governmental agencies, publications, networks, corporations, and foundations that can play significant roles in the nation's cultural life. Often former students of literature, sociology, or psychology, these people also may be graduates of drama departments and art institutes. They are the ones who have taken over the mass media. What do these humanities and behavioral sciences students do when ensconced in their new seats of power? Why, they plot with their former teachers against their more creative literary contemporaries. "The mass media and the university-sponsored quarterlies," complains Bellow, "have between them swallowed up literary journalism. The salaried professor will supply literary articles cheaply and has all but wiped out his professional competitors."[4] Bellow sees no need to support his implication that practicing poets or novelists are better able to write "literary journalism" than are academic critics or scholars – and are in fact more entitled to do so.

Many commentators are pained and surprised by Bellow's attacks against those who seemingly make up his own intellectual (and academic) constituency. But professional thinkers and liberal-arts academics are for Bellow primarily responsible for this nation's arid new cultural bureaucracy. Too many in the media and academe, he feels, are driven by narrow needs and ambitions and behave in a greedy, self-serving fashion. The resulting media culture, fed and shaped by the university and its half-educated graduates, has established itself within America's liberal society. Many influential American "intellectuals," Bellow notes wryly, have a strong need for such a media culture. Certainly this urge surpasses their "need for novels and poems."[5] Who else is ultimately responsible for this sorry state of affairs? Bellow is specific: "Upperclass Protestant America." He makes this clear most pointedly in *Mr. Sammler's Planet* (1970), *The Dean's December* (1982), and *More Die of Heartbreak* (1987). Although "heavily armed," this long-dominant group now feels so weak in authority, he declares, that it "freely, even excessively, confesses its failures." Its last great leader was F.D.R., and while the group retains much power, it is "floundering" (CN, p. 176). The WASP community has allowed itself to be replaced, in part, by the new class of publicity intellectuals who dominate certain of its industries.

To make matters worse, these media hustlers differ sharply from Depression-era intellectuals. The latter, lacking employment, truly "lived as intellectuals" (CN, p. 176). But today's college-educated media managers, complains Bellow, "have never lived as [independent or impoverished] writers, painters, composers or thinkers." They have no need to do so. Since World War II they have increased "in number and influence," he notes. "They are now spoken of with respect, even with awe, as indispensable to the government as makers of educated opinion, as sources of symbolic legitimacy." In effect, they are, as Walt Whitman might put it, "replacing the clergy." Despite their lack of imagination or creativity, these media manipulators organize the "writing, art, thought and science in publishing houses, in museums, in foundations, in magazines, in newspapers." Utilizing also the art and thought of others more creative than they in television, advertising, and the fashion industry, states Bellow, they make these varied media activities "pay and pay handsomely."[6] In fact, the top management of newspapers and magazines, once so autocratic, now seeks their favor and their intercession with a youthful or youth-worshipping public. A yellowing journalism results. Even the staid and grave *New York Times* has surrendered without even a fight to this new class.

2. A Sorry Moral Climate

The cumulative result is a sorry moral and cultural climate in which literature is consistently exploited. For these culture executives, states

Bellow, "have passed from contemplative reading to movement, to action, politics and power struggles." Ironically, they derive from their actions neither personal status nor meaningful public importance. No, it is primarily "from the study of literature," explains Bellow, that they gain "the prestige they enjoy and exploit." The late Marshall McLuhan exemplifies for him the fame to be garnered from a clever fusion of literature and popular media. Of course McLuhan was merely a symptom, he concedes, of the varied social forces pressuring literature. Indeed literature now is confronted by numerous rivals, generally in the form of "great public questions." Since around 1914, such tangible social issues as "war, revolution, fascism, communism, depression, unemployment, devastation, reconstruction," Bellow states, have deflected mankind's imagination from the creative arts. Consequently, writers, poets, dramatists, artists have had to develop ways of coping with great public changes and events. This is especially true of the more venturesome or experimental artists and writers. The avant-garde – which Bellow defines as "a minority resistance movement, a small-public movement" (CN, p. 163) – has reacted by reflecting its times in imaginative works like James Joyce's *Ulysses* or T. S. Eliot's *The Waste Land*. These writings are not designed, says Bellow, for mass readers but for a cultural elite. Hence their cultural impact is very limited.

Here journalists and media specialists could make a positive difference. But the sad truth for Bellow is that these people have been of no more help than the avant-garde. In interview and essay, and most pointedly in *The Dean's December,* he reiterates his unhappiness with journalism and journalists. He finds highly suspect the claim of newspaper and magazine writers that they alone deal with daily life's "real" social or political questions. Journalists offer no greater degree of reality than do other purveyors of the media or even the avant-garde. In fact, he considers the journalistic "sphere" to be like that of the "small-public" writer: essentially "an imaginative sphere, a realm of fictions" (CN, p. 164). For life's hard daily issues form for most journalists, says Bellow, a "turbulent, anxious, agitated" drama filled with "phantasms." These phantasms – whether as individuals or events – excite, depress, confuse, and corrupt an embroiled citizenry. In short, modern journalists, like fiction writers, rely upon the imagination. The trouble is they make inadequate use of that very special faculty, despite dealing with subjects crying out for the imagination's most creative expression.

Albert Corde exemplifies most directly the aesthetic distance between journalist and artist. Bellow makes this clear when he talks about his depiction in *The Dean's December* of the American city's "demoralized . . .

inner slum." A mere journalistic knowledge of life's sordid daily facts, he emphasizes, does not render them meaningful. In his novel he was after something deeper. "What I meant was there is a correspondence between outer and inner, between the brutalized city and the psyche of its citizens." American life has become intolerable, but its leaders and experts respond with glib generalities. "Given their human resources I don't see how people today can experience life at all," complains Bellow. "Politicians, public figures, professors address 'modern problems' solely in terms of employment." These titular leaders "assume that unemployment causes incoherence, sexual disorders, the abandonment of children, robbery, rape, and murder. Plainly, they have no imagination of these evils. They don't even *see* them." So in *The Dean's December* he chose to speak to this blindness. What he did there, he explains, "was to say, 'Look!' The first step is to display the facts. But the facts, unless the imagination perceives them, are *not* facts." His Dean, although a journalist, is an exceptional one. "As an artist does, Mr. Corde, the Dean, passionately takes hold of Chicago and writes his articles like an artist rather than a journalist. He's an in-between type, perhaps like the Orwell who wrote *Down and Out* or the *Wigan Pier* book."[7]

Explaining his Dean in these terms, Bellow clarifies some of the problems he sees now confronting the sensitive artist whose mind has been shaped by books. "Corde is a man who has had an 'aesthetic' upbringing and who has never found a life appropriate to such an upbringing. After all, to have been brought up on Baudelaire, on the French novelists from Stendhal to Proust, on Joyce, etc., is not only to have read books but [also] to have received a kind of spiritual training." Yet what is an individual to do with such a training? asks Bellow. What is he to do "with the tastes, the outlook, the demands, the passions that have been created by years of immersion in poems, novels, paintings"? Bellow is explicit: the resultant outlook and passions are not to be "hoarded." Indeed, "they demand use." Such qualities and experiences having combined to form a sensitive individual like Albert Corde, the good Dean is obligated to employ his special sensibility to improve his city. The irony is that all this happens to Corde "in the barbarous boondocks of faraway Chicago." To make matters worse, "it happens not only to a reader like Corde, who has never found a life appropriate to his upbringing, but also to writers whose native heath happens to be in the barbarous boondocks, Carl Sandburg's 'city of broad shoulders.'"[8]

Obviously, Saul Bellow is speaking of himself as well as of other serious writers. Only contemporary literature and those who create it are able to deal honestly and creatively, he believes, with the "new kind of consciousness" American society needs. He recognizes that reshaping communal sensibilities is difficult. Serious writers have to absorb and articulate a social awareness not only distorted by partisan interests but also "streaked with fantasy" (CN, p. 164). Sensing a major revolution in human consciousness, these writers now try hard to create a fiction reflecting this psychological shift. Even the most creative artists may not always succeed, Bellow concedes. But they alone are making a sincere effort to capture in their art this age's societal and cultural dynamics. The media people – or, as he likes to term some among them, the publicity and literary intellectuals – do not even try. They are too busy responding to different, more pragmatic, impulses.

Bellow is not suggesting that all America's cultural ills are attributable to its humanities professors or their students (these same media intellectuals). Still, academics and popular-media operatives do appear to impoverish rather than enrich humanistic values and standards. They do so in part by concocting an unceasing flow of literary fads and fashions. Yet instead of being new or avant-garde, most of their supposed innovations are merely repetitious and derivative. "I don't see any real avant-garde in sight," complains Bellow, "maybe because there isn't sufficient stability."[9] Certainly today's intelectuals, whether literary or media, appear to him to offer little cultural or social stability. Having started with "an avant-garde bias against the great public" (CN, p. 164), a bias they likely acquired as undergraduates, these aesthetically inclined young people quickly changed their minds and tactics upon graduating. Ironically, during the postwar years most intellectuals "expressed nothing but horror of mass media," Bellow recalls, "but now, just as violently, that's what they're embracing." This behavior reveals "their faddishness, not to say their sneakiness and cowardice."[10] Occasionally they do reach out to the masses, but they do so not as sensitive, conscientious writers but as "demagogues." They offer their countrymen not literature but a culture containing mere "literary elements." For the true interests of these pseudo-literary intellectuals, Bellow insists, are not artistic but "exclusively social and political." Their tunnel vision has resulted in the long estrangement of the avant-garde from the larger community and has brought experimental art to "a curious end." What now passes as avant-garde art or literature has been swallowed up by greedy media intellectuals who hunger again "for contact with the tribe," complains Bellow. This is the same "tribe to whose words a century ago the Mallarmés were trying to give a more pure sense" (CN, p. 164). But such purity of aesthetic motive is lacking today in America's self-appointed cultural leaders.

But if serious writers (despite their obvious faults) are not major cultural malefactors, and if America's cultural ills are not all to be blamed on its humanities professors or their students (the media intellectuals), or even on Upperclass Protestant America, who else is at fault? Well, in addition to all of the aforementioned, there is also postwar American society itself: its debased mass tastes encourage – if not demand – a steady diminishing of cultural tastes and standards. Not surprisingly, this sad state of affairs proves beneficial to the publicity intellectuals. For civilization's disappointments or failures, declares Bellow, provide these people with their base for personal success. In other words, if civilization is a failure, the media functionaries are profiting by the failure. Whatever civilization salvages or accumulates, he complains, these culture opportunists "treat as fuel and burn up." In recent years they merely have shifted society's major energy sources. The nineteenth-century power-seekers derived their "industrial fuel from coal, from the combustion of carboniferous forests." But today's "successful operators burn up the culture of the nineteenth, the eighteenth, the seventeenth centuries, of all the centuries, of all the ages." Even as they voice complaints of a "consumer culture," they are themselves busy consuming man's total past (CN, p. 174).

These people have no problem with guilt. They think they are doing nothing wrong. Their "sanction," explains Bellow, is their secular belief in the "Contemporaneous." Convinced that "whatever is not Contemporaneous is worthless," and that "dead civilizations are to be cremated," they look to the conflagration that promises their version of "peace and wisdom" (CN, pp. 174–75). In short, these culture vultures favor that which works to their advantage and disparage anything that does not. Yet even more viciously anti-intellectual than even these media opportunists are those spokesmen of the underground press who advocate narcotics and excremental language. The "most potent of primordial materials" for this group, Bellow declares, is feces and its related terms and images. Hence a comic entertainer like Lenny Bruce, who combined both narcotics and excremental humor, has become a talismanic figure. Bellow cites as literary validators of Bruce's use of language two writers whom in the past he has praised: George Orwell and Henry Miller.[11] He recalls that George Orwell, in his essay "Inside the Whale," lauds Henry Miller for replacing the old "language of literary protocol" with the "real language" spoken by "real men" in streets and shipping-rooms. Now the "Miller victory," says Bellow, "is complete." The resonance of the street words has become great, and excremental verbiage exudes "a moral force like that of Church Latin." For the underground does not lack religion, though it takes a blasphemous form. Hence Lenny Bruce proved "a Jesus who died for our sins. He was caught while taking the narcotics sacrament and his (or His) pure spirit was destroyed." Can this not be termed, asks Bellow facetiously, "an excrement-sacrament?" (CN, p. 176).

3. Art and Narcissism Equals Amusement

What then is art's role in this vulgarized, bohemianized society? Bellow's answer: "It is a toy" (CN, p. 170). For the nation's prevailing cultural standard is the "amusement standard." More precisely, it is the "amusement-boredom standard." In the past, avant-garde art belonged not to a great public but to the few. Such art was born of "solitude and twilight." Only a small public saw and read the "group masterpieces" resulting from the artists' "pure subjectivity or inwardness" – that is, from their "dissociation and solitary reflection." Now art is beholden to "a great public with small-public attitudes." This "great-small public" has interests less aesthetic than social and narcissistic. Not wanting true art, its members prefer "art-tinctured ideas and suggestions for the conduct or misconduct of life" (CN, p. 177). His use of "narcissistic," Bellow explains, echoes Tocqueville, who insisted that in a democracy ordinary people desire "primarily to view themselves." Each free citizen finds "nothing more fascinating than – himself" (CN, p. 170.).

At present, too, Americans are given to "staring" at themselves. In this "new self-consciousness," says Bellow, "art is a key element." The mass media take advantage of this general need to pamper and entertain the self. They assimilate the methods and discoveries of talented modern artists and spread these borrowings throughout society. Large corporations also have been quick to cash in. They offer the general public "techniques of shock, violent dissociation, gratuitous acts, monstrous beauties, *Ubu* barbarities." Huge numbers of people and profits are involved, and with the population explosion has come a "consciousness explosion" that induces "vast amounts of fantasy." All this expanded self-awareness and strong, widespread "feelings of solidarity" convince Americans we all are at life's vital center. We know our lives and actions are what make up art; indeed, we feel we are more important than art. What need then have we for the "authority" or art of artists? "We recognize no such authority," declares Bellow. "As Protestantism denied the power of priests, We deny the power of these priest-substitutes, the artists, who wish to cast a magical spell over Us and to invest their work with sacredness. There is no such sacredness now" (CN, p. 170).

In the United States, then, art and literature have shrunk in importance. Most people are interested primarily in "glorious self-realization." "Americans have never been very bookish," Bellow explains, "and in books they generally sought the usable." In the last century, literature did help transform social life and character. Now people wish to make practical use of imaginative art but to avoid being influenced by it. "They want to cook their meals over Pater's hard gemlike flame," he jokes, "and they light their cigarettes at it." They wish to erase the boundaries between literature and life, stage and audience. Some spectators disrobe and mingle with the actors. "What the actors have, the spectators have too. Significance is thus dispersed." Thousands believe they share whatever qualities merit attention. Many observers have noted that everyone is "in the act," with poet Wallace Stevens pointing up literature's essential "theatricality." Authors are actors, Stevens argued, and books are theaters. Bellow agrees. Still he cannot help wondering: "if the theatre is everywhere, and everyone is acting, where are exemplary events to be seen?" In short, he worries that this "theory of creative equality" advocated by popular media and underground press may imply "the death of art." If we are not careful, art could become "the problem . . . for the census taker, not the critic" (CN, pp. 177–78).

The basic problem is that a powerful nation of unequaled "energy and practicality" has fashioned an industrial society without historical precedent. What can or should the artist do in this society? Bellow believes his best step is "to take a common-sense view of things." No longer can the artist play such Sixties roles as "the Child, the Primitive, the Romantic Agonist, the Rebel, the Drugged Visionary." Such roles and plots are shattered and gone. Today, demagogues, dunces, businessmen, and publicity intellectuals in effect own "modernism," whereas the artist has lost "contact with his modernist predecessors." He has been deprived of valuable impulses and a needed creative verve. Yet despite being surrounded by "lunatics," the artist has to "make rational judgments." He is not suggesting the artist be limited or bound by the rational, says Bellow. "The operations of common sense are only preliminary." He must begin, however, by grasping to what degree "fantasy prevails in the country" and how "art-polluted" is his environment. Only then is the artist or writer free to receive again new imaginative impulses. "The depths of the spirit," Bellow reminds his readers, "is never overcrowded" (CN, p. 178).

Still, most Americans do have reason to seek escape, Bellow concedes, whether in fantasy, pseudo art, or otherwise. Our cities and suburbs *are* so overcrowded that their inhabitants feel increasingly closed-in, fearful, and in need of entertainment and distraction. The American artist or writer must accept the grim truth that American society, "like decadent Rome, is an amusement society." Hence art's "business" and usefulness are valued before its intrinsic beauty. This situation suggests to Bellow that art's aesthetic qualities "cannot and should not compete with amusement." He recalls R. G. Collingwood's argument that the artist must function as a prophet. Collingwood explained he was not suggesting the artist "'foretells things to come,'" but only that by nature of being an artist he informs "'the audience, at risk of their displeasure, the secrets of their own hearts.'" The artist exists to be his community's spokesman. This view of the artist's function, Bellow acknowledges, is an old one, "much older than Collingwood." But now it is a view not often recalled. He feels it should be, for "'no community,'" as Collingwood reminded us, "'altogether knows its own heart.'" On a later occasion, Bellow challenges Collingwood's view of the artist's social responsibilities. But here he agrees with the philosopher that this failure of human knowledge jeopardizes a community's well being. The remedy for this failure, both Collingwood and Bellow insist, lies in art itself or "'the poem itself.'" Art provides "'medicine'" for the communal mind's "'worst disease,'" quotes Bellow, by which they both mean "'the corruption of consciousness'" (CN, p. 178).

Having concurred in this view of the artist's social responsibilities, Bellow nevertheless detects a flaw in Collingwood's logic. The artist cannot always play social prophet, warns Bellow, even when he wishes to do so. Many cultural factors and institutions help corrupt a community's sensibility or consciousness. They change constantly, for example, the artist's status and function, his perceptions and audience. Indeed, these factors too have not remained the same in recent years. For one thing, the serious young writer today, says Bellow, generally does not expect to win a large readership; instead he looks to a small, discriminating one. He even has to convince people he is truly a writer. In place of the "proper credentials" flaunted by members of other professions, the writer has only "a self-anointed look." His initial task, therefore, "is to legitimize himself." His struggle to do so varies sharply from that of a literary aspirant of fifty or sixty years ago. The American literary (or even journalistic) scene was then very different. An ambitious novelist "from Sioux Falls or Lincoln, Nebraska," Bellow states, "headed for St. Louis, New Orleans, or Chicago." If he had "the gift of words," he could work as a newspaper reporter and live in "a little bohemia" on the Mississippi banks or Chicago's Near North Side. In short, having made his choice, "he became a writer." But such opportunities exist no longer. The gathering and dissemination of news, laments Bellow, "have been rationalized, mechanized, electronified." Newspapers bulge with advertisements, canned news items, and syndicated columns to the point where they have little space for writing and none for "reflective personal reporting." Gone are the old, easy informality, the idle scribbling in saloons, the "Front Page razzle dazzle." Life, earnest and real, Bellow complains, "has caught up with us."[12]

4. The City as Setting

Bellow is also acutely aware of this century's literary geography. He repeatedly emphasizes the vital role geography has played in the American writer's development – or in his lack of proper development and growth. By the end of the 1920s, says Bellow, writers had left New Orleans and Chicago for Hollywood, New York, and Paris. Today, New York is considered America's literary capital. "But it is really that?" he asks. The writer arriving from Paducah or Topeka feels he has finally escaped "from the barren periphery" and arrived at "the center." The question is, at "the center of what? Of new literary ideas, new impulses?" (SDL, p. 15). Does the newcomer truly have reason to believe he will encounter new ideas and impulses in New York? For Bellow the answer is no: a writer carries his geography with him. Theodore Dreiser is an example. One source of Dreiser's appeal for Bellow is that he too made the city (often Chicago) a central element of his fiction. It was the focal point of his characters' hopes and fears, successes and failures. "Dreiser was the starstruck country boy madly excited by the provincial capital," explains Bellow. "I find it very agreeable, at times truly moving, to read books like *Sister Carrie* or *Dawn*. How deeply the Hoosier kid feels the power of the great city – the purposeful energy of the crowds." Everything there fascinates Dreiser: the "factories, horse-cars, hotel lobbies, a machine which makes keys, a hardware warehouse, luxury shops, fast women, plausible salesmen, exponents of social Darwinism and other bookish ninnies, sturdy railroad men." Dreiser grows "drunk with all this." He considers "the Windy City the most marvelous thing that ever happened."[13]

When he reads Dreiser then, says Bellow, he is "inclined to think so, too." Many of the same things intrigue him, and at times he regrets their passing. Dreiser's pages provide him with an instant montage of the Chicago that was. "The crass, dirty, sinful, vulgar, rich town of politicians, merchant princes and land speculators, the Chicago of Yerkes and Samuel Insull, has vanished. Suddenly the 'Hog Butcher for the World' was there no longer." Bellow has never been able to decide "whether Sandburg's 'Chicago' was a poem or an advertising man's effusion." What he does realize is that in this city "Europeans – even New Englanders – were able to let themselves go." The changes continue, however, and in recent years "a new population of Third World immigrants has settled in Chicago," as have "internal immigrants from the South."[14] So despite some vestigial landmarks, Bellow too often feels himself a stranger in his own town.

His critics and reviewers frequently over-simplify and distort Bellow's views on the city. He does rely heavily upon the city as setting and metaphor. He does point repeatedly to urban life as a serious inten- sifier of modern man's chaotic mental and emotional condition. But he rejects the notion that the city itself is the prime *cause* of contemporary pressures or evils. The "evils" of modern existence, Bellow argues, now engage people everywhere and easily and are hardly confined to the city. They can reach people and "annihilate their minds and souls just as well out in the sticks as they can in New York." The truth is that the city's "characteristic life," at least as drawn by James Joyce in *Ulysses,* says Bellow, is no longer truly "visible" in America. "People are not out in the streets as Leopold Bloom was in 1904"; instead, they are "in the suburbs. The inner city is blighted, the scene of violence, crime and horror." Clearly its residents "are not reading books."[15]

Most are leading a harrowing urban existence. "People today in the cities," Bellow declares, "feel isolation and powerlessness. They can feel their weakness, their impotency and their entrapment. They don't know what to do." Yet who even bothers to discuss their plight? "Who has the answers?" he asks. "People sit at home in terror and read horror stories for diversion or watch violent TV programs." What else are they to do? "Really, matters have gotten out of hand."[16] The Chicago of his own youth and earlier, he insists, despite the horrific tales of violence in popu- lar folklore and media, was a much safer place. Serious writers who did not truly understand Chicago only added to the distortion. Sherwood Anderson was among those professing shock at the violence and sin. But Anderson "was an artistic small-towner," says Bellow. "He had left the provinces because his sensibilities required more culture, more ideas, conversation and refinement. In Winesburg he found only psychopath- ology in Freudian (sexual) forms." Bellow considers Anderson "characteristic of the small-town American with esthetic inclination, circa

1910." He is not suggesting that Anderson "lacked talent, only that he was a provincial, craving big-time esthetic and cultural horizons. That Chicago should seem awful to him is easy to understand." Not only did Anderson lack adequate knowledge to grasp the city as it truly was, adds Bellow, but he also "applied to it standards of 'refinement' and 'art' which today make us a bit uncomfortable."[17]

Sadly enough, that folklore of violence is more valid today than earlier. For obviously "Chicago is a far more dangerous place now," laments Bellow, than even during Prohibition. "In the twenties the Capone guys shot up the O'Banion guys. Only one innocent died in the Valentine's Day massacre. You knew when a body was found in a sewer which gang the victim belonged to." Rarely did such killings extend beyond the gangs. "The circulation wars sometimes affected the newspaper guy on the corner because he might lose all his teeth if he carried the *Examiner* instead of the *Tribune*. Most ordinary citizens – civilians, if you like – were not greately affected." Conditions today offer a sharp contrast, as "over a recent Thanksgiving weekend no less than nine murders were reported."[18]

What has happened to his city, declares Bellow, is that "Black politicians and white city-council crooks who have taken over the old Daley Machine have between them divided the city on racial lines." These shrewd politicos have made it difficult even to determine if the crime rate has increased. "The police fiddle with the records on orders from our mayors, so it is impossible to obtain reliable figures. Impossible also to get an accurate breakdown of the statistics." The papers are not helpful. "Newspapers, when they report abominable crimes," he states, "do not refer to the race of the suspects. The public, which understands only too well, is resigned to the imposition of this taboo. Right thinking liberal citizens, hoping for future improvements, recalling past injustices, counsel themselves to be patient." To them "'patience' sounds better than 'intimidation' or 'surrender,' and nicer than 'cowardice.'" There may not be "more muggings, knifings, shootings and murders than there used to be," concedes Bellow, "but the crimes seem to be more outlandish." They are "committed in a more demonic spirit. You are robbed, and locked in the trunk of your car; raped, and also forced to go down on the rapist; or sodomized."[19]

Therefore newcomers, from the crime standpoint alone, find a Chicago very different from the city that welcomed earlier generations. "Consider the hazards new immigrants must now face," laments Bellow. "Different? Of course Chicago is different! The public schools are now eighty-five or eighty-seven percent Negro and Hispanic." No longer are they the melting pot of earlier decades. "What sort of democratic education do you suppose such schools afford?" he asks. "There's no way to compare the experience of old and new ethnic groups." Now the basic scenario is that "the Central Americans, Koreans, Pakistanis, Iranians come here seeking employment, peace, stability. A refugee from the terrors of Beirut opens a grocery store in Chicago, thrives, and then is shot in a holdup." This is "not an uncommon story," complains Bellow. "The funny misfortunes and torments of *Candide* are the literal facts of modern experience. The older 'ethnics,' the Poles, Czechs, the Italians, the Irish, the Germans and the Scandinavians, live in heavily-defended districts, clinging to the properties in which their parents and grandparents invested so much labor. They organize neighborhood watch-groups, and they buy arms." But this tragic "division into blacks and ethnics is a disaster. A second disaster is the swift rise of the demagogues in both factions. They expose each other's corruption and criminal connections." This exposure serves little purpose, says Bellow, for "the more the public learns, the more its paralysis increases."[20]

Yet despite his dirge about life in Chicago and other American urban centers, he is "not saying," Bellow hastens to add, "that cities are doomed places." But he does suggest "that the hard core of the welfare society is doomed." These people have "no prospects." No one has taken "the trouble to teach them anything. They live in a kind of perpetual chaos, in a great noise. And, you know, they really are startled souls. They cannot be reasoned with or talked to about anything." Bellow offers no solutions for such serious urban problems, but he does think a candid acknowledgement of city terrorism and fear will help. Is it not time, he asks, that we admit such a condition exists? "For a long time, the subject lay under a taboo. Nobody was going to talk about it. Now people are beginning to do so. Though I consider myself a kind of liberal, I have to admit that the taboos were partly of liberal origin." Liberals believed it was "wrong to speak with candor. But lying in a good cause only aggravates disorder." Still, mass deception is easier than getting people to admit that major changes are needed in city life. "There's a scheme of evasion which has gotten into everybody," declares Bellow. "It's as though people were to say: 'I get home dog tired after a terrible day out in that jungle, and then I don't want to think about it. Enough! I want to be brainwashed. I'm going to have my dinner and drink some beer, and I'm going to sit watching TV until I pass out—because that's how I feel."[21]

Interestingly enough, such biting candor about their city has impressed rather than angered his fellow Chicagoans. At a recent Art Institute dinner hosted by the city's political and social leaders to salute Bellow's 75th birthday, the speakers repeatedly acknowledged his unflinching honesty. Mayor Richard Daley (the younger) declared the city fathers' recognition of Bellow to be "long overdue." He thanked Bellow not merely for "adding a great deal of vitality to the city" but also for moving him personally by his fiction and by their private conversations to be "a more compassionate man." Novelist Eugene Kennedy noted that Bellow's searingly honest depictions of all aspects of Chicago life "bring out the best in this city." Allan Bloom, author of *The Closing of the American Mind* and Bellow's colleague at the University of Chicago, put the occasion into clear perspective. "Bellow is to Chicago what Balzac was to Paris," Bloom stated. "Saul has always understood that even if you are on your way from Becoming to Being, you still have to catch the train at Randolph Street." Bellow then offered his own explanation. "My roots in Chicago are more like tangled wires," he observed. "Because I've loved the city, I've never been able to write lies about it. World-class cities like Chicago don't need phony promotion."[22]

5. A Cry of Anger

Certainly he avoids idle civic flattery. The TV-and-beer attitude he describes suggests to Bellow that inhabitants of Chicago and other inner cities are reluctant to put up a struggle "for the human part of themselves." Instead they have chosen to organize "the terror in such a way as to expel it from their lives with doormen, security precautions, alarm systems." They practice avoidance. "They don't go out at night. They avoid walking in certain streets. Many are only half aware that they have done this." Their actions are for them "only half conscious, not fully real. What's real is the daily grind, hardships and ailments, tax questions, the traffic, how long you have to wait for the elevator – all these little things. Those are real." Has their failure to face up to ugly modern facts caused Bellow to sour on his fellow men? No. As so often in the past, he emphasizes human nature's positive potential. Despite their too frequent negative behavior, he states, "when we think of what human beings really are, the sublimity of their greatest powers, the capacities of the least of them, even the most criminal – human powers in an inverted form – we can't fail to be impressed. We can't help it."[23]

Still, his faith in man's capacity for good does not stop Bellow from expressing his anger at his countrymen's failure to deal with urban blight. He lashes out in essay, interview, and especially in novels like *Mr.*

Sammler's Planet and *The Dean's December.* The latter book, he declares, literally "was a *cri de coeur.* I just could no longer stand the fact that the city and the country were in decay under our very eyes and people would not talk about the facts. They might talk about money to change things, but never about what was actually happening. No one levels any more. So it was a cry. But I don't know whether anyone heard it." [24] To make matters worse, the physical decay and moral blight have spread unimpeded from inner city to suburb and countryside. Bellow finds rural life only a small improvement at best over inner-city life. He will concede, he notes somewhat wryly, that most "bucolic dreams" are "rather touching," and that it is pleasant "to go where the air is fresher." He even will acknowledge that destroying one's brain "with dope out in the quiet countryside is probably more agreeable than doing it in the city." Otherwise, he sees little value there in what he has referred to on several occasions as the rural communes of the young. In fact, there were times in the 1960s and '70s when he joked that if he were a "capitalist," he would consider investing "in old people's homes for the young." The way some of their communes were going, the young people, he then thought, were fated to prove "prematurely decrepit" and that there would "be a big business in rehabilitation" (LC, p. 15). [25]

So *where* an individual finds himself is not for Bellow the key factor. He also rejects the claim that modern life is intense and vulnerable only in the city. "The volume of judgments one is called upon to make," he argues, depends not upon location but upon "the receptivity of the observer." What matters most is the individual and his powers of perception. Still, it is not easy anywhere to be a creative person. For anyone today who is sensitive and receptive to the life about him, warns Bellow, will have "a terrifying number of opinions to render." He will be asked: "What do you think about this, about that, about Viet Nam, about city planning, about expressways, or garbage disposal, or democracy, or Plato, or pop art, or welfare states, or literacy in a 'mass society'?" Bellow wonders whether modern conditions ever again will provide tranquillity enough for a "contemporary Wordsworth to recollect anything." Art is related to quietude, he insists, to "the achievement of stillness in the midst of chaos." He refers to the stillness that characterizes both prayer and "the eye of the storm." Conversely, true art can result also in "an arrest of attention in the midst of distraction." [26] But for Bellow the basic question remains: Where in this country, in this age, can the artist attain such tranquillity?

Bellow cautions that true art, at least in novelistic form, and even at its most "melioristic" or social-minded, is limited in what it can accomplish. He once had expressed his belief that social distraction or urban chaos directly challenges the novel and limits the novelist. He had reasoned that as a result certain expressive modes appropriate to music or poetry are not available to the novelist, especially the realistic novelist. But he since has had second thoughts. "I'm no longer so sure of that," he admits. "I think the novelist can avail himself of similar privileges. It's just that he can't act with the same purity or economy of means as the poet. He has to traverse a very muddy and noisy territory before he can arrive at a pure conclusion. He's more exposed to the details of life." Still, a true artist can transform societal exposure into art. For Bellow, the "modern masterpiece" of such urban confusion is James Joyce's *Ulysses*. In it Joyce delineates a receptive mind that is "unable to resist experience." Human experience in all "its diversity, its pleasure and horror, passes through [Leopold] Bloom's head like an ocean through a sponge. The sponge can't resist; it has to accept whatever the waters bring. It also notes every microorganism that passes through it." What he means to say, Bellow explains, may be better expressed as a question: "How much of this must the spirit suffer, in what detail is it obliged to receive this ocean with its human plankton?" Joyce makes it appear at times as if the sheer volume of experiences has nullified the mind's power. Yet Joyce here has assumed a high degree of passivity. "Stronger, more purposeful minds" than that of a Leopold Bloom, states Bellow, "can demand order, impose order, select, disregard." But society's torrent of particulars threatens even the most disciplined mind with "disintegration." However, "a Faustian artist" like James Joyce, he declares, "is unwilling to surrender to the mass of particulars."[27]

A sensitive, gifted novelist, then, may fashion art from urban disorder, but even he can do little through his writing to reform or ameliorate that disorder. He himself had once harbored reformist tendencies, recalls Bellow. Now, in his late years, he knows better. "Like many American writers I was always pulling for something. I wanted to add my mite to the general improvement fund. But I am much less concerned now. I have done my duty by democracy." The reasons for his harder, more realistic outlook are clear to him. "After all, I have seen how ineffective all this meliorism has been for two centuries, beginning with the Romantics and continuing right down through the bourgeois critics." He is thinking of well-meaning social-improvers "like Shelley, Emerson, William Morris." He wonders if there ever has been "a writer in English who has not been an improving one?" Certainly earlier American writers exhibited a strong desire to improve things. Bellow can understand why: "The country was wild and untutored, and it needed advice." Walt Whitman was a prime example. The venerable bard even thought "he had to invent archetypes for the whole nation. He had a vision of what the country should be and he did his best to improve it." Of course, some Americans always feel compelled to advise their countrymen. He has in mind, notes Bellow, such self-appointed sages as "Teddy Roosevelt, Hugh Hefner, [and] old Bernarr McFadden, the health faddist."[29]

But most Americans today have goals less sweeping and more self-centered and pragmatic than in past years. At present the national "emphasis has shifted to making it," says Bellow. "People have surrendered their personal moral objectives to government or schools or psychologists." This change was "accelerated with the boom" following World War II. People found themselves unexpectedly having "to play roles without a pattern or precedent. They might be yanked up suddenly to become manager of a plant or head of a company, so they needed advice." In effect, their behavior proved a collective "surrender to pragmatism." They realized that "the true is what makes you successful and the false is what makes you fail." In a situation like that, wonders Bellow, "what happens to faith, hope and charity?" For Americans have turned in recent years to forming "their moral ideas not in the old way but by their professions and guilds." This approach diminishes any sense of personal guilt as it "tends to transfer sin to the corporation." He cites as example a "recent F.B.I. sting operation to uncover corruption among Chicago judges." What resulted was informative if disheartening: "all the lawyers in town were terribly indignant about members of their own profession cooperating with the F.B.I. There was no indignation about the fraud, only about the cooperation." While saddening, their behavior was predictable. "People think now about disloyalty to the group, not the offense, and actually disloyalty to the group is rather rare." But perhaps it is merely "the character of cynicism that's changed," suggests Bellow; "maybe this means a wiping out of hypocrisy."[29]

He suggests a possible source of this moral malaise. Much of this cynicism may derive directly from what "Americans are being told," reasons Bellow. "Every American thinks he has a right to the best of everything. That includes the best opinions, which are obviously those of the best people. So you see how received opinion works." He finds this a "comic" situation, but one with non-comic overtones. "[A]s in all good comedy," he warns, "the obverse side is grim; there is a lot of cant. It all makes a man unhappy – but also glad to be in Chicago." He then asks rhetorically: "Who would not prefer the vulgarity of Chicago to the finesse

of the East Coast literary establishment? You have to count your bless-
ings, you know."[30]

6. New York—"That Glittering City"

Chicago and New York are the two cities of Bellow's fiction and psyche,
and he does not hesitate to criticize either. Yet he repeatedly makes clear
that his visceral home, for better or worse, is Chicago. Of the New York
he has known at first hand Bellow is much less forgiving. He is convinced
that much of what is culturally wrong with this country can be seen in—if
not traced to—New York City. He does concede that years ago, especially
in the early postwar years, the intellectual scene there was much different. By the late 1940s, he recalls, postwar New York had a thriving "literary intellectual life" that included *Partisan Review*, Columbia University,
and "many independent writers, painters, and critics." Even more significant were the many things that had not yet happened. "The big money
had not yet hit, the media had not yet developed their full power, the
universities had not yet entered the picture as patrons of the arts." But
the media and the universities were soon to assert their influence, and
between them, as Bellow sees it, this country's literary life was annihilated (LC, p. 12). Eager young writers then left or avoided the spartan
or bohemian lifestyles their predecessors had taken for granted. Opting
instead for comfort and security, these ambitious newcomers migrated
to *Time* magazine or the networks and advertising agencies—or to the
university literature departments.

   Bellow remained in New York for a decade, but in the late 1950s he
began to think about leaving the east coast. "I didn't like living in New
York," he says of those years. "I hated the New York literary Establishment." He considers New York now to be "not the cultural center of
America, but the business and administrative center of American culture."[31] He recognizes that the Big Town helped many talented postwar
writers to get started, but he insists it now poses a persistent danger to
many writers. New York often tempts and transforms the most gifted into Major Literary Figures. These individuals then do little more for the
rest of their lives other than grant "solemn interviews to prestigious
journals or serve on White House committees or . . . participate in international panel discussions on the crisis in the arts" (SDL, pp. 16–17). In
short, the Literary Figure absorbs the writer so that his "social struggle"
proves more important than his art.

Bellow does confess to a certain nostalgia for "the New York that might have been: a city of great culture." But the city he actually sees he describes vividly and scornfully in key episodes in *Mr. Sammler's Planet.* These episodes, he explains, "are meant to be typical of the madness in New York City middle-class life."[32] He had tried to make this point earlier in *Herzog,* says Bellow, but in the later novel he catalogues more fully his dismay at the city's postwar physical clutter and confusion. Elderly, world-weary Artur Sammler lives in a Manhattan littered by smashed outdoor pay telephones and booths used as urinals. He guesses that Manhattan now exceeds Naples or Salonika in its decayed fluorescence. Sammler is neither dismayed nor gratified. He realizes that people are given to exaggerating "the tragic accents of their condition." They insist on using the dissolution of former conventions to rationalize their own shallowness, vulgarity, foolishness, and lust—thereby "turning former respectability inside out."[33] Yet if displeased by such moral blight, he is hardly shocked. He has seen much worse than filthy phone booths. So has Saul Bellow. He too observes the modern social disorder with keen interest but emotional detachment. "Today you can simply be distracted to death," he states. "Tearing the self apart has become a social duty."[34]

Bellow finds it ironic that New York remains the business center for American culture. Here the nation's "culture is prepared, processed, and distributed," he complains. Here also America's major publishers, with their complex modern commercial, editing, printing, and advertising apparatus, as well as their personnel specialists, "wait for manuscripts" (SDL, p. 15). With their tremendous expenses, says Bellow, these publishers cannot afford to wait long. They have to find material by attracting writers—or fabricating books in their own editorial offices. By "New York," in this context, Bellow also means Washington and Boston. In fact, many of the city's "literary mandarins," he explains, live in Cambridge, New Haven, Bennington, New Brunswick, Princeton, with a few in London and Oxford. These high-culture officials write for the newspapers, sit on editorial committees, advise-define-consult and set standards. They also drink cocktails and gossip. By these frenzied actions they contribute "to New York's appearance of active creativity," its seemingly "substantial literary life" (SDL, pp. 15–16).

But even that description, he realizes, is not precise. New York is more accurately the nation's "amusement or frivolity center, the excitement center, perhaps even the anxiety center." For in truth the city does not provide, Bellow cautions, any semblance of "independent and original intellectual life"; it offers to artists "no equilibrium [and] no mental space." "Ideas are no longer truly discussed or tested here" (NYCD, p. 12). In short, New York lacks for Bellow any true "intellectual substance." The city does not nurture a valid cultural life but merely the "idea of a cultural life" (SDL, p. 16). For what intellectual life the country may still possess has moved, for better or worse, out into the universities.

So Bellow cautions the aspiring writer who insists on flying into the Big Town "from Boise, Idaho" not to expect to find a welcoming commit- tee of other writers moved by a pure love of poetry. He will not find writers awaiting him "on the steps of the Public Library like Athenians to discuss existence or justice." What the literature-minded newcomer will find instead of philosophical discussions, declares Bellow, is a city thriving "on a sense of national deficiency" (NYCD, p. 12). For no matter at what he looks, Bellow discerns in postwar New York little significant cultural or aesthetic activity. Yes, the city may exhibit considerable phys- ical and emotional action, but this action derives from "manipulations, rackets, power struggles . . . infighting," with personal reputations "in- flated and deflated." Thus Bellow considers the emotions and gestures that dominate this accepted national culture center to be "bluster, vehe- mence, swagger, fashion, image-making, [and] brain-fixing." Still the aspiring writer from the provinces can do some things in New York City. He can "lead the *life* of a poet or a novelist." In other words, the neophyte can acquire "a pad, go to bars, wear the clothes, and make the scene." Ob- viously, this lifestyle has little to do with art; it is "to poetry," says Bellow, "what an ad for bread is to nourishment." Such calculated behavior offers merely "the picture" of the real thing. Yet some people ask nothing more. They find the "idea of being a writer or of leading the art-life" far more appealing than the perfecting of an art. The art itself is demanding and difficult, while most artists are "beset by detractors, challenged by change, threatened with obsolescence by the prophets of electronics and by snooty college professors who want to pick up the marbles of tradition and break up the game." In addition, the typical, moderately educated American feels he has all of the literature he needs and therefore has lit- tle interest in the novels of his contemporaries. To a degree the citizen is right. Novels today too often are "indeed irrelevant to his real concerns," laments Bellow, being "derivative feeble things" (SDL, p. 16).

7. The Writer as Shaman

What then should the writer today do? Bellow suggests he begin by real- izing he can expect little help from other people, literary or non-literary, at home or abroad. So what are his options? A respected friend once confided to Bellow, only half-facetiously, that "possession" may provide the answer: writers, in these difficult times, "should be more shamanistic." Bellow explains that shamans were "primitive Siberian priests, given to trances, dream-utterances," who tended to be "androgynous, homosexual, creatures of mystery, uninhibited, antinomian." Most likely his friend was not making a serious proposal that civilized writers behave precisely like those shamans, thinks Bellow. He was probably implying writers should turn more readily to their intuitive or instinctive feelings of social revolt against the comfortable, established order of things. Bellow appears to agree, cautiously. For "when things are tough," he reasons, "when the knowledge needed for realistic analysis is out of reach, some form of intuitive daring may seem best." Are there not sufficient literary precedents? Was not Rimbaud "a sort of Druidic figure"? Was not D. H. Lawrence, "with his Dionysian apocalyptic insights . . . something of a shaman"? Clearly, even some negative aspects of shamanism appeal to the modern temper, says Bellow. He refers to contemporary life's abundant "connotations of squalor, neurotic sexuality, mesmerism, charlatanism, and so forth." Those socially defiant beings who most wish to resist today's "glib poster-world of packaging and public relations" seem to him to find a "healthy antidote" to current problems in shamanism's "blood, spittle, excrements, and swoons." For them "defacement and smearing" are not out of line, nor is "blasphemy." Indeed the problem for these culture rebels is to "find things sacred enough to blaspheme" (SDL, pp. 26–27).

Their stance may not be his, Bellow concedes, but he does find their refractory attitude intriguing. He is hardly alone. Shamanism now appeals to numerous disquieted moderns living within society's "elaborate systems of compromise," he states. The desire or need of these discontented Americans for some form of social "defiance" suggests to them the possibility of penetrating magically "the fortifications of organization, tyranny, established falsehood, and dulness." Hence a degree of shamanistic skepticism, he argues, could benefit American literature. For the shamanistic idea hints at the tremendous longing by writers to "be free enough to tell off the State and all its organizations." These dissatisfied individuals wish to strike back at the State's "ruling industries and the enormous apparatus of persuasion, information-misinformation, manipulation, and control." Their desire for changes is a reminder that even reasonably prosperous and free people harbor a strong "need for defiance and even subversion." It also implies a turn by creative people "toward the sacred, if only in the shaggy, dubious, inferior form of shamanism." Their accumulated hungers suggest to Bellow a reversed Platonism: "the artist must pray to be possessed by spirits, that he may utter in his rapture the truth which patient reason can no longer hope for." Such literary fervor would hardly be new. Artists and writers have long been associated, Bellow notes, with the divine and mystical. At one point in nineteenth-century America, for instance, church influence began to wane and clergymen to experience definite doubts; poets, novelists, and essayists stepped to "the center of the spiritual crisis and assumed spiritual obligations." Walt Whitman saw the priests replaced by the "divine literati." Henry James proclaimed the writer's "paramount charge" to be the curing of souls, even if this meant the "subjugation" or even the "exclusion of the picturesque" (SDL, p. 27).

But that was in the last century. How should the American writer now view his social or cultural obligation? Bellow has responded to this question in varied ways. At times he has declared that society should not expect its writers or artists to provide moral or even cultural leadership. "We must be in a rather sad position," he states in one interview, "when we expect novelists to supply us with ethical statements which should properly be offered by society, by firm ideas of right and justice." The trouble is that "in our great need for consolation we seize upon every utterance of every writer and examine it for auguries of good or evil." As a result, an unfair "burden is thrown upon the writer, who is asked to feel himself a prophetic personality." Obviously so great a social responsibility is too much for a writer like himself – that is, a writer "who considers himself a comedian."[35]

Bellow is not suggesting that the writer is without social responsibilities. Indeed, on another occasion he declares that "If there's anything good that he can do the writer should certainly do it at once." Yet the truth is that most writers are narrowly focused and absorbed in their own writing, says Bellow. They are not given to thinking about "holding the line for civilization" against the forces of barbarism. University professors are the ones worrying about this society's "cultural assignment." He himself has mixed feelings on the subject. "Sometimes I'm on one side of the matter and sometimes I'm on the other." If occasionally he worries "about what's happening to culture in the United States, at other times he thinks "there is no culture in the United States, and there's no point in worrying about it." Yes, he knows he once had agreed with the philosopher R. G. Collingwood that the artist "is the one who tells the audience, at the risk of their displeasure, the secrets of their own hearts." He had liked and quoted that statement when he read it. Now he worries about the moral and didactic responsibilities society thrusts upon the writer. "After all, we are, most of us," he states, "frail vessels: how much do we think we can do, what the devil do we think we are doing anyway? Do we really believe, in a country, a society, a civilization like this, that we can make that much difference?" Bellow does not care for "the feeling of super-erogation that goes with this. I don't even know how many times Shelley would have said poets are the unacknowledged legislators of mankind, if he had lived beyond the age of forty." Had he done so, Shelley might well have grown tired of "saying it over and over again. Possibly he would have changed his mind" (LC, pp. 6–7).

Still, societal pressures on the creative individual persist. What the modern writer does feel, complains Bellow, is the public's demand "that he should be a legislator and that he should perform a moral function." People even expect him to "provide emotional, spiritual stuff." For Bellow such expectations derive from "rather old fashioned ideas," and they confirm his conviction that people do not wish to give up such old views. Yes, in public they may "scoff at them," but in private "they continue to live by them. And I include writers in this." The writer, however, is in a predicament. He feels the public's desire that he play teacher and legislator, but at the same time he is nagged by the sense few are paying attention. This feeling is valid, says Bellow, as "hardly anybody is heard very much." American society is essentially "an amusement society," and he does not think most writers harbor "too many illusions about how seriously they are being harkened unto" (LC, p. 7).

The American writer who does succumb to the temptation to act the legislator or prophet should not expect to be taken seriously. For even those who should extend him a sympathetic ear generally fail to do so. He refers once again to the professors and critics, says Bellow, who serve as this nation's literary and media intellectuals and who do much to shape public opinion. He is not suggesting that the creative writer allow himself to be bullied into becoming a passive yea-sayer or affirmer of current social fads, customs, or institutions. When writers no longer serve their society as intellectual and cultural gadflys, warns Bellow, that role is seized by those far less suited for the task. That is precisely what has happened in postwar America. Using an Irving Kristol article as text, Bellow notes that in recent years not novelists or poets but "literary intellectuals" help determine, in Kristol's phrase, "'the opinions of the educated classes.'" These critics and professors play a crucial role in "'defining the moral quality of our society.'" He also cites Kristol's observation that "'there is surely no more important task than to question or affirm the legitimacy of a society's basic institutions, to criticize or amend the original assumptions on which political life proceeds.'" Being himself a social critic and essayist rather than a literary critic or creative writer, Kristol is moved to ask: "'How well equipped are our literary intellectuals for this job? Not, it must be confessed, as well equipped as they ought to be.'"[36] Bellow agrees. Thanks to their selfishness and shortsightedness, America's literary critics and professors have failed to "question or affirm" adequately the legitimacy of their society's key institutions. What is worse, complains Bellow, their failure has affected the nation's creative writers. Literature is now an agent of expediency, having become "important for what one can do with it," he declares. "It is becoming a source of orientations, postures, lifestyles, positions." These postures and positions derive from the "odds and ends of Marxism, Freudianism, existentialism, mythology, surrealism, absurdism, *undsoweiter*." Such fragments represent "the debris of modernism, with apocalyptic leftovers added" (CC, pp. 44–45).

Let no one argue that this was always the American literary condition. Even in this century things were different. During the Depression, notes Bellow, writers "were still concerned with social problems and problems of justice." But this regard for society and justice, he states, fled the United States at the start of the Second World War "and has never returned to reclaim its own lost significance." Bellow recognizes the danger inherent "in the artist's becoming so involved with institutions that he absorbs institutional attitudes and fails to question the power of the ruling class and matters of justice." This was certainly not true of 1930s writers, he points out, and "it need not be the condition of writers today, either." The problem is that at present political concepts, like political positions, tend to be confused. "Many people in the social sciences whose own intuitions are conservative are being pressed continually to make radical discoveries and to announce them. But then Bellow has to consider that "perhaps their radical discoveries are more genuinely radical than those of the would-be writers of protest who don't seem to have any substance." The latter are people "whose hearts may be in the right place but who make no real study of the conditions they protest against."[37]

Here, as elsewhere, Bellow's prime targets are those "educated and indeed supercivilized people" who champion a self-defeating nihilism because they "believe that a correct position makes one illusionless." Such individuals hold "that to be illusionless is more important than anything else." They believe "that it is enlightened to expose, to disenchant, to hate and to experience disgust." As he does so often, Bellow cites

Wyndham Lewis, who, he feels, "had an excellent term for this last phenomenon." Lewis alluded to "the vulgarization of once aristocratic disgust by the modern romantics." But Romanticism is for a traditional humanist like Bellow hardly the only earlier intellectual movement to be distorted in recent times. The "skepticism of the Enlightenment," he complains, "has also been vulgarized." In fact, that once true questioning spirit has been altered to where now it is deemed enlightened and sophisticated to discard conventional emotions. In other words, "it is at present thought blessed," states Bellow, "to see through to the class origins of one's affection for one's grandfather, or to reveal the hypocritical weakness and baseness at the heart of friendships." As always, Bellow rejects such negativism to argue that human beings instinctively persist in their "friendships, affinities, natural feelings." They also retain their "rooted norms," as witness their general agreement "that it is wrong to murder. And even if they are unable to offer rational arguments for this, they are not necessarily driven to commit gratuitous acts of violence." So it occurs to Bellow "that writers might really do well to start thinking about such questions again." But it is evident to him writers will have to do so without the help of critics. Most critics are simply "too romantic to deal with these problems" (CC, p. 45). Writers today, then, like creative artists so often in the past, are primarily on their own. Saul Bellow finds this artistic isolation in America a sorry cultural condition in the century's last decade.

NOTES

1. Saul Bellow, "A Matter of the Soul," *Opera News,* 11 January 1975: 28.

2. Jim Douglas Henry, "Mystic Trade – the American Novelist Saul Bellow Talks to Jim Douglas Henry," *The Listener,* 22 May 1969: 706.

3. Henry, p. 706.

4. Saul Bellow, "Cloister Culture," *New York Times Book Review,* 10 July 1966, p. 2. Subsequent references to this source, abbreviated as CC, are given parenthetically in the text.

5. Saul Bellow, "Culture Now: Some Animadversions, Some Laughs," *Modern Occasions* 1 (Winter 1971): 163. Subsequent references to this source, abbreviated as CN, are given parenthetically in the text.

6. Saul Bellow, "New York – At a Comfortable Distance: 'World Famous Impossibility,'" *New York Times,* 6 December 1970, Sec. A.: 12. Subsequent references to this source, abbreviated as NYCD, are given parenthetically in the text.

7. Matthew C. Roudané, "An Interview with Saul Bellow," *Contemporary Literature,* 25 (Fall 1984): 273.

8. Roudané, pp. 274–75.

9. Jane Howard, "Mr. Bellow Considers His Planet," *Life,* 3 April 1970: 58.

10. Howard, p. 58.

11. See Saul Bellow, "Literature," in *The Great Ideas Today 1963,* ed. Robert M. Hutchins and Mortimer J. Adler (Chicago: Encyclopedia Britannica, Inc., 1963), p. 161.

12. Saul Bellow, "Skepticism and the Depth of Life," in *The Arts & the Public,* ed. James E. Miller and Paul D. Herring (Chicago: Univ. of Chicago Press, 1967), pp. 14–15. Subsequent references to this source, abbreviated as SDL, are given parenthetically in the text.

13. Rockwell Gray, Harry White and Gerald Nemanic, "Interview with Saul Bellow," *TriQuarterly,* 60 (Spring/Summer 1984), p. 637.

14. Gray, et al., p. 657.

15. Robert Boyers *et al,,* "Literature and Culture: An Interview with Saul Bellow," *Salmagundi,* 30 (Summer 1975), p. 15.

16. Alvin P. Sanoff, "'Matters Have Gotten Out of Hand' in a Violent Society: A Conversation with Saul Bellow," *U.S. News and World Report,* 28 June 1982: 49–50.

17. Gray, White and Nemanic, pp. 638–39.

18. Gray, et al., pp. 637–38.

19. Gray, et al., p. 638.

20. Gray, et al., p. 638.

21. Sanoff, pp. 49–50.

22. Jerry Nemanic, "Politicians Sing of Bellow's Gift to Fiction City," *Chicago Tribune,* 9 October 1990, Sec. 1: 14.

23. Sanoff, p. 50.

24. D. J. Bruckner, "A Candid Talk with Saul Bellow," *New York Times Magazine,* 15 April 1984: 52.

25. Bellow commented somewhat similarly, for example, in a 1970 *Life* magazine interview. "These kids, I predict," he stated there, "will face a lot more trouble than their elders. If I were an enterprising real estate man in California I'd build a colony not for the old but for the soon-to-be senile young" (Howard, p. 60).

26. Gordon Lloyd Harper, "Saul Bellow," *Writers at Work: The Paris Review Interviews,* Third Series, ed. George Plimpton (New York: Viking Press, 1968), p. 190.

27. Harper, pp. 190–91.

28. Bruckner, p. 52.

29. Bruckner, p. 52.

30. Bruckner, p. 54.

31. Henry, p. 705.

32. Unsigned, "Some People Come Back Like Hecuba," *Time,* 8 February 1970: 82.

33. Saul Bellow, *Mr. Sammler's Planet* (New York: Viking Press, 1970; rpt. New York: Viking Compass Books, 1973), p. 9.

34. "Some People Come Back Like Hecuba," p. 82.

35. David D. Galloway, "An Interview with Saul Bellow," *Audit-Poetry,* 3 (Spring 1963): 21–22.

36. Irving Kristol, "The Troublesome Intellectuals," *The Public Interest,* 2 (Winter 1966), p. 6.

37. Galloway, p. 20.

Saul Bellow Bibliography (Selected)

Gloria L. Cronin and
Blaine H. Hall

S AUL BELLOW'S stature as a postwar American novelist can only
be compared to that of James, Hemingway, and Faulkner in the
preceding periods. As a Nobel Laureate, winner of several fiction awards, and the subject of over three thousand articles,
Bellow's reputation seems assured. Thus far, he has written sev-
enteen volumes of fiction including novels, novellas, and volumes
of short stories, with at least two more major novels promised.
This is a remarkable body of work which qualifies him not only as
a major American writer but also as an international heavyweight.

The first wave of scholarly interest in Bellow occurred between
1965 and 1974. Critics like Brigitte Scheer-Schäzler (1965), Keith
Opdahl (1967), Irving Malin (1967), John J. Clayton (1968), David D.
Galloway (1970), Nathan Scott (1973), Sarah Blacher Cohen (1974),
M. Gilbert Porter (1974), and Earl Rovit (1974) and (1975) established the dominant critical paradigm through which Bellow is still
largely read. All shared in the celebration of Bellow as neo-
humanist, or contemporary transcendentalist who restored to the
American novel its lost sense of the value of the private life, a feeling for the mystery of human existence, and a healthy American
contempt of the nihilistic effects of European philosophy. They
readily grasped his uniquely Jewish affirmations and welcomed
them as an antidote to the prevailing modernist angst of an American culture they perceived to be overly enamored of modernist
aesthetics, French existentialism, and historicist assumptions. In so
doing, they placed Bellow within the contemporary scene and
broadly distinguished his thematic concerns, stylistic techniques,
and philosophical interests.

The second wave of scholarly interest occurred between 1975 and 1979. Critics like Peter Bischof (1975), Robert Kegan (1976), Tony Tanner (1978), Yuzaburo Shibuya (1978), Chirantan Kulshreshtha (1978), Edmund Schraepen (1978), and Stanley Trachtenberg (1979) amplified the work of earlier scholars by bringing their own national and international perspectives to bear on the task. However, they only slightly modified the by-now-orthodox reading paradigm of Bellow the anti-modernist neo-humanist and contemporary "Yea Sayer."

With the advent of the 1980s a third wave of critical interest produced book-length studies which opened up new avenues of inquiry and attempted to fill in some of the gaps. Joseph McCadden (1980) produced the first treatment of women characters in the Bellow novel. Mark Harris (1980) published the results of his unsuccessful attempt to do a biography on Bellow. Malcolm Bradbury (1982) located Bellow more accurately within the historiography of modernism. Claude Levy (1983) wrote a structuralist treatment of Bellow's style, and Liela Goldman (1983) examined Bellow's debt to Jewish philosophy and ethics. Jan Bakker (1983) compared Bellow to Hemingway, and Jeanne Braham (1984) explored his connection with the American transcendentalists. Daniel Fuchs (1984) produced the first textual study of the novels, being one of the few scholars allowed access to the manuscripts. Jonathan Wilson (1985) expressed his frustration with the "Bellow the humanist" reading paradigm and explored the novels as evidence of Bellow's affinities with the nihilists. Ellen Pifer (1990) turned to the more orthodox view of Bellow, but filled the picture out more thoroughly. In 1991, the Ruth Miller biography was published.

With Bellow's publication in 1989 of two new novellas, *A Theft* and *The Bellarosa Connection,* and in 1991 of a new short story, "Something to Remember Me By," plus the promise to his publishers of two new novels, no doubt another wave of Bellow criticism will focus on "Bellow, the late phase." Present work-in-progress in the early 1990s is beginning to focus on Bellow's political commentary and his European involvement. Likewise the investigation into gender issues and ideologies in Bellow's fiction is underway. James Atlas is working on a major biography of Bellow which is to be published within the next two years. However, still to be explored much more thoroughly is Bellow the playwright, Bellow the essayist, and Bellow the short story writer. Also, while many influence studies have traced Bellow's debts to the British and English romantics, to some Eastern thinkers, and to a few major European philosophers, much remains to be done with his fictional use of a host of other major and minor thinkers of many nationalities and time periods.

It is also clear from the majority of materials represented here that Bellow criticism is still seriously undertheorized. We are yet to see the emergence in significant numbers of critics willing to use poststructuralist theory, reader-response criticism, Marxist theory, rhetorical criticism, feminist and gender approaches, and postmodern theory in order to provide us with new reading paradigms of this rewarding and complex writer.

Included in this selected bibliography are articles representing the major critical lines of inquiry on each of the novels, short stories, plays, and novellas. In the case of recently published materials there is a preponderance of reviews rather than the kind of scholarly articles and major chapters which represent earlier works. In some cases, materials in preparation and work-in-progress have been included for the sake of currency and completeness.

PRIMARY SOURCES

Books

The Adventures of Augie March. New York: Viking, 1953.

The Bellarosa Connection. New York: Penguin, 1989.

Dangling Man. New York: Vanguard, 1944.

The Dean's December. New York: Harper, 1982.

Henderson the Rain King. New York: Viking, 1959.

Herzog. New York: Viking, 1964.

Him With His Foot in His Mouth and Other Stories. New York:
Harper & Row, 1984.

Humboldt's Gift. New York: Viking, 1975.

The Last Analysis. New York: Viking, 1965.

Mosby's Memoirs and Other Stories. New York: Viking, 1968.

More Die of Heartbreak. New York: Morrow, 1987.

Mr. Sammler's Planet. New York: Viking, 1970.

Seize the Day. New York: Viking, 1956.

Something to Remember Me By. New York: Signet, 1991.

A Theft. New York: Penguin, 1989.

To Jerusalem and Back. New York: Viking, 1976.

The Victim. New York: Vanguard, 1947.

SECONDARY SOURCES

Books

Bradbury, Malcolm. *Saul Bellow.* Contemporary Writers. London and
New York: Methuen, 1982.

Clayton, John J. *Saul Bellow: In Defense of Man.* Bloomington: Indiana Univ. Press, 1968. 2nd ed. 1979.

Cohen, Sarah Blacher. *Saul Bellow's Enigmatic Laughter.* Urbana: Univ. of Illinois Press, 1974.

Dutton, Robert R. *Saul Bellow.* Twayne's United States Author Series 181. New York: Twayne, 1971. Rev. ed. 1982.

Fuchs, Daniel. *Saul Bellow: Vision and Revision.* Durham: Duke Univ. Press, 1984.

Goldman, Liela H. *Saul Bellow's Moral Vision: A Critical Study of the Jewish Experience.* New York: Irvington, 1983.

Kiernan, Robert F. *Saul Bellow.* Literature and Life. American Writers. New York: Continuum, 1989.

Malin, Irving. *Saul Bellow's Fiction.* Crosscurrents/Modern Critiques. Carbondale: Southern Illinois Univ. Press, 1969.

McCadden, Joseph F. *The Flight from Women in the Fiction of Saul Bellow.* Washington: Univ. Press of America, 1981.

Newman, Judie. *Saul Bellow and History.* New York: St. Martin's; London: Macmillan, 1984.

Opdahl, Keith M. *The Novels of Saul Bellow: An Introduction.* University Park: Pennsylvania State Univ. Press, 1967.

Pifer, Ellen. *Saul Bellow Against the Grain.* Philadelphia: Univ. of Pennsylvania Press, 1990.

Porter, M. Gilbert. *Whence the Power? The Artistry and Humility of Saul Bellow.* Columbia: Univ. of Missouri Press, 1974.

Roderigues, Eusebio L. *Quest for the Human: An Exploration of Saul Bellow's Fiction.* Lewisburg, Pa.: Bucknell Univ. Press, 1981.

Scheer-Schaezler, Brigitte. *Saul Bellow.* Modern Literature Monographs. New York: Ungar, 1972.

Tanner, Tony. *Saul Bellow.* Writers and Critics. Edinburgh and London: Oliver and Boyd; New York: Barnes, 1965; New York: Chips, 1978.

Wilson, Jonathan. *Herzog: The Limits of Ideas.* Twayne's Masterwork Studies 46. Boston: Twayne, 1990.

Biographies

Harris, Mark. *Saul Bellow: Drumlin Woodchuck*. Athens: Univ. of Georgia Press, 1980.

Miller, Ruth. *Saul Bellow: A Biography of the Imagination*. New York: St. Martin's Press, 1991.

Collected Essays

Bach, Gerhard in cooperation with Jakob J. Kollhofer. *Saul Bellow at Seventy-five: A Collection of Critical Essays*. Köllhofer. Tübingen: Narr, 1991.

Bloom, Harold, ed. *Saul Bellow*. Modern Critical Views. New York: Chelsea, 1986.

Cronin, Gloria L., and L. H. Goldman, eds. *Saul Bellow in the 1980s: A Collection of Critical Essays*. East Lansing: Michigan State Univ. Press, 1989.

Hollahan, Eugene, ed. *Philosophical Dimensions of Saul Bellow's Fiction. Studies in the Literary Imagination*. 17 (Fall, 1984).

Malin, Irving, ed. *Saul Bellow and the Critics*. New York: New York Univ. Press, 1967.

Rovit, Earl. *Saul Bellow: A Collection of Critical Essays*. Twentieth Century Views. Englewood Cliffs: Prentice-Hall, 1975.

Trachtenberg, Stanley, ed. *Critical Essays on Saul Bellow*. Critical Essays on American Literature. Boston: G. K. Hall, 1979.

Interviews

Bellow, Saul. "Bellow on Himself and America." *Jerusalem Post Magazine*, 3 July 1975: 11–12; 10 July 1975; 12.

————. "Interview with Myself." *New Review* 2.18 (1975): 53–56.

————. "On John Cheever: Speech to the American Academy of Arts and Letters." *New York Review of Books*, 30 (17 Feb. 1983): 38.

Boyers, Robert T. "Literature and Culture: An Interview with Saul Bellow." *Salmagundi*, 30 (Summer 1975): 6–23.

Bragg, Melvin. "Off the Couch by Christmas: Saul Bellow on His New Novel." *Listener* 94 (20 Nov. 1975): 675–76.

Brandon, Henry. "Writer versus Readers: Saul Bellow." *Sunday Times,* 18 Sept. 1966, 24.

Brans, Jo. "Common Needs, Common Preoccupations: An Interview with Saul Bellow." *Southwest Review* 62 (Winter 1977): 1–19.

Breit, Harvey. "A Talk with Saul Bellow." *New York Times Book Review,* 20 Sept. 1953: 22.

Bruckner, D. J. R. "A Candid Talk with Saul Bellow." *New York Times Magazine,* 15 Apr. 1984: 2.

Bushinsky, Jay. "Saul Bellow on the Firing Line." *Chicago Daily News Panorama,* 13–14 Dec. 1975: 2.

Carroll, Paul. "Q & A – Saul Bellow Says a Few Words about His Critics and Himself." *Chicago Sun Times – Bookweek,* 9 Nov. 1975: 8.

Clemons, Walter, and Jack Kroll."America's Master Novelist: Interview with Saul Bellow." *Newsweek,* 1 Sept. 1975: 33–35.

Cook, Bruce. "Saul Bellow: A Mood of Protest." *Prospective on Ideas and the Arts,* 12 Feb. 1963: 46–50.

Cromie, Robert. "Saul Bellow Tells (among other things) the Thinking Behind Herzog." *Chicago Tribune – Books Today,* 24 Jan. 1965: 8–9.

Dommergues, Pierre. "Recontre avec Saul Bellow." *Prevues,* 17 (Jan. 1967): 38–47.

Ellenberg, Al. "Saul Bellow Picks Another Fight." *Rolling Stone,* 4 Mar. 1982: 14+ .

Enck, John. "Saul Bellow: An Interview." *Wisconsin Studies in Contemporary Literature,* 6:2 (1965): 156–60.

Epstein, Joseph. "A Talk with Saul Bellow." *New York Times Book Review,* 5 Dec. 1976: 3+ .

Galloway, David D. "An Interview with Saul Bellow." *Audit* 3 (Spring 1963): 19–23.

Gray, Rockwell, Harry White, and Gerald Nemanic. "Interview with Saul Bellow." *TriQuarterly,* 60 (1985): 12–34.

Gutwillig, Robert. "Talk with Saul Bellow." *New York Times Book Review,* 20 Sept. 1964: 40–41.

Harper, Gordon Lloyd. "Saul Bellow." *Paris Review,* 9.36 (1965): 48–73.

Henry, Jim Douglas. "Mystic Trade: The American Novelist Saul Bellow Talks to Jim Douglas Henry." *Listener,* 22 May 1969: 705–07.

Heyman, Harriet. "Q & A with Saul Bellow." *Chicago Maroon,* 4 Feb. 1972.

Hogue, Alice Allbright. "Saul Bellow Revisited at Home and at Work." *Chicago Daily News Panorama,* 18 Feb, 1967: 5.

Howard, Jane. "Mr. Bellow Considers His Planet." *Life,* 3 Apr. 1970: 57–60.

Illig, Joyce. "An Interview with Saul Bellow." *Publishers Weekly,* 22 Oct. 1973: 74–77.

Kakutani, Michiko. "A Talk with Saul Bellow: On His Work and Himself." *New York Times Review of Books,* 13 Dec. 1981: 28–30.

Kulshreshtha, Chirantan. "A Conversation with Saul Bellow." *Chicago Review,* 23.4-24.1 (1972): 7–15.

"Literature and Culture: An Interview with Saul Bellow." *Salmagundi,* 30 (Summer 1975): 6–3.

Medwick, Cathleen. "A Cry of Strength: The Unfashionably Uncynical Saul Bellow." *Vogue,* Mar. 1982: 368+ .

Nachman, Gerald. "A Talk with Saul Bellow." *New York Post Magazine,* 4 Oct. 1964: 6.

Nash, Jay, and Ron Offen. "Saul Bellow." *Chicago Literary Times,* Dec. 1964: 10.

Pryce-Jones, David. "One Man and His Minyan." *Daily Telegraph Magazine,* 3 Oct. 1975: 26–30.

Robinson, Robert. "Saul Bellow at 60 – Talking to Robert Robertson." *Listener,* 13 Feb. 1975: 218–19.

Roudané, Matthew. "An Interview with Saul Bellow." *Contemporary Literature* 25.3 (1984): 265–80.

Sanoff, Alan P. "A Conversation with Saul Bellow – Matters Have Gotten Out of Hand in a Violent Society." *U. S. News and World Report,* 28 June 1982: 49–50.

Saporta, Marc. "Interview avec Saul Bellow." *Le Figaro Litteraire,* 17 Mar. 1969: 24–25.

Simmons, Maggie. "Free to Feel: Conversations with Saul Bellow." *Quest,* Feb.–Mar. 1979: 30–36.

"Some Questions and Answers: An Interview with Saul Bellow." *Ontario Review,* 3 (1975): 51–61.

Steers, Nina. "Successor to Faulkner: An Interview with Saul Bellow." *Show* (Sept. 1964): 36–38.

Steinem, Gloria. "Gloria Steinem Spends a Day in Chicago with Saul Bellow." *Glamour,* July 1965: 98+ .

General Articles,
Chapters and Reviews

Abbott, H. Porter. "Saul Bellow and the 'Lost Cause' of Character." *Novel: A Forum on Fiction,* 13 (1980): 264–83.

Alter, Robert. "Kafka's Father, Agnon's Mother, Bellow's Cousins." *Commentary,* Feb. 1986: 46–52.

Anderson, David D. "The Novelist as Playwright: Saul Bellow on Broadway." *Saul Bellow Journal,* 5.1 (1986): 48–62.

———. "Saul Bellow and the Midwestern Tradition: Beginnings." *Midwestern Miscellany,* 16 (1988): 59–68.

Bach, Gerhard. "Saul Bellow's German Reception. Part I." *Saul Bellow Journal,* 5.2 (1986): 52–65.

———. "Saul Bellow's German Reception. Part II." *Saul Bellow Journal,* 6.1 (1987): 40–51.

Bakker, J. "Saul Bellow: A Writer's Despair." *Essays on English and American Literature and a Sheaf of Poems Offered to David Wilkinson on the Occasion of His Retirement from the Chair of English Literature in the University of Groningen.* Ed. J. Bakker et al. *Costerus,* n.s. 63. Amsterdam: Rodopi, 1987. 177–90.

Bawer, Bruce. "Talking Heads: The Novels of Saul Bellow." *New Criterion,* Sept. 1987: 8–24.

Bloomberg, Edward. "Saul Bellow Looks at France." *Saul Bellow Journal,* 9.2 (1990): 68–81.

Borrus, Bruce J. "Bellow's Critique of the Intellect." *Modern Fiction Studies,* 25.1 (1979): 29–45.

Bouson, J. Brooks. "The Narcissistic Self-Drama of Wilhelm Adler: A Kohutian Reading of Bellow's *Seize the Day.*" *Saul Bellow Journal,* 5.2 (1986): 3–14.

Bradbury, Malcolm. "The Nightmare in Which I am Trying to Get a Good Night's Rest': Saul Bellow and Changing History." *Saul Bellow and His Work.* Ed. Edmond Schraepen, Brussels: Centrum Voor Taal En Literatuurwetenschap, Vrije Universiteit Brussels, 1978. Symposium held at the Free University of Brussels (V.U.B.) on 10–11 Dec. 1977. Rpt. as "Saul Bellow and Changing History" in *Saul Bellow.* Ed. Harold Bloom. Modern Critical Views. New York: Chelsea, 1986. 129–46.

Brookner, Anita. "The Depth of His Potato Love." *Spectator,* 31 Oct. 1987: 36–37.

Chase, Richard. "The Adventures of Saul Bellow: Progress of a Novelist." *Commentary,* 27.4 (1959): 323–30. Rpt. in *Saul Bellow and the Critics.* Ed. Irving Malin. New York: New York Univ. Press, 1967. 25–38; *Saul Bellow.* Ed. Harold Bloom. Modern Critical Views. New York: Chelsea, 1986. 13–24.

Chavkin, Allan. "Bellow and English Romanticism." *Studies in the Literary Imagination,* 17.2 (1984): 7–18.

Chavkin, Allan, and Nancy Feyl Chavkin. "Bellow's Dire Prophecy." *Centennial Review,* 33.2 (1989): 93–107.

Clayton, John J. "Alienation and Masochism." Bloomington: Indiana Univ. Press, 1968. 2nd ed. 1979. Rpt. in *Saul Bellow.* Ed. Harold Bloom. Modern Critical Views. New York: Chelsea, 1986. 6

———. "The Unity and Development of Bellow's Fiction." *Saul Bellow: In Defense of Man.* John J. Clayton. Bloomington: Indiana Univ. Press, 1968. 2nd ed. 1979. 287–310. Rpt. in *Der Amerikanische Roman Nach 1945.* Wege der Forschung 639. Ed. Arno Heller. Darmstadt: Wissenschaftliche Buchgesellschaft, 1987. 364–84.

Cohen, Sarah Blacher. "The Comedy of Urban Low Life: From Saul Bellow to Mordecai Richler." *Thalia,* 4.2 (1981–82): 21–24.

———. "Saul Bellow's Chicago Humor." *Saul Bellow Journal,* 6.1 (1987): 9–17.

Cronin, Gloria L. "The Purgation of Twentieth Century Consciousness." *Interpretations: A Journal of Ideas, Analysis and Criticism,* 16.1 (1986): 8–20.

―――. "Holy War Against the Moderns: Saul Bellow's Antimodernist Critique of Contemporary American Society." *Studies in American Jewish Literature,* 8.1 (1989): 77–94.

Dougherty, David C. "Finding Before Seeking: Themes in *Henderson the Rain King* and *Humboldt's Gift." Modern Fiction Studies,* 25.1 (1979): 93–101.

Field, Andrew. "The Sustained Voice of Saul Bellow: De Tocqueville as Novelist." *Quadrant,* Sept. 1987, 23–27.

Field, Leslie. "Saul Bellow: From Montreal to Jerusalem." *Studies in American Jewish Literature,* 4.2 (1978): 51–59. Joint issue with *Yiddish* 3.3 (1978).

Fuchs, Daniel. "Bellow and Freud." *Studies in the Literary Imagination,* 17.2 (1984): 59–80.

Galloway, David D. "Culture-Making: The Recent Works of Saul Bellow." *Saul Bellow and His Work.* Ed. Edmond Schraepen. Brussels: Centrum voor Taal-en Literatuurwetenschap, Vrije Universiteit Brussel, 1978. 49–60. Proceedings of a symposium held at the Free University of Brussels (V.U.B.) on 10–11 Dec. 1977.

Gitenstein, Barbara. "Saul Bellow and the Yiddish Literary Tradition." *Studies in American Jewish Literature,* 5.2 (1979): 24–46. Joint issue with *Yiddish* 4.1 (1979).

Glenday, Michael K. "Some Versions of the Real: The Novellas of Saul Bellow." *The Modern American Novella.* Ed. Robert A. Lee. New York: St. Martin's: London: Visions, 1989. 162–77.

Goldman, Liela H. "The Holocaust in the Novels of Saul Bellow." *Modern Language Studies,* 16.1 (1986): 71–80.

―――. "'Shuffling Out of My Vulgar Origins': The Masculinist-Elitist Language of Saul Bellow's Fiction." *Melus,* 16 (Mar. 1989): 33–42.

―――. "Saul Bellow and the Philosophy of Judaism." *Studies in the Literary Imagination,* 17.2 (1984): 81–95.

Gullette, Margaret Morganroth. "Saul Bellow: Inward and Upward, Past Distraction." *Safe at Last in the Middle Years: The Invention of the*

Midlife Progress Novel—Saul Bellow, Margaret Drabble, Anne Tyler, and John Updike. Berkeley: Univ. of California Press, 1988. 120–45.

Hirsch, David H. "Jewish Identity and Jewish Suffering in Bellow, Malamud and Philip Roth." *Saul Bellow Journal,* 8.2 (1989): 47–58.

Hynes, Joseph. "The Fading Figure in the Worn Carpet." *Arizona Quarterly,* 42.3 (1986): 321–30.

Ichikawa, Masumi. *"Herzog* from a Buddhist Perspective." *Studies in American Jewish Literature,* 8.1 (1989): 95–103.

Johnson, Gregory. "Bellow's Bellows." *Saul Bellow Journal,* 6.2 (1987): 3–18.

Knight, Karl F. "Bellow's Shawmut: Rationalizations and Redemption." *Studies in Short Fiction,* 24.4 (1987): 375–80.

Kraus, Joe. "Dissertations about Saul Bellow: A Supplementary List." *Saul Bellow Journal,* 7.2 (1988): 84–87.

Kremer, S. Lillian. "Scars of Outrage: The Holocaust in *The Victim* and *Mr. Sammler's Planet." Witness Through the Imagination: Jewish American Holocaust Literature.* S. Lillian Kremer. Detroit: Wayne State Univ. Press, 1989. 36–62.

Leveson, J. C. "Bellow's Dangling Men." *Critique* 3.3 (1960), 3–14. Rpt. in *Saul Bellow and the Critics.* Ed. Irving Malin. New York: New York Univ. Press, 1967. 39–50.

Lyons, Bonnie. "From *Dangling Man* to 'Colonies of the Spirit.'" *Studies in American Jewish Literature,* 4.2 (1978): 45–50. Joint issue with *Yiddish,* 3.3 (1978).

————. "American Jewish Fiction Since 1945." *Handbook of American-Jewish Literature: An Analytical Guide to Topics, Themes, and Sources.* Ed. Lewis Fried, Gene Brown, Jules Chametsky, and Louis Harap. Westport: Greenwood, 1988. 61–89.

Malin, Irving. "Seven Images." *Saul Bellow and the Critics.* Ed. Irving Malin. New York: New York Univ. Press, 1967. 142–76.

Marovitz, Sanford E. "The Panorama of America in American-Jewish Fiction." *Zeitschrift für Anglistik und Amerikanistik,* 36.1 (1988): 47–61.

Maver, Igor. "The Delicate Balance of Tension in Saul Bellow's *The Dean's December:* An Attempt at Interpretation from a European

Perspective." *Cross Cultural Studies: American, Canadian and European Literatures, 1945–1985*. Ed. Mirko Jurak. Ljubljana: English Dept., Filozofska Fakulteta, 1988. 107–13.

McConnell, Frank D. "Saul Bellow and Terms of our Contract." *Four Postwar American Novelists: Bellow, Barth, and Pynchon*. Frank McConnell. Chicago: Univ. of Chicago Press, 1977. 1–57. Rpt. in *Saul Bellow*. Ed. Harold Bloom. Modern Critical Views. New York: Chelsea, 1986. 101–14.

McSweeney, Kerry. "Saul Bellow and the Life to Come." *Critical Quarterly*, 18.1 (1976): 67–72.

Newman, Judie. "Bellow's Sixth Sense: The Sense of History." *Canadian Review of American Studies*, 13.1 (1982): 39–51.

Nilsen, Helge Normann. "Bellow and Transcendentalism: From *The Victim* to *Herzog*." *Dutch Quarterly Review of Anglo-American Letters*, 14.2 (1984): 125–39.

———. "Helt eller klov? Omkring noe uloste konflikter i Saul Bellows forfatterskap." [Hero or Clown? On Certain Unresolved Conflicts in Saul Bellow's Work]. *Edda* (1980): 93–102. Cited in *MLA Bibliography*, 1980.

Opdahl, Keith M. "Stillness in the Midst of Chaos: Plot in the Novels of Saul Bellow." *Modern Fiction Studies*, 25.1 (1979): 15–28.

Pifer, Ellen. "If the Shoe Fits: Bellow and Recent Critics." *Texas Studies in Literature and Language*, 29.4 (1987): 442–57.

Pinsker, Sanford. "Saul Bellow and the Special Comedy of Urban Life." *Ontario Review*, 8 (1978): 82–94. Cited in *MLA Bibliography*, 1978.

———. "Saul Bellow, Soren Kierkegaard and the Question of Boredom." *Centennial Review*, 24.1 (1980): 118–25.

Pollin, Burton R. "Poe and Bellow: A Literary Connection." *Saul Bellow Journal*, 7.1 (1988): 15–26.

Porter, M. Gilbert. "Hitch Your Agony to a Star: Bellow's Transcendental Vision." *Saul Bellow and His Work*. Ed. Edmond Schraepen. Brussels: Centrum voor Taal-en Literatuurwetenschap, Vrije Universiteit Brussel, 1978. 73–88. Proceedings of a symposium held at the Free University of Brussels (V.U.B.), 10–11 Dec. 1977.

Quayum, M. A. "Finding the Middle Ground: Bellow's Philosophical Affinity with Emerson in *Mr. Sammler's Planet.*" *Saul Bellow Journal,* 8.2 (1989): 24–38.

Rodrigues, Eusebio L. "Beyond All Philosophies." *Studies in the Literary Imagination,* 17.2 (1984): 97–110.

Rovit, Earl. "Saul Bellow and the Concept of the Survivor." *Saul Bellow and His Work.* Ed. Edmond Schraepen. Brussels: Centrum voor Taal-en Literatuurwetenschap, Vrije Universiteit Brussel, 1978. 89–101. Proceedings of a symposium held at the Free University of Brussels (V.U.B.), 10–11 Dec. 1977.

Satlof, Marilyn R. "Bellow's Modern Lamed *Vovniks.*" *Saul Bellow Journal,* 8.2 (1989): 39–46.

Shaked, Gerson. "Shadows of Identity: A Comparative Study of German Jewish and American Jewish Literature." *The Shadows Within: Essays on Modern Jewish Writers.* Gerson Shaked. Philadelphia: Jewish Publication Society, 1987. 57–82.

Shechner, Mark. "Saul Bellow and Ghetto Cosmopolitanism." *Studies in America Jewish Literature,* 4.2 (1978): 33–44. Joint issue with *Yiddish* 3.3 (1978).

————. "Down in the Mouth with Saul Bellow." *After the Revolution: Studies in the Contemporary Jewish American Imagination.* Mark Schechner. Bloomington: Indiana Univ. Press, 1987. 121–58.

Shibuya Yuzaburo. "Saul Bellow: Politics and the Sense of Reality." *The Traditional and the Anti-Traditional: Studies in Contemporary American Literature.* Ed. Kenzaburo Ohashi. Tokyo: Tokyo Chapter of the American Literature Society of Japan, 1980. 43–56.

Siegel, Ben. "Saul Bellow and the University as Villain." *Missouri Review* 6.2 (1983): 167–88.

Tripathy, Biyot K. "End-Game: Terminal Configuration in Bellow's Novels." *Modern Fiction Studies* 33.2 (1987): 215–31.

Walden, Daniel. "Urbanism and the Artist: Saul Bellow and the Age of Technology." *Saul Bellow Journal,* 2.2 (1983): 1–14.

————. "Saul Bellow's American Dream: Technology, the Artist, and the Machine in the Ghetto." *Bulletin of Science Technology & Society,* 7.4 (1987): 469–75.

Weinstein, Mark. "Bellow's Imagination-Instructors." *Saul Bellow Journal,* 2.1 (1982): 19–22.

Wisse, Ruth R. "The Schlemiel as Liberal Humanist." *The Schlemiel as Modern Hero.* Ruth R. Wisse. Chicago: Univ. of Chicago Press, 1971. 91–107. [Paperback ed. 1980.] Rpt. in *Saul Bellow: A Collection of Critical Essays.* Ed. Earl Rovit. Twentieth Century Views. Englewood Cliffs, NJ: Prentice, 1975. 90–100.

————. "The New York (Jewish) Intellectuals." *Commentary,* Nov. 1987: 28–38.

Yetman, Michael G. "Toward a Language Irresistible: Saul Bellow and the Romance of Poetry." *Papers on Language & Literature,* 22.4 (1986): 429–47.

The Adventures of Augie March

Aldridge, John W. "The Society of Three Novels." *In Search of Heresy: American Literature in an Age of Conformity.* John W. Aldridge. New York: McGraw-Hill, 1956. 126–48. Rpt. as "The Society of Augie March" in *The Devil in the Fire: Retrospective Essays on American Literatue and Culture, 1951–1971.* John W. Aldridge. New York: Harper Magazine Press, 1972. 224–30.

Alter, Robert. "Heirs of the Tradition." *Rogue's Progress: Studies in the Picaresque Novel.* Robert Alter. Harvard Studies in Comparative Literature, 26. Cambridge, MA: Harvard Univ. Press, 1964. 106–32.

Frohock, W. M. "Saul Bellow and His Penitent Picaro." *Southwest Review,* 53 (Winter 1968): 36–44.

Fuchs, Daniel. *"The Adventure of Augie March:* The Making of a Novel." *Americana-Austriaca: Beitrage zur Amerikakunde.* Ed. Klaus Lanzinger. Vol. 5. Vienna: Universitats-Verlagsbuchandlung, 1980. 27–50.

Goldberg, Gerald Jay. "Life's Customer, Augie March." *Critique,* 3.3 (1960): 15–27.

Hart, Jeffrey. "Bellow's Best." Rev. of *The Bellarosa Connection. National Review,* 5 Mar. 1990: 52–53.

Lewis, R. W. B. "Recent Fiction: *Picaro* and Pilgrim." *A Time of Harvest: American Literature 1910–1960.* Ed. Robert E. Spiller. American Century Series 50. New York: Hill and Wang, 1962. 144–53.

Newman, Judie. "Saul Bellow and Ortega y Gasset: Fictions of Nature, History and Art in *The Adventures of Augie March*." *Durham University Journal,* 77.1 (1984): 61–70. (n. s. 46.1).

Overbeck, Pat Trefzger. "The Women in *Augie March*." *Texas Studies in Literature and Language,* 10.4 (1968): 471–84.

Pearce, Richard. "Looking Back at *Augie March*." *Yiddish,* 6.4 (1987): 35–40.

Pizer, Donald. "Saul Bellow: *The Adventures of Augie March*." *Twentieth-Century American Literary Naturalism: An Interpretation.* Donald Pizer. Crosscurrents/Modern Critique/New Series. Carbondale, IL: Southern Illinois Univ. Press, 1982. 133–149.

Rodrigues, Eusebio L. "Augie March's Mexican Adventures." *Indian Journal of American Studies,* 8.2 (1978): 39–43.

Shaw, Patrick W. "History and the Picaresque Tradition in Saul Bellow's *The Adventures of Augie March*." *CLIO,* 16.3 (1987): 203–19.

Trilling, Lionel. Introduction. *The Adventures of Augie March.* New York: Modern Library, 1965.

The Bellarosa Connection

Bawer, Bruce. "Change of Pace for a Pair of Heavyweights." Rev. of *The Bellarosa Connection. Wall Street Journal,* 29 Sept. 1989, A12.

Coates, Joseph. "Saul Bellow's Country." Rev. of *The Bellarosa Connection. Chicago Tribune,* 8 Oct. 1989, sec. 14, 3.

Denby, David. "Memory in America." Rev. of *The Bellarosa Connection* and *A Theft. New Republic,* 1 Jan. 1990: 37–40.

Eder, Richard. "Recalling Memory of the Spirit." Rev. of *The Bellarosa Connection. Los Angeles Times,* 5 Oct. 1989, sec. V: 22.

Feeney, Mark. "Bellow's 'Bellarosa': Memory within Memory." Rev. of *The Bellarosa Connection. Boston Globe,* 28 Sept. 1989: 93.

Fenster, Coral. "Ironies and Insights in *The Bellarosa Connection*." *Saul Bellow Journal,* 9.2 (1990): 20–28.

"Fiction." Rev. of *The Bellarosa Connection*. *Jim Kobak's Kirkus Review*, 1 Feb. 1989: 140.

French, Sean. "Bellow's Gift." Rev. of *The Bellarosa Connection*. *New Statesman & Society*, 20 Oct. 1989: 46.

Gray, Paul. "A Child in the New World." Rev. of *The Bellarosa Connection*. *Time*, 2 Oct. 1989: 8.

Johnson, Greg. "Saul Bellow's Short 'Bellarosa' Long on Quality." Rev. of *The Bellarosa Connection*. *Atlanta Journal/Constitution*, 8 Oct. 1989: L11.

Jospovici, Gabriel. "The Work of Memory." Rev. of *The Bellarosa Connection*. *Times Literary Supplement*, 27 Oct. 1989: 1181.

Lehmann-Haupt, Christopher. "Of the Forgetfulness of a Memory Expert." Rev. of *The Bellarosa Connection*. *New York Times*, 28 Sept. 1989: C22.

Leonard, John. "Book Notes." Rev. of *The Bellarosa Connection*. *Nation*, 27 Nov. 1989: 652–53.

Nesanovich, Stella. *The Bellarosa Connection*. *Magill's Literary Annual*: Ed. Frank N. Magill. 2 vols. Pasadena: Salem, 1990. 1: 53–57.

Pritchard, William H. "Blackmailing Billy Rose." Rev. of *The Bellarosa Connection*. *New York Times Book Review*, 1 Oct. 1989: 11.

Sudrann, Jean. "Goings and Comings." Rev. of *The Bellarosa Connection*. *Yale Review*, 79.3 (1990): 414–20.

Taylor, D. J. "Memories Are Made of This." Rev. of *The Bellarosa Connection*. *Spectator*, 14 Oct. 1989: 34–35.

Wills, Garry. "Mr. Memory." Rev. of *The Bellarosa Connection*. *New York Review of Books*, 12 Oct. 1989: 34.

Yardley, Jonathan. "Bellow at His Best." Rev. of *The Bellarosa Connection*. *Washington Post*, 20 Sept. 1989: D2.

Dangling Man

Anderson, David D. "The Room, the City and the War: Saul Bellow's *Dangling Man*." *Midwestern Miscellany*, 11 (1983): 49–58.

Baim, Joseph. "Escape from Intellection: Saul Bellow's *Dangling Man*." *University Review*, 37 (Autumn 1970): 28–34.

Donoghue, Denis. "Commitment and the *Dangling Man.*" *Studies: An Irish Quarterly Review of Letters, Philosophy and Science,* 53 (1964): 174–87. Expanded version rpt. in *The Ordinary Universe: Soundings in Modern Literature.* Ed. Denis Donoghue. New York: Macmillan, 1968. 194–220.

Glenday, Michael K. "'The Consummating Glimpse': *Dangling Man's* Treacherous Reality." *Modern Fiction Studies,* 25.1 (1979): 139–48.

Kaler, Anne K. "Use of the Journal/Diary Form in the Development of the Odyssean Myth in *Dangling Man.*" *Saul Bellow Journal,* 5.1 (1986): 16–23.

Kulshreshtha, Chirantan. "Affirmation in Saul Bellow's *Dangling Man.*" *Indian Journal of American Studies,* 5 (1975): 21–36.

Lehan, Richard. "Existentialism in Recent American Fiction: The Demonic Quest." *Texas Studies in Literature and Language,* 1.2 (1959): 181–202. Rpt. in *Recent American Fiction: Some Critical Views.* Ed. Joseph J. Waldmeir. Boston: Houghton, 1963. 63–83.

Mellard, James. "*Dangling Man:* Saul Bellow's Lyrical Experiment." *Ball State University Forum,* 15.2 (1974): 67–74.

Pinsker, Sanford. "*Rameau's Nephew* and Saul Bellow's *Dangling Man.*" *Notes on Modern American Literature,* 4 (1980): Item 22.

Saposik, Irving S. "*Dangling Man:* A Partisan Review." *Centennial Review,* 26.4 (1982): 388–95.

Schwartz, Delmore. "A Man in his Time." Rev. of *Dangling Man.* *Partisan Review,* 11.3 (1944): 348–50.

Wilson, Edmund. "Doubts and Dreams: *Dangling Man* Under a Glass Bell." *New Yorker* 1 Apr. 1944: 78+.

The Dean's December

Atlas, James. "Interpreting the World." Rev. of *The Dean's December.* *Atlantic,* Feb. 1982: 78–82.

Bach, Gerhard P. "The Dean Who Came in from the Cold: Saul Bellow's America of the 1980s." *Studies in American Jewish Literature,* 8.1 (1989): 104–14.

Beatty, Jack. "A Novel of East and West." Rev. of *The Dean's December. New Republic,* 3 Feb. 1982: 38–40.

Bragg, Melvyn. "Eastward Ho!" Rev. of *The Dean's December. Punch,* 31 Mar. 1982: 536.

Chavkin, Allan. "The Feminism of *The Dean's December." Studies in American Jewish Literature,* 3 (1983): 113–27.

Cronin, Gloria L. "Through a Glass Brightly: Dean Corde's Escape from History in *The Dean's December." Saul Bellow Journal,* 5.1 (1986): 24–33.

Goldman, Liela H. "*The Dean's December:* A Companion Piece to *Mr. Sammler's Planet." Saul Bellow Journal,* 5.2 (1986): 36–45.

Hall, Joe. "*The Dean's December:* A Separate Account of a Separate Account." *Saul Bellow Journal,* 5.2 (1986): 22–31.

Harmon, William. Rev. of *The Dean's December. Southern Humanities Review,* 17.3 (1983): 280–81.

Johnson, Greg. "A Winter's Tale." Rev. of *The Dean's December. Southwest Review,* 67.3 (1982): 342–45.

Newman, Judie. "Bellow and Nihilism: *The Dean's December." Studies in the Literary Imagination,* 17.2 (1984): 111–22.

Pinsker, Sanford. "A Kaddish for Valeria Raresh: Dean Albert Corde's Long Dark Month of the Soul." *Studies in American Jewish Literature,* 3 (1983): 128–37.

Pugh, Scott. "Preemptive Defense of Narrative and the Designs of *The Dean's December." Kyushu American Literature,* 27 (1986): 87–95. Cited in *MLA Bibliography* 1986.

Roudané, Matthew C. "A *Cri De Coeur:* The Inner Reality of Saul Bellow's *The Dean's December." Studies in the Humanities,* 11.2 (1984): 5–17.

Updike, John. "Toppling Towers Seen by a Whirling Soul." Rev. of *The Dean's December. New Yorker,* 22 Feb. 1982: 120–28.

Weinstein, Mark. "Communication in *The Dean's December." Saul Bellow Journal,* 5.1 (1986): 63–74.

Wilson, Jonathan. "Bellow's Dangling Dean." *Literary Review,* 26.1 (1982): 165–75.

Wolcott, James. "Dissecting our Decline." Rev. of *The Dean's December. Esquire,* Mar. 1982: 134+.

Henderson the Rain King

Alter, Robert. "Jewish Humor and the Domestication of Myth." *Defenses of the Imagination: Jewish Writers and Modern Historical Crisis.* Robert Alter. Philadelphia: Jewish Publication Society of America, 1977. 155–67. Rpt. from *Harvard English Studies,* 3 (1972).

Anderson, David D. "Hemingway and Henderson on the High Savannas, or Two Midwestern Moderns and the Myth of Africa." *Saul Bellow Journal,* 8.2 (1989): 59–75.

Axelrod, Stephen Gould. "The Jewishness of Bellow's Henderson." *American Literature,* 47.3 (1975): 439–45.

Baim, Joseph, and David P. Demarest, Jr. "*Henderson the Rain King:* A Major Theme and a Technical Problem." *A Modern Miscellany.* Carnegie Series in English 11. Pittsburgh: Carnegie-Mellon Univ. Press, 1970. 53–63.

Billy, Ted. "The Road of Excess: Saul Bellow's *Henderson the Rain King." Saul Bellow Journal,* 3.1 (1983): 8–17.

Brophy, Robert J. "Biblical Parallels in Bellow's *Henderson the Rain King." Christianity and Literature,* 23.4 (1974): 27–30.

Butler, Robert James. "The American Quest for Pure Movement in Bellow's *Henderson the Rain King." Journal of Narrative Technique,* 14.1 (1984): 44–59.

Campbell, Jeff H. "Bellow's Intimations of Immortality: *Henderson the Rain King." Studies in the Novel,* 1.3 (1969): 323–33.

Cecil, L. Moffitt. "Bellow's Henderson as American Imago of the 1950's." *Research Studies,* 40.4 (1972): 296–300.

Cronin, Gloria L. "*Henderson the Rain King:* A Parodic Exposé of the Modern Novel." *Arizona Quarterly,* 39.3 (1983): 266–76.

Detweiler, Robert. "Patterns of Rebirth in *Henderson the Rain King." Modern Fiction Studies,* 12.4 (1966–67): 405–14.

Goldfinch, Michael. "A Journey to the Interior." *English Studies,* 43.5 (1962): 439–43.

Guttman, Allen. "Bellow's Henderson." *Critique,* 7.3 (1965): 33–42. Rpt. in *The Jewish Writer in America: Assimilation and the Crisis of Identity,* Ed. Allen Guttman. New York: Oxford Univ. Press, 1971. 201–10.

Hughes, Daniel J. "Reality and the Hero: *Lolita* and *Henderson the Rain King."* *Modern Fiction Studies,* 6.4 (1960–61): 345–64. Rpt. *Saul Bellow and the Critics.* Ed. Irving Malin. New York: New York Univ. Press, 1967. 69–91; *Saul Bellow.* Ed. Harold Bloom. Modern Critical Views. New York: Chelsea, 1986. 25–43.

Kehler, Joel R. "Henderson's Sacred Science." *Centennial Review,* 24.2 (1980): 232–47.

Knight, Karl F. "Bellow's Henderson and Melville's Ishmael: Their Mingled Worlds." *Studies in American Fiction,* 12.1 (1984): 91–98.

Kuzna, Faye I. "Mental Travel in *Henderson the Rain King."* *Saul Bellow Journal,* 9.2 (1990): 54–67.

Leach, Elsie. "From Ritual to Romance Again: *Henderson the Rain King."* *Western Humanities Review,*14.2 (1960): 223–24.

Majdiak, Daniel. "The Romantic Self and *Henderson the Rain King."* *Bucknell Review,* 19.2 (1971): 125–46.

Markos, Donald W. "Life Against Death in *Henderson the Rain King."* *Modern Fiction Studies,* 17.2 (1971): 193–205.

Michelson, Bruce. "The Idea of *Henderson."* *Twentieth Century Literature,* 27.4 (1981): 309–24.

Moss, Judith. "The Body as Symbol in Saul Bellow's *Henderson the Rain King."* *Literature and Psychology,* 20.2 (1970): 51–61.

Pearce, Richard. "Harlequin: The Character of the Clown in Saul Bellow's *Henderson the Rain King* and John Hawkes' *Second Skin."* *Stages of the Clown: Perspective on Modern Fiction from Dostoevsky to Beckett.* Richard Pearce. Crosscurrents/Modern Critique. Carbondale, IL: Southern Illinois UP; London: Feffer, 1970. 103–16.

Pifer, Ellen. "Beyond History and Geography: *Henderson the Rain King."* *Saul Bellow Journal,* 7.2 (1988): 16–34.

Rodrigues, Eusebio L. "Bellow's Africa." *American Literature,* 43.2 (1971): 242–56.

Rodrigues, Eusebio L. "Reichianism in *Henderson the Rain King.*" *Criticism*, 15.3 (1973): 212–33.

———. "Saul Bellow's Henderson as America." *Centennial Review*, 20.2 (1976): 189–95.

Schur, Ellen. "Eugene Henderson's Many Selves." *Saul Bellow Journal*, 7.2 (1988): 49–57.

Trachtenberg, Stanley. "Saul Bellow's *Luftmenschen:* The Compromise with Reality." *Critique*, 9.3 (1967): 37–61.

Herzog

Axthelm, Peter M. "The Full Perception: Saul Bellow." *The Modern Confessional Novel*. Peter M. Axthelm. New Haven: Yale Univ. Press, 1967. 128–79.

Baruch, Franklin R. "Bellow and Milton: Professor Herzog in his Garden." *Critique*, 9.3 (1967): 74–83.

Boulot, Elisabeth. "Rupture, revolte et harmonie dans *Herzog* de Saul Bellow." *Visates de l'harmonie dans la litterature Anglo-Americaine*. Reims: Centre de Recherce sur l'imaginaire dans le litterature de langue anglaise, University of Reims, 1982. 153–66.

Boyers, Robert T. "Attitudes Toward Sex in American 'High Culture.'" *Annals of the American Academy of Political and Social Sciences*, 376 (1968): 36–52.

Bradbury, Malcolm. "Saul Bellow's *Herzog.*" *Critical Quarterly*, 7.3 (1965): 269–78.

Chavkin, Allan. "Bellow's Alternative to the Wasteland: Romantic Theme and Form in *Herzog.*" *Studies in the Novel*, 11.3 (1979): 326–37.

———. "Bellow's Investigation of the 'Social Meaning in Nothingness': Role Playing in *Herzog.*" *Yiddish*, 4.4 (1982): 48–57.

Cixous, Hélène. "Situation de Saul Bellow." *Les Lettres Nouvelles*, 58 (Mar.-Apr. 1967): 130–45.

Colbert, Robert E. "Satiric Vision in Herzog." *Studies in Contemporary Satire*, 5 (1978): 22–33.

Cronin, Gloria L. *"Herzog:* The Purgation of Twentieth Century Consciousness." *Interpretations: A Journal of Ideas, Analysis and Criticism,* 16.1 (1985): 8–20.

Fisch, Harold. "The Hero as Jew: Reflections on *Herzog." Judaism,* 17.1 (1968): 42–54.

Fuchs, Daniel. *"Herzog:* The Making of a Novel." *Critical Essays on Saul Bellow.* Ed. Stanley Trachtenberg. Critical Essays on American Literature. Boston: Hall, 1979. 101–21. Longer version rpt. in *Saul Bellow: Vision and Revision.* Daniel Fuchs. Durham, NC: Duke Univ. Press, 1984. 121–54.

Galloway, David D. "Moses-Bloom-Herzog: Bellow's Everyman." *Southern Review,* 2.1 (1966): 61–76.

Goldman, Liela H. "On the Character of Ravitch in Saul Bellow's *Herzog." American Notes and Queries,* 19.7–8 (1981): 115–16.

Howe, Irving. "Odysseus Flat on His Back." *New Republic,* 19 Sept. 1964: 21–26. Rpt. as "Herzog." *The Critic as Artist: Essays on Books 1920–1970.* Ed. Gilbert A. Harrison. New York: Liveright, 1972. 181–91; as "Down and Out in New York and Chicago: Saul Bellow, Professor Herzog, and Mr. Sammler." *The Critical Point: On Literature and Culture,* ed. Irving Howe. New York: Horizon, 1973. 121–36, and in *Herzog: Text and Criticism.* Ed. Irving Howe. Viking Critical Library. New York: Viking, 1976. 391–400. Rpt. with original title in *Saul Bellow.* Ed. Harold Bloom. Modern Critical Views. New York: Chelsea, 1986. 45–51.

Josipovici, Gabriel. "Bellow and Herzog." *Encounter,* 37.5 (1971): 49–55. Rpt. in *Herzog: Text and Criticism.* Ed. Irving Howe. Viking Critical Library. New York: Viking, 1976. 401–15; as "Herzog: Freedom and Wit" in *The World and the Book: A Study of Modern Fiction.* Ed. Gabriel Josipovici. London: Macmillan, 1971, 2nd ed., 1979. 221–35.

Lundquist, Susan Evertsen. "The Ontic, Epistemic, and Semantic Nature of Saul Bellow's *Herzog." Saul Bellow Journal,* 9.2 (1990): 38–53.

Mellard, James M. "Consciousness Fills the Void: Herzog, History, and the Hero in the Modern World." *Modern Fiction Studies,* 25.1 (1979): 75–91.

Mosher, Harold F., Jr. "Herzog's Quest." *Le Voyage dans la litterature anglo-saxonne. Actes du Congres de Nice* (1971). Paris: Didier, 1972. 169–72.

Newman, Judie. "*Herzog:* History as Neurosis." *Delta,* 19 (1984): 131–53.

Pinsker, Sanford. "Moses Herzog's Fall into the Quotidian." *Studies in the Twentieth Century,* 14 (Fall 1974): 105–15.

Poirier, Richard. "*Herzog,* or Bellow in Trouble." *Saul Below: a Collection of Critical Essays.* Ed. Earl Rovit. Twentieth Century Views. Englewood Cliffs, NJ: Prentice, 1975. 81–89.

Porter, M. Gilbert. "*Herzog:* A Transcendental Solution to an Existential Problem." *Forum,* 7.2 (1969): 32–36.

Read, Forrest. "Notes, Reviews, and Speculations." Rev. of *Herzog. Epoch,* 14.1 (1964), 81–96. Rpt. in *Herzog: Text and Criticism.* Ed. Irving Howe. Viking Critical Library. New York: Viking, 1976. 416–39.

Rovit, Earl. "Bellow in Occupancy." *American Scholar,* 34.2 (1965): 292+ Rpt. in *Saul Bellow and the Critics.* Ed. Irving Malin. New York: New York Univ. Press, 1967. 177–83.

Sale, Roger. "Provincial Champions and Grandmasters." *Hudson Review,* 17.4 (1964–65): 608–18.

Schraepen, Edmond. "*Herzog:* Disconnection and Connection." *Saul Bellow and His Work.* Ed. Edmond Schraepen. Brussels: Centrum voor Taal-en Literatuurwetenschap, Vrije Universiteit Brussel, 1978. 119–29. Proceedings of a symposium held at the Free University of Brussels (V.U.B.), 10–11 Dec. 1977.

Shulman, Robert. "The Style of Bellow's Comedy." *PMLA,* 83.1 (1968): 109–17. Rpt. in *Herzog: Text and Criticism.* Ed. Irving Howe. Viking Critical Library. New York: Viking, 1976. 489–509.

Tanner, Tony. "Saul Bellow: The Flight from Monologue." *Encounter,* Feb. 1965: 58–70. Rpt. in *Herzog: Text and Criticism.* Ed. Irving Howe. Viking Critical Library. New York: Viking, 1976. 445–65.

Van Egmond, Peter G. "Herzog's Quotation of Walt Whitman." *Walt Whitman Review,* 13.2 (1967): 54–56.

Vardaman, James M., Jr. "Herzog's Letters." *Journal of the English Institute,* 9-10 (1979): 129–49.

Weinstein, Norman. *"Herzog,* Order and Entropy." *English Studies,* 54.5 (1973): 336–46.

Young, James Dean. "Bellow's View of the Heart." *Critique,* 7.3 (1965): 5–17.

Humboldt's Gift

Baker, Carlos. "Bellow Gift." *Theology Today,* Jan. 1976: 411–13.

Bartz, Fredrica K. *"Humboldt's Gift* and the Myth of the Artist in America." *South Carolina Review,* 15.1 (1982): 79–83.

———. "The Role of Rudolph Steiner in the Dreams of *Humboldt's Gift." Ball State University Forum,* 24.1 (1983): 27–29.

Brackenhoff, Mary. *"Humboldt's Gift:* The Ego's Mirror – A Vehicle for Self Realization." *Saul Bellow Journal,* 5.2 (1986): 15–21.

Bradbury, Malcolm. "The It & the We: Saul Bellow's New Novel." *Encounter,* Nov. 1975: 61–67.

Bragg, Melvyn. "'Off the Couch by Christmas': Saul Bellow on his New Novel." *Listener,* 20 Nov. 1975: 675–76.

Chavkin, Allan. "Baron Humboldt and Bellow's Von Humboldt Fleisher: Success and Failure in *Humboldt's Gift." Notes on Contemporary Literature,* 10.2 (1980): 11–12.

———. *"Humboldt's Gift* and the Romantic Imagination." *Philological Quarterly,* 62.1 (1983): 1–19.

Clayton, John J. *"Humboldt's Gift:* Transcendence and the Flight from Death." *Saul Bellow and His Work.* Ed. Edmond Schraepen. Brussels: Centrum voor Taal-en Literatuurwetenschap, Vrije Universiteit Brussel, 1978. 31–48. Proceedings of a symposium held at the Free University of Brussels (V.U.B.), 10–11 Dec. 1977.

Cronin, Gloria. "Art vs. Anarchy: Citrine's Transcendental Experiment in *Humboldt's Gift." Indian Journal of American Studies,* 15.1 (1985): 33–43.

Goldman, Mark. *"Humboldt's Gift* and the Case of the Split Protagonist." *Modern Language Studies,* 11.2 (1981): 3–16.

Kernan, Alvin B. "Mighty Poets in their Misery Dead: The Death of the Poet in Saul Bellow's *Humboldt's Gift."* Alvin B. Kernan. Princeton:

Princeton Univ. Press, 1982. 37–65. Abridged version rpt. in *Saul Bellow*. Ed. Harold Bloom. Modern Critical Views. New York: Chelsea, 1986. 161–77.

Kerner, David. "The Incomplete Dialectic of *Humboldt's Gift*." *Dalhousie Review*, 62.1 (1982): 14–35. Rpt. in *Saul Bellow*. Ed. Harold Bloom. Modern Critical Views. New York: Chelsea, 1986. 161–77.

McSweeney, Kerry. "Saul Bellow and the Life to Come." *Critical Quarterly*, 18.1 (1976): 67–72.

Mowat, John. "*Humboldt's Gift*: Bellows 'Dejection Ode.'" *Dutch Quarterly Review of Anglo-American Letters*, 8 (1978): 184–201. Cited in *MLA Bibliography*, 1978.

Rosenfeld, Alvin H. "Poet, Magician, and Anthroposophist: Saul Bellow's Latest Fiction." *Midstream*, Dec. 1975: 62–67.

Ryan, Steven T. "The Soul's Husband: Money in *Humboldt's Gift*." *Money Talks: Language and Lucre in American Fiction*. Ed. Roy R. Male. Norman: Univ. of Oklahoma Press, 1981. 111–21.

Schraepen, Edmond. "*Humboldt's Gift*: A New Bellow." *English Studies*, 66.2 (1981): 164–70.

Siegel, Ben. "Artists and Opportunities in Saul Bellow's *Humboldt's Gift*." *Contemporary Literature*, 19.2 (1978): 143–64. Rpt. in *Critical Essays on Saul Bellow*. Ed. Stanley Trachtenberg. Critical Essays on American Literature. Boston: Hall, 1979. 158–74.

Updike, John. "Draping Radiance with a Worn Veil." *New Yorker*, 15 Sept. 1975: 122+.

Weinstein, Mark. "Charles Citrine: Bellow's Holy Fool." *Saul Bellow Journal*, 3.1 (1983): 28–37.

Yetman, Michael G. "Who Would Not Sing for Humboldt?" *ELH*, 48.4 (1981): 935–51.

More Die of Heartbreak

Blades, John. "Mellow Bellow." Rev. of *More Die of Heartbreak*. *Chicago Tribune*, 31 May 1987, sec. 14: 1, 3.

Bluestein, Gene. "Kinky Times." Rev. of *More Die of Heartbreak*. *Progressive*, Nov. 1987: 30.

Brookhiser, Richard. Rev. of *More Die of Heartbreak American Spectator,* Sept. 1987: 43–44.

Carpenter, David A. *"More Die of Heartbreak." Magill's Literary Annual: 1988.* Ed. Frank N. Magill. 2 vols. Pasadena: Salem, 1988. 2: 583–88.

Clemons, Walter. "A Comedy of Marriage and Manipulation." Rev. of *More Die of Heartbreak. Newsweek,* 8 June 1987: 79+.

Cunliffe, Marcus. "Saul Bellow's Family Affairs." Rev. of *More Die of Heartbreak. Washington Post Book World,* 7 June 1987: 1+.

Fuchs, Daniel. "More Die of Heartbreak: A Reading." *Saul Bellow Journal,* 11.1 (Fall 1992).

Freeney, Mark. "No Ordinary Authorial Voice But a Bellow." Rev. of *More Die of Heartbreak. Boston Globe,* 31 May 1987: B14–B15.

Field, Leslie. Rev. of *More Die of Heartbreak. Saul Bellow Journal,* 6.2 (1987): 71–75.

Gaddis, William. "An Instinct for the Dangerous Wife." Rev. of *More Die of Heartbreak. New York Times Book Review, 24 May 1987: 1+.*

Gray, Paul. "Victims of Contemporary Life." Rev. of *More Die of Heartbreak. Time,* 15 June 1987: 71.

Kazin, Alfred. "Trachtenberg the Brain King." Rev. of *More Die of Heartbreak. New York Review of Books,* 16 July 1987: 3–4.

Meyers, Jeffrey. "The Marriage Hearse." Rev. of *More Die of Heartbreak. National Review,* 17 July 1987: 49–50.

Michaud, Charles. Rev. of *More Die of Heartbreak. Library Journal,* July 1987: 92.

Newman, Judie. "From Psyche to *Psycho:* Saul Bellow and the Degradation of Love." *Saul Bellow Journal,* 11.1 (Fall 1992).

Rafferty, Terrence. "Hearts and Minds." Rev. of *More Die of Heartbreak. New Yorker,* 20 July 1987: 89–91.

Schulz, Dieter. "The Poe Connection in *More Die of Heartbreak." Saul Bellow Journal,* 11.1 (Fall 1992).

Siegel, Ben. "Clearing His Desk: Saul Bellow's *More Die of Heartbreak." Saul Bellow Journal,* 11.1 (Fall 1992).

Strawson, G. "Professor Crader's Satellite." Rev. of *More Die of Heartbreak*. *Times Literary Supplement*, 23–29 Oct. 1987: 1157–58.

Tanner, Stephen L. Rev. of *More Die of Heartbreak*. *Saul Bellow Journal*, 7.1 (1988): 70–76.

Mr. Sammler's Planet

Bayley, John. "By Way of Mr. Sammler." *Salmagundi*, 30 (Summer 1975), 24–33. Rpt. in *Salmagundi Reader*. Eds. Robert T. Boyers and Peggy Boyers. Bloomington: Indiana Univ. Press, 1983: 394–93.

Berger, Alan L. "Holocaust Survivors in *Anya* and *Mr. Sammler's Planet*." *Modern Language Studies*, 16.1 (1986): 81–87.

Bilik, Dorothy Seidman. "Bellow's Worldly 'Tsadik'." *Immigrant Survivors: Post Holocaust Consciousness in Recent Jewish-American Literature*. Dorothy Seidman Bilik. New York: Wesleyan Univ. Press, 1981. 137–66.

Bolling, Douglass. "Intellectual and Aesthetic Dimensions of *Mr. Sammler's Planet*." *Journal of Narrative Technique*, 4.3 (1974): 188–203.

Cronin, Gloria L. "Faith and Futurity: The Case for Survival in *Mr. Sammler's Planet*." *Literature and Belief*, 3 (1982): 97–108.

Cushman, Keith. "Mr. Bellow's *Sammler:* The Evolution of a Contemporary Text." *Studies in the Novel*, 7.3 (1975): 425–44.

Galloway, David D. "*Mr. Sammler's Planet:* Bellow's Failure of Nerve." *Modern Fiction Studies*, 19.1 (1973): 17–28.

Gittleman, Sol. "*Mr. Sammler's Planet* Ten Years Later: Looking Back of Crises of 'Mishpocha.'" *Judaism*, 30 (Fall 1981): 480–83.

Glickman, Susan. "The World as Will and Idea: Comparative Study of *An American Dream* and *Mr. Sammler's Planet*." *Modern Fiction Studies*, 28.4 (1982–83): 569–82.

Guttman, Allen. "Saul Bellow's *Mr. Sammler*." *Contemporary Literature*, 14.2 (1973): 157–66.

Harris, James Neil. "One Critical Approach to *Mr. Sammler's Planet*." *Twentieth Century Literature*, 18.4 (1972): 235–50.

Kremer, S. Lillian. "The Holocaust in *Mr. Sammler's Planet*." *Saul Bellow Journal*, 4.1 (1985): 19–32.

Newman, Judie. *"Mr. Sammler's Planet:* Wells, Hitler and the World State." *Dutch Quarterly Review of Anglo-American Letters,* 13.1 (1983): 55–71.

Pifer, Ellen. "'Two Different Speeches': Mystery and Knowledge in *Mr. Sammler's Planet." Mosaic,* 18.2 (1985): 17–32.

Sacks, June. "Questioning of a Survivor: A Reappraisal of the Role of Mr. Sammler." *Unisa English Studies,* 26.2 (1988): 21–26.

Siegel, Ben. "Saul Bellow and Mr. Sammler: Absurd Seekers of High Qualities." *Saul Bellow: A Collection of Critical Essays.* Ed. Earl Rovit. 75. 122–34.

Sloss, Henry. "Europe's Last Gasp." *Shenandoah,* 22.1 (1970): 82–86.

Weinstein, Mark A. "The Fundamental Elements in *Mr. Sammler's Planet." Saul Bellow Journal,* 1.2 (1982): 18–26.

Wirth-Nesher, Hana, and Andrea Cohen Malamut. "Jewish and Human Survival on Bellow's Planet." *Modern Fiction Studies,* 25.1 (1979): 59–74.

Plays

Anderson, David D. "The Novelist as Playwright: Saul Bellow on Broadway." *Saul Bellow Journal,* 5.1 (1986): 48–62.

Weales, Gerald. "Saul Bellow and Some Others." *The Jumping Off Place: American Drama in the 1960s.* New York: Macmillan; London: Collier-Macmillan, 1969. 195–223.

Seize the Day

Alhadeff, Barbara. "The Divided Self: A Laingian Interpretation of *Seize the Day." Studies in American Jewish Literature,* 3.1 (1977): 16–20.

Bach, Gerhard P. "'Howling Like a Wolf from the City Window': The Cinematic Realization of *Seize the Day." Saul Bellow Journal,* 7.2 (1988): 71–83.

Bordewyk, Gordon. "Saul Bellow's Death of a Salesman." *Saul Bellow Newsletter,* 1.1 (1981): 18–21.

Chavkin, Allan. "'The Hollywood Thread' and the First Draft of Saul Bellow's *Seize the Day*." *Studies in the Novel,* 14.1 (1982): 82–94.

———. "Suffering and Wilhelm Reich's Theory of Character-Armoring in Saul Bellow's *Seize the Day*." *Essays in Literature,* 9.1 (1982): 133–37.

Clayton, John J. "Alienation and Masochism." *Saul Bellow: In Defense of Man.* John J. Clayton. Bloomington: Indiana Univ. Press, 1968. 2nd ed. 1979. 49–76. Rpt. in *Saul Bellow.* Ed. Harold Bloom. Modern Critical Views. New York: Chelsea, 1986. 65–85.

———. "Saul Bellow's *Seize the Day*: A Study in Midlife Transition." *American Literature in Belgium.* Ed. Gilbert Debusscher and Marc Maufort. Amsterdam: Rodopi, 1988. 135–47.

———. "Wordsworth's Ode and Bellow's *Seize the Day*." *American Notes and Queries,* 3 (1990): 121–24.

Costello, Patrick. "Tradition in *Seize the Day*." *Essays in Literature,* 14.1 (1987): 117–31.

Cronin, Gloria L. "The Seduction of Tommy Wilhelm: A Post-Modernist Appraisal of *Seize the Day*." *Saul Bellow Journal,* 3.1 (1983): 18–27.

Giannone, Richard. "Saul Bellow's Idea of Self: A Reading of *Seize the Day*." *Renascence,* 27.4 (1975): 193–205.

Handy, William J. "Bellow's *Seize the Day*." *Modern Fiction: A Formalist Approach.* William J. Handy. Crosscurrents/Modern Critiques. Carbondale, IL: Southern Illinois Univ. Press, 1971. 119–30.

———. "Saul Bellow and the Naturalistic Hero." *Texas Studies in Literature and Language,* 5.4 (1964): 538–45.

Ikeda, Choko. "Human Relations in Saul Bellow's *Seize the Day*." *Kyusha American Literature,* 30 (1989): 21–26.

Jefchak, Andrew. "Family Struggles in *Seize the Day*." *Studies in Short Fiction,* 11.3 (1974): 297–302.

Kremer, S. Lillian. "*Seize the Day*: Intimations of Anti-Hasidic Satire." *Yiddish,* 4.4 (1982): 32–40.

Loe, Thomas. "Modern Allegory and the Form of *Seize the Day*." *Saul Bellow Journal,* 7.1 (1988): 57–66.

Marshall, Sarah. "Bellow's *Seize the Day*." *Notes on Contemporary Literature,* 20.1 (1990): 9–10.

Morahg, Gilead. "The Art of Dr. Tamkin: Matter and Manner in *Seize the Day*." *Modern Fiction Studies,* 25.1 (1979): 103–16.

Raper, J. R. "Running Contrary Ways: Saul Bellow's *Seize the Day*." *Southern Humanities Review,* 10.2 (1976): 157–68.

Richmond, Lee J. "The Maladroit, the Medico, and the Magician: Saul Bellow's *Seize the Day*." *Twentieth Century Literature,* 19.1 (1973): 15–25.

Rodrigues, Eusebio L. "Reichianism in *Seize the Day*." *Critical Essays on Saul Bellow.* Ed. Stanley Trachtenberg. Critical Essays on American Literature. Boston: Hall, 1979. 89–100.

Scrafford, B. L. "Water and Stone: The Confluence of Textual Imagery in *Seize the Day*." *Saul Bellow Journal,* 6.2 (1987): 64–70.

Shear, Walter. "*Steppenwolf* and *Seize the Day*." *Saul Bellow Newsletter,* 1.1 (1981): 32–34.

Sicherman, Carol M. "Bellow's *Seize the Day:* Reverberations and Hollow Sounds." *Studies in the Twentieth Century,* 15 (1975): 1–31.

Trowbridge, Clinton W. "Water Imagery in *Seize the Day*." *Critique,* 9.3 (1967): 62–73.

Weiss, Daniel. "Caliban on Prospero: A Psychoanalytic Study of the Novel *Seize the Day* by Saul Bellow." *American Imago,* 19.3 (1962): 277–306. Rpt. in *Saul Bellow and the Critics.* Ed. Irving Malin. New York: New York Univ. Press, 1967. 114–141; *Psychoanalysis and American Fiction.* Ed. Irving Malin. New York: Dutton, 1965. 279–307.

West, Ray B., Jr. "Six Authors in Search of a Hero." *Sewanee Review,* 65.3 (1957): 498–508.

Short Fiction

Alter, Robert. "Kafka's Father, Agnon's Mother, Bellow's Cousins." *Commentary,* Feb. 1986; 46–52.

Demarest, David P., Jr. "The Theme of Discontinuity in Saul Bellow's Fiction: 'Looking for Mr. Green' and 'A Father-to-Be.'" *Studies in Short Fiction,* 6.2 (1969): 175–86.

Dietrich, Richard F. "The Biological Draft Dodger in Bellow's 'A Father-to-Be.'" *Studies in the Humanities,* 9.1 (1981): 45–51.

Fuchs, Daniel. "On *Him with His Foot in His Mouth and Other Stories.*" *Saul Bellow Journal,* 5.1 (1986): 3–15.

Ikeda, Choko. "Narrative Devices in Saul Bellow's 'A Silver Dish.'" *Kyusha American Literature,* 29 (1988): 31–39.

Johnson, Gregory. "Jewish Assimilation and Codes of Manners in Saul Bellow's 'The Old System.'" *Studies in American Jewish Literature,* 9.1 (1990): 48–60.

————. "Bellow's Victor Wulpy: The Failure of Intellect." *Saul Bellow Journal,* 6.2 (1987): 26–35.

————. "The Rhetoric of Bellow's Woody Selbst: Religion and Irony." *Saul Bellow Journal,* 8.1 (1989): 35–43.

————. "Sexual Irony in Bellow's 'What Kind of Day Did You Have?'" *Notes on Contemporary Literature,* Mar. 1987: 10–12.

Newman, Judie. "Saul Bellow and Trotsky: 'The Mexican General.'" *Saul Bellow Newsletter,* 1.1 (1981): 26–31.

Ozik, Cynthia. "Farcical Combat in a Busy World." Rev. of *Him with His Foot in His Mouth and Other Stories. New York Times Book Review,* 20 May 1984: 3. Rpt. in *Saul Bellow.* Ed. Harold Bloom. Modern Critical Views. New York: Chelsea, 1986. 235–41.

Rodrigues, Eusebio L. "A Rough-Hewn Heroine of Our Time: Saul Bellow's 'Leaving the Yellow House.'" *Saul Bellow Newsletter,* 1.1 (1981): 11–17.

Rooke, Constance. "Saul Bellow's 'Leaving the Yellow House': The Trouble with Women." *Studies in Short Fiction,* 14.2 (1977): 184–87.

Roudané, Matthew C. "Discordant Timbre: Saul Bellow's 'Him with His Foot in His Mouth.'" *Saul Bellow Journal,* 4.1 (1985): 52–61.

Shear, Walter. "'Leaving the Yellow House': Hattie's Will." *Saul Bellow Journal,* 7.1 (1988): 51–56.

Stevick, Philip. "The Rhetoric of Bellow's Short Fiction." *Critical Essays on Saul Bellow.* Ed. Stanley Trachtenberg. Critical Essays on American Literature. Boston: Hall, 1979. 73–82.

A Theft

Appelo, Tim. "Smart Talk Reviews: Saul Bellow Turns Paperback Writer." *A Theft. Savvy Woman,* Apr. 1989: 24.

Banville, John. "Altogether Different; and Her Tears Seem a Celebration." Rev. of *A Theft*. *London Review of Books*, 30 Mar. 1989: 21.

Benedictus, David. "109–Page Culture." Rev. of *A Theft*. *Punch*, 10 Mar. 1989: 6.

"Bookshelf." Rev. of *A Theft*. *Wall Street Journal*, 14 Mar. 1989: A22.

Boyers, Robert. "Losing Grip on Specifics." Rev. of *A Theft*. *Times Literary Supplement*, 24 Mar. 1989: 299.

Brookner, Anita. "Ring of Falsehod." Rev. of *A Theft*. *Spectator*, 15 Apr. 1989: 29–30.

Chavkin, Allen. "Bellow's *A Theft*." Rev. of *A Theft*. *Saul Bellow Journal*, 8.1 (1989): 68–70.

Cheuse, Alan. "Saul Bellow's Ring of Truth." Rev. of *A Theft*. *Chicago Tribune Books*, 5 Mar. 1989: 1+.

Conarroe, Joel. "The Laureate's Latest, on Love." Rev. of *A Theft*. *Washington Post*, 24 Feb. 1989: C3

Eder, Richard. "Love in Gogmagogsville." Rev. of *A Theft*. *Los Angeles Times Book Review*, 19 Mar. 1989: 3.

Feeney, Mark. "What Made Frederic Seize the Ring?" Rev. of *A Theft*. *Boston Globe*, 5 Feb. 1989: 86+.

Fender, Stephen. "Hero into Heroine." Rev. of *A Theft*. *Manchester Guardian Weekly*, 23 Apr. 1989, 30.

"Fiction." Rev. of *A Theft*. *Jim Kobak's Kirkus Review*, 1 Aug. 1989: 1087.

Gray, Paul. "An Old Master in Soft-Covers." Rev. of *A Theft*. *Time*, 6 Mar. 1989: 70.

Johnson, Greg. "Bellow's 'Theft' Is a Deft, Contained Work." Rev. of *A Theft*. *Atlanta Journal/Constitution*, 2 Apr. 1989: N10.

Lehmann-Haupt, Christopher. "Saul Bellow's Small Book of Outsized Characters." Rev. of *A Theft*. *New York Times*, 2 Mar. 1989: C23.

Marin, Rick. Rev. of *A Theft*. *American Spectator*, July 1989, 47.

Novak, Ralph. "Picks & Pans – Pages." Rev. of *A Theft*. *People Weekly*, 24 Apr. 1989: 28+.

Oates, Joyce Carol. "Clara's Gift." Rev. of *A Theft*. *New York Times Book Review*, 5 Mar. 1989: 3.

Packer, George. "Less Brains, Better Legs." Rev. of *A Theft. Nation,* 15 May 1989: 674–75.

Pinsker, Sanford. "Mr. Bellow's Planet Through Female Eyes." Rev. of *A Theft. Midstream,* June/July 1989: 62–63.

Prescott, Peter. "Ring Around Park Avenue." Rev. of *A Theft. Newsweek,* 20 Mar. 1989: 80.

Pritchard, William H. "Realism without Magic." Rev. of *A Theft. Hudson Review,* 42.3 (1989): 490.

Quinn, Anthony. "Clara's Conversion." Rev. of *A Theft. New Statesman & Society,* 31 Mar. 1989: 35.

Raban, Jonathan. "Lost Emerald City." Rev. of *A Theft. Observer,* 2 Apr. 1989: 45.

Safer, Elaine B. "Degrees of Comic Irony in *A Theft* and *The Bellarosa Connection.*" *Saul Bellow Journal,* 9.2 (1990): 1–19.

Timson, Judith. "It Takes a Thief." *Maclean's,* 24 Apr. 1989: 66

Towers, Robert. "Mystery Women." Rev. of *A Theft. New York Review of Books,* 27 Apr. 1989: 50–52.

Travisano, Thomas. "A Theft." *Magill's Literary Annual: 1990.* Ed. Frank N. Magill. 2 vols. Pasadena: Salem, 1990, 2: 792.

Updike, John. "Nice Tries." Rev. of *A Theft. New Yorker,* 1 May 1989: 113–14.

To Jerusalem and Back

Bird, Christine, M. "The Return Journey in *To Jerusalem and Back.*" *Melus,* 6.4 (1979): 51–57.

Chomsky, Noam. "Bellow's Israel." *New York Arts Journal* (Spring 1977): 29–32. Rpt. as "Bellow, *To Jerusalem and Back.*" *Towards a New Cold War: Essays on the Current Crisis and How We Got There.* Noam Chomsky. New York: Pantheon, 1982. 299–307.

Cohen, Sarah Blacher. "Saul Bellow's Jerusalem." *Studies in American Jewish Literature,* 5.2 (1979): 16–23. Joint issue with *Yiddish* 4.1 (1979).

Ehrenkrantz, Louis. "Bellow In Jerusalem." *Midstream,* Nov. 1977: 87–90.

Grossman, Edward. "Unsentimental Journey." *Commentary,* Nov. 1976, 80, 82–84.

Lavine, Steven David. "On the Road to Jerusalem: Bellow Now." *Studies in American Jewish Literature,* 3.1 (1977): 1–6.

Libowitz, Richard. "Of Sights and Vision." *Reconstructionist,* Mar. 1977: 24.

Pinsker, Sanford. "Jerusalem Without Fictions." *Jewish Spectator,* 42.1 (1977): 36–37.

Saposnik, Irving S. "Bellow's Jerusalem: The Road Not Taken." *Judaism,* 28.1 (1979): 42–50.

Wilson, Robert F., Jr. "The Politics of Massage: Moshe the Masseur in *To Jerusalem and Back.*" *Notes on Modern American Literature,* 2.4 (1978): Item 26.

The Victim

Aharoni, Ada. "*The Victim:* Freedom of Choice." *Saul Bellow Journal,* 4.1 (1985): 33–44.

Baumbach, Jonathan. "The Double Vision: *The Victim* by Saul Bellow." *The Landscape of Nightmare: Studies in the Contemporary American Novel.* Jonathan Baumbach. New York: New York Univ. Press, 1965. 35–54.

Bradbury, Malcolm. "Saul Bellow's *The Victim.*" *Critical Quarterly,* 5.2 (1963): 119–28.

Chavkin, Allan. "Ivan Karamazov's Rebellion and Bellow's *The Victim.*" *Papers on Language and Literature: A Journal for Scholars and Critics of Language and Literature,* 16.3 (1980): 316–20.

Dittmar, Kurt. "Realitat und Fuktion in der zeitgenossischen amerikanischen Erzahlliteratur." *Literarische Ansichten der Wirklichkeit: Studien zur Wirklichkeitsckonstitution in englischsprachiger Literatur.* Eds. Hans-Heinrich Freitag and Peter Huhn. Anglo American Forum 12. Frankfurt aM: Lang, 1980. 401–27.

Gilmore, Thomas B. "Allbee's Drinking." *Twentieth Century Literature,* 28.4 (1982): 381–96.

Glicksberg, Charles I. "The Theme of Alienation in the American Jewish Novel." *Reconstructionist,* 29 Nov. 1957: 8–13.

Greenberg, Martin. "Modern Man as Jew." *Commentary,* Jan. 1948: 86–87.

Kremer, S. Lillian. "Acquiescence to Anti-Semitism in *The Victim:* An Alternate Reading of Bellow's Daniel Harkavy." *Saul Bellow Journal,* 1.2 (1982): 27–30.

————. "The Holocaust in *The Victim." Saul Bellow Journal,* 2.2 (1983): 15–23.

Nilsen, Helge N. "Anti-Semitism and Persecution Complex: A Comment on Saul Bellow's *The Victim." English Studies,* 60.2 (1979): 183–91.

Shastri, N. R. "Self and Society in Saul Bellow's *The Victim." Osmania Journal of English Studies,* 82 (1971): 105–12.

Bibliographies and Checklists

Cronin, Gloria L. "Saul Bellow Selected and Annotated Bibliography." *Saul Bellow Journal,* 4.1 (1985): 80–89.

Cronin, Gloria L., and Liela H. Goldman. "Saul Bellow." *American Novelists.* Detroit: Gale, 1986. 83–155. Vol. 1 of *Contemporary Authors Bibliographical Series.* 3 vols to date. 1986–

Cronin, Gloria L. and Blaine H. Hall. *Saul Bellow: An Annotated Bibliography.* 2nd ed. New York Garland, 1987. 313 pp.

Cronin, Gloria L. "Selected Annotated Critical Bibliography for 1984," *Saul Bellow Journal,* 6.1 (1987): 55–68.

————. "Selected Annotated Critical Bibliography for 1985," *Saul Bellow Journal,* 6.2 (1987): 76–80.

Cronin, Gloria L., and Blaine H. Hall. "Selected Annotated Critical Bibliography for 1986," *Saul Bellow Journal,* 7.1 (1988): 79–95.

Cronin, Gloria L., and Blaine H. Hall. "Selected Annotated Critical Bibliography for 1987," *Saul Bellow Journal,* 8.1 (1989): 74–96.

Cronin, Gloria L. and Blaine H. Hall. "Selected Annotated Critical Bibliography for 1988," *Saul Bellow Journal,* 10.2 (1990): 82–94.

Cronin, Gloria L., and Blaine H. Hall. "Selected Annotated Critical Bibliography for 1989," *Saul Bellow Journal,* 10.2 (1992).

Field, Leslie, and John Z. Guzlowski. "Saul Bellow: A Selected Checklist." *Modern Fiction Studies,* 25.1 (1979): 149–71.

Galloway, David D. "A Saul Bellow Checklist." *The Absurd Hero in American Fiction: Updike, Styron, Bellow, Salinger.* Austin: Univ. of Texas Press, 1966. 210–26; Rev. ed. 1970, 220–39.

Lercangee, Francine. *Saul Bellow: A Bibliography of Secondary Sources.* Brussels: Center for American Studies, 1977.

Nault, Marianne. *Saul Bellow: His Works and His Critics: An Annotated International Bibliography.* Garland Reference Library of the Humanities 59. New York: Garland, 1977.

Noreen, Robert G. *Saul Bellow: A Reference Guide.* A Reference Publication in Literature. Boston: Hall, 1978.

INDEX

269